In memory of my Sephardic and Mizrahi families. They inspired me to write this collection of recipes in the hope that future generations will remember an important part of their heritage.

Content

Introduction   p 6

Cook's notes   p 11

A few words about the   p 12
spices and condiments

Recipes

Salads and dips   p 19
Salatas y mezes
Salaata we maza

Soups   p 45
Supas
Shorba

Gratins and egg dishes   p 65
Komidas con keso y uevos
Atbakh jibnah wa beid

Fish   p 85
Pishkado
Samak

Meat   p 105
Carne
Lahmah

Poultry   p 133
Poyo
Ferakh

Vegetarian dishes   p 155
Komidas sin carne
Atbakh nabatiah

Egyptian dishes   p 191
Atbakh masria

Passover   p 225
Pessah

Savoury and sweet pastries   p 245
Cosas de orno/Cosas de masa
Almoajanat/Moajanat helwa

Cakes   p 291
Pasteles
Cake

Desserts   p 319
Dulcerias
Halaweyaat

Jams and miscellaneous   p 339
Mermelada
Murabba

Glossary   p 354

Bibliography   p 355

Index   p 356

Introduction

My maternal grandparents were born and lived in Aleppo, which had been the centre of the camel-caravan trade and a vital stop along the Silk Road, until its importance diminished greatly with the opening of the Suez Canal in 1869. They decided to leave for economic reasons and settled in Egypt in 1910. My father's family originates from Toledo and were expelled from their home during the time of the Inquisition, when an edict from Isabel of Castile and her husband Ferdinand of Aragon decreed that all Jews must leave, unless they agreed to convert to Christianity. They eventually settled in Constantinople, known today as Istanbul. As with the Jews of Aleppo, the gradual collapse of the Ottoman Empire left them struggling financially and my grandparents chose to move and seek their fortune in Egypt, where they arrived in 1908.

The only grandparent I ever knew was my maternal grandmother and I wish she had taught me how to cook, but I was too young and far from interested. Fortunately, she had passed on her wonderful Syrian Jewish recipes to my mother and aunt, so the memories of the dishes they liked have been my inspiration. In contrast, my father's family was strongly influenced by their Judeo Spanish upbringing, which was reflected in their style of cooking.

This recipe collection is not about reinventing the wheel, but is first and foremost a legacy to my family, especially the younger generation. They may one day be curious to find out what their ancestors cooked in their kitchens in Aleppo, Constantinople and Cairo. Their heritage is a unique blend of three different cultures and styles of cooking, which I have tried to amalgamate in my book. I only became aware of this rich legacy later on in life, when the people who could have taught me properly were long gone. A few years ago, I felt a sudden longing for one of my mother's menenas, the wonderful date filled ma'amoul. I had absolutely no idea how to go about it, so I looked up one of Claudia Roden's recipes and, somehow managed to produce a decent batch. It seemed to take forever, but the next time was easier. This was the beginning of my culinary journey, when the memories of all the dishes I had tasted as a child came flooding back.

I am grateful for the inspiration provided by the many cookbooks written about Sephardic and Middle Eastern cooking, in particular Claudia Roden. There was a lot of excitement amongst the Egyptian Jewish community when her Book of Middle Eastern cooking was first published in 1968 - hers were all the recipes we all knew and remembered with much fondness. A Fistful of Lentils, by Jennifer Abadi and Flavours of Aleppo by Poopa Dwek were very useful sources. Their Syrian Jewish recipes are what my family knew and cooked. I would also like to mention Gil Marks, as his book Olive Trees and Honey has been a great help with regard to soups and vegetarian dishes.

I wrote this recipe collection in lockdown during the Covid 19 pandemic. I suddenly had a lot of time on my hands and this encouraged me to experiment and reproduce some of the dishes which had been part of my childhood. We were all in self isolation and there was therefore no opportunity to try what I made with friends and experts, as I would have done under normal circumstances. The recipes should therefore be used as a guide and inspiration and tweaked according to taste. It is always about personal preference and trial and error. For instance, I have used Claudia Roden's recipe to make a particular dough for borekas, but the choice of fillings and quantities is entirely mine. Although the instructions for some of the pastries such as borekas ma'amoul and filo pastries are spelt out clearly, it will take time and patience to perfect the shape.

Poopa Dweck, in her book Aromas of Aleppo, explains that cooking in the Aleppian Jewish style goes beyond fine ingredients and customs. It's about opening your home to family and friends and sharing. Historically, the role of women in the Jewish community was to keep the home in good order. Nowadays, ladies of Aleppian origin still take pride in being good cooks and excellent hostesses. These qualities are embodied in the concept of suffeh, which literally translated means 'orderliness'. It is also understood to mean warmth and the ability to make

people feel welcome, along with adhering to a certain etiquette. To say that a woman has suffeh is one of the highest compliments you could pay her. The equivalent Ladino expression is necutchera. The word represents an accomplished woman with a refined sense of taste, spirituality and intuitive wisdom.

The food of Aleppo is known for its delicacy of seasoning and elaborateness. Dishes are seasoned with coriander, garlic, allspice, cinnamon, cumin and Aleppo pepper and many have a sweet-and-sour flavour, provided by the balance of citrus fruits, pomegranates, tamarind and dried fruits. Rice, legumes and vegetables feature prominently and olive oil is used much less frequently than in other parts of the Levant.

I also feel very close to my Judeo Spanish heritage. It goes as far back as the golden age of Jews in Medieval Spain and it is important to preserve and cherish what is left of those traditions and cuisine. As with Syrian Jews, it is a remarkable culture that has hung onto its origins with pride and tenacity throughout the years. The Jews of Spain have managed to keep many aspects of their heritage, whilst adopting the flavours and recipes of the countries they lived in. These have been passed down through the generations, along with a rich source of Ladino songs and proverbs, poetry, folktales and more.

Ladino, also called Judeo Spanish and Judezmo, is the language which was spoken by the Jews of Spanish origin. Its phonology derives, for the most part, from pre-16th-century Spanish. It also has words mixed in from Portuguese, French, Italian, Arabic, Greek, Turkish and Hebrew. From the Spanish Inquisition until World War II, Ladino was the primary language spoken by thousands and thousands of Jews throughout the Mediterranean. Although my father's family often conversed in Ladino, which they spoke fluently, it is no longer used anywhere as a first language and estimates put speakers at only just 200,000 worldwide.
Turkish cooking is the style which has mostly influenced my father's family, since they had lived in the Ottoman Empire for many generations, before moving to Egypt. They adapted their Spanish dishes to the Turkish cuisine and learnt new ones. It was their capacity to absorb new cultures, whilst remaining true to their roots, that enabled them to adjust the recipes brought back by the Moors in Spain. It is said that, when they arrived in Turkey, they were delighted to find that the Turkish borek was very similar to their empanadas, so they changed it slightly and called it borekas, hence the origin of the name. Bread was a staple, as was rice, often served in the form of seasoned and garnished dishes.

The appreciation of food and an openhearted sense of hospitality was the essence of their approach to life. In Sephardic custom, homemade sweet treats were part of everyday fare and were also offered at celebratory events. They were aptly named dulces de alegria, meaning sweetness and joy. That is mostly how I remember my father's family. They welcomed you with a smile and a sense of excitement, though they may have seen you the day before and they always had some wonderful treat on offer, even if they were not expecting you.

Jews of Spanish origin had a variety of sweets and pastries, each with a unique origin. Their love for almonds was inherited from their ancestors in Spain and handcrafted marzipan, called massapan, was emblematic of their confectionery. Doughnuts soaked in a honey syrup, called bimuelos, date back to the Golden Age of Spain and an almond semolina cake soaked in citrus syrup, called shamali, still appears in Greek, Turkish and Middle Eastern cooking. In addition, the influence of the Ottoman Empire added more variety to desserts and sweets, such as frangipane-filled filo triangles, filas de almendra and almond-filled crescents called travados.

Egypt is where I was born and grew up. It's always close to my heart and cooking some of the traditional dishes takes me back to blue skies and sunny days. Many of those dishes are far better known nowadays than they were years ago, but I have tried to include less familiar ones. Middle Eastern people attach a lot of importance to leisure and peace of mind, which they call keif. Roughly translated, it means tranquil

enjoyment and there is nothing they like more than sitting on their balconies or in their courtyards, sipping drinks and savouring various mezze.

Cooking and eating were an intricate and integral part of our lives in Egypt, as they still are throughout the Middle East. They were essentially social activities and each dish held within it centuries of culture and tradition. Hospitality was important and people entertained constantly and warmly. The well know Jewish cookery author Claudia Roden also grew up in Cairo in a Sephardic community, so we had roughly the same experiences and share similar memories. In The New Book of Middle Eastern cooking, she emphasises that 'the ultimate aim of good manners was to welcome and please one's guests. To this end, there were rules strictly laid down by tradition, such as welcome, generosity and cheerfulness. The amount of food offered was considered as a compliment to the guest and failure to offer would offend, as well as bring disrepute to the host.'

We always turned to food to mark important events, such as weddings, religious festivals, new arrivals, etc; in fact most occasions, however small, were a reason to celebrate. The extraordinary choice of Mediterranean fruit gave rise to the art of making sweet preserves and jams, capturing the essence of each season in a jar. There were a variety of sweet pastries and desserts, each with a unique origin and evolution. Cooks were constantly encouraged to surpass themselves and come up with another secret ingredient for a particular family recipe. In our community, cooking was one of the highly rated female accomplishments and it was widely believed that a woman held her husband first and foremost by his stomach, rather than her pretty face.

Food was an important topic of conversation and family and friends often discussed what they were serving for lunch and sometimes helped each other prepare dishes which required time and skill. Claudia Roden explains that 'cooking was an inherited art and was traditional, rather than experimental or precise. Along with the respect for custom and convention, there was a deep attachment to dishes of the past and those which had been passed down from generation to generation. Cooking was therefore instinctive rather sophisticated, which left room for some improvisation within the boundaries of tradition'.

I still remember the scents which filled the kitchen when I was growing up - the smell of cumin and coriander seeds, freshly roasted, savoury biscuits just baked, strawberry jam slowly cooking on the stove and orange blossom water. The smell I loved most was that of sofrito - this was a method of frying meat and vegetables with olive oil and garlic, before slowly adding water. Potatoes were cubed and fried before being combined with the meat or chicken and powdered turmeric was an important spice, which gave the dish a unique deep yellow colour.

Cakes were scented with rose water and filo pastries filled with nuts. Food was cooked fresh daily and required an early morning trip to the market, which was one of the duties of our manservant. The vegetables were chemical-free and had been nestled into the ground only hours before coming to market. No leftovers were kept overnight and the purpose of our large fridge kept in the dining room was to store the numerous preserves my mother made on a regular basis. Every seasonal fruit was made into jam - figs, dates, apricots, Seville oranges and even grapes. I follow this tradition and always try to make my own jam, though of course I don't have the wonderful choice we had in Egypt.

Cooking was generally done over a type of primus called fatayel. It was a long, slow procedure and pans were sometimes left to simmer overnight. We had a small oven, but cakes and pastries were usually sent to be baked in the ovens of the local bakery. This was a feature of every day life and I remember people hurrying about in the streets, with huge trays and casseroles, sometimes balancing them on their heads. This task was always left to the servants and they performed it with diligence and good humour.

In Egypt, the first and most important step when cooking was to obtain the freshest ingredients available. This was not difficult, as there was always a vast array to choose from, which varied according to the season. Oranges, apricots, guavas, cherries, peaches, figs, from bright green to deep crimson and black, dates, grapes, guavas, prickly pears, plums and melons of all kinds were all offered for sale at the roadside or heaped on the seller's cart. Walnuts, hazelnuts, pistachios and fresh or dried almonds were also available and were bought fresh rather than stored at home. Because of this, meals concluded with fresh fruit and, in fact, there is no Arabic

word for 'dessert'. Sugary treats were usually an accompaniment to coffee or a drink in mid afternoon and were also enjoyed on special occasions and offered to visitors.

Collecting these recipes has been about trying to recall a world that has vanished and holding on to an identity which is about to disappear. It's important to preserve the culture of the Jews of Syria and Spain, two slowly disappearing communities. By giving some of the recipes their original name, I feel I am keeping alive the memory of all my departed relatives.

Thinking about my food heritage keeps me connected and safe. It triggers off memories, many of which had long been forgotten, or so it seemed. Fish is associated with long summer holidays by the sea, when it was always freshly caught and simply cooked with olive oil and lemon. There were so many varieties and we took them all for granted at the time. Olives, feta cheese, aubergine dips and the various arrays of appetisers known as mezze, remind me of the tearooms, bars and restaurants of Cairo, where drinks were always accompanied by a selection of those, as well as roasted salted nuts, almonds and pumpkin seeds. The longer you stayed, the more of these little plates appeared at the table. They were a wonderful social ritual and represented a way of living which, together with the balmy weather, encouraged many convivial gatherings.

My mother and aunts had what I call 'the touch'. They seemed to know instinctively how to make the perfect pastry, whether savoury or sweet. Theirs were not elaborate dishes, yet they looked and tasted wonderful. They were probably the result of years of experience and recipes handed down from generation to generation. Their deep deference to the past was perhaps one of the main reasons for their unwavering attachment to ancestral dishes.

Whatever they made turned out well. I remember an amusing incident when we first came to England. My mother had bought some flour to make a cake, but it had not risen and was very dense, which puzzled us - until we looked at the packet and realised why. She had bought potato flour, instead of ordinary flour, not aware of the difference. Yet, miraculously, the cake tasted good and somehow we never forgot it, though she did not attempt to made it again.

I have discovered many interesting facts through exploring recipes, which I had not paid much attention to before. There are only so many ways vegetables can be cooked and what differentiates one culture from another are the ingredients and spices used. Judeo Spanish cooking is relatively simple, with the use mainly of olive oil, lemon juice and very few spices. The Syrian Jewish cuisine is richer and more elaborate. Sweet and sour dishes are favourites, the tartness of pomegranate molasses and tamarind sauce balanced by the addition of brown sugar and dried fruit, such as apricots and prunes.

Many Sephardi cookery books have already been written and Claudia Roden's The Book of Jewish Food is the definitive one on all the different styles of Sephardic cooking. I wanted to write something more personal, mainly for my family, in the hope that, in the future, they may want to experiment with some of the recipes. Perhaps, one day and with the help of this cookbook, they may be encouraged to carry on with some of the traditions.

My love for both my families lives on when I reproduce some of their favourite dishes. It is a way of preserving their culinary legacy and an important link to their past. Ladino is a language rich in sayings and blessings. At the end of a meal, the guests will thank the cook by saying bendichas manos - it is a compliment and an expression of gratitude to the cook, as well as a wish that the hands that produced such wonderful food will continue to be blessed. The Arabic expression, which means the same, is yesalem edeki. I hope that, by opening my home and sharing my recipes, I can continue with some of those traditions.

Cook's notes

All recipes are designed to serve 4-6 people, unless otherwise stated.

Eggs are large, unless otherwise specified.

Teaspoons, tablespoons and teacups are the sizes most commonly found in English households.

It is possible to substitute oil for butter in almost every dish, including filo pastry. This is important for those who wish to reduce their consumption of butter.

Onions and garlic may be used in large quantities or simply omitted from a dish. Fresh parsley may be used if coriander is not available (and vice versa) - use the flat-leaf variety, not the curly one, which is bitter and chewy.

To reheat rice, sprinkle about 1 tablespoon hot water over the rice and place on a low heat. Cook until piping hot, killing any bacteria.

Spices may be interchanged and soups may be made thick or thin, according to preference. Dishes requiring lots of lemon can be made less lemony, depending on taste.
As with all cooking, it is mostly about experimenting and many recipes should be used as a guide, rather than interpreted too literally. You may choose to use slightly different ingredients for a dish, with equal success.

There are many recipes for making the dough for savoury pastries such as borekas, borekitas, samosas, etc. Some use a combination of oil and butter, or flour and semolina or just flour and water. They are totally interchangeable and it is a matter of experimenting and finding out which dough mixture you prefer.

In the Middle East, soups can be a meal in themselves, served with Arab bread or pita. In Sephardic cooking, soups, stews and one-pan meals, collectively referred to as komidas, are the cornerstone of every day food. They are rich with vegetables, pulses and rice and meat is often also added. They are often cooked for so long that you can no longer distinguish what is in the pan and they look the same as stews, except that they have much more liquid. The vegetables used depends on what is available or in season and often includes aubergines and peppers, or different varieties of beans.

There are infinite combinations when it comes to soups, such as spinach and lentils, spinach and yoghurt or rice, yoghurt and barley, and so on. Soups are greatly enhanced by spices, lemons and garlic. Whatever you choose to improvise with, the soup will always turn out well, especially if prepared a day ahead, allowing for the flavours to develop.

In Egypt, lunch was always the main meal of the day and frequently consisted of a rich vegetable stew with a little meat, always accompanied by rice. Any vegetable could be used in a stew and cheaper cuts of meat were good enough, provided they were allowed to cook for a long time. The meat was seared first in oil or butter until lightly coloured, before stewing it. This added richness and a deeper colour to the dish and helped to keep the meat juices. Small amounts of spices were used to begin with and more added after the stew has been cooking for some time. There were many things which were also thrown in for flavouring, such as fresh parsley and coriander, spring onions, celery, garlic, as well as chick peas and lentils to bulk up the dish. The sauce was thickened using a tablespoon of flour mixed well into the stew or ground almonds.

A few words about the spices and condiments

Ahwa (Arabic coffee)
In the Middle East, the drinking of coffee still retains a strong religious and social mystique about it. It is an activity enmeshed in ritual, practised at all times throughout the day. Also known as Turkish coffee, it requires a special long-handled coffee pot called kanaka to make it. It is served to guests in espresso coffee cups, along with a glass of water and a selection of pastries. It is important to learn how to make 'proper coffee' or ahwa. The skill lies in producing a thick layer of foam on the top, called wesh in Arabic. One way to increase the foam is to pour it slowly and try to lift the pot higher and higher as the pouring continues. You can have Turkish coffee with sugar, without sugar and with spices.

Aleppo pepper
This flaky red spice comes from a variety of red peppers that are grown in Aleppo, then dried and coarsely ground. The flavour is somehow hot, with a smoky taste. Aleppo pepper is not easy to find, so it is often replaced with cayenne pepper or paprika.

Amardeen
This is a sticky apricot paste also known as fruit leather. The thick sheets are stuck together and are sold in a pack which looks like a folded letter inside a bright orange cellophane. In Egypt, we used to make a drink with it in summer, because it was sweet and refreshing. It is also popular all over the Middle East during Eid el-Fitr, the holiday just after Ramadan.

Allspice (Baharat)
This is a generic term for shop-bought spice mix, which includes ground cardamom, clove, black pepper, cinnamon, coriander, cumin, paprika and nutmeg. In Syrian cooking, ground allspice is mixed with ground cinnamon and added to sauces and meat dishes.

Anise
Anise is one of the most ancient spices. Its yellowish brown seeds resemble cumin, but the taste is completely different. Anise has a flavour reminiscent of liquorice and is normally used in sweet fare.

Apricots (mish mish or mish mosh)
Apricots take a life of their own when it comes to Aleppian Jewish cuisine. They are very often added to cooking, whether it's a meat or chicken stew or a simple vegetable one. Syrians use dried apricots, rather than fresh ones. Together with dried prunes, they are an important ingredient, required to achieve the perfect balance of sweet and tart. They usually need to be soaked in cold water for 10-20 minutes before using, then drained. Apricots remind me of one of my favourite Egyptian expression, bokra fil mishmish. Literally translated, it means 'tomorrow when the apricots blossom', but more precisely, when hell freezes over, in other words it will never happen.

Artichokes
Artichokes, together with leeks, are the favourite vegetables of Sephardic Jews of Spanish descent. Artichokes are used in salads and vegetable stews, with lots of lemon and olive oil. The bottoms are stuffed, with beef mince and rice or a combination of cheeses. Fresh artichokes were abundant in Egypt, but required a lot of patience, as all the leaves had to be painstakingly removed first. Tinned artichoke hearts are available in most supermarkets and produce excellent results. Artichokes bottoms are available frozen or in large jars in Middle Eastern supermarkets.

Aubergines
One of the mainstays of Sephardic and Middle Eastern cuisines, aubergines are incredibly versatile. They are used in soups, make excellent dips and salads and are stuffed with meat and/or rice. They also features in many stews, casseroles and gratins. Choose aubergines that are firm, with a dark, glossy skin, as these are less likely to be filled with bitter seeds.

Burgul
Burgul was very popular in all the regions of the Ottoman Empire and was included mainly as a bulking component to recipes. It is a whole grain that is high in fibre and nutty in flavour and the two varieties, coarse and fine bulgur, are used very differently. For instance, I have used fine burgul to make kibbeh bil sanieh (layered bulgur and meat pie) and coarse burgul to make burgul

bi kousa (cracked wheat with courgettes).

Cardamom
This spice, which is called hail in Arabic, originates from countries such as India, Bangladesh, Indonesia and Nepal. The ground variety is often used in the traditional Arabic coffee to give it a distinct flavour, as well as in Middle Eastern cakes and desserts. The green cardamom pods add taste to rice dishes and meat stews.

Chickpeas
The tinned variety is often used for ease and to save time, but on certain occasions they are too soggy or waterlogged for a recipe and the dried variety is far better - for instance, if using chickpeas instead of fava beans for making falafel. They have to be soaked overnight and then boiled the next day for 20-30 minutes. Tinned chickpeas hold too much water for a recipe like this and the resulting falafel would fall apart when moulding and frying them.

Cinnamon
Dried cinnamon is available in sticks or ground. Occasionally, the sticks are used in stews, such as chicken with prunes, to obtain a more mellow flavour. Ground cinnamon can be combined with allspice to create a sweet, yet mild spicy mixture that is often used in savoury stews and meat dishes. When used in desserts, ground cinnamon adds colour as well as a little natural sweetness.

Citrus fruit
Oranges and lemons abound in the cuisine of Mediterranean and Middle Eastern Jews. Lemon enhances other foods and gives it a special acidic flavour. Sephardic Jews favours the presence of orange in savoury dishes and cakes.

Coriander
This is a nutty tasting spice ground from the dried seeds of the coriander flower. You can buy it ground or, for a sharper taste, buy the seeds whole and grind them yourself in a pestle and mortar or in a spice or coffee grinder. Keep grinding until the consistency is very fine.

Couscous
A staple in countries of the Maghreb - Morocco, Tunisia and Libya - couscous was prepared at home in earlier days, but is now available packaged. It consists of semolina, salt, water and oil. When steamed or soaked in water, couscous expands to about three times its original size.

Cumin
Cumin dates back as far as the second millennium BC and is mentioned in the Bible in the New and Old Testaments. It has been used in cooking for its flavour, as well as for medicinal purposes. Cumin seeds come from a plant native to the Nile valley in Egypt. It adds a slightly hot and spicy flavour to dishes and can be purchased as seeds or ground. Cumin and coriander are the most used spices in Egyptian cooking and, in my mother's kitchen, they were added to many dishes. We often included Arabic words or expressions when conversing in French and cumin and coriander were always called by their Arabic name, so we referred to them as courcoum and cosbara respectively.

Dates
Dates are used mostly to stuff pastry or to make the Sephardic date and raisin paste for Passover, called haroset. The average ones sold in supermarkets are small and dry and Middle Eastern grocery stores have a great variety to choose from. They also sell date paste in blocks (although this is not made entirely of dates), which is ideal for making the stuffed pastries called ma'amoul. Medjool dates are more expensive, but they are moister and meatier, so it is preferable to use them in cakes.

Fava beans (Broad Beans)
These are used to make ful medames, one of Egypt's traditional dishes, which is pre-Ottoman and pre-Islamic and thought to be as old as the Pharaohs. They are dark brown broad beans and you can find the dried and tinned varieties in Middle Eastern stores, where they are called ful medames on the tin. In Egypt, they are the main ingredient for bessara (fava bean and herb dip) and are also used in preference to chickpeas to make ta'amiya (falafel).

Filo pastry
These are the very thin unleavened sheets of dough sold to make pastries such as baklava. The filo pastry sold in Middle Eastern grocery stores is different from the one which can be found in English supermarkets. The sheets are much

thinner and longer, which means they are more difficult to handle. They are much better value, though, as they work out at half the price and are ideal for making a large tray of baclava. I use the filo pastry from standard supermarkets to make dishes like courgette and filo pie, as it is enough to serve 4-6 people.

Freekeh
Freekeh is very popular in Palestine, but also throughout the Middle East. It is a young toasted green wheat that is harvested in the sun and then set on fire to create a charred effect on the outside, while protecting the seeds. It then goes back in the sun to intensify the flavour. This process is called rafik, which literally means rubbed, and gives freekeh its name. It has at least four times more fibre than other grains, hence its popularity.

Ginger
Ginger is available in a variety of forms - fresh, dried, crystallised, preserved and pickled. Ground ginger is powdered ginger, which has a different flavour from fresh and the two do not generally serve as substitutes for each other.

Halva or Halawa
The word simply means sweet. It is basically a sweetmeat which has sesame seeds as one of the main ingredients. The other ingredients vary, but include sugar, vanilla and nuts of choice. Halva can be purchased from Middle Eastern stores and the best quality is from Egypt, Syria and Lebanon.

Karkadeh (Hibiscus tea)
This tea has been enjoyed since the time of ancient Egyptians, who drank it hot in winter and cool as a refreshing drink in summer. It is known for its remarkable ruby red colour and subtle floral flavour. It is made from the dried sepals that form around the seed pods of the Roselle, or Hibiscus flower. In Egypt, it is drunk mainly for its medicinal benefits, as recent scientific studies have confirmed that it is high in Vitamin C and antioxidants. When buying the dried roselle (also sold as hibiscus flowers), look for the dark variety, as the light red kind has less flavours and contains more acid.

Labneh
Labneh is a yoghurt that has been strained to remove its whey, becoming thick and creamy and slightly tart. I have used Greek yoghurt in all the recipes, but labneh can be eaten with za'atar and olive oil and dipped with bread.

Lemons
The Sephardim have a predilection for the tart flavour of lemon juice. It is added to many dishes as a flavour heightener and often cooked with eggs and chicken broth as a sauce, such as avgolemono and agristada.

Ma'azahr (orange blossom water)
This is distilled water infused with fresh orange blossoms. Ma'azahr is synonymous with the Middle East and has a wonderfully distinctive aroma. It was used in most of our desserts and sugar syrups, which would not have tasted the same without it. In Egypt, we used the essence of orange blossom water, which is much stronger and has the most beautiful smell. Unfortunately, all you can find nowadays is the watered down variety, which will do, but is not the same. It is advisable to buy it from Middle Eastern shops, as the ones sometimes found in supermarkets are expensive and smell rather medicinal.

Mahlab
Mahlab is black cherry kernels and gives a special taste to breads and pastries. It is sold already ground in Middle Eastern stores and is often added when making ma'amoul. A little goes a long way.

Matza or matzos
Unleavened bread, the only type permitted during the Jewish festival of Passover.

Matzo meal
Ground matza, used instead of breadcrumbs.

Mint
Mint is an aromatic herb which has been part of Jewish cooking since biblical times. Although in the West it is generally associated with lamb, in other parts of the world it plays an important culinary role, especially in savoury dishes. Dried mint adds a refreshing touch, which is appreciated in the hot climate of the Middle East. Moroccans use it to make their national beverage, mint tea. The dried mint found in

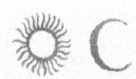

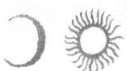

Middle Eastern stores is far superior to the one sold in supermarkets.

Paprika
This is made from the dried chilli peppers from the capsicum family. It is a popular spice, as it is smoky and sometimes hot. It is used as a flavour and also to add colour to dishes.

Pine nuts
The best variety are the slender and long ones, which can be found in Middle Eastern shops. However, the ones sold in standard supermarkets will do. Pine nuts are often toasted and scattered over the top of dishes as a garnish, but in reality the dish would not be the same without them. They are beautifully subtle in favour and, although expensive to buy, carry their weight and are well worth the extra cost. Toast them in a little butter or oil in a hot frying pan until they just turn brown, as it releases their flavour.

Pistachios
Pistachios are one of the oldest flowering trees, dating back to even earlier than 500 BC. They are used most commonly in desserts and not in main savoury meals, as you would find in Persian cuisine. They taste wonderful crushed over sweet syrupy desserts such as konafa and aish el saraya (the palace bread).

Pomegranate molasses
This is pomegranate juice that has been gently reduced, with or without added sugar, to make a syrup. It has a tangy sweet-sour flavour and is used in both savoury and sweet dishes, most traditionally in the Middle East. When buying, check the label to make sure no extra sugar has been added, that way you can control the sweet and sharp balance of your dishes. Middle Eastern supermarkets have a wide choice of brands so it's difficult to choose. They are all equally good, but I favour the label Sofra. It offers a wide range of products, including dairy and the quality is consistently good. I also like the name, as it reminds me of the Egyptian expression sofra dayma, which is said at the end of a meal and roughly translated means 'may we always have such delicious food'.

Quince
Quince is believed to predate the apple. Many references to fruit in ancient texts, such as the forbidden fruit of the Garden of Eden, were probably referring to the quince. Greek mythology associates it with Aphrodite, the goddess of love, and many believe that the golden apple given to her by Paris was a quince. It is shaped like a hybrid of an apple and pear and is at its best when slightly fragrant and a golden yellow colour. It is inedible when raw, but becomes sweet and luscious when cooked, when it acquires a deep red colour. In the Middle East, it is added to chicken and meat stews and made into a jam called safargel.

Ras El Hanout
Literally translated, this means 'the grocer's head'. It is a blend of spices very popular in North Africa. The most common one is a mixture of 12 aromatics, which generally includes cinnamon bark, whole nutmeg, dried rose buds, pieces of dried ginger, cloves and different peppers, all pounded together in a mortar. Ras El Hanout has a very distinctive aromatic scent and can be purchased in Middle Eastern grocery stores.

Rose water
This perfumed liquid is made by mixing together water and fragrant rose petals, leaving them to infuse before heating them for about 1-1½ hours to intensify the flavour. I remember the vendor of rose petals in Cairo. He used to walk the streets shouting el ward, the Arabic name for rose petals. The best quality of rose was only available one month of the year and rose water and petal jam were made on the roof of our apartment building. It was a yearly ritual which took most of the day, as it required a lot of time and patience. Like orange blossom water, it is a popular enhancer in Middle Eastern desserts.

Safffron
The red threads of the stigmas of crocus flowers tint food a rich yellow-gold and infuses it with a delicate flavour. It is a key flavouring in numerous rice and fish dishes. The threads are usually soaked in a little hot water before being added to a dish, as this helps the spice blend with the other ingredients.

Semolina
This is a finely ground wheat with a consistency like that of cornmeal. It is pale yellow in colour and can be purchased as fine or coarse in Middle Eastern supermarkets. It is used in sweet and savoury pastry dough, along with plain flour, to add a crunchy, flaky consistency - be careful not to use too much, or the dough will not be pliable enough to work with. Fine semolina is used when

making a pastry dough and I have used a mixture of coarse and fine semolina for the Egyptian dessert called basbousa.

Sesame seeds

They add a nutty flavour to savoury pastries and also look pretty as a garnish. I have used them to sprinkle on top of borekas and pasteles before baking. To bring out their aroma, dry toast over medium heat. Stir frequently until they begin to turn golden brown.

Sha'riyeh (Vermicelli nests)

This type of pasta is commonly cooked with rice in Egypt, which almost makes it a dish on its own. The sha'riyeh is toasted and then boiled with the rice, creating a nutty backdrop.

Spice mixtures

Every household had its favourite spice mixtures which they blended to taste and kept in jars as a ready condiment. In Egypt, the most popular mixture was what we called les quatre épices (the four spices). This was a ground mixture of cloves, cinnamon, nutmeg and pepper.

Sumac

Sumac is a spice which comes from the sumac tree. It goes well with pretty much everything, from salads to meat and fish and is often used as a garnish in dips such as houmous. A few sprinkles of sumac adds colour and makes all the difference to its appearance.

Tahini

This is probably the ingredient most associated with the Middle East. It is a creamy, nutty toasted sesame paste used in a countless number of dishes, which wouldn't work without it. It is great mixed with tomatoes, parsley and lemon juice and drizzled over salads, or used as a dip for bread. It is so diverse and flavourful that I have even used it in my recipe for halva and tahini brownies. When buying tahini, look for Middle Eastern brands, available in larger tubs in Middle Eastern grocery shops. Avoid the grey, sludgy-looking stuff in jars, generally sold in supermarkets. Good tahini is creamy coloured and silky. Mix in the layer of oil before using.

Tamarind

You can find this in Indian and Middle Eastern shops. It is sold as a sauce, a ready made paste or as a sticky mass of broken pods and seeds which, macerated in hot water, produces a sour, dark brown juice. The commercial paste available is easier to use. Tamarind is added to pomegranate molasses to give the dish a tart taste, which is balanced with brown sugar and dried fruit to produce the contrasting sweetness required in many of the sour-sweet Syrian dishes.

Turmeric

This is called courcoum in Arabic and is often added when cooking stews and vegetables. It is usually sold in ground form and its bright golden-yellow root gives a wonderful warming colour to a dish. It has a mildly fragrant flavour, however it is bitter in quantity, so it is important not to overuse. Used properly, it contributes a bridge between other spices, helping to blend their flavours. Although sometimes suggested as an alternative to saffron, these flavours have nothing in common, and so turmeric should never be used as a substitute, unless it is purely for colour. The fresh root variety is small finger-sized, like a minimal ginger root.

Worcestershire sauce

This comes in handy when tamarind paste is not available and it can be mixed with lemon juice to achieve a similar tart flavour. The combination of pomegranate molasses, sugar, salt, pepper and, most importantly tamarind in a sauce, gives it a tangy flavour.

Yoghurt

Yoghurt has been an important part of the Middle Eastern diet for more than five thousand years. It is mixed into salads, spooned over plates of rice and lentils and drizzled with honey for dessert. It is also customary to place a bowl of yoghurt on the dinner table, for people to help themselves. Greek yoghurt is the best, as it has been strained to remove most of its whey, resulting in a thicker consistency than unstrained yoghurt, whilst still preserving the distinctive taste of yoghurt.

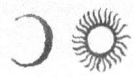

SALADS & DIPS

Salatas y mezes
Salaata we maza

Aubergine salad with dates and chickpeas

Served over a bed of couscous, this salad makes a substantial lunch. It is important to use a good quality tahini paste, so if possible buy one of the many brands available in Middle Eastern grocery stores. They are lighter and much creamier than the ones found in standard supermarkets.

Ingredients
   3 aubergines, weighing about 750g in total
   3 small onions, peeled
   6 tablespoons olive oil
   3 teaspoon ground cumin
   2 teaspoons Aleppo pepper
   salt to taste
   1 x 400g tin chickpeas, drained and rinsed
   juice of ½ lemon
   10g coriander leaves only, roughly chopped
   1½ tablespoons date syrup
   8 medjool dates, stoned and roughly chopped
   15g almonds, toasted

For the dressing
   50ml tahini
   50ml extra virgin olive oil
   1 fat garlic clove, chopped
   4 tablespoons Greek yoghurt
   juice of ½ lemon
   50ml water

Preheat the oven to 190C/ Gas Mark 5.

Prepare the vegetables - cut the aubergines horizontally into slices, about 2cm (1 inch) thick, then halve the larger slices. Halve the onions and cut each into crescent-shaped wedges.

Put the aubergines and the onions in a roasting tin, drizzle with 5 tablespoons olive oil and add the ground cumin, Aleppo pepper and salt. Mix all the ingredients and roast for 45 minutes in the preheated oven, tossing everything around every so often – the aubergines will shrink a lot.

Prepare the dressing - put all the ingredients together into a blender with 50ml water and blitz. It should be the consistency of thick cream and pourable. Add more water if it's too thick.

Cook the chickpeas while the aubergines are nearly cooked - heat the final tablespoon of oil in a frying pan and warm the chickpeas through. Season and add the juice of ½ lemon.

To serve - tip the warm chickpeas into a shallow serving bowl. Stir the coriander leaves into the aubergines and pile these on top of the chickpeas. Drizzle the tahini dressing first, then the date syrup Scatter the dates and nuts over the top.

Serve with couscous.

Betingan bil firan

Fried aubergine sandwiches

This traditional dish, called mafrum in Libya, is said to represent the biblical manna, which fell between two layers of dew. It has traditionally been served on Shabbat by many North African Jews.

3 medium aubergines, weighing about 300g each
2 tablespoons coarse sea salt
3 tablespoon olive or vegetable oil or more

Filling
  225g feta cheese, crumbled
  1 large egg yolk
  60g shredded mozzarella cheese
  salt to taste
  2 eggs, lightly beaten

Prepare the aubergines - cut them crosswise into 1cm (½ inch) slices Put in a colander, sprinkle with salt and let them stand for at least 1 hour. Rinse under cold water and squeeze out all the bitter juices until the slices feel firm and dry.

In a large frying pan, heat about 3 tablespoons oil over a medium heat. Fry the aubergine slices in batches, turning and adding more oil between each batch, until golden brown, but still slightly undercooked, about 2-3 minutes each side. Using a slotted spoon, transfer to paper towels to drain.

Make the filling – in a medium bowl, beat together the crumbled feta cheese and egg yolk and add the shredded mozzarella.

Preheat the oven to 180c/Gas Mark 4.

Make the aubergine sandwiches - using a knife, spread the cheese stuffing over half the aubergine slices and top with the remaining slices to form sandwiches. Arrange the slices in a large and slightly oiled baking dish.

Pour 2 lightly beaten eggs over the top, drizzle with a little olive oil and bake until golden brown, about 40 minutes. Serve warm or at room temperature

Note – I have used baby aubergines available in Middle Eastern groceries.

Butternut squash, sweet potato, chickpea and freekeh salad

This is a very easy salad to make and requires a minimum of work if you buy a ready to cook diced butternut squash and sweet potato mix. Pre-cooked microwavable freekeh is also available.

350g pack diced butternut squash and sweet potato mix
400g can chickpeas, drained and rinsed
2 tablespoons olive oil
¼ teaspoon nutmeg
½ teaspoon salt
1 teaspoon pomegranate molasses
1 teaspoon honey
1 cup water
250g pack microwavable cooked freekeh
1 tablespoon lemon juice
extra virgin oil

Heat the oil in a large shallow pan and fry the butternut squash and sweet potato mix with the chickpeas for 2 minutes. Add the nutmeg, salt, pomegranate molasses, honey and water.

Lower the heat, cover and cook for 15 minutes or until the water has been absorbed and the vegetables are tender.

Microwave the freekeh for 2 minutes or according to instructions. Add to the vegetables with 1 tablespoon lemon juice and stir through.

Drizzle with a little extra virgin oil.

Serve at room temperature or slightly warmed.

Note – packs of microwavable precooked freekeh are now available from most supermarkets, as are prepared diced butternut squash and sweet potatoes.

Lentil, red pepper and feta cheese salad

The Arabic word for lentils is ads and dishes cooked with lentils were very popular in Egypt, especially in the cooler months, when shorbet ads (lentil soup) often appeared at the dinner table. This dish can be served either as a salad or as a substantial accompaniment to a main course.

**200g brown lentils
1 medium onion, finely chopped
3 red peppers, deseeded and cut into 2cm (1½ inch) strips
4 tablespoons olive oil
juice of ½ lemon or to taste
1 tablespoon apple cider vinegar
75g feta cheese, crumbled
150g red or yellow cherry tomatoes, quartered (optional)
salt and pepper to taste
extra virgin oil to drizzle**

Preheat the oven to 180C/Gas Mark 4

Wash the lentils and cook in a saucepan of simmering water until they are soft, but still have some bite. This should take about 20-25 minutes. Drain and set aside.

Place the pepper strips on a baking tray, drizzle with 3 tablespoons olive oil and cook in the preheated oven for 25 minutes or until they are soft. Remove from the oven, put the peppers in a plastic bag and close it tightly. This will make it easier to remove the skins. Remove those when the peppers have cooled.

Heat 1 tablespoon olive oil in a pan and fry the chopped onion until soft and translucent, about 5 minutes.

Mix the lemon juice with the apple cider vinegar and add salt and pepper to taste. Place the cooked lentils on a large serving dish, add the fried onions, red peppers and cherry tomatoes, if using. Pour the lemon and vinegar mixture over the surface, mix well, taste and adjust the seasoning.

Crumble the feta cheese over the surface and drizzle with extra virgin oil.

Apio
(Lemony celeriac and carrots)

This is a popular Judeo Spanish dish which originates from Turkey. The lemon sauce gives it a special tang and it can be served over a bowl of rice or eaten at room temperature. Celeriac was a favourite with Sephardic Jews living in the Ottoman Empire and was often served at the Passover table in a lemony stew combined with other vegetables.

**4 cups cold water
juice of 2 lemons
900g celeriac, peeled, washed and cut into 1cm (½ inch) pieces
1/3 cup olive oil
2 medium onions, finely chopped
4 cups hot water or vegetable stock
3 medium carrots, diced
1 tablespoon sugar
½ teaspoon turmeric
salt and pepper to taste**

Combine the cold water and juice of 1 lemon in a saucepan. Peel the celeriac and cut into 1 cm (½ inch) pieces. Add to the pan, bring to the boil and cook for 10 minutes. Drain and set aside.

Heat the oil and fry the onions for 5 minutes, until translucent. Add the hot water or vegetable stock and the carrots, juice of 1 lemon, sugar, turmeric and salt and pepper to taste.

Cover, lower the heat and simmer for 20 -25 minutes until the vegetables are tender and the liquid has been absorbed. Add more lemon to taste.

Artichoke and broad bean salad

If you didn't grow up eating artichokes, they might seem a little intimidating. All but the innermost leaves are tough and you have to scrape them with your teeth to eat the tender parts, having boiled the artichoke first. They are certainly labour intensive if used as a vegetable in cooking, as it involves removing all the leaves before getting to the heart, which is completely edible and delicious. Fortunately, canned artichoke hearts are now widely available and provide an excellent alternative.

1 x 390g tin artichoke hearts, drained and rinsed
500g frozen broad beans
2 shallots, finely chopped
1 tablespoon olive oil
30g raisins, soaked in boiling water for 20 minutes, then drained (optional)
2 tablespoons pine nuts, toasted
1 teaspoon dried mint
salt and pepper to taste

For the dressing
  juice of ½ lemon
  a few saffron strands
  ½ teaspoon balsamic vinegar, preferably white
  1 teaspoon honey
  60ml extra virgin oil
  salt and pepper

Cook the artichokes for 5 minutes in boiling water. Drain and place in a large shallow serving dish In the same saucepan, cook the frozen broad beans in boiling water for 8 minutes. Drain and add to the artichokes.

Heat the oil in a pan and fry the shallots for about 5 minutes, until soft but not brown.
Add them to the artichokes and broad beans, followed by the raisins, if using, the pine nuts, dried mint and salt and pepper.

Prepare the dressing – heat the lemon juice, balsamic vinegar and saffron strands in the microwave for 1-2 minutes or in a small saucepan over a low heat for 30 seconds. Remove from the heat and cool.

Whisk in the honey and olive oil and season to taste.

Toss gently into the artichoke and broad bean mixture to combine.
Taste for seasoning – you should have a balance of sweet and savoury.

Salata matbucha

(Cooked salad)

This is more of an accompaniment to dishes than a salad on its own. It can refrigerated for a few days and should ideally be served over a bed of couscous.

2 tablespoons olive oil
1 medium onion, finely chopped
3 mixed peppers, seeded, cut into medium strips and grilled first
3 celery sticks, cut into 1cm (½ inch) pieces
1 cup water
½ teaspoon salt
½ teaspoon ground turmeric
1 teaspoon dried oregano
4 medium tomatoes, blanched in boiling water, peeled and sliced
2 tablespoons tomato paste

Preheat the oven to 180C/ Gas Mark 4

Place the pepper strips on a baking tray, drizzle with oil and cook in the preheated oven for 15 minutes or until they are softened – you can also grill them. Set aside.

Boil some water in a saucepan and blanch the tomatoes. Cool, gently remove their skin and cut into slices.

Heat 2 tablespoons olive oil in a large non stick pan and fry the onion until soft and translucent. Add the chopped celery and fry for another few minutes. Add the pepper strips, water, turmeric, oregano and salt and mix well. Cover and simmer for 15 minutes, stirring now and then.

Add the tomatoes and simmer for 15 minutes more or until the vegetables are very soft and the liquid has evaporated. Add the tomato paste, stir and remove from the heat.

Cool, refrigerate and serve with any kind of couscou.s

Note – a simpler version is to fry the onions first in a large pan, then throw in all the chopped vegetables, tomato paste and flavourings. Add the water, cover and simmer, stirring frequently, for about 30 minutes, or until all the liquid has evaporated and the vegetables are soft.

Sephardi leeks and carrots

This dish can be eaten at room temperature as a salad or served as a side dish. The balance of rice and vegetables is just right for a salad, but you can add another 20g rice for a more substantial dish. Sephardic Jews like a lot of lemon in their cooking.

2 medium leeks
3 medium carrots
40g basmati rice
4 tablespoons olive oil
juice of 1-2 lemons
1 teaspoon sugar
200ml water

Wash the leeks well, cut them lengthwise and into 2½cm (1 inch) pieces. Wash the rice, rinse and drain. Cut the carrots in 1cm (½ inch) cubes.

Heat the oil and sauté the carrots and rice for 5 minutes.

Add the leeks, lemon juice, sugar, salt and pepper and stir for 5 minutes. Pour about 200ml water, enough to cover the rice and vegetables.

Lower the heat, cover and simmer for 15 minutes or until the water has been absorbed - you may have to add a little more water. Taste and adjust the seasoning.

Add salt and pepper to taste.

Muhammara
(Walnut and red pepper paste)

4 large peppers
3 slices wholemeal bread, crusts removed
175g walnut pieces
1 garlic clove, crushed
3 tablespoons pomegranate molasses
juice of 1 lemon
1 teaspoon sugar
½ teaspoon salt
¼ teaspoon Aleppo chilli flakes
½ teaspoon ground cumin (optional)
125ml extra virgin oil

Muhammara is a spicy pepper dip that originated from Aleppo, Syria, with one of the ingredients being Aleppo chilli flakes. There are many different versions and this is my favourite, a mix of savoury, sweet and smokey.

Roast the peppers - place them in a hot preheated oven 200C/Gas mark 5 for 30 minutes, turning once, until they are soft.

Remove and place them in a strong plastic bag, twisting it closed - this will make it easier to remove the skin. When the peppers have cooled, remove the skin, stems and seeds. Squeeze to remove any excess juice.

Place the peppers in a food processor with all the other ingredients. Blitz until the mixture is blended to a creamy paste. Eat with pita bread.

Note - Use paprika if you can't find Aleppo pepper or chilli flakes.

Smoked aubergine salad with fig, feta cheese and bulgur

This is a Syrian recipe, where dried fruit is used as a balance against the saltiness of the feta cheese. You can substitute the figs with dates or leave them in and add a few dates. Medjool dates are by far the best variety, they are more expensive but go a long way.

Ingredients
   2 medium aubergines
   1 green pepper
   1 yellow pepper
   2 tablespoons olive oil
   50g dried figs
   150g bulgur wheat
   300ml boiling water
   100g feta cheese, crumbled

For the dressing
   2 garlic cloves
   juice of ½ lemon
   150g yoghurt
   2 tablespoons olive oil

   2 tomatoes, diced
   handful flat-leaf parsley
   sea salt and ground pepper

Preheat the oven to 200C/ Gas Mark 7

Trim the tops off the aubergines and cut them into bite-size chunks. Place in a colander and sprinkle some salt. Leave for 30 minutes, then squeeze out the bitter juices.

Halve the peppers and remove the seeds and white membrane. Cut them into strips. Place the peppers and aubergines in a roasting tin. Drizzle over 2 tablespoons oil and add some salt and pepper. Toss well to coat, then place in the oven and roast for 45 minutes, until tender.

Meanwhile, tip the bulgur wheat into a heatproof bowl and sprinkle with salt. Chop the dried figs into small pieces and stir into the bulgur wheat. Pour in 300ml water and cover with a large plate. Set aside to soak the water for 15 minutes.

Prepare the dressing - peel the garlic cloves, finely chop or grate them and place them in a bowl. Squeeze in the juice of ½ lemon, stir in the yoghurt, 2 tablespoons of olive oil, and a little salt and pepper. Mix well to combine and set aside.

Dice the tomatoes and finely chop the parsley, both leaves and stalks. Use a fork to fluff up the bulgur wheat, add the crumbled feta cheese and mix well. Stir through the roasted aubergines and peppers, along with the diced tomatoes, chopped parsley and half the yoghurt dressing.

Pile on serving plates and serve drizzled with the remaining yoghurt dressing.

Mango and pepper salad on a bed of couscous

'Instant couscous' is widely available and the advantage is that it requires no additional steaming or lengthy cooking, but only soaking in hot water. It does not fluff up as nicely as the traditional unprocessed medium-grain variety found in Middle Eastern stores, but it works well in salads.

150g instant couscous
200ml hot water
3 tablespoons olive oil
1 large onion, finely chopped
2 large yellow peppers, cut into small pieces
1 large unripe mango, cut into small pieces
½ teaspoon ras-el-hanout spice
½ teaspoon allspice
½ teaspoon ground cinnamon
1 teaspoon sugar
juice of ½ lemon, or to taste
salt and pepper to taste
handful of raisins (optional)
extra virgin olive oil for sprinkling

Place the couscous in a medium bowl and pour over 200ml boiling water. Cover and leave for 10 minutes or more until all the water is absorbed.

Heat the oil in a large pan and fry the onion until translucent, about 10 minutes. Add the pepper and continue frying for another 10 minutes, until they are well coated and soft. Add the mango, ras-el-hanout, allspice and cinnamon. Mix well to combine, add salt and pepper and lemon juice to taste.

Fluff up the couscous and place in a serving bowl. Spread the onion, pepper and mango mixture on top and scatter a handful of raisins, if using. Taste and adjust the seasoning and sprinkle with a little extra virgin oil.

Note - it is important to use an underripe firm mango, as it will disintegrate otherwise.

Baby spinach salad with tomatoes and mozzarella

Summer salads should be easy to make and this one can be prepared in a matter of minutes. Mozzarella, tomatoes and basil are classics combinations and baby spinach adds colour and extra flavour.

125g baby spinach, washed and ready to eat
2 vine tomatoes, cut thinly crosswise
125g mozzarella cheese, buffalo or in a ball
2 teaspoons balsamic vinegar
2 tablespoons extra virgin olive oil
a few basil leaves, cut into thin strips
4 large green olives (optional)
4 artichoke hearts (optional)
salt to taste

Alternate layers of spinach and tomatoes across a plate. Top with the mozzarella cheese and basil leaves. Add the green olives and artichoke hearts if using.

Drizzle with oil and vinegar. Season to taste with salt and pepper.

Serve immediately.

Fennel, apple and pomegranate salad

The sweetness of the apples works well against the aniseed flavour of the fennel and the salad looks very pretty with the pomegranate seeds sprinkled through. I like to roast the fennel first in a little olive oil, but that is entirely optional.

2 fennel bulbs, sliced
4 red apples, sliced
juice of 1 lemon
seeds of 1 pomegranate
small bunch fresh dill, roughly chopped

For the dressing
150ml extra virgin oil
75ml apple cider vinegar
2 tablespoons caster sugar
1 teaspoon sea salt

Cut the fennel bulbs into half moon slices and roast in a preheated over for 15 minutes – that is optional

Put the fennel and sliced apples in a bowl and squeeze over the lemon juice. Turn them in the juice to prevent them going brown.

Add the pomegranate seeds and dill and mix together well.

Mix the dressing ingredients together in a small bowl. Pour this over the salad and toss so that it is well combined.

Note – you can add some cooked basmati rice to this salad. Only add room temperature or cold rice, otherwise the heat will make the salad go limp.

Cauliflower salad with tahini and onions

The combination of roasted cauliflower, sweet onions and tangy lemon tahini dressing is one of my favourites. It is important that the cauliflower florets retain a bite and are not allowed to get mushy. I blanch them first for 3 minutes in boiling water to soften them, then roast them drizzled with olive oil.

1 head cauliflower, broken into florets
2 tablespoons olive oil
1 medium red onion, sliced and cut into crescents
1 teaspoon zaatar spice
100g large green olives
1 tomato, cut into wedges
salt and pepper to taste

For the dressing
   3 tablespoons tahini
   2 tablespoons Greek yoghurt
   Juice of 1-2 lemons
   1 teaspoon sea salt

Preheat the oven to 200C/ Gas Mark 7.

Blanch the cauliflower florets in boiling water for 3 minutes. Drain, rinse with cold water and drain again.

Put the florets on a baking tray. Pour over 2 tablespoons oil and scatter the onions, the zaatar spice and a little salt. Mix well so that it is all coated. Bake for 20-25 minutes.

Remove the cauliflower florets and onions from the baking tray when cooked and cool for 10 minutes in a bowl. Add the tomato and green olives and mix together.

To make the dressing, mix the tahini, yoghurt, lemon juice and salt. Adjust the seasoning and add a little more water if needed – the dressing should have the consistency of double cream.

Transfer the cauliflower to a serving dish. Drizzle the dressing over the top and serve warm or at room temperature.

Fig, walnut and goat's cheese salad

This salad is perfect for a light lunch or served as a summer course. You can prepare all the components ahead and assemble just before serving. The goat's cheese can be substituted with feta cheese.

4 large ripe figs, cut into quarters or 8 small ones cut into halves
50g walnut halves
185g goat's cheese log, broken into pieces
1 teaspoon honey
juice of ½ lemon
2 tablespoons extra virgin oil
½ teaspoon Dijon mustard
2 pears, cored and thickly sliced
70g bag of rocket or baby leaf salad

Heat the grill to medium. Place the figs, walnut halves and goat's cheese on a lined baking tray. Grill for 5-6 minutes, to soften the figs and cheese.

In a small bowl, whisk together the honey, lemon juice, olive oil and mustard.

Place the pears and rocket or baby leaf salad on a serving dish and toss together with the dressing. Top with the grilled figs, walnuts and goat's cheese.

Note – if using feta cheese instead, do not grill the cheese but crumble it over the salad at the last minute.

Lentil and tahini dip

400g canned or cooked lentils, rinsed and drained
70g sundried tomatoes
3 tablespoons tahini
1 tablespoon soy sauce
½ teaspoon ground cumin
3 tablespoons water
juice of ½ lemon

This Middle Eastern inspired dish only take a few minutes to prepare and is loaded with healthy ingredients and protein. Lentils are high in fibre, vitamins B, iron and folate, amongst other things. The dip is the perfect appetiser or snack, accompanied by pita bread or other vegetables.

Place all the ingredients in a food processor or blender and blend until smooth.

Note – the dip can be kept in the fridge in a sealed container for up to one week.

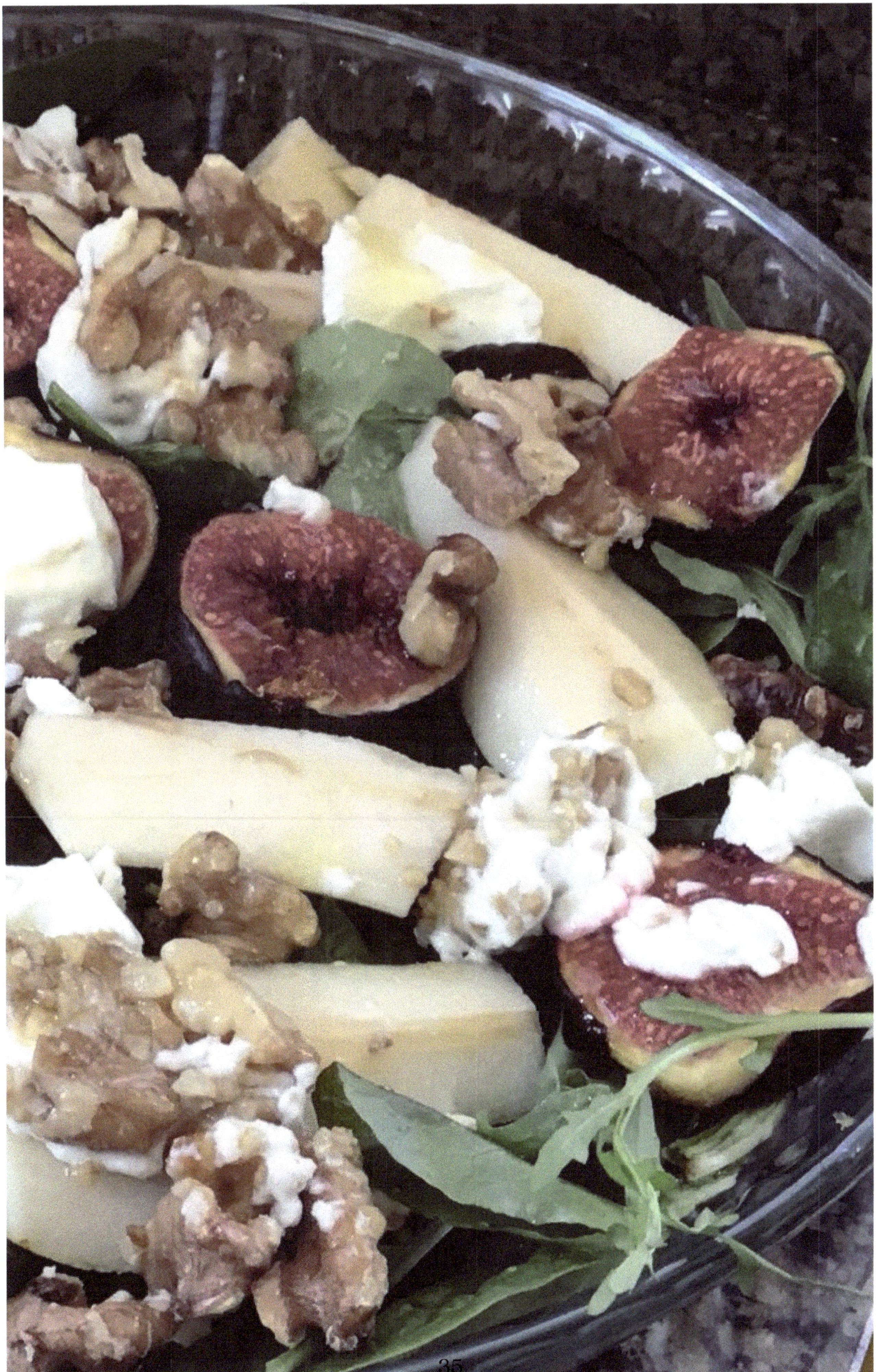

Mutabbal
(Aubergine dip)

2 large aubergines
1 tablespoon coarse sea salt
oil for drizzling
2 tablespoons tahini paste
4 tablespoons Greek yoghurt
juice of 2 lemons
1 garlic clove
salt to taste
pomegranate seeds, to serve

Mutabbal is a very popular Middle Eastern dip made with smoky roasted aubergines, tahini and garlic. Many people would recognise it as babaganoush, but the difference is that mutabbal contains yoghurt, whereas babaganoush does not. I prefer mutabbal, as the end result is creamier.

Preheat the oven to 200C/Gas Mark 6

Prick the the aubergines all over with a fork. Drizzle with salt and olive oil and cook in the preheated oven for about 30 minutes, until they are soft.

Remove from the oven, cool and peel them. Open the skin, scoop out the flesh and and chop into small pieces. Put in a sieve and set aside for- about 5 minutes to drain the excess water away.

Put the chopped aubergines in a bowl and add the tahini, yoghurt, lemon juice, garlic and salt. Mix it all together and adjust the seasoning - you may wish to add more salt or yoghurt.

Drizzle with some olive oil and top with pomegranate seeds.

Taramasalata
(Fish roe dip)

A proper taramasalata dip is nothing like the sweet, lurid pink, full of preservative ones sold under that name in supermarkets. Traditional taramasalata is a soft creamy colour and bread is added to the roe, to give it a milder taste and a thicker consistency. It is perfect on pita bread, accompanied by a salad.

250g smoked fish roe
½ small onion
100g stale, crustless white bread
2-3 tablespoons lemon juice
200ml extra virgin oil, plus extra to serve

Finely grate the onion, then drain through a sieve and discard the solids. Put the bread in a dish, cover with cold water, drain immediately and squeeze out the excess water.

Put the onion juice, bread and roe in a food processor and pulse together until relatively smooth. Slowly add the lemon juice and oil until well combined, checking the mixture all the time. Season and add more lemon juice to taste.

Note – add 2 tablespoons of chopped smoked salmon to the taramasalata in the food processor to give the dip an extra layer of flavour and richness.

Courgette, leeks and walnut salad

Summer salads are often about combining what you have left over in your fridge. This is a simple salad of leeks and courgettes, with the addition of walnuts, to give it some crunchiness. The vegetables should be cooked al dente, otherwise they will go floppy.

**1/3 cup walnuts
1 garlic clove, finely grated
2 tablespoons lemon juice
5 tablespoons olive oil, divided
2 large leeks, white and pale green parts only
2 large courgettes (about 400g)
small bunch flat-leaf parsley**

Halve the leeks lengthwise and leave some root attached. Halve the courgettes lengthwise.

Preheat the oven to 180C/Gas Mark 4.

Toast the walnuts in the warm oven for about 10 minutes, or use a small dry skillet over medium heat, tossing them for 3-4 minutes.

In a small bowl, combine the warm walnuts with the garlic, lemon juice and 3 tablespoons olive oil. Season with salt and pepper.

Brush the leeks and courgettes with the remaining 2 tablespoons oil. Season with salt and pepper and roast the vegetables until tender, about 15 minutes.

Transfer to a cutting board. Trim the roots from the leeks and cut them into bite-size pieces. Do the same with the courgettes.

Add the leeks and courgettes to the bowl with the walnuts and dressing and toss to combine. Adjust the seasoning, add more lemon juice if desired and drizzle with a little extra virgin oil.

Salatet il Rahib

(Monk's aubergine salad)

This salad originates from Lebanon and is thought to be named after a monk who created the dish from the produce he tended in his garden. It is based on a recipe I found in a book called Palestine on a Plate by Joudie Kalla, and it has become a summer staple ever since.

2 large aubergines
130/140ml olive oil, plus extra for rubbing
1 small red pepper, deseeded
½ green pepper, deseeded
3 medium vine tomatoes, chopped
½ onion, chopped
3 spring onions, chopped
20g fresh flat-leaf parsley, chopped
1 small garlic clove, crushed
2 small teaspoons dried mint
juice of 1-2 lemons
1 pomegranate, seeded
salt to taste
1 teaspoon zaatar

Preheat the oven to 220C/Gas Mark 7 and line a baking tray with baking parchment.

Use a sharp knife to pierce the aubergines on all sides and rub them with some oil. Place the aubergines on the prepared baking tray. Bake for about 35-40 minutes, until they are charred and brown.

Meanwhile, prepare the rest of the salad. Mix the peppers, tomato, onion and spring onions in a bowl. Add the parsley, garlic, zaatar and dried mint and mix together.

Squeeze in the lemon juice and add the olive oil and salt to taste.

When the aubergines are ready, take them out of the oven and leave them until they are cool enough to handle. Cut them in half and scoop out the fresh, discarding the skin. Squeeze well to get rid of the bitter juices. Roughly chop the flesh and add it to the salad.

Mix everything together, adjust the seasoning to taste and add more salt or lemon juice if needed. Top with the pomegranate seeds and serve with pita bread.

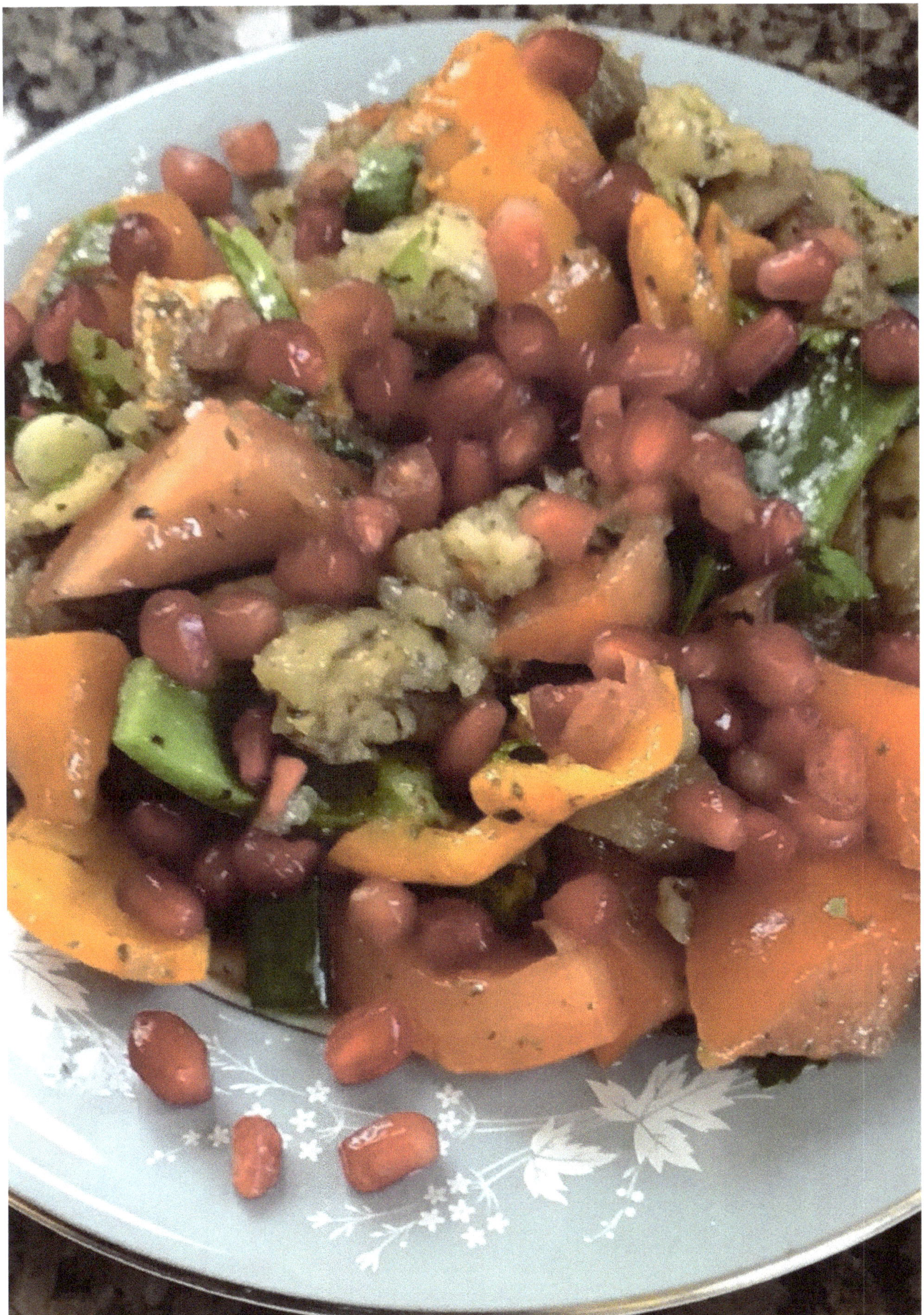

Salmon salad with honey dressing

This summer salad can be served as a starter or a main course. Use ripe nectarines and strong honey, such as eucalyptus, to give the salmon a richer flavour.

6 salmon fillets, weighing about 150g each
3 tablespoons olive oil
salt and pepper
1 tablespoon clear honey
3 tablespoons water
3 ripe nectarines
200g mixed salad leaves

For the dressing
    6 tablespoons extra virgin olive oil
    1 tablespoon clear honey
    juice of 1 orange
    1 teaspoon balsamic vinegar
    salt and pepper to taste
    1 red apple, cored and chopped into small pieces

Preheat the oven to 200C/Gas Mark 6.

Place the salmon fillets on a baking tray and season with salt and pepper. Mix the honey with 3 tablespoons water and pour over the salmon. Cover and bake for 20 minutes. Remove from the oven and leave to cool.

Prepare the dressing – combine the olive oil, honey, orange juice and balsamic vinegar. Add salt and pepper to taste.

To serve, line a serving dish with the mixed salad leaves. Add the nectarines and chopped apple. Place the cooled salmon fillets on top and pour over the dressing.

Note – add the apple just before serving. The dressing will keep up to three days in the fridge.

Spinach and artichoke dip

This is a no cook, no bake version of a spinach and artichoke dip, which is useful if you don't like last minute preparations. It's great as a starter and can be made the day before and refrigerated, covered with foil. It's also a good party dip.

250g fresh spinach or 140 frozen spinach, thawed
150g canned artichokes, drained and rinsed
1 garlic clove, grated
100g cream cheese
50g feta cheese
2 tablespoons Greek yoghurt
½ tablespoon lemon juice
salt and pepper to taste

Remove the stems from the spinach and chop it very roughly if the leaves are large. Wash well and pat dry. Place the spinach in a pan with a splash of water over medium heat and let it wilt gently, about 4 minutes. Stir a few times in between.

If using frozen spinach, place it in a saucepan and let it thaw on low heat, covered, for about 5 minutes. Stir occasionally.

In both cases, place the spinach in a colander. Once cool enough to handle, take handfuls of spinach and squeeze them well in your hand in order to remove as much moisture as possible. Chop the spinach finely or purée it for 10 seconds in a food processor.

Place the spinach in a bowl. Drain the artichokes, rinse well and drain again. Pat dry with kitchen paper, chop finely and add them to the bowl with the spinach.

Add the grated garlic, cream cheese, crumbled feta, yoghurt and lemon juice. Add salt and pepper, stir well and adjust the taste. Add more lemon juice if necessary.

Spinach and orzo salad

Orzo is a rice shaped pasta that can traditionally be prepared as pasta or cooked and served in much the same way as rice. It can be enjoyed hot or cold and is commonly a part of soups and salads. This dish can be eaten at room temperature, so is a great addition to picnics. All by itself, it makes for a light, but substantial lunch and it's a distinctive looking dish on the dinner table.

1 head garlic
5 tablespoons extra virgin oil
(plus extra for roasting the garlic)
2 teaspoons salt
225g orzo pasta
225g washed spinach, divided
2 tablespoons lemon juice
80g gruyère cheese
50g grated parmesan cheese
small bunch flat-leaf parsley, finely chopped

Preheat the oven to 190C/Gas Mark 5

Roast the garlic – slice off the top of the bulb, exposing the cloves. Lightly drizzle with oil and roast in the preheated oven for about 30 minutes, or until the cloves are lightly browned and tender. Once cool, peel the garlic cloves.

While the garlic is roasting, bring a saucepan of water to the boil. Add 1 teaspoon salt and the orzo pasta. Cook, stirring s couple of times to prevent sticking, until al dente, about 8 minutes. Drain and set aside.

Place half the spinach, 1 tablespoon lemon juice and 4 tablespoons olive oil in a food processor and purée until smooth.

Heat the remaining 1 tablespoon olive oil in a small sauté pan over medium heat. Add the remaining spinach and sauté for 1-2 minutes until wilted. Remove from the heat.

In a large bowl, fold the spinach purée into the orzo pasta. Add the wilted spinach, roasted garlic cloves, gruyère cheese, parmesan, chopped parsley and remaining 1 tablespoon lemon juice. Toss to combine and add salt and pepper to taste.

Note- this dish can be stored in the fridge for up to 3 days. Washed ready to eat spinach available in packs from supermarkets is easier to use.

43

SOUPS
Supas
Shorba

Tandir Corbasi
(Turkish mixed légume soup)

This is a mixed bean soup, similar to a Lebanese version called makhlouta. The name tandir is derived from the Persian word for a clay oven (tandor), which is where this soup was traditionally cooked. The Turkish word corba comes from shorba, the Persian and Arabic word for soup. This is an ideal winter soup.

2 tablespoons olive oil
2 onions, finely chopped
3 garlic cloves, minced
1 tablespoon tomato paste
2 litres water or vegetable stock

400g can chickpeas
120g red lentils
1 small courgette or leek, chopped
1 teaspoon ground coriander
1 teaspoon ground cumin
120g bulgur wheat, preferably coarse
400g can cannellini beans or pinto beans
1 teaspoon salt
ground black pepper
2 teaspoons dried mint (optional)
small bunch of flat leaf parsley, finely chopped (optional)

In a large pot, heat the oil over medium heat. Add the onions and garlic and sauté until soft and translucent, 5-10 minutes. Add the tomato paste and stir until slightly darkened, about 1 minute.

Stir in the stock, chickpeas, courgette or leek, red lentils, ground coriander, cumin and salt and pepper. Bring to a boil, reduce the heat, cover and simmer for about 45 minutes.

Add the bulgur wheat and cannellini or pinto beans and simmer for a further 15 minutes, stirring occasionally, until all the vegetables are tender and the soup has thickened. Add more water if necessary.

If using, add the mint and parsley just before serving.

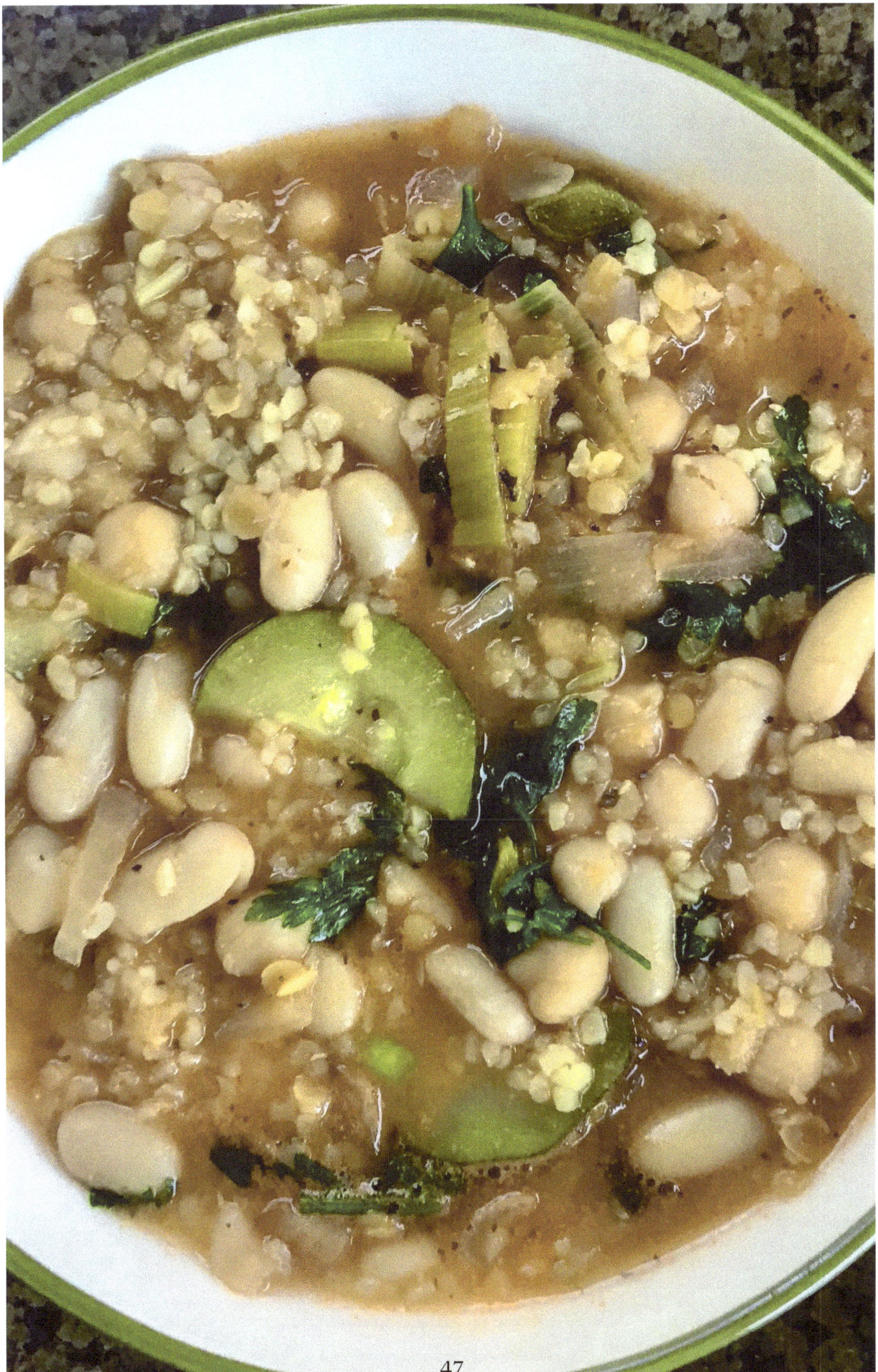

Artichoke and vegetable soup

Along the Mediterranean, artichokes are plentiful and inexpensive, with the first crop appearing in early Spring. Tinned artichoke hearts or frozen artichoke bottoms are a good alternative. The soup can be kept chunky or puréed in a blender.

30g butter
1 medium onion, finely chopped
2 medium carrots, finely chopped
4 celery sticks, chopped
3 garlic cloves, crushed
3 tablespoons flour
1000 (1 litre) vegetable stock
1 medium courgette, chopped
300g frozen artichoke bottoms
OR 380g can artichoke hearts, drained and rinsed
2 teaspoons dried mint
juice of ½ lemon
celery leaves (optional)
salt and pepper
150ml single cream

Melt the butter in a large saucepan and add the chopped onion. Fry for a couple of minutes, then add the garlic, chopped carrots and celery Fry for 5 minutes and add the flour. Mix well until all the flour is well blended.

Add the vegetable stock, courgette and artichokes bottoms or hearts, dried mint, lemon juice and celery leaves (if using). Add salt and pepper to taste, cover and cook on a low heat for 30 minutes. Blend in the single cream, stir well and turn off the heat.

Note - If using artichoke bottoms, you will have to cut them up when the soup has cooled.

Carrot and sweet potato soup

I love this thick and creamy soup, it's easy to make, but the most important thing is to get a pleasing balance between the sweet potatoes and the carrots. I have used the same quantity for both, but it's a matter of taste and you can adjust this according to your preference.

60g unsalted butter
500g carrots
500g sweet potatoes
1 small white potato
½ teaspoon ground cumin
1 litre water
salt and pepper

Wash and peel the carrots, sweet potato and potato. Cut into small chunks.

In a large saucepan, melt the butter. Fry the vegetables for a few minutes until they are all coated.

Add the water, ground cumin and salt and pepper. Cover, lower the heat and simmer for 25-30 minutes until the vegetables are tender.

Blend the soup in a food processor or in an electric blender.

Artichoke and rice soup

Although artichoke cultivation dates back to Roman times, it was the Moors who first fell in love with this vegetable, beginning to cultivate it in Spain around 800. It subsequently became a frequently used ingredient in Sephardic cooking, prepared in countless recipes

400g can artichokes hearts
2 tablespoons olive oil or unsalted butter
1 large onion, chopped
2 garlic cloves, minced
1000ml (1 litre) chicken or vegetable stock
1 celery stick (optional)
100g long grain rice
juice of ½ lemon
salt to taste

Drain and rinse the artichoke hearts. Wash and drain the rice

In a large saucepan, bring the chicken or vegetable stock to the boil Throw in the rice, lower the heat to medium, cover and cook for 20 minutes

In a small frying pan, heat the oil or butter and fry the chopped onion until golden Add the minced garlic and fry for a couple more minutes Stir the onion and garlic mixture into the stock and rice, cover and cook for 20 minutes on a low heat

Add the artichoke hearts, the celery if using, lemon juice and salt to the pan - you may have to add more water to the stock Lower the heat and cook for a further 30 minutes until the stock has reduced and the rice is tender

When cool, purée the soup in a blender or food processor until smooth

Avgolemono
(Egg-lemon chicken soup)

Avgolemono or egg-lemon is a family of sauces and soups made with egg yolk and lemon juice, mixed with broth and heated until they thicken. In Sephardic cuisine, it is also called agristada and in Arabic beida bi lemoune. This is a Judeo Spanish recipe and a delicious alternative to the traditional chicken soup served at the start of the Shabbat meal.

4 chicken legs, weighing about 1kg
25g flour
3 eggs, beaten
juice of 1½ lemons
salt and pepper to taste

Boil the chicken legs for about 1 hour until tender. Remove from the chicken from the pan, cool and shred it into small pieces.

Transfer all the chicken stock to a jug. Remove about 120ml of the stock and slowly blend it into the flour in a bowl until the mixture is smooth.

In another bowl, mix the beaten eggs and lemon juice.

Transfer both the flour and stock mixture and the egg and lemon mixture to a large saucepan. Simmer, stirring constantly. When it begins to thicken a little, gradually and very slowly start adding the remaining stock in the jug– one ladle at a time to begin with, then gradually increasing the quantity until all the stock has been used.

Remove from the heat when the sauce has thickened, but still has a pouring consistency and add salt and pepper to taste.

Transfer to a bowl and add the chicken pieces. Serve hot.

Note - some people like adding 250g cooked rice to the soup just before serving.

Eshkaneh
(Persian onion soup)

Persian dishes often contain sweet and sour flavours. In this dish, the sweetness of the onions and sugar is balanced by the tartness of the lemon and the flavour of dried mint. Eshkaneh is usually eaten with lavash or pita bread and the soup is customarily garnished with parsley.

3 tablespoons vegetable oil
4 large onions, thinly sliced, weighing about 1kg
40g sugar
1 tablespoon flour
4 cups water
¼ teaspoon ground turmeric
1 teaspoon salt
¼ teaspoon ground black pepper
100-120ml fresh lemon juice
2 teaspoons dried mint
¼ teaspoon ground cinnamon
2 large eggs, lightly beaten
chopped fresh parsley to garnish

In a large saucepan, heat the oil over medium heat. Add the onions and fry until translucent, about 10 minutes. Sprinkle with 1 tablespoon of the sugar and sauté until golden, about 5 minutes.

Stir in the flour and cook, stirring, for about 3 minutes. Gradually add 1 cup of the water, scraping to loosen any brown bits. Add the remaining 3 cups water, ground turmeric, salt and pepper.

Bring to a boil, cover, reduce the heat to low and simmer, stirring occasionally, until all the flavours have blended, about 40 minutes.

Add the lemon juice and the remaining sugar, tasting to adjust the tartness. Simmer for 10 minutes and stir in the mint and cinnamon.

Just before serving, gradually whisk 1 cup of the hot soup into the beaten eggs. Add the egg mixture to the soup and simmer, stirring constantly until thickened, about 3 minutes. Do not allow the soup to boil.

Serve warm, garnished with the parsley.

Celeriac and Jerusalem artichoke soup

The Jerusalem artichoke, despite its name, is not an artichoke at all and has nothing to do with the Holy Land, nor does it taste like an artichoke. It looks like a tuber with lumpy knots and a brownish skin. It has a sweet-nutty flavour when cooked. Similar in flavour to celery, celeriac is ideal mashed or added to stews.

2 tablespoons olive oil
1 large onion, diced
500g celeriac, peeled and cut into 1cm (½ inch) pieces
800g Jerusalem artichokes, peeled and cut into 1cm (½ inch) pieces
2 large carrots, peeled and left whole
½ teaspoon dried thyme
5 cups vegetable broth
salt and pepper to taste

Heat the oil in a large pan and sauté the onion until translucent, about 5 minutes.

Add the celeriac, Jerusalem artichokes and carrots and continue to sauté for a few more minutes. Add the vegetable broth, dried thyme, salt and pepper, lower the heat, cover and simmer for 15 minutes.

Remove the lid and continue simmering for a further 15 minutes or until the vegetables are completely soft. Discard the carrots.

Pulse the soup in a blender or food processor, leaving about a fourth of the soup chunky.

Chicken and rice soup

Chicken soup is undoubtably symbolic of Jewish cuisine and is often referred to as the 'Jewish Penicillin'. As early as the 13th century, Maimonides, the Judeo-Spanish philosopher and physician, had advocated the health properties of this broth. This flavoursome and nutritious version is thickened with rice and is a comfort food guaranteed to lift your spirits on a cold winter evening.

750g chicken thighs or legs
3 celery stalks
bunch of celery leaves (optional)
125g rice
juice of 1 lemon
½ teaspoon ground turmeric
1 teaspoon cinnamon
4 cardamom pods or ½ teaspoon ground cardamom

Put the chicken thighs or legs in a saucepan with 2½ litres (4 pints) of water. Bring to the boil and remove the scum.

Add in all the remaining ingredients, cover and simmer for 1½ hours until the rice has softened. The texture should be creamy.

When cool, remove the skin and bones from the chicken, cut into chunks and put back in the soup.

Corn soup

This is one of the easiest soups to make and requires a minimum of preparation. You can use 2 x 325g cans of sweetcorn if you don't have any frozen - just drain, wash well and cook in the same way..

900g frozen corn kernels
450g potatoes, peeled and cut into 2cm (1 inch) pieces – about 3 large potatoes
1 medium onion, peeled and chopped
900ml chicken or vegetable stock
42g butter
240ml double cream
2 teaspoons sugar (optional)
salt and pepper to taste

Place the corn, onion, potatoes and broth in a large saucepan over medium heat. Bring to the boil, reduce then heat and cook covered for 15-20 minutes, or until the potatoes are tender.

Stir in the butter and cream. Mix to combine and simmer for 2-3 minutes. Turn off the hea.t

Cool for a few minutes, transfer to a blender or food processor and purée in batches until smooth. If the soup is too thick, add some water or milk to reach the desired consistency.

Add sugar, salt and pepper to taste.

Leek and potato soup

Potato and leek soup is a classic and there is nothing better than a bowl of this hearty soup on a chilly day. I like adding crème fraîche or cream to give it a richer taste

500g potatoes
500g leeks
1 litre water
500ml milk
250ml crème fraîche (optional)
salt and pepper

Peel and cut the potatoes in 2cm (1 inch) cubes.

Trim the leeks and chop them very finely into a food processor – they should look almost puréed.

Place the leeks and potatoes in a large saucepan. Add the water, milk and salt and pepper to taste. Simmer for 1 hour.

Cool and lightly mash the potatoes with a masher.

Serve with crème fraîche.

Green vegetable and lemon soup with rice

The most important ingredients in this soup are the rice and lemons. With regard to the vegetables, you can substitute the leeks and/or celery with other green vegetables, such as courgettes or swish chard.

4 tablespoons sunflower oil
3 large leeks
2 medium onions sliced lengthwise to form thin crescents
5 celery sticks
150g kale (optional)
18 litres chicken or vegetable stock (3 pints)
200g cooked rice
juice of 2 lemons
salt and pepper to taste

Wash the rice well and drain. In a medium saucepan, bring 400ml water to the boil, add the rice and a little salt. Cover, lower the heat and simmer for 12-15 minutes, or until all the water has evaporated and the rice is tender.

Prepare the vegetables - peel the onions and cut them in thin slices lengthwise. Wash the leeks and celery thoroughly and cut them into thin slices. If using kale, chop into small chunks.

Heat the oil in a large saucepan and fry the onions until translucent. Add the leeks and celery and fry for 5 minutes. Add the prepared chicken or vegetable stock and the kale if using, then the cooked rice and lemon juic. Add salt and pepper to taste.

Cook covered on a low heat for 30 minutes or until some of the liquid has been absorbed.

Kale, chickpeas and freekeh soup

This is much more than just a soup, because of the variety of ingredients. The freekeh is a delicious addition and gives the soup a rich and nutty flavour It can easily be served as a main course.

3 tablespoons sunflower oil
1 small onion finely chopped
2 garlic cloves crushed
2 teaspoon ground coriander
1 teaspoon ground cumin
1 teaspoon baharat spice
1 teaspoon salt
1 litre warm vegetable stock
2 carrots, diced
200g cooked freekeh or 250g packet of precooked freekeh
1 teaspoon salt
400g can chickpeas, drained and rinsed
200g kale
3 tablespoons lemon juice
2 tablespoons extra virgin olive oil
natural yoghurt to serve

Cook the freekeh in a medium saucepan with 400ml water until tender. Alternatively microwave the packet of precooked freekeh for 2 minutes and set aside.

Heat the sunflower oil in a small frying pan. Add the chopped onion and crushed garlic and fry over medium heat for 4 minutes. Add the coriander, cumin and baharat spice and continue cooking for a further 3 minutes, stirring constantly.

Place the onion and spice mixture into a large saucepan containing the warm vegetable stock. Add the salt, diced carrots and cooked freekeh. Cover and cook for about 15 minutes or until the carrots are tender.

Add the drained chickpeas and cook for a further 10 minutes. Finally, add the kale, lemon juice and extra virgin oil and cook covered for a further 10 minutes.

Serve with a dollop of natural yoghurt on the side.

Shorba fireek
(Syrian pinto bean and freekeh soup)

Pulses, such as lentils, chickpeas, haricot, broad beans and pinto beans, lend themselves beautifully to make rich soups, which are enhanced by the use of spices, lemon, garlic and herbs. There are infinite combinations and you can vary the spices and add more or less lemon and garlic, according to taste.

2 tablespoons olive oil
1 onion finely chopped
1 teaspoon ground coriander
½ teaspoon ground cumin
½ teaspoon sumac
¼ teaspoon Aleppo pepper
600ml vegetable or chicken stock
2 large carrots, finely chopped
2 celery sticks, finely chopped
400g can tinned chopped tomatoes
150g freekeh
400g can pinto beans, drained and rinsed
bunch of chopped coriander
salt and pepper to taste

Wash and cut the carrots and celery in small pieces. Rinse and drain the freekeh.

Chop the onion and fry in the olive oil for 10 minutes. Add the coriander, cumin, sumac and Aleppo pepper. Stir well and cook for 3 minutes.

Add the vegetable or chicken stock, carrots, celery and chopped tomatoes. Cook for 5 minutes and add the freekeh, pinto beans, chopped coriander, salt and pepper. Cover and cook on a low heat for 45 minutes or until the freekeh is tender.

Drizzle with extra virgin olive oil and lemon juice to taste. Serve with natural yoghurt on the side.

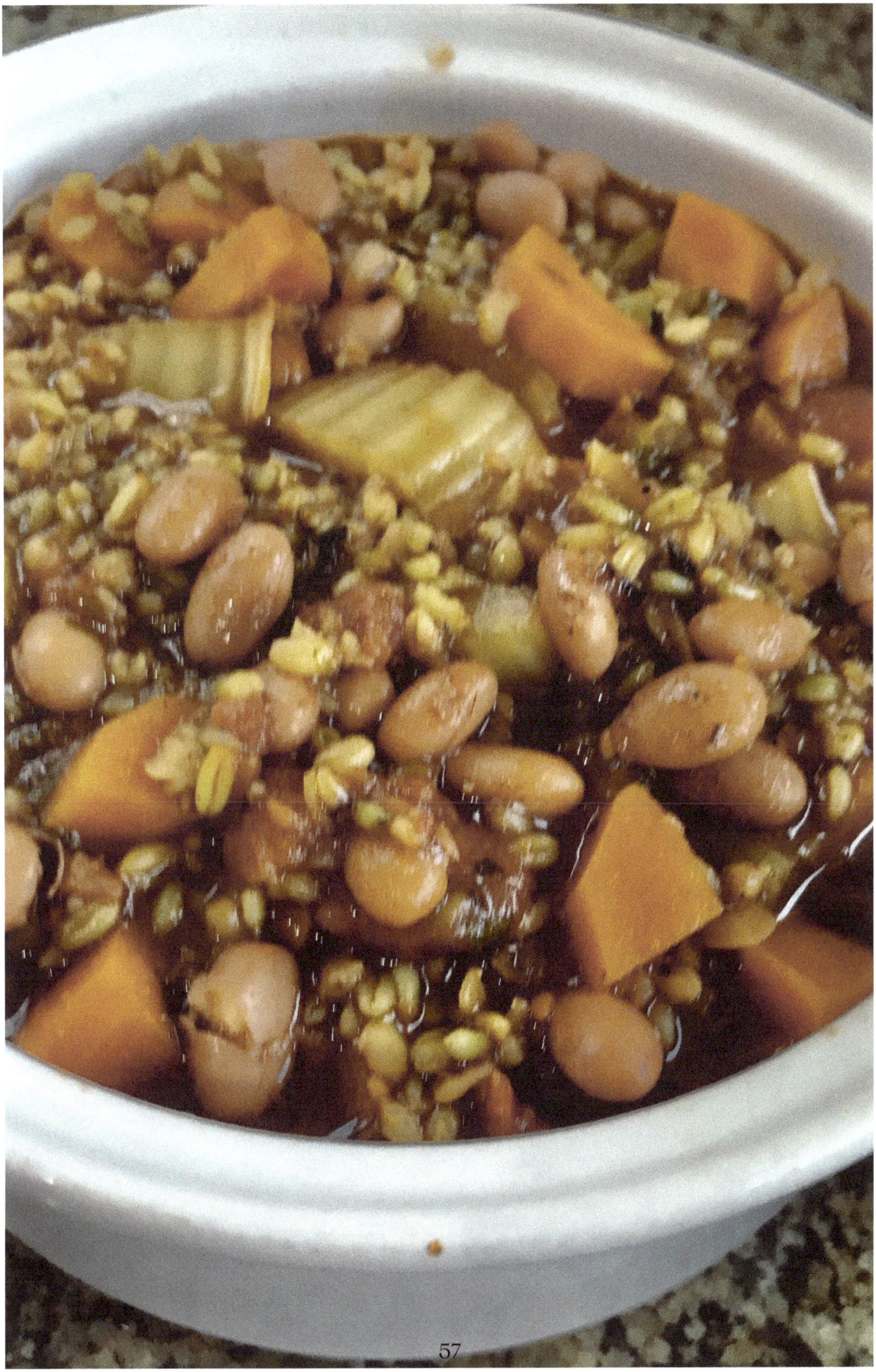

Shorbah Sabanekh

(Syrian spinach and yoghurt soup)

"Spinach soup is popular in spring and summer in many parts of the Middle East, as it is light and can be served at room temperature. Syrians usually favour dried mint, but other herbs can be used, as well as ginger. The yoghurt can be stirred into the soup or a few dollops added just before serving. The soup is usually eaten with pita bread.

50ml vegetable oil
2 onions, coarsely chopped
3 -4 garlic cloves, minced
800g fresh spinach or 2 x 400g packs frozen spinach, squeezed dry
6 cups vegetable stock
180g basmati or long grain rice
2 teaspoons dried mint
1 teaspoon salt
½ teaspoon pepper
juice of 1 lemon
2-4 cups plain yoghurt

In a large saucepan, heat the oil over medium heat. Add the onions and garlic and sauté until soft and translucent, 5-10 minutes. Gradually add the spinach, stirring until wilted, about 5 minutes.

Add the stock, rice, dried mint, lemon juice, salt and pepper. Bring to the boil, cover, reduce the heat to medium low and simmer until the rice is tender, about 20 minutes.

Leave the soup with a chunky texture or process in a blender or food processor until nearly smooth. If too thick, add a little more stock.

Top each portion with several dollops of yoghurt or stir the yoghurt into the soup. Serve hot or chilled.

Note - If reheating after the yoghurt has been added, do not boil.

Sopa de cebada

(Greek barley soup)

Barley was not often used by the Sephardim and only occasionally to thicken soups or in a dessert called sleehah. When used in soups, it was enhanced with fresh herbs, cheese and milk or yoghurt, giving the dish a creamy texture.

2 tablespoons vegetable or sunflower oil
2 medium onions, chopped
1 garlic clove, minced
2 tablespoons dried marjoram
1 teaspoon dried rosemary
20g fresh flat-leaf parsley, finely chopped
6 cups vegetable stock or water
200g pearl barley
1 medium potato, peeled and cut into small chunks
2 carrots, peeled and chopped
500ml milk
3 egg yolks, lightly beaten
50g grated parmesan
salt and pepper

In a large pot, heat the oil over medium heat. Add the onions and sauté until soft and translucent, about 5 minutes. Stir in the garlic, marjoram, rosemary and chopped parsley and sauté for 1 minute.

Add the stock or water, pearl barley, carrots, potato and salt and pepper. Bring to the boil, lower the heat, cover and simmer for 50 minutes until the barley is tender, but still chewy. Add the milk and heat through. Remove the soup from the heat and cool for 10 minutes

Pour 1 cup of the soup into a small jug and mix in the beaten egg yolks. Stir this into the soup pan and add the cheese.

Place the pan over a low heat and simmer, stirring constantly until the soup thickens, about 3 minutes. Do not boil.

Sopa de Endjinaras

(Artichoke soup)

This soup makes use of seasonal artichokes, which were available in Egypt in late spring and summer. Fresh artichokes are hard to get in England and are also expensive, so canned artichoke hearts will do well. You can keep the soup chunky, in which case omit the potatoes and replace with 200g fresh tomatoes and a fennel bulb. I have opted for the smooth texture version. For extra flavour, serve with grated parmesan cheese.

400g can artichoke hearts, drained and rinsed
3 tablespoons olive oil
1 large onion, finely chopped
2 large garlic cloves, minced
1 large potato, peeled and chopped 2cm (1inch) cubes
2 celery sticks, chopped into 1cm (½ inch) pieces
1 teaspoon salt
2 teaspoons lemon juice
1 litre vegetable stock

In a large heavy pan, heat the oil and fry the onions until translucent, about 5 minutes. Add the garlic and sauté for another 3 minutes. Stir in the artichoke hearts, celery and potato and sauté until shiny, about 2-3 minutes. Add the vegetable stock, salt and lemon juice.

Bring to the boil, reduce the heat and cover. Simmer for 30 minutes or until the vegetables are tender.

When cool, purée the soup in a blender or food processor. You may have to add a little water if you prefer a thinner texture.

Note: I make the vegetable stock by mixing 1 tablespoon bouillon powder with some boiling water. More vegetable bouillon powder may be needed, according to taste.

Tomato and rice soup

A perfect summer soup, which can be served at room temperature. Use fresh ripe tomatoes for best results.

2 tablespoons olive or sunflower oil
1kg ripe tomatoes, peeled, seeded and coarsely chopped
3 cups chicken or vegetable stock
2 celery sticks, chopped very finely
10g flat leaf parsley, finely chopped
50g long grain rice
salt and pepper to taste

Heat the oil in a large pan and add the tomatoes. Cook, stirring often and mashing them down with a wooden spoon, until they break down into a purée – about 10 minutes.

Heat the chicken or vegetable stock in a separate saucepan. Add the rice, tomatoes, celery and parsley. Add salt and pepper to taste.

Bring the mixture to a boil over a high heat. Lower the heat and simmer uncovered for about 20 minutes, stirring occasionally, until the rice is tender.

Sopa de huevos y bulgur

(Sephardic egg and bulgur soup)

Egg-and-lemon soups are prevalent in Sephardic cooking, particularly during the summer. Many versions contain chicken. This one uses bulgur instead, which makes it a hearty winter soup. The eggs give it an extra richness and creaminess.

40ml olive oil or vegetable oil
340g coarse bulgur
2 litres vegetable stock or water
about 1½ teaspoons salt
700g fresh tomatoes, peeled, seeded and chopped or 2 x 400 g cans chopped tomatoes
juice of 1½-2 lemons
4 large eggs
bunch of parsley, chopped
30g grated emmental or gruyère (optional)

In a large saucepan, heat the oil over medium heat. Add the bulgur and sauté until well coated and lightly coloured, about 5 minutes. Add 1 litre of the stock or water and ½ teaspoon of salt. Bring to the boil, lower the heat and cover. Simmer until the liquid is absorbed and the bulgur is tender, about 20 minutes.

Add the remaining 1 litre stock or water, the tomatoes with their juices or chopped tomatoes and the remaining salt. Bring to the boil, lower the heat and simmer, stirring occasionally until the tomatoes are tender, about 5 minutes. Remove from the heat.

Whisk the lemon juice into the eggs. Gradually whisk 1 cup of the hot soup into the eggs and stir the egg and stock mixture into the pan.

Place over a low heat and simmer, stirring constantly, until the soup begins to thicken, about 5 minutes. Do not boil or the soup will curdle.

Serve hot, sprinkled with the parsley and the cheese.

Lentil and chickpea soup

In the Middle East, soups are often eaten as a meal in itself either for lunch or dinner, accompanied by Arab bread. They are rich with vegetables, meat, pulses, cereals and rice and are sometimes indistinguishable from stews, except for the fact that they have very much more liquid. The beauty of soups is that you can add anything to them, as long as you allow time for the cooking. This soup can equally be served as a starter in winter or a main course in spring and summer.

2 red onions, finely chopped
2 tablespoons sunflower or vegetable oil
150g brown lentils
400g can chickpeas, drained and rinsed
400g chopped peeled tomatoes
1 tablespoon tomato purée
1 teaspoon turmeric
¼ teaspoon ground ginger
20g chopped parsley
20g chopped coriander (optional)
1 tablespoon bouillon powder
1 litre water
80g orzo pasta
juice of ½ lemon

Rinse the brown lentils, cover with water and let them soak for 30 minutes. Wash and drain the canned chickpeas.

Heat the oil in a large saucepan and fry the red onions for 5 minutes. Add the drained lentils and chickpeas, followed by the peeled tomatoes, tomato purée, ground ginger, turmeric and chopped parsley and coriander, if using. Add the bouillon powder, water and salt to taste.

Bring to the boil, lower the heat, cover and simmer for around 45 minutes until the lentils are tender. Keep checking as you may have to add some water.

After 45 minutes, add the orzo pasta and lemon juice and cook for a further 10 minutes.

My special chicken soup with vegetables

There is nothing more comforting than a hearty chicken and vegetable soup in winter. This soup, along with the Egyptian mmolokheya are my favourites when the weather turns colder. I have made it with chicken, but the vegetarian version works just as well — simply add some bouillon and a couple of onions to the water, then proceed with the rest of the vegetables.

4 chicken legs
2 litres water
3 celery sticks, cut into 2cm (1 inch) pieces
a few celery leaves (optional)
3 carrots, cut into medium chunks
1 large courgette, thickly cut
1 large leek, cut into 2cm (1 inch) pieces
100g orzo pasta

Pour 2 litres of water in a large saucepan and add the chicken legs. Bring to the boil and remove any scum which rises to the surface. Add the celery leaves, if using. Cover and cook for 15 minutes.

Wash the carrots and celery sticks and cut them into chunks or pieces. Add them to the saucepan and cook for another 15 minutes.

Add the leeks and courgettes and cook for 10 minutes. Finally add the orzo pasta and cook for a further 10 minutes.

Uncover and check that the chicken and all the vegetables are cooked. When the soup has cooled, remove the chicken legs, cut into small chunks and return to the pan.

Note - I add the vegetables gradually as carrots and celery take longer to cook than leeks or courgettes. I try to buy celery from Turkish or Middle Eastern shops as their celery is the long variety with a lot of leaves, which is ideal for this soup.

GRATINS & EGG DISHES

Komidas con keso y uevos
Atbakh jibnah wa beid

Prasa quajado
(Potato and leek bake)

Quajado is most often prepared by Sephardic Jews for Passover, although it's a dish which can be made all year round. The name comes from asquajado, which means coagulated in Ladino. This version uses leeks, very popular in Sephardic cooking, but you can mix and match any vegetables.

400g potatoes
600g leeks, white part only, sliced and washed well
4 large eggs, lightly beaten
100g grated Emmental or cheddar
salt and pepper to taste
3 tablespoons olive oil

Preheat the oven to 180C/ Gas Mark 4.
Put 2 tablespoons oil in the bottom of 22 x 22 cm (9 x 9 inch) baking dish and swirl to cover the bottom and sides.

Bring a pot of salted water to a boil. Peel and cut the potatoes into even chunks. Cook in the boiling water until tender, about 10-15 minutes. Drain, lightly mash and set aside.

Place the leeks in a steamer set into a pot with a few inches of boiling water that does not reach the bottom of the steamer. Cover the pot, turn the heat to medium and let the leeks cook for about 10-15 minutes until softened. Take them out, put in a colander and squeeze out as much water as possible with the back of a spoon.

Mash together the leeks and potatoes. Add the eggs, salt, pepper and cheese and mix well.

Place the oiled baking dish in the preheated oven for 3-4 minutes, as this will help create a crisp crust on the bottom. Spread the mixture evenly in the baking dish and gently brush with the remaining 1 tablespoon olive oil.

Bake for 25-30 minutes until the top is golden brown.

Serve at room temperature with a salad for a light lunch, or as a vegetarian side dish.

Note – the dish will keep in the fridge for 3 - 4 days. It can also be frozen.

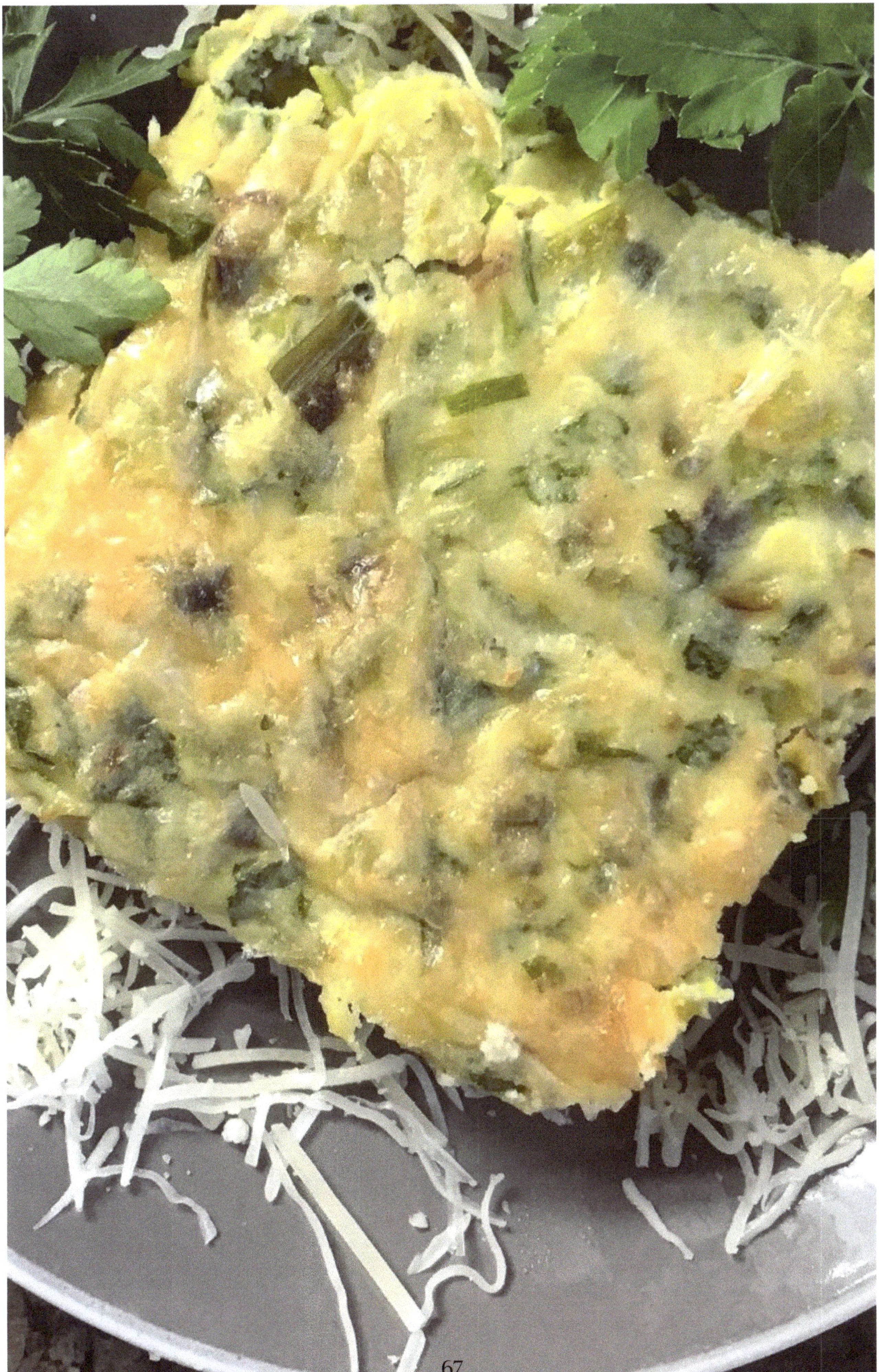

Berendjenas con keso

(Baked aubergines with cheese)

This dish reminds me of many holidays spent in Italy as a teenager, of the warm Mediterranean sea and the Italian songs that were popular at the time. We didn't have much money when we first came to England and the highlight of the year was spending three weeks in August in a villa my aunt, who lived in Milan, had rented for the family. The dish made a light and satisfying lunch, ideal after a morning spent on the beach. The aubergines were grilled and mashed the evening before, quickly assembled with the rest of the ingredients in the morning, then put it in the oven for 40 minutes while we freshened up before lunch.

4 aubergines
300g mozzarella
100g grated cheese, gruyère, emmental or cheddar
2 eggs, lightly beaten
2 large slices bread, crusts removed
4 tablespoons oil
juice of ½ lemon
50g parmesan cheese

Preheat the oven to 180C/Gas Mark 4.

Wash the aubergines and prick them all over with a fork. Place them under the grill of a hot oven until the skin is soft, about 25 minutes. Cool, peel them and squeeze as much of the dark juices as you can. Mash with with a fork until they are soft (do not put in the food processor as this will change the consistency).

In a separate bowl, shred the mozzarella cheese. Mix with the lightly beaten eggs, the bread (soaked in water and squeezed dry) grated cheese, juice of ½ lemon and 4 tablespoons oil. Add the mashed aubergines and combine.

Put the mixture in an oiled baking dish and sprinkle with the parmesan cheese.

Transfer to the preheated oven and cook for about 40 minutes until lightly coloured.

Note: this is a slightly different version from the aubergine flan (Almodrote de berendjenas) recipe, as it uses bread to bind and no onions. Also, I substituted the feta cheese with mozzarella - this is the Italian cheese my aunt used and it has the advantage of melting nicely in the oven.

Courgette filo pie

Filo is a very versatile pastry, used to make sweet and savoury dishes, from baklava and almond cigars to filo triangles filled with cheese, spinach or meat. It was difficult to get when we first came to England in the late 1950's and could only be found in a handful of specialised supermarkets. Nowadays, it is widely available, but the quality varies greatly. The filo pastry sold in Middle Eastern supermarkets is the thinnest and therefore gives a lighter and flakier result.

1 standard packet filo pastry (270 grams, 7 sheets)
4 tablespoons sunflower oil
1 large onion, chopped
600g courgettes
about 70g butter or margarine, melted
200g feta cheese
4 large eggs
salt and pepper
a handful of grated cheddar cheese

Preheat the oven to 180C/Gas Mark 4.

Peel and chop the onion and fry in hot oil for 5 minutes. Wash the courgettes, cut them into very small pieces and fry them with the onion, adding a little more oil if necessary Continue cooking for 10 minutes until the courgettes have softened. Cool.

In a small saucepan, melt the butter or margarine. Brush the base of a baking dish with some of the melted butter I used a 28 x 22cm (11 x 9 inch) rectangular dish as the length of the filo pastry sheets fits well into it.

Place one sheet of the filo pastry at the base of the buttered dish. Brush liberally with the melted butter. Add another 3 sheets of filo pastry, brushing each sheet with the melted butter.

Place the courgette mix over the filo pastry and crumble the feta cheese over the surface. Beat the eggs lightly and spoon over the feta cheese. Add the last 3 sheets of filo pastry, always brushing each sheet with melted butter. Press gently to flatten.

Mould the filo pastry that's hanging over the edges and crimp it. Brush with the remaining melted butter and scatter a handful of grated cheese over the top.

Bake in a preheated oven for 40 minutes until the top is golden.

Feta, aubergine and sweet potato bake

I like the combination of feta cheese, fried aubergines and sweet potatoes, as they seem to blend together. I have added carrots, but that is entirely optional.

2 medium sized aubergines
3 tablespoons sunflower oil
2 medium sized sweet potatoes
3 small carrots (optional)
200g feta cheese
4 large eggs
120ml milk
½ teaspoon mixed spice
salt and pepper
30g parmesan cheese

Preheat the oven to 180C/Gas Mark 4.

Wash the aubergines and cut into 3cm (1½ inch) chunks, sprinkle with salt and leave for 30 minutes. Rinse and squeeze out the bitter juices. Fry in 2 tablespoons sunflower oil until brown on both sides. Set aside.

Peel the sweet potatoes, wash and cut into small chunks. Place on a baking tray, sprinkle 1 tablespoon oil and cook in a moderate oven for 20 minutes until they have softened. Set aside.

Wash and peel the carrots, cut them into small chunks and boil for 5 minutes. Wash under cold water and drain.

Beat the eggs and add the milk, mixed spice, salt and pepper.

Assemble the dish - in a 22 x 22 cm (9 x 9 inch) baking dish place half the aubergines, sweet potatoes and carrots. Crumble half the feta cheese on top and pour over half the egg and milk mixture. Continue with the remaining vegetables and feta cheese and pour the remaining egg and milk over the surface.

Sprinkle with parmesan cheese and bake in the preheated oven for 30 minutes until the top starts to brown.

Kalavassas reynadas con keso

(Courgettes stuffed with cheese)

Courgettes contain 95% water, so it is recommended to extract some of the moisture before sautéing. In this recipe, you can do this by squeezing out any excess water before frying the pulp. The prevalent Middle Eastern way of stuffing courgettes is to hollow out the whole squash, using a naqqara (a thin long-handled scoop). A melon baller or apple corer are good substitutes, but attention must be paid not to damage the sides or the bottoms. The labour involved is quite intensive and the Sephardic way is simply to halve them, which is what I have done in this recipe.

4 large courgettes, weighing about 1kg
3 tablespoon oil
3 medium tomatoes
1 tablespoon tomato purée
1 cup water
200g feta cheese, crumbled
150g grated cheese, cheddar or emmental
50g mozzarella cheese
1 egg
100g mashed potatoes
bunch of parsley, finely chopped
4 tablespoons flour
1 egg, beaten
3 tablespoons sunflower or vegetable oil to fry
20g parmesan cheese

Preheat the oven to 180C/Gas Mark 4

Prepare the courgettes - cut them in half vertically. Carefully take out the pulp inside, working from both sides and leaving ½ cm of flesh. Fry the courgette pulp with the tomatoes and tomato purée in 1 tablespoon hot oil. Add 1 cup water and cook until the water is absorbed. Spread the mixture on the base of a lightly oiled ovenproof casserole dish. Set aside.

Prepare the cheese mixture - peel the potatoes, cut them into chunks and boil them until cooked. Mash them and add the crumbled feta cheese, grated cheese, mozzarella and egg. Add salt to taste and some chopped parsley.

Next cut the hollowed courgettes into 12cm (5 inch) pieces. Toss them first in the flour, then in the beaten egg. Heat 2 tablespoons oil and fry the courgettes.

Place the fried courgettes over the cooked pulp in the casserole dish, then fill each one with some of the cheese and egg mixture. If you have any mixture left, spread it amongst the courgettes.

Cover with a lid or foil and bake in the preheated oven for 1 hour or until the courgettes are soft. Check midway through the cooking and add a little water if necessary.

Sprinkle some parmesan cheese just before serving.

Keftes de prasa y patatas

(Leek and potato patties)

Makes 25 fritters

Leeks have a special place in my heart, probably because they were my father's favourite vegetable and were cooked in various dishes by his family. Leeks are loved all over the Mediterranean and one of the most traditional ways of enjoying them is in the form of leek patties.

500g leeks, ends trimmed and dark green tops removed
1 medium onion, peeled
300g potatoes, peeled and quartered
2 eggs, lightly beaten
3 tablespoons finely chopped flat-leaf parsley
1 tablespoon finely chopped dill
4 tablespoons breadcrumbs or matzo meal
salt and pepper to taste

For shallow frying:
vegetable or sunflower oil

Remove the outer layers of the leeks. Cut into half lengthwise and across into chunks. Wash thoroughly.

Put the leeks, whole onion and potatoes in a pan of salted hot water. Bring to a boil, cover, reduce the heat and simmer for 30 minutes or until tender. Drain in a colander and let the vegetables cool. Squeeze out as much water as possible.

Blitz them in a food processor, pulsing a few times until combined - the mixture should not be puréed and should retain some consistency. Combine the leek potato mixture with the eggs, parsley and dill. Add salt and pepper and enough breadcrumbs or matzo meal for the mixture to hold its shape. Chill in the fridge for 30 minutes.

Shape the patties – with a small bowl nearby, dampen your hands and shape the mixture into round patties, about 5cm (2inch) wide. Place on a lined tray.

Heat some oil in a large frying pan over medium heat. When it is hot, gently drop the patties and fry 3- 4 minutes on each side. Lower the heat if they are browning too quickly, as they must cook through, but not burn, adding more oil if necessary. Scoop out with a slotted spoon and drain on paper towels.

Serve hot with a tomato sauce or garlic dip.

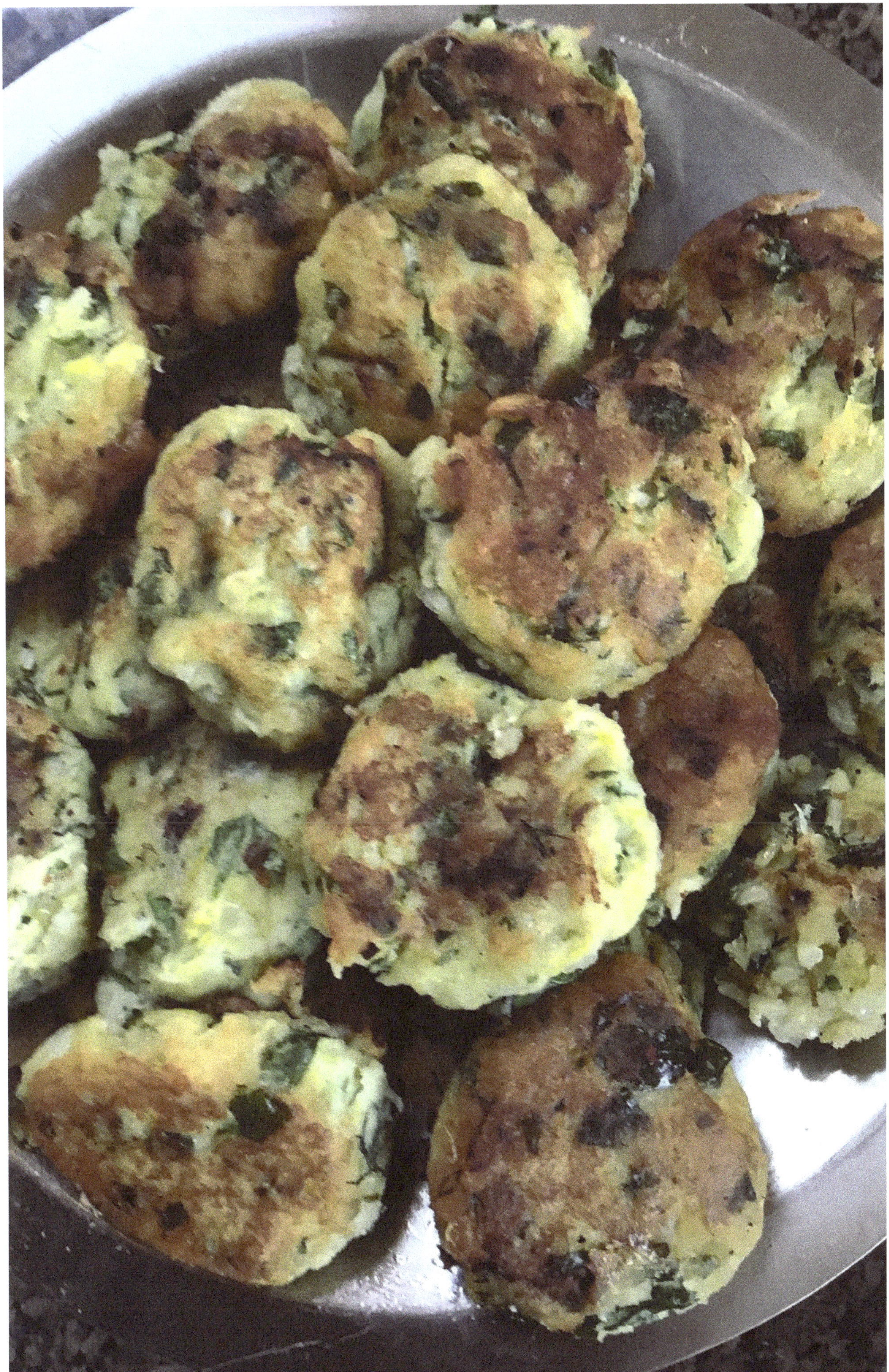

Leek and courgette pie

The Ladino word for leek is prasa. Also known as Judeo-Spanish, Ladino is the spoken and written language of Sephardi Jews of Spanish origin. My father often conversed in Ladino with his family and leeks were very often used in their cooking.

200g red or brown onions, finely chopped
400g courgettes, finely chopped (about 2 courgettes)
600g leeks, finely chopped (about 3 large leeks)
4 tablespoons sunflower or vegetable oil
60g flat leaf parsley, finely chopped

100g unsalted butter, melted
10 sheets filo pastry
finely grated zest of 1 lemon
1 teaspoon dried mint
100g mozzarella cheese, shredded
100g grated cheese
3 large eggs, beaten
2-3 teaspoons sesame seeds

Preheat the oven to 170C/Gas Mark 3.
Grease the base of a 28 x 22cm (11 x 9 inch) deep baking dish.

Heat 3 tablespoons oil in a large heavy pan or frying pan, add the onions and leeks and turn the heat down. Cook gently for 10 minutes, until softened. Add the remaining 1 tablespoon of oil, the courgettes and parsley and continue to cook over a low heat for a further 15 minutes, stirring occasionally.

Lay one sheet of filo pastry over the base of the prepared tin and mould gently into its shape, allowing the ends to fall over the edge of the tin. Don't worry if it breaks a little. Brush well with melted butter Repeat this with 5 more sheets of pastry, brushing each sheet with the melted butter as you go. Press down gently over the 6 sheets of filo pastry to flatten them.

Add the lemon zest and dried mint to the leek and courgette mixture and spoon over the filo pastry. Sprinkle the shredded mozzarella and grated cheddar over the surface and pour in the beaten eggs.

Add the remaining 4 layers of filo pastry, brushing each filo sheet with melted butter first. Fold the hanging edges over the top of the pie, brushing down gently. Brush the top filo sheet with a little more melted butter and scatter sesame seeds.

Bake in the preheated oven for 30 minutes until golden on top.
Serve hot or cold.

Leek and matza bake

3 medium leeks
60g butter
½ teaspoon salt
½ teaspoon black pepper
¼ teaspoon nutmeg
200ml double cream
5 large eggs
3 matzah sheets
115g grated cheddar cheese

This recipe is similar to the Sephardic Mina de prasa, but it's more like a pie, as the matzah is mixed with eggs and cream, rather than layered. It's also richer, because of the cream.

Preheat the oven to 180C/Gas Mark 4.
Grease and line a 22cm (9 inch) square pan.

Discard the green leaves of the leeks, cut lengthwise and rinse. Cut into thin rings and sauté in the butter for 15 minutes until the leeks are tender. Add salt, pepper and nutmeg.

In a small bowl, mix the eggs with the cream.

In a medium bowl, break the matzah and soak it in one cup of warm water for 3 minutes. Squeeze dry. Mix the matzah with a third of the cream and egg combination and line the bottom of the pan with this.

Mix the leeks with the remaining cream and egg mixture, add the cheese and spread over the matzah in the pan.

Bake for 1 hour or until the mixture sets and is golden brown.

Carchof jiben
(Syrian artichoke and cheese casserole)

2 x 390g cans artichoke hearts
3 tablespoons olive oil or unsalted butter
1 large onion, chopped
340g grated cheddar or gruyère cheese
6 large eggs
salt and pepper to taste
20g grated parmesan cheese

This dish reflects the common Sephardic practice of cooking vegetables with cheese and eggs. Artichokes and cheese have a great affinity and the texture of this dish is firm and custard-like. It is commonly served with pita bread.

Preheat the oven to 180C/Gas Mark 4.
Lightly grease a 22 x 22cm (9 x 9 inch) casserole dish.

Drain and wash the artichoke hearts and chop each one into quarters
In a large, heavy base saucepan, heat the oil and fry the onion until translucent, about 5 minutes. Add the artichokes and sauté for another 5 minutes.

In a large bowl, mix together the cheese, eggs, salt and pepper and stir in the artichokes and onions. Spoon the mixture in the prepared casserole dish and sprinkle with parmesan cheese.

Bake until golden brown, about 40 minutes. Place on a wire rack and allow to cool and set for 5 minutes and serve warm.

Almodrote de kalavassa

(Courgette flan)

Many recipes for almodrote have survived from fourteenth and fifteenth century Spain. Casseroles consisting of eggs, vegetables and cheese remain a mainstay of Sephardic cooking and go by many names, such as almodrote, frittada, quajado and sfongo. Almodrote hails from Turkey and can be made with eggplant, spinach or courgettes. It differs from frittada in that it contains a lower ratio of eggs, with a heavier focus on the vegetables.

3 medium courgettes, weighing about 800g in total
4 tablespoons flour
½ teaspoon baking powder
2 large eggs
4 tablespoons olive oil
200g mozzarella cheese, grated
130g feta cheese, crumbled
salt and pepper to taste
grated parmesan for sprinkling

Preheat the oven to 180C/Gas Mark 4.
Lightly oil a 22 x 33cm (9 x 13 inch) baking dish.

Peel and grate the courgettes. Press with your hands to squeeze out as much water as possible.

Place the grated courgettes in a large bowl and add the eggs, shredded mozzarella, feta cheese, oil, salt and pepper and mix well. Add the flour and baking powder and combine.

Pour the mixture in the baking dish and sprinkle the top with some grated parmesan.

Bake in the preheated oven for 45-60 minutes, until the top is lightly coloured.

Note – you can substitute the mozzarella cheese with 150g grated cheddar or emmental.

Prasifutchi

(Leek and potato gratin)

Leeks were a favourite in my father's family, as were all green vegetables; that was probably due to their Judeo Spanish heritage, where leeks were often included in many dishes. Their ancestors were expelled from Spain in 1492 and many settled in the Ottoman Empire, where they were welcomed. My father's favourite lunch was a simple leek omelette, which my mother often made for him. I put this recipe together long after he had passed away and I know he would have appreciated it, so making it somehow keeps his memory alive.

2 - 3 large leeks
3 tablespoons olive oil
4 large potatoes
4 large eggs
250g grated cheese
 (emmental is better, but any grated cheese is fine)
50g grated parmesan cheese
salt and pepper
two handfuls of breadcrumbs

Preheat the oven to 180C/Gas Mark 4.

Begin by washing the leeks and removing the green stalks. Cut them lengthwise, then chop into small pieces. Transfer to a baking tray and sprinkle with olive oil and some salt. Place in the oven for 15 minutes or until soft. Remove, cool, then press to remove any excess water.

Meanwhile, peel the potatoes, cut them into small pieces and cook them with some boiling water. Mash, adding a little milk and butter.

Transfer the mashed potatoes into a large mixing bowl, add the leeks, eggs, salt and pepper and 250g grated cheese. Mix well and transfer to an oiled baking dish. Spread the mixture evenly and sprinkle with the breadcrumbs and parmesan cheese.

Bake for about 20 minutes or until browned.

Almodrote de berendjena

(Aubergine flan)

This dish originates from Turkey, and even earlier from Spain. In the Ottoman Empire, Sephardic vegetable-egg-and-cheese casseroles became known as almodrote, which is Ladino for 'hodgepodge'. Aubergine has a great affinity with cheese, which enhances its flavour and helps to bind it. Blending with eggs helps to create a custardy texture. Use feta cheese for a strong flavour and cream cheese for a milder consistency. I like to use a combination of cheeses.

1 large aubergine
2 medium onions, finely chopped
2 tablespoons sunflower or vegetable oil
2 large eggs, beaten
300g sieved cottage cheese
100g crumbled feta cheese
150 grated cheese, gruyère or cheddar
salt and pepper

Preheat the oven to 180C/Gas Mark 4.

Prick the aubergine with a fork and cook on a baking sheet in a pre-heated oven 190C/Gas mark 5 for 30 minutes or until the flesh is soft. Turn the aubergine several times during baking. Remove from the oven and cool. Cut in half and scrape the soft flesh away from the skin.

Heat the oil and fry the onions until translucent, about 5 minutes Mash the aubergine and place in a bowl. Add the remaining ingredients, reserving about 25g of the grated cheese. Mix well.

Pour into a greased baking dish and sprinkle the remaining 25g of cheese.

Bake in the preheated oven for 45 minutes.

Sfongo
(Spinach and potato pie)

This is a good dairy meal for Passover, although it can be served all year round.

12kg potatoes
50g butter
125ml milk
2 eggs, lightly beaten
100g cottage cheese
50g grated parmesan
¼ teaspoon nutmeg
salt and pepper
750g fresh spinach
2 tablespoons olive oil

Preheat the oven to 200C/Gas Mark 6.

Peel the potatoes, cut into chunks and boil until soft. Mash them and add the butter, milk, eggs, cottage cheese, 30g of the parmesan cheese, nutmeg and salt and pepper. Mix well until blended.

Wash the spinach, drain and squeeze out the excess water(or use pre washed spinach). Cook over a low heat in a pan for 3 minutes, until the leaves soften. Cool and remove any excess water again.

Cover the base of 22 x 22cm (9 x 9 inch) baking dish with 2 tablespoons oil. Spread half the potato mixture over the surface, followed by the spinach and finally the remaining potato mixture. Sprinkle the top with the remaining 20g parmesan cheese.

Bake in the preheated oven for 40 minutes, until the top is lightly coloured.

Spinach and potato frittata

This is a useful recipe for a quick lunch, as all the ingredients are mixed together in a bowl. You can prepare the mixture a couple of hours in advance and refrigerate it until ready to cook.

4 large eggs
1 large potato, grated
1 small onion, finely chopped
200g spinach leaves, chopped
50g grated cheddar cheese
small bunch flat-leaf parsley, chopped
salt and pepper to taste

Prepare the frittata mixture by mixing all the ingredients well.

Heat enough sunflower or vegetable oil so the frittata mixture does not stick to the pan (about 3 tablespoons). When the oil is hot, throw in the mixture, spread it all over the frying pan and fry over a low heat for 10 minutes.

Transfer the frying pan to a pre heated oven at 180C/Gas mark 4 or place under a grill for a further 10 minutes or until the top is cooked.

Remove from the oven and carefully turn over the frittata (you may have to cut it into two halves to do that). Return to the hob and cook over a low heat for a further 3 minutes.

Mina de prasa

(Sephardic Leek-and-cheese matzah pie)

Minas are Passover pies, lasagne-like pastries using soaked matzo instead of pasta. They can be filled with vegetables, cheeses or meat. If making a layered bake, it is important to soak the matzah for no longer than 2 minutes, otherwise it will disintegrate and fall apart. The leeks can be substituted with courgettes, or a mixture of both.

5 medium leeks
50g unsalted butter or vegetable oil
1 onion, chopped
250g ricotta cheese
150 grated cheddar or gruyère cheese
4 large eggs
1 teaspoon nutmeg
1 teaspoon salt or to taste
4-5 matzah sheets

Preheat the oven to 180C/Gas Mark 4.
Lightly oil at 20 x 20cm (8 x 8 inch) square baking pan.

Cut away the root ends from the leeks and most of the green part and discard. Cut the leeks in half lengthwise and then crosswise into thin slices. Soak in cold water, swish around to loosen any dirt and drain well in a colander.

Heat the butter or oil in a large sauté pan over medium heat. Add the leeks and onion and cook, stirring often, until the leeks are very tender, about 20 minutes. You may have to add water to help soften them Remove from the heat and set aside. When cool, make sure all the water has evaporated and drain well if it has not.

Mix the leeks with the ricotta cheese, 50g of grated cheese, 2 eggs, salt, nutmeg.

Beat the remaining 2 eggs in a shallow bowl large enough to hold a sheet of matzah. Pour cold water in another bowl. Soak the matzah in the water for about 2 minutes, then drain. Dip the matzah in the egg, then place it in the prepared baking pan. Repeat with a second matzah sheet and, if necessary, use additional matzah to fill in any spaces in the pan.

Sprinkle 50g grated cheese over the matzah and top with the leek mixture. Dip the remaining 2 matzahs in water for 2 minutes, drain, dip in the egg and place on top of the leek mixture. Top with the remaining 50g grated cheese.

Bake in the preheated oven for 30-40 minutes, until browned. Remove from the oven, let rest for 10 minutes and cut into squares.

Kurraath b' saniyah

(Leek dill pie)

Kurraath is the Arabic word for leeks and this recipe is not much different from other Judeo Spanish ones with prasa, the Ladino name for leeks. Leeks are a member of the onion family, so you can adapt the recipe to taste, using more onions and less leeks. Similarly, cheeses can easily be interchanged, according to what you have in your fridge.

4 large leeks
1 large onion, finely chopped
4 tablespoons sunflower oil
250g cottage cheese
150g grated cheese, cheddar or emmenthal
2 tablespoons finely chopped dill
2 large eggs, lightly beaten
¼ teaspoon cayenne pepper or Aleppo pepper
1 teaspoon salt

Preheat the oven to 180C/Gas Mark 4.

Wash the leeks thoroughly, cut lengthwise and chop into 1cm (½ inch) pieces. Chop the onion. Heat the oil in a large pan and fry the onion and leeks until soft and golden, about 5 minutes.

In a bowl, combine the cottage cheese, 100g of the grated cheese, eggs, dill, pepper and salt. Mix well. Add the sautéed onions and leeks and combine.

Transfer the mixture into a 22cm (9 inch) pie dish. Sprinkle the remaining 50g grated cheese over the surface.

Bake in the preheated oven for about 40 minutes until the pie is golden brown on top and the centre is firm.

Poached eggs in creamed spinach

Spinach is very healthy, as it is loaded with nutrients and antioxidants It's a low calorie vegetable, which means it's okay to add a milk based sauce to give the dish more substance. Buying washed and ready to use spinach, which I often do, means that you don't have to spend time washing and patting it dry.

1½kg fresh spinach
60g butter
500ml cold milk
½ teaspoon each salt and pepper
3 tablespoons flour
4 large eggs

Wash the spinach, dry and chop medium fine.

In a saucepan, combine the butter and 175ml milk, salt and pepper and cook over a low heat until the butter has melted. Add all the spinach at once and stir. Cook for 3-5 minutes, stirring occasionally. Continue to cook uncovered for about 5 minutes, until very little liquid remains.

Mix the flour and remaining milk into a smooth mixture. Add to the spinach and continue to cook, stirring until the mixture is creamy and has thickened, about 5-10 minutes.

Make four evenly spaced hollows in the creamed spinach and crack an egg into each, taking care not to break the yolk. Cover the pan and simmer for 3 minutes over a low heat until the eggs are done. The whites should be firm and the yolks liquid.

Serve over mashed potatoes.

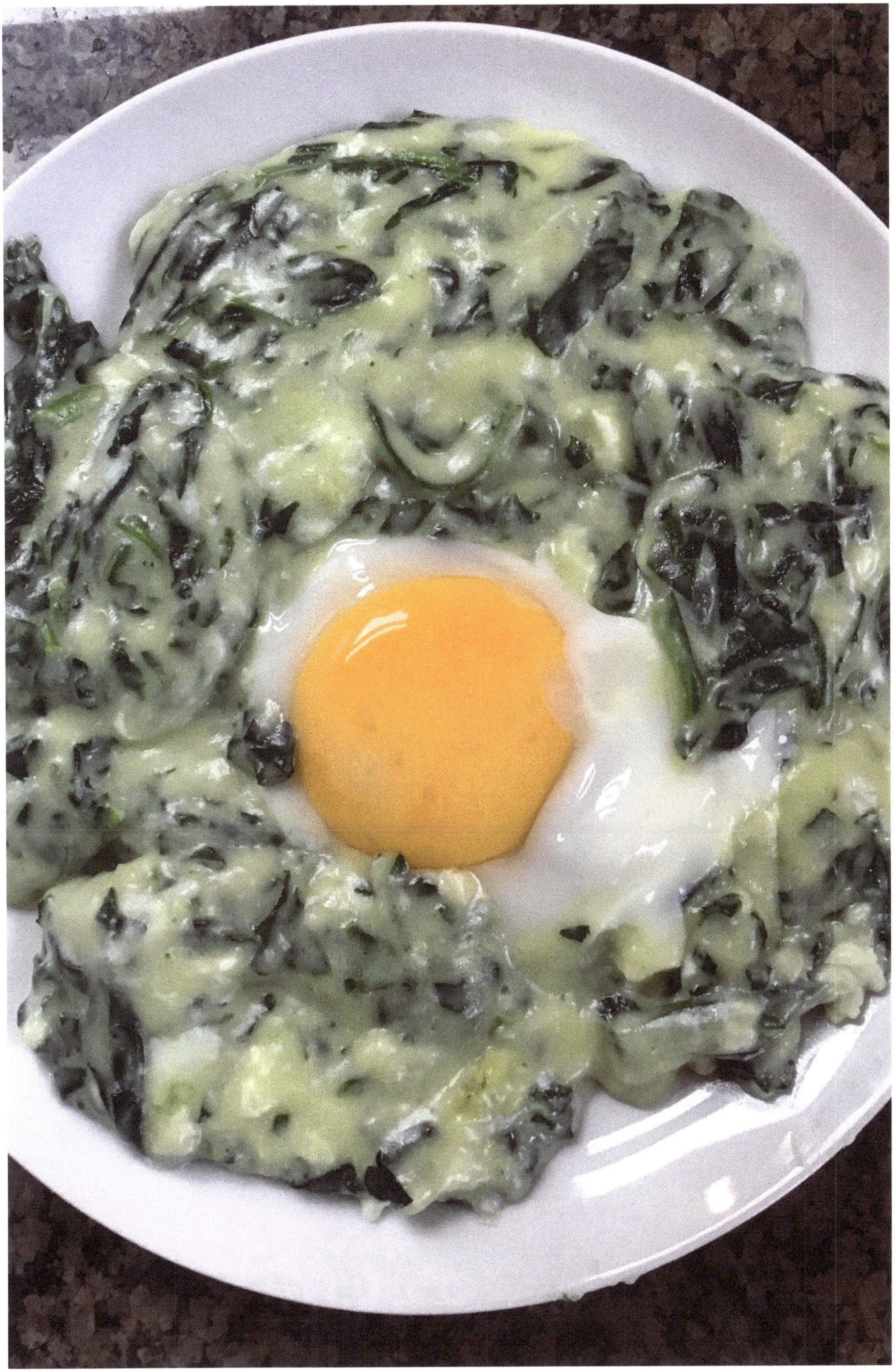

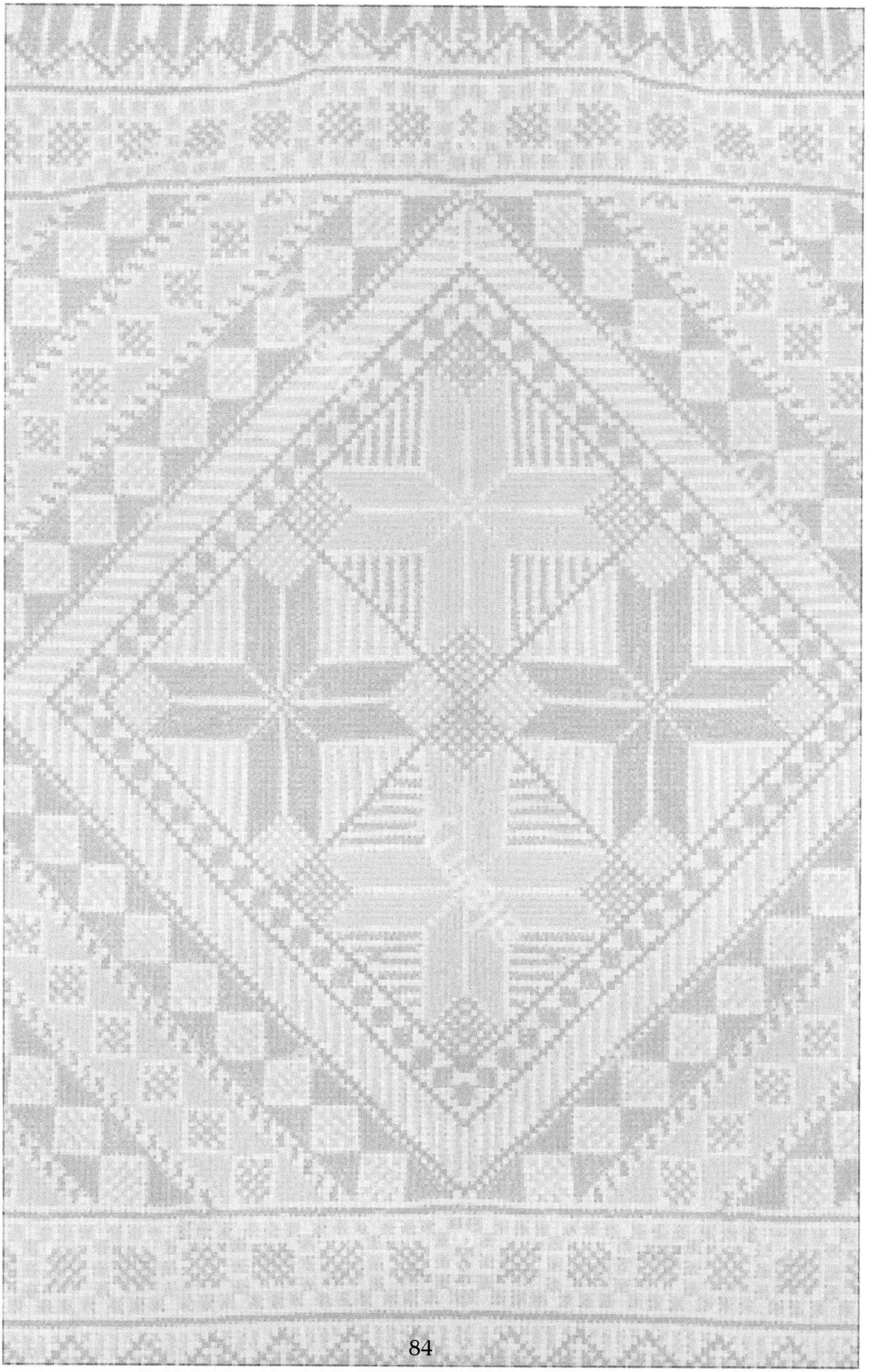

FISH DISHES

*Pishkado
Samak*

Albondigas de pishkado

(Fish balls in tomato sauce)

Makes around 18

These fish balls remind me of summer, as we often had them while on holiday. They are easy to make and cook in a very short time. They make a great light meal, served with white rice and a simple cucumber and tomato salad.

For the sauce
- 2 garlic cloves, finely chopped
- 3 tablespoons sunflower oil
- 400g can tomatoes, peeled and chopped
- 4 teaspoons tomato purée
- 1 teaspoon ground coriander
- 1 teaspoon turmeric
- 2 teaspoons sugar
- juice of ½ lemon
- 1 cup water

For the fish
- 500g minced white fish
- 20g tablespoons breadcrumbs or matzo meal
- 1 egg, lightly beaten
- 1 teaspoon nutmeg
- ¼ teaspoon ground ginger
- 4 tablespoons finely chopped coriander or flat leaf parsley
- salt and pepper to taste

Make the sauce - in a large shallow pan, heat the oil and fry the chopped garlic for 2 minutes. Add the tomato purée and peeled tomatoes (or fresh tomatoes if using). Add the ground coriander, turmeric, sugar, lemon juice and 1 cup water. Stir, bring to the boil and remove from the heat.

Prepare the fish - blitz it very quickly in a food processor – not too long or it will turn to a paste. Transfer to a large bowl and add the beaten egg, nutmeg, ground ginger, matzo meal or breadcrumbs. Add the chopped coriander or parsley and salt and pepper.

Take small lumps of the mixture, the size of a walnut, and roll into little balls. Drop them one by one into the pan with the sauce. Cover and simmer for 20 minutes, carefully turning them over once.

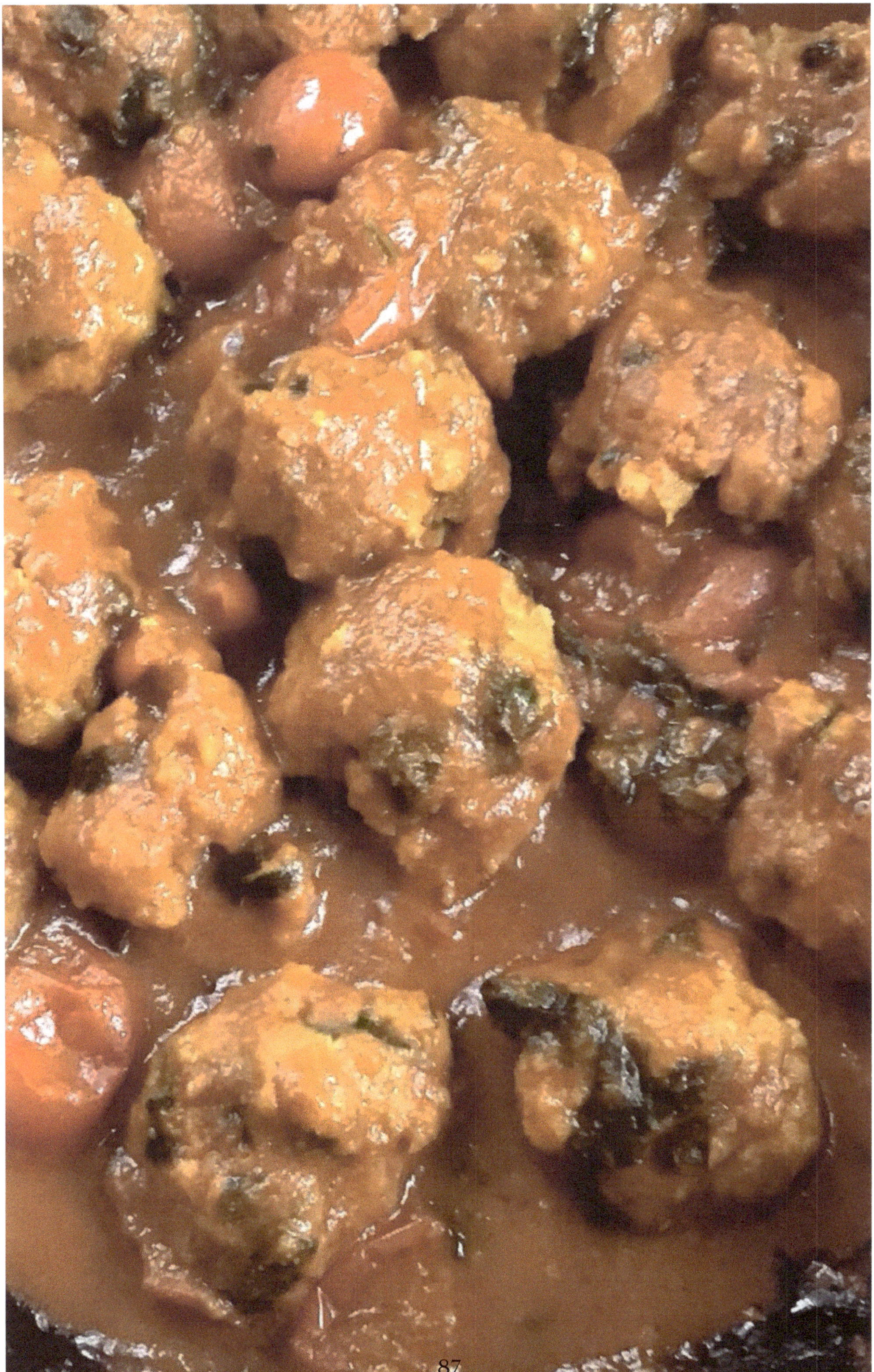

Tuna croquettes in tomato sauce

This is another Turkish favourite, using ordinary ingredients with great results

Makes 12 croquettes

2 x 160g cans tuna
¼ cup matzo meal or breadcrumbs
2 eggs, beaten
2 tablespoons chopped parsley
1 onion, grated
salt and pepper
oil for deep frying

For the sauce
1 x 400g can chopped tomatoes
1 tablespoon tomato purée
juice of 1 lemon or to taste
1 teaspoon sugar
½ cup water

Drain and flake the tuna. Add the matzo meal or breadcrumbs, eggs, parsley, grated onion, salt and pepper. Form balls with wet hands.

Heat the oil in a large skillet or deep frying pan and fry the croquettes on both sides until golden brown, about 3 minutes each side. Transfer to a plate.

In a medium saucepan, mix all the sauce ingredients and bring to a boil. Add the croquettes, lower the heat and simmer for 10 minutes, until the sauce has slightly reduced.

Fish with walnut sauce

This is one of my favourite Middle Eastern fish recipes. The combination of walnuts, tamarind sauce and cider vinegar give a lot of taste to an otherwise bland fish.

For the fish
6 cod, haddock or halibut fish steaks or fish fillets, weighing about 200g each
oil for shallow frying

For the walnut sauce
2 large onions, finely chopped
4 tablespoons sunflower or vegetable oil
4 garlic cloves, crushed
1 tablespoon tamarind paste
200g walnuts, ground or finely chopped
salt to taste
½ teaspoon cayenne pepper
1 tablespoon cider vinegar
250-350ml water

Prepare the walnut sauce – heat the oil in a frying pan and fry the onion until soft, about 10 minutes. Add the garlic, stir and cook for a further 3 minutes.

Add the tamarind paste, stirring until it dissolves, then the walnuts, salt and cayenne pepper and finally the vinegar and enough water to make a creamy sauce. Cook for a further 5 - 10 minutes more, stirring frequently.

Preheat the oven to 180C/Gas Mark 4.

Shallow fry the fish in hot oil for 10 minutes, turning once. Arrange the pieces on a baking dish and spoon over the walnut sauce. Cover with foil and bake for 20 minutes.

Pishkado con agristada

(Fish with a lemon and egg sauce)

Agristada is a lemon-infused sauce, which originated with the Jews in Spain before the Inquisition. It was often used as a dressing for fish and the sauce became synonymous with the dish, so we referred to it simply as agristada.

For the fish
- 750g cod, haddock or hake fillets
- 1 large egg
- 3 tablespoons flour
- oil for frying

For the agristada sauce
- 250ml cold water
- 2 tablespoons flour
- 2 large eggs
- juice of 1 large or 2 small lemons
- salt and pepper to taste

Prepare the sauce - put all the ingredients, except the lemon juice in a blender. Blend until smooth.

Transfer to a saucepan and cook very slowly over a low heat, stirring constantly, until the sauce has thickened. Stir in the lemon juice, very slowly and drop by drop. Remove from heat and set aside.

Cook the fish - heat the oil in a large frying pan. Dip the fish fillets in the beaten egg and then coat with the flour. Fry until golden brown, about 5 minutes each side.

Drain on paper towels and arrange over the warm agristada sauce in a shallow dish.

Variation (this is my preferred method).
Bake the fish fillets in a preheated oven with a little oil, lemon juice and salt. When cooked, pour the warm agristada sauce over the fillets.

Fish tagine

Tagine is a dish which originated in Morocco. It gets its name from the conical pot that is placed on top of a gas hob or put in the oven. The secret of a good tagine is in its spices and an essential one is called ras el hanout (literally, the grocer's head). It is a combination of up to 27 different spices and available from all Middle Eastern stores. No tagine would be complete without the inclusion of ras el hanout and dried fruits, such as dates, figs or apricots are also usually added.

3 tablespoons olive oil
3 red onions, finely sliced
4 garlic cloves, finely chopped
1½ teaspoon ground turmeric
1 teaspoon ras- el- hanout
1 teaspoon ground cinnamon
150ml water
400g butternut squash slices, cut into 2cm (1 inch) pieces
100g dried apricots
50g dates
zest and juice of 1 lemon
6 white fish fillets, such as sea bream, sea bass, cod or haddock
400g cherry tomatoes
100ml white wine or water
1 teaspoon sugar
salt and pepper

For the couscous
500g couscous
1000ml (1 litre) water or vegetable stock

Heat the oil in a large non stick pan or frying pan. Add the onions and garlic and sauté for 3 minutes over medium heat, until they are soft but not brown. Add the turmeric, ras- el -hanout and cinnamon and stir well to combine. Add the butternut squash, apricots and dates, the zest of a lemon and 150ml water. Bring to the boil, reduce the heat, cover and simmer for 15 minutes.

Add the fish fillets, tomatoes, sugar, lemon juice and 100ml white wine or water. Season with salt and pepper, cover and continue to cook for a further 15 minutes or until the fish and butternut squash are tender.

Prepare the couscous – place it in a large bowl and pour over the water or vegetable stock. Season with salt and pepper, cover with clingfilm and leave until the stock or water is absorbed. Fluff up with a fork.

Transfer the couscous to a serving dish and spoon over the fish tagine.

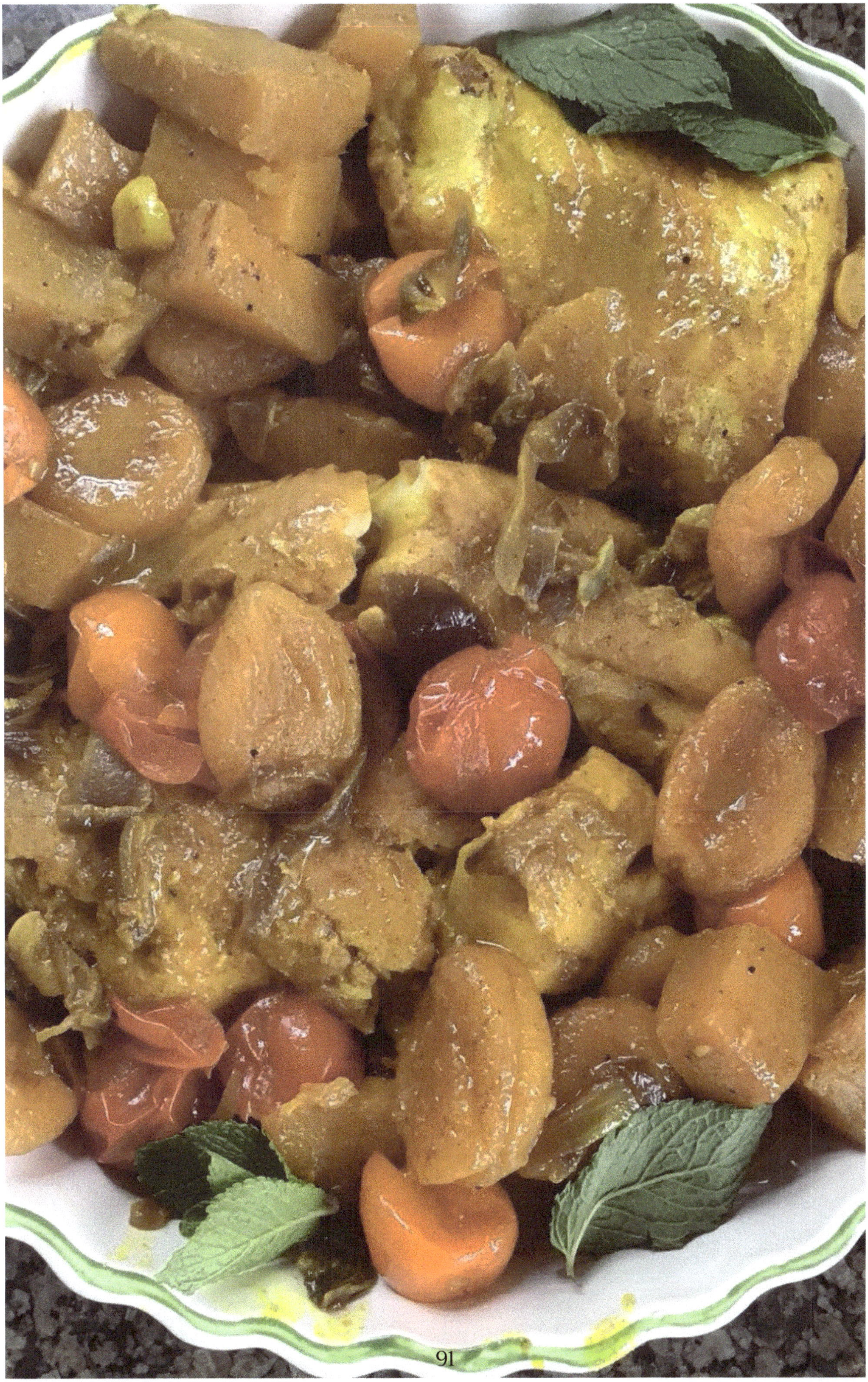

Salmon with a creamy dill sauce

Fresh dill has a distinctive taste which is likened to fennel and celery. Its fresh, citrus-like flavour particularly complements fish and works well with garlic. You can use less cream, which will result in a thinner sauce, but won't affect the overall result.

4 salmon steaks or fillets, weighing around 250g each
2 tablespoons olive oil
2 garlic cloves
160ml double cream
juice of 1 lemon
½ cup vegetable bouillon
1 tablespoon cornflour, mixed into a smooth paste with 1 tablespoon water
2 tablespoons finely chopped dill
salt and pepper

Prepare the salmon - place it in a baking dish and drizzle with 1 tablespoon olive oil and a few drops of lemon juice. Bake in a preheated oven 180C/Gas Mark 4 for 15 minutes until the salmon is cooked.

Place the salmon fillets on a serving dish.

Prepare the sauce – in a small pan, fry the garlic cloves in 1 tablespoon olive oil. Add the vegetable bouillon, cream, lemon juice, cornflour paste, salt and pepper. Stir continuously until the sauce thickens, about 3 minutes. Add the chopped dill.

Pour the sauce over the salmon fillets.

Salmon with a honey and garlic sauce

Salmon is ideal for a last minute meal, as it cooks quickly in the oven and has a distinctive enough taste to be served as it is, with a dash of olive oil, lemon juice and sea salt. However, I prefer to serve it in a sauce and a honey based one is a favourite.

4 salmon fillets, weighing about 200g each
30g butter
3 garlic cloves, finely chopped
1 teaspoon paprika
4 tablespoons honey
1 tablespoons water
2 teaspoons soy sauce
1 tablespoon lemon juice
salt and pepper

Cook the salmon fillets- place them on an oiled baking tray, add salt and a dash of lemon juice. Cook in a preheated oven 180C/Gas Mark 4 for 10 minutes, until the fillets are partially cooked. Remove from the oven.

Prepare the sauce – heat the butter in a pan until melted. Add the chopped garlic and sauté for a few minutes, until fragrant. Add the honey, water, paprika, lemon juice, soy sauce, salt and pepper.

Add the salmon fillets to the pan and baste for a few minutes, until the salmon is cooked and well coated with the sauce.

Samak b'kamoun

(Baked fish with a cumin-coriander tomato sauce)

A favourite way of cooking fish in Egypt was to bake it in a simple tomato and lemon sauce, with coriander and cumin, the most popular spices. I have added crushed ginger and brown sugar because they blend well with the other ingredients.

4 cod or haddock steaks, weighing approx 200g each
3 tablespoons olive oil
1 onion finely chopped
2 teaspoons crushed garlic
2 teaspoons crushed ginger
3 tablespoons tomato purée
1 teaspoon ground coriander
½ teaspoon ground cumin
1 teaspoon turmeric
juice of ½ lemon
1 cup water
1 tablespoon brown sugar
bunch of chopped coriander
salt to taste

Heat the oil and fry the chopped onion for 5 minutes. Add the crushed garlic and ginger and continue frying for a few minutes. Add the coriander, cumin and turmeric and make sure they are well blended.

Stir in the tomato purée and lemon juice, combine well and finally stir in the water, brown sugar, salt and chopped coriander. Heat the sauce for 3 minutes until all the ingredients are blended.

Coat the bottom of a shallow ovenproof dish with some of the sauce. Place the fish steaks on top and cover with the rest of the sauce.

Cover and cook in a preheated oven 180C/Gas Mark 4 for 45 minutes.

Cod roe fritters
(Taramokeftedes)

These fritters are great as a mezze in summer, served with a taramasalata or tahini dip, olives, pitta bread and a green salad.

250g fresh cod roe
2 slices stale white bread, crusts removed, soaked in cold water and well squeezed
2 spring onions, finely chopped
1 garlic clove, minced
small bunch flat- leaf parsley, finely chopped
juice ½ lemon
2 tablespoons self raising flour
1 teaspoon baking powder

flour for coating
sunflower or olive oil for frying

Put the roe in a pan of salted water and bring to the boil. Lower the heat and simmer for 15-20 minutes. Remove from the pan and allow to cool.

Place the roe in a large bowl, add 2 tablespoons hot water and mix well. Add all the remaining ingredients and combine. The mixture should be thick, if not add a little more flour. Refrigerate for ½ hour.

Shape the mixture into small patties, roll them in flour and shake off the excess.

Heat about 3 tablespoons oil in a large frying pan and when it starts to sizzle fry the patties in small batches. With a spoon or spatula, lightly flatten the balls, this way they will not absorb too much oil. Cook each side for 2-3 minutes, or until golden brown.

Drain on kitchen paper. Serve immediately with a few drops of lemon juice.

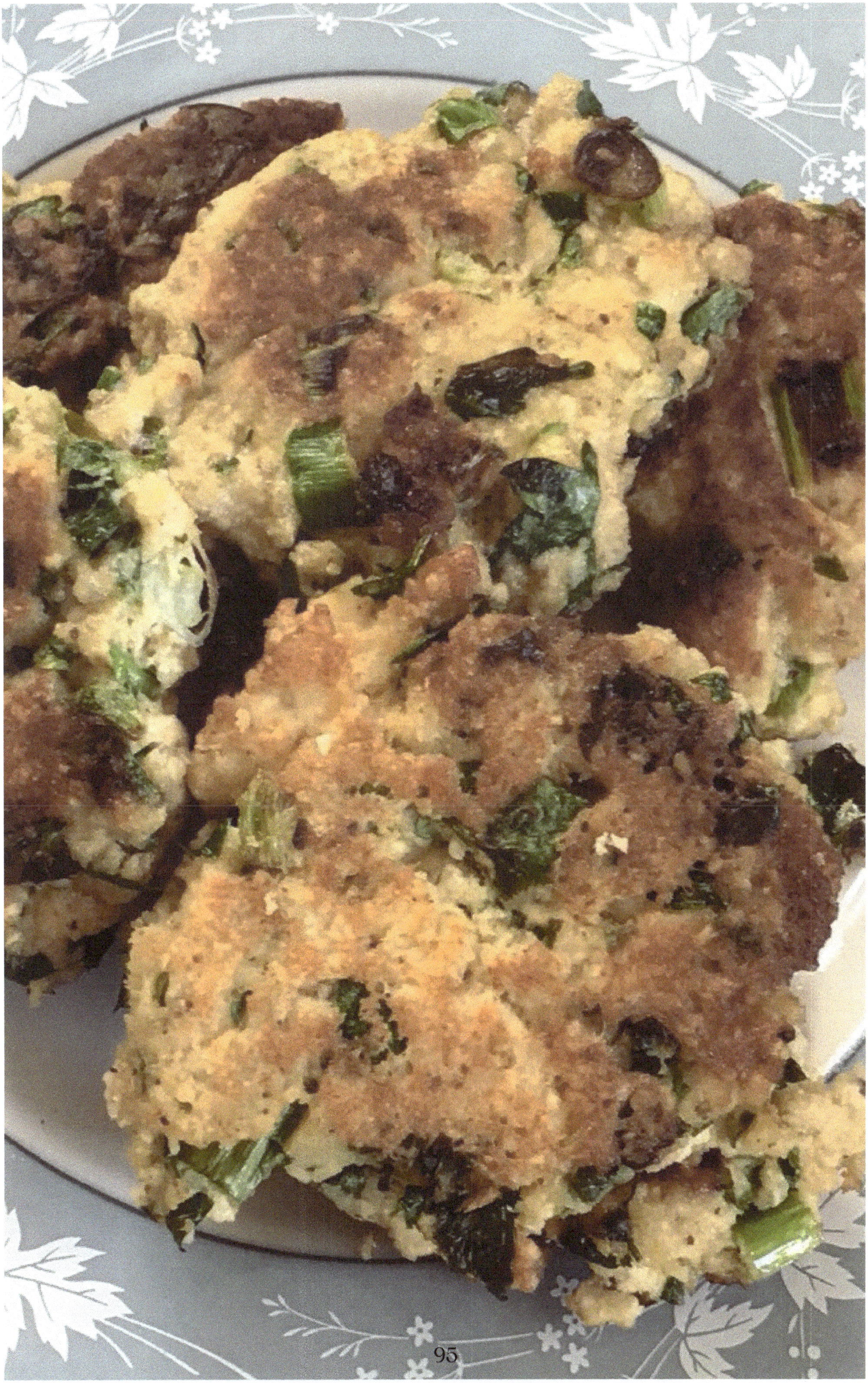

Sea bass fillets with tahini sauce

Tahini is now widely available in many supermarkets. However, the brands sold in Middle Eastern and Turkish grocery stores are the best and the creamiest. This sesame seed paste is a tasty, healthy and dairy-free alternative to butter. It is also high in calcium and a richer source of protein than milk.

For the fish
    4 sea bass fillets, weighing approximately 400g in total
    2 tablespoons olive oil
    1 tablespoon lemon juice
    1 teaspoon dried herbs
    salt and pepper

For the sauce
    4 tablespoons tahini paste
    ½ cup hot water
    juice of 1 lemon
    2 garlic cloves, finely chopped
    2 tablespoons olive oil
    2 tablespoons flat leaf parsley, chopped
    salt to taste

Preheat the oven to 180C/Gas Mark 4.

Put all the ingredients for the tahini sauce in a food processor and blitz for a few seconds.
Check the consistency of the sauce and add a little water if it's too thick. Pour it into a microwaveable dish and set aside.

Place the sea bass fillets on a baking tray. Drizzle olive oil and lemon juice over each fillet.
Cover with foil and bake in the preheated oven for 15 minutes or until the fillets are cooked.
Place the fillets on a serving dish.

Heat the tahini sauce in the microwave for 1 minute. Pour the sauce over the fillets and serve immediately.

Samak fil forn be fireek

(Baked fish with fereek)

Fereek (also known as freekeh and farika) is a grain harvested from green, immature durum wheat. It is widely used in the Middle East and, as well being a great stuffing for chicken, it makes for a substantial main course when cooked with trout or sea bass.

4 whole firm white-flesh fish, such as trout, bream or sea bass
flour for coating
vegetable or sunflower oil for shallow frying

For the fish marinade
  2 garlic cloves, crushed
  1 teaspoon ground coriander
  1 teaspoon ground cumin
  juice of 1 lemon

For the fereek ingredients
  200g fereek
  2 tablespoons tomato paste
  220ml water
  1 teaspoon ground cumin
  salt and pepper
  1 tablespoon olive oil

Preheat the oven to 180C/Gas Mark 4.

Wash the fish and pat dry with paper towels. Rub the marinade in and around the fish, making sure it is well coated. Place it in a bowl and refrigerate for 1-2 hours.

Wash and drain the fereek and place it in a large ovenproof baking dish. Combine the tomato paste with 250ml (1 cup) water. Add the ground cumin, season with salt and pepper and pour the mixture over the fereek.

Put a little flour on a board and dip the fish into it, coating it on all sides. Shake off any excess flour. Heat some vegetable or sunflower oil in a frying pan, enough for shallow frying. Add the fish and fry for 3-4 minutes on each side.

Place the fried fish on top of the fereek, drizzle 1 tablespoon olive oil and place the dish in the oven. Bake for 20-25 minutes until the fereek is tender.

Samak fil forn
(Baked fish)

As a child, I was lucky enough to spend the summer months by the seaside in Alexandria, as the Cairo heat became unbearable in July and August. Alexandria is a port, so freshly caught fish was always available. We occasionally had lunch in one of the many restaurants in the nearby bay of Aboukir, where you could go into the kitchen and choose your fish. Mostly, we had lunch at home and this is one of the dishes my mother used to prepare.

600g white fish fillets, any
2 tablespoons flour
3 tablespoons vegetable or sunflower oil, for shallow frying

For the sauce
  4 shallots, cut lengthwise and in half
  300g cherry tomatoes
  small bunch flat leaf parsley, finely chopped (stalks discarded)
  1 tablespoon Worcestershire sauce
  juice of ½ lemon
  ½ teaspoon sugar
  1 teaspoon ground cumin
  2 tablespoons tomato paste
  120ml water
  salt and pepper to taste
  sprinkling olive oil

Preheat the oven to 180C/Gas Mark 4.

Coat the fish fillets with flour. Heat the oil in a large pan and fry each fillet for 2 minutes. Set aside.

Prepare the sauce - in the same pan, fry the shallots for 5 minutes until soft and translucent. Add the cherry tomatoes, tomato paste, sugar, lemon juice, ground cumin, parsley, Worcestershire and water. Add salt and pepper and turn off the heat.

Assemble the dish – place the fish fillets in a large, shallow ovenproof casserole dish. Arrange the shallots and tomato mixture around the fish. Add a little more water if necessary and sprinkle some olive oil over the surface.

Cover and bake in the preheated oven for 25-30 minutes.

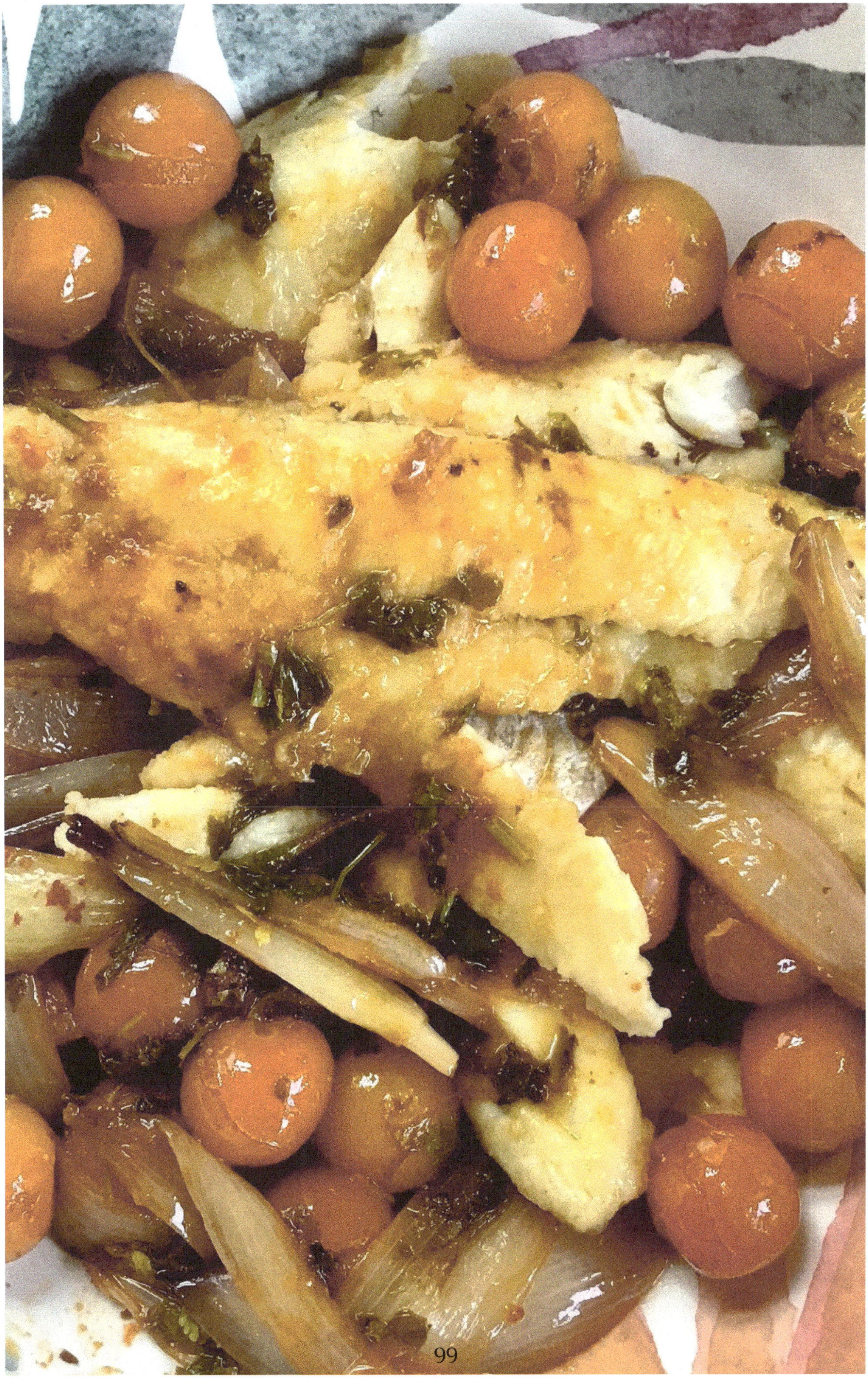

Salmon couscous

The addition of couscous makes the fish go a long way. I have kept with the Middle Eastern touch by adding, ginger, turmeric and saffron. The quantity of spices is given only as a guide and you can increase one particular seasoning or leave it out. Serve with a green salad.

**3 tablespoons olive oil
4 salmon fillets, weighing about 600g in total
2 red onions, thinly sliced
5cm (2 inch) piece of fresh root ginger, peeled and finely chopped
juice and grated zest of 1 orange
2 medium tomatoes, sliced
50g raisins
1 tablespoon tomato purée
2 teaspoons ground cinnamon
1 teaspoon ground turmeric
1 teaspoon saffron threads
300g couscous
750ml boiling water
salt and pepper to taste**

Preheat the oven to 180C/Gas Mark 4.

Place the salmon fillets in a large baking tray, drizzle with 1 tablespoon olive and cook in the preheated oven for 10 minutes. Remove from the oven and set aside.

Infuse the saffron threads in some warm water for 10 minutes.

Heat 2 tablespoons oil in a large pan and fry the onions for 5 minutes. Add the sliced tomatoes, tomato purée, turmeric, cinnamon, ginger, raisins, juice and zest of the orange and infused saffron. Add salt and pepper and 150ml boiling water. Bring to the boil, reduce the heat and simmer, covered, for 5 minutes.

Prepare the couscous – place it in a bowl and cover with the remaining 600ml water. Cover with cling film and leave for 5 minutes.

Stir the salmon into the vegetable mixture in the pan and simmer uncovered for 5 minutes until the salmon has absorbed the flavours. Add a little more water if necessary.

Place the couscous in a serving dish. Pour the salmon and vegetable mixture over the couscous.

Sea bream roasted on a bed of baby potatoes

This is another fish dish we often had while on holiday. We cooked it with freshly caught red snapper roasted on a bed of potatoes and topped with Mediterranean vegetables. Red snapper is not always available here, so I have substituted it with sea bream.

4 whole sea bream, weighing about 250g each
1 tablespoon olive oil, plus extra for brushing
4 whole garlic gloves
2 teaspoons fresh thyme leaves
salt and pepper

450g baby potatoes
1 large fennel bulb, trimmed
1 large red onion, thinly sliced lengthways
5 ripe plum tomatoes or 400g can chopped tomatoes
1 red pepper, cored and cut into strips
1 tablespoon tomato paste
1 teaspoon dried oregano

2 tablespoons fresh lemon juice
2 tablespoons olive oil
1 cup vegetable stock

Preheat the oven to 200C/Gas Mark 6.

Rinse the fish and pat dry with paper towels. Brush well with oil and sprinkle both the inside and outside with salt and pepper. Stuff the cavities with the fresh thyme and garlic cloves and refrigerate.

Oil a shallow roasting pan, large enough to lay the fish whole.

Put the unpeeled potatoes in a pan of salted water. Bring to the boil, cover and cook over medium heat for about 20 minutes or until tender. Drain and cut the potatoes in half. Lay the potatoes in the prepared roasting pan. Season with salt and pepper and drizzle with a little olive oil.

Cut the fennel bulb lengthways and into 4mm (¼ inch) thick slices. Blanch in hot water for 1 minute and drain.

Combine the red onion, tomatoes, fennel, red pepper strips, tomato paste and oregano in a bowl. Add salt to taste and a few thyme leaves. Spread the mixture over the potatoes.

Remove the fish from the fridge and lay it on top of the vegetables. Combine the olive oil, lemon juice and vegetable stock and pour around the fish. Cover the pan with foil, sealing it well and bake for 20 minutes, basting 3 or 4 times with the pan juices, until the vegetables and fish are cooked through.

Remove the foil and bake for a further 15 minutes. Top up with hot water if the fish and vegetables start to dry out.

Drizzle with a little olive oil before serving.

Baked fish with tahini sauce

Tahini mixed with tabasco sauce adds an unusual and pleasant flavour to the fish. Serve with rice or burghul on the side.

4 whole trout or sea bream
¼ cup tahini paste
6 tablespoons cold water
juice of ½ lemon
¼ teaspoon tabasco sauce
¼ teaspoon salt
1 tablespoon pine nuts (optional)
handful pomegranate seeds (optional)

Preheat the oven to 180C/Gas Mark 4.

Rinse the fish in cold water and pat dry with paper towels.

Line a large baking dish with aluminium foil and drizzle a little olive oil on the bottom. Place the fish on the oiled baking sheet.

Measure the tahini paste into a small bowl. Add the cold water, 1 tablespoon at a time, stirring well with a fork and mashing any lumps. Add the lemon juice, tabasco sauce and salt and mix well.

Cover the fish with the sauce, setting aside a few tablespoons to spoon over the fish right before serving. Sprinkle with pine nuts, if using.

Cover loosely with aluminium foil and bake in the preheated oven for 40 minutes. Remove the foil and continue to bake until the fish is cooked through, 15-20 minutes – the thicker the fish, the longer it will take.

Transfer to a serving plate and drizzle the remaining sauce over the fish. Garnish with pomegranate seeds, if using.

MEAT DISHES
Carne
Lahmah

Kibbeh bil sanieh

(Layered bulgur and meat pie)

Kibbeh are the hallmark of Syrian cooking and the standard by which housewives were judged once upon a time. They represented refinement and elegance and the biggest compliment you could pay a lady was to say that she had 'kibbeh fingers'. They remind me of my grandmother, who taught my mother and aunt how to make perfectly shaped ones. They were the foremost food served to guests and reserved for special occasions. Making them was a time consuming task, so kibbeh on a tray (sanieh in Arabic) was the simplified, every day version and took far less time. In Egypt, we called them kobeba.

For the shell
- 250g fine bulgur wheat
- 2 large onions, cut into quarters
- 250g beef or lamb mince
- 1 teaspoon salt
- ½ teaspoon black pepper
- 1 teaspoon ground nutmeg or allspice
- 1 teaspoon cinnamon

For the hashweh (filling)
- 15g butter
- 1 medium onion, finely chopped
- 250g beef or lamb mince
- 1 teaspoon cinnamon or mixed spice
- ½ teaspoon nutmeg or allspice
- ½ tablespoon pomegranate molasses
- salt and pepper
- 125ml water
- 1 tablespoon pine nuts (optional)
- 50g butter, softened

Preheat the oven to 180C/Gas Mark 4.
Grease a 22cm (9 inch) round baking dish or a 25 x 20cm (10 x 8 inch) square dish.

Boil some water in a kettle. Place the bulgur wheat in a large bowl and cover with boiling water. Leave for 30 minutes until the water has been absorbed and the wheat has doubled in volume. Remove any excess water by straining it with a sieve and place the bulgur in a large bowl.

Prepare the hashweh (spiced meat filling) – in a large pan, melt the butter and fry the onion for 2 minutes until golden. Add the meat and brown over medium heat for 5 minutes. Add the spices, pomegranate molasses and salt and pepper to taste. Cover the meat with 125 ml water. Bring to the boil on a high heat, then simmer until all the liquid has evaporated. Add the pine nuts (optional) and cook for a further 2 minutes.

Prepare the bulgur mixture for the shell - combine the raw beef or lamb, onion quarters, salt and pepper, spices and the cooked bulgur. Mince the mixture to obtain a fine paste - if you don't have a mincer, you can use a food processor.

Assemble the dish for baking - place half the bulgur mixture into the prepared baking dish and flatten it, using the palm of your hand. Spread the hashweh over this and cover with the remaining bulgur mixture - you may need to wet your hands to flatten the top layer.

Cut the kibbeh (kobeba) into squares or diamonds. Place a few dollops of butter on top and bake for 30-40 minutes until the top is golden brown.

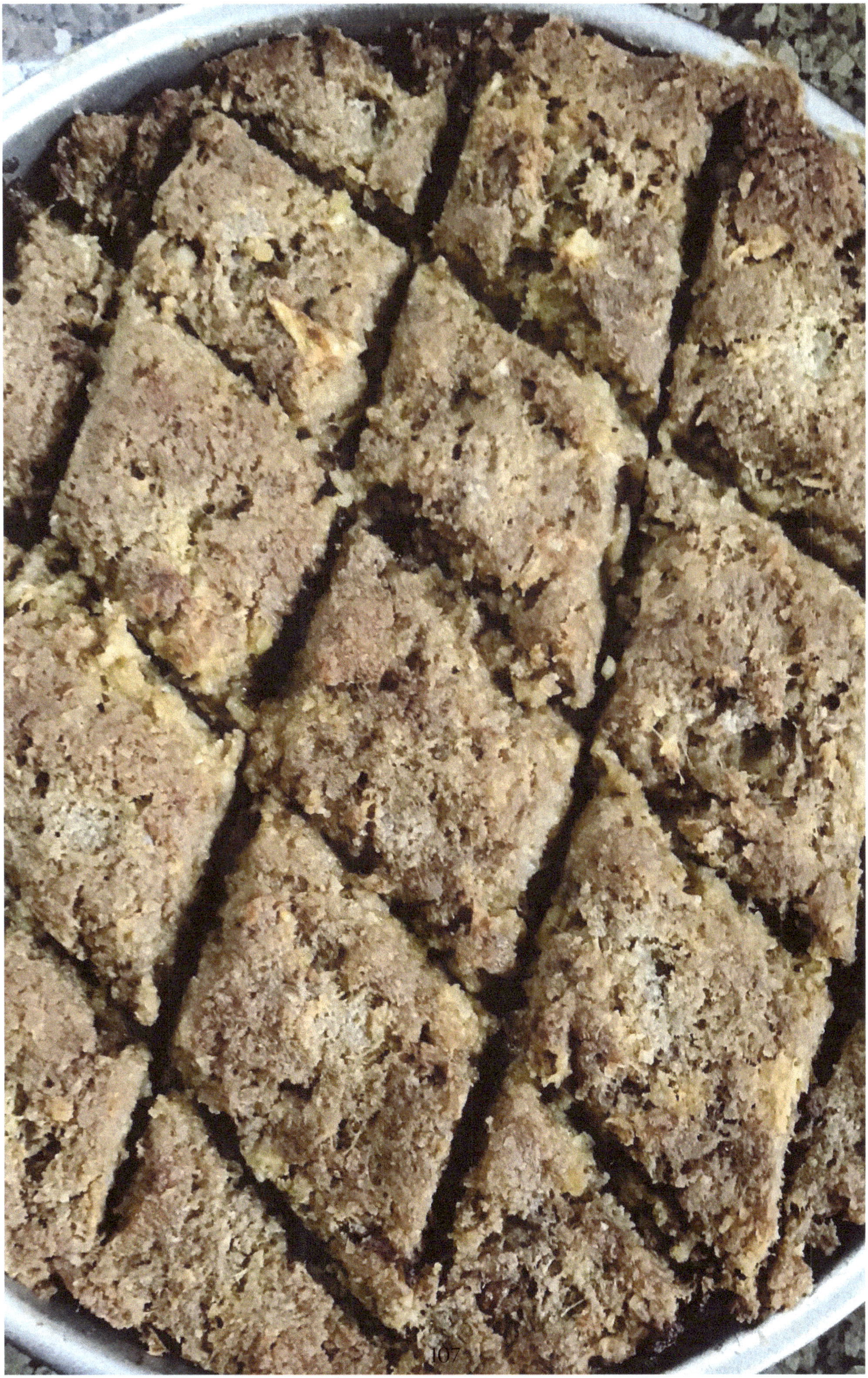

Apio kon avos

(Veal stew with cannellini beans and celery)

4 tablespoons olive oil
1kg veal chunks, cut into 5cm (2 inch) pieces
1 large onion, finely chopped
2 cups hot chicken stock
50g celery stalks, trimmed and sliced into 2cm (1 inch) pieces
400g can chopped tomatoes
1 tablespoon tomato purée
½ teaspoon sugar
1 teaspoon ground turmeric
2 x 400g cans cannellini beans, drained and rinsed
1 tablespoon lemon juice
salt and pepper to taste

This is a hearty one-pot stew which can be served accompanied with rice. The veal can be substituted with diced lamb or beef.

Heat the oil in a large, heavy based pan over a medium high heat. Add the veal and cook in batches until lightly browned. Remove from the heat and set aside. Add the onion to the pan and cook for 3 minutes, stirring frequently, until softened. Return the browned meat to the pan and pour in the hot stock. Cover, reduce the heat and cook for 1 ½ - 2 hours until the veal is very tender. Add hot water as necessary.

Stir in the celery, peeled tomatoes, tomato purée, ground turmeric, sugar, salt and pepper. Bring to the boil, cover and cook for 30 minutes. Add the drained cannellini beans and lemon juice and cook uncovered for a further 10 minutes.

Beef stew Aleppo style

1 large onion, finely chopped
1 tablespoon sunflower oil
500g stewing beef or beef steak, cut into 5cm (2 inch) chunks
2 cups water
400g can chopped tomatoes
3 tablespoons tomato purée
1 large potato, peeled and cut into small chunks
1 large carrot, sliced into 2cm (1 inch) pieces
1 green pepper, cut into medium strips
½ large aubergine, peeled and cubed
2 tablespoons tamarind concentrate
juice of 1 ½ lemons
1 teaspoon sugar
salt and pepper

My father did not like the addition of dried fruit to savoury dishes, which was the hallmark of Syrian Jewish cooking, so my mother compromised by leaving them out, whilst still maintaining a balance of tart and sweet - hence the use of tamarind concentrate and lemons, contrasted with the tomato purée and sugar.

Heat the oil in a medium saucepan and fry the onion until soft and translucent, about 5 minutes. Add the beef chunks to the onions and continue to fry, stirring constantly, for 5 minutes. Pour 2 cups of water, cover, reduce the heat to medium low and cook for 30 minutes.

Add the chopped tomatoes, tomato purée, vegetables and all the remaining ingredients. Reduce the heat, cover and simmer for about 1 hour or until the vegetables are tender and the liquid has thickened.

Sweet and sour beef and aubergine stew

This dish is based on a Claudia Roden recipe called Ingriyi, which has Turkish Jewish origins. I have adapted it and added more ingredients to the sauce.

1kg lamb or beef, diced
900ml water
2 large aubergines weighing about 1 kg, cut into slices of 1.25cm (½ inch)
2 large onions sliced
3 tablespoons sunflower or vegetable oil
1 kg tomatoes, peeled and sliced

For the sauce
  2 tablespoons tamarind paste
  2 tablespoons sugar
  1 tablespoon pomegranate molasses
  1 tablespoon honey
  juice ½ lemon
  Salt and pepper

Preheat the oven to 180C/Gas mark 4.

Sprinkle the aubergines with salt, place in a colander and leave for 1 hour. Squeeze out the bitter juices. Rinse and pat dry with paper towels.

Place the meat in a large saucepan, cover with water and simmer for about 1 hour or until tender.

Heat 3 tablespoons oil in a frying pan, fry the onions until brown and set aside. Fry the aubergines briefly in the same oil until lightly brown on both sides, adding more oil if necessary. Drain on paper towels.

Remove the meat from the saucepan, leaving the stock. Place it with the aubergines in a large ovenproof casserole and add the fried onions and sliced tomatoes on top.

For the sauce, mix the stock with the tamarind paste, sugar, pomegranate molasses, honey, lemon juice, salt and pepper. Bring to the boil, then pour it evenly over the meat and aubergine dish.

Transfer to the preheated oven and cook for 1 hour or until the sauce has reduced - you may have to cook uncovered for a further 15 minutes.

Beef stew with chickpeas, kale and tahini

This tangy stew is perfect for autumn days when it's still warn outside but the evenings are starting to feel chilly. The recipe also works well with lamb.

3 tablespoon olive oil
1 onion, finely chopped
4 garlic gloves, crushed
500g stewing beef
2 tablespoons flour
1 teaspoon ground coriander
1 teaspoon allspice
1 teaspoon turmeric
2 tablespoons tomato purée
500ml chicken or vegetable stock
salt and pepper
400g can chickpeas, drained and rinsed
400g can cannellini beans, drained and rinsed (optional)
300g chopped kale

For the sauce
2 tablespoons pomegranate molasses
2 tablespoons tahini
1 tablespoon sumac
½ cup water

Preheat the oven to 180C/Gas mark 4

Heat the oil in a heavy ovenproof casserole. Add the chopped onions and fry over a medium heat for 5 minutes. Add the garlic and cook for a further 2 minutes. Coat the meat with the flour and add to the onion and garlic, stirring until the meat is well coated. Add the ground coriander, all spice, turmeric and tomato purée. Cook, stirring well for 5 minutes, then add the drained chickpeas, 500ml stock and salt and pepper to taste. Make sure the meat is covered, if not add some water.

Transfer to the preheated oven and cook for 1 ½ - 2 hours until the meat is tender. After 1 hour add the cannellini beans, if using. Boil the chopped kale for 5 minutes until it's tender and set aside.

Prepare the sauce by mixing all the ingredients. Heat in a saucepan until it's smooth, adding more water if necessary. Add the sauce and kale to the meat and stir well. Return to the oven and cook for a further 10 minutes.

Endjinaras con patatas y carne

(Artichokes with potatoes and meat)

Endjinaras is the Ladino name for artichokes. They are widely used in Sephardic cooking, either stuffed or with other vegetables, such as broad beans or carrots. Their flavour is perfectly balanced by the lemon juice and sugar and I have added some turmeric powder - we often used it in cooking in Egypt and it gives the dish a lovely golden colour.

4 tablespoons olive oil
500g veal or beef, cubed
600g potatoes, peeled and cut into small chunks
380g can artichoke hearts, drained and rinsed
juice of 1 large lemon or 2 small lemons
2 teaspoons sugar
1 teaspoon turmeric powder (optional)
salt and pepper
1 cup water

Heat 4 tablespoons olive oil in a large non stick casserole dish and fry the meat for 3 minutes on each side. Add the cut potatoes and continue frying for a few minutes, then add the drained artichokes, lemon juice, sugar, salt and pepper and turmeric powder, if using.

Pour 1 cup of water over the meat and vegetables, making sure they are all covered.

Cover and cook on a low heat for 1 - 1 ½ hours or until the meat is tender and most of the juice has been absorbed.

Hamin de kastanya
(Lamb with chestnuts)

This is a Judeo Spanish dish which originated in Turkey. The recipe calls for roasted and peeled fresh chestnuts, but frozen ones work equally well and make life easier.

500g diced lamb, or neck of lamb cut into 3cm (1¼ inch) cubes
1 large onion, chopped
2 tablespoons sunflower or vegetable oil
salt and pepper
1 teaspoon ground cinnamon
½ teaspoon allspice
450g frozen chestnuts
juice of ½ lemon

Heat the oil in a large frying pan or heavy base saucepan. Add the chopped onion and fry on a very low heat, stirring occasionally, until golden, about 5 minutes. Add the meat and turn to brown it all over. Add salt, pepper, cinnamon and allspice.

Pour some water over the meat, enough to cover it, and bring to the boil. Remove the scum, lower the heat, cover and simmer for 1 ½ - 2 hours until the meat is tender. You will have to check every 30 minutes and add more water if necessary.

15 minutes before the end of cooking the lamb, add the chestnuts and lemon juice.

Lamb and quince stew

1 large onion, coarsely chopped
3 tablespoons oil
1kg lamb, beef or veal cut into chunks
1½ teaspoon cinnamon
½ teaspoon mixed spice
100g yellow split peas
1 large carrots cut into small pieces
1 large quince, cut into 8 or 12 pieces
2 tablespoons tomato purée
juice of ½ lemon
1 tablespoon honey
1 tablespoon pomegranate molasses
1½ cups water
salt and pepper

Quince is an autumn fruit and at its best when its colour changes from light green-yellow to a golden colour, usually in October or November. Quinces are coming back into culinary fashion in England, but at home we always used them in savoury dishes. They are hard to cut, so I find that blanching them in boiling water for a few minutes softens their skin and makes the task much easier.

Heat the oil and fry the onions until golden Add the meat and fry until brown on all sides.
Add the cinnamon, mixed spice, tomato purée and lemon juice and continue to fry for a couple of minutes, stirring all the time.

Transfer the meat to a large casserole dish. Add the chopped carrots, yellow split peas and quince, arranging them around the meat.

Mix in the honey, pomegranate molasses, salt and pepper. Cover with the water and simmer on a low heat for 1-1½ hours or until the meat is tender.

113

Hashweh
(One pot rice dish)

Hashweh is a one pot rice dish, loaded with minced beef or lamb, raisins, spices and pine nuts. It is delicious cooked and served as a side dish, but in Egypt and throughout the Middle East, it is the stuffing base for all sorts of vegetables. If using this way, do not cook the meat and the rice- simply soak the rice for 30 minutes, drain, add the remaining ingredients, mix well and use to stuff the vegetables.

300g long grain rice
3 tablespoons olive oil
1 small red onion, finely chopped
500g minced beef or lamb
1 ½ teaspoon all spice
½ teaspoon ground cloves
1 teaspoon ground cinnamon
salt and pepper
80g dark raisins
small bunch flat leaf parsley, chopped
3 cups water
30g pine nuts, toasted

Rinse the rice thoroughly and soak in water for 20 minutes. Drain.

Heat the olive oil in a heavy, shallow pan Fry the onion for 5 minutes until translucent. Add the minced beef or lamb and cook until brown, about 10 minutes, constantly stirring and breaking up any pieces with a wooden spoon.

Add the all spice, ground cloves, cinnamon, salt and pepper. Once the meat is cooked, add the rice, raisins, chopped parsley and 3 cups water. Drizzle with a little olive oil and sprinkle a little more ground cinnamon and allspice.

Bring to the boil and cook uncovered until half the water has been absorbed. Cover, lower the heat and simmer for 20 minutes or until all the water has been absorbed - check after 15 minutes and, if necessary, add a little more water. Leave the pan undisturbed for 10 minutes before uncovering.

Toast the pine nuts dry in a small frying pan. Turn the rice onto a plate and sprinkle with the toasted nuts.

Kharshouf Mahshi

(Artichoke bottoms stuffed with meat)

This was a big favourite at home, as artichokes were plentiful in Egypt. They were always fresh ones and a lot of time and patience were required to cut away all the leaves, leaving only the bottom for stuffing. Nowadays frozen artichoke bottoms can be purchased in large supermarkets and Middle Eastern stores, making the preparation much easier.

500g frozen artichoke bottoms (about 10)
1 medium onion, chopped
2 tablespoons sunflower oil
2 tablespoons pine nuts
300g minced beef
2 tablespoons finely chopped flat-leaf parsley
½ teaspoon salt
pinch of pepper
¼ teaspoon ground nutmeg
½ teaspoon cinnamon
1 small egg, beaten
juice of ½ lemon
150ml water

Preheat the oven to 180C/Gas mark 4.

Defrost the artichoke bottoms and blanch. Fry the onion in the oil until translucent, about 5 minutes. Add the pine nuts and stir until coloured.

With your hands, mix the minced beef with the parsley, salt, pepper, nutmeg, cinnamon and egg and work in the onion and pine nuts. Take lumps of the meat mixture and fill the artichoke bottoms, making little mounds. Place them in a shallow baking dish, mix the lemon juice with 150ml of water and pour over the artichokes.

Cover with foil and bake in the preheated over for 30 minutes or until the meat is cooked.

Serve hot or at room temperature.

Khoresh betingan
(Aubergine khoresh)

This is an aubergine and meat stew normally served with rice Its origin is Persian.

2 aubergines, sliced into medium slices
1 large onion, finely chopped
3 tablespoons sunflower or vegetable oil
1 tablespoon sunflower or vegetable oil
500g stewing beef or lamb, cubed
60g brown lentils or yellow split peas, soaked for a few hours
600 -1000ml water
salt and pepper
1 teaspoon ground turmeric (optional)
½ teaspoon cinnamon
½ teaspoon ground nutmeg

Garnish
½ tablespoon vegetable or sunflower oil
reserved chopped onion
2 tablespoons dried mint
1-2 garlic cloves, crushed

Sprinkle the aubergine slices with salt and leave them to drain in a colander for at least 30 minutes. Wash, squeeze out the bitter juices and pat them dry. Set aside.

Set aside 1 tablespoon of the chopped onion for garnish. Fry the remainder in 1 tablespoon of sunflower or vegetable oil until soft and golden, about 5 minutes. Add the meat cubes and brown on both sides. Add the drained lentils or split peas and cover with about 600 - 1000ml water. Season to taste with salt and pepper, cover, lower the heat and simmer for 1 ½ - 2 hours until the meat is tender and the lentils or yellow split peas are soft. Add the cinnamon, nutmeg, and ground turmeric, if using.

Sauté the aubergines in about 2 tablespoons of oil until soft and golden. Add them to the stew and cook for 15 minutes longer.

Prepare the garnish – fry the remainder of the onion in a little oil until soft and golden, add the dried mint and garlic and fry for 1 minute longer.

Serve in a bowl with the garnish, as an accompaniment to a dish of plain white rice or couscous.

Kofta bil karaz
(Meatballs with a sour cherry sauce)

This is another Syrian Jewish dish with a balance of sweet and sour, a favourite method of cooking. It can be served on toast or over a bed of rice. It is best to use sour cherries if you can find them, but fresh morello cherries will also work.

500g minced lamb
1 teaspoon cinnamon
1 teaspoon allspice
3 tablespoons finely chopped parsley
vegetable oil for shallow frying

For the sauce
1 large onion, coarsely chopped
2 tablespoons sunflower or vegetable oil
500g morello cherries, pitted or 250g sour cherries
juice of ½ lemon
1 tablespoon tamarind paste
1-2 tablespoons sugar to taste
salt and pepper to taste

If using dried sour cherries, soak them in half a cup of water overnight.

Prepare the meatballs - work the lamb mince with your hands to soften it. Add the cinnamon, allspice, salt and chopped parsley. Take lumps of paste the size of small walnuts and roll them into little balls.

Heat some vegetable oil in a frying pan, enough for shallow frying, and quickly fry the meatballs on both sides until lightly browned and slightly pink inside. Remove from the pan and set aside. Wash the frying pan as you will need to use it again.

Prepare the sauce - heat 2 tablespoons oil in the frying pan and fry the onion for 5 minutes, until translucent. Add the sour cherries with the water they have been soaked in (if using morello cherries, add half a cup of water to the pan).

Add the juice of ½ lemon, 1 tablespoon of tamarind paste, 1-2 tablespoons of sugar, salt and pepper and the meatballs. Make sure the meatballs are covered, so you may have to add some more water. Simmer for 20 minutes until the sauce has reduced.

Serve on slices of toast, crusts removed or over a bed of plain rice.

Lamb with broad beans and almonds

2 tablespoons vegetable or sunflower oil
500g diced lamb
2 celery sticks, chopped in 1cm (½ inch) pieces
300ml water
salt and pepper
½ teaspoon mace
1 onion, chopped
300g beans, fresh (weighed after shelling) or frozen
100g blanched almonds, roasted
1 tablespoon honey

This was a dish we often had at Passover, as it is believed that the Hebrews ate beans when they were slaves in Egypt. We used fresh broad beans, but frozen ones are fine.

Heat 1 tablespoon oil in a large saucepan and fry the meat, turning it until slightly brown. Add the celery and water and bring to the boil Season with salt and pepper and mace.
Simmer for 1½-2 hours, adding a little water if necessary.

In a separate pan, fry the onions in 1 tablespoon oil until golden and stir in the almonds. Add these and the broad beans to the meat and stir in the honey.

Cook on a low heat for 15 minutes, or until the beans and almonds are tender.

Slow roast leg of lamb with spices

1½ - 2 kilo leg of lamb
3 tablespoons olive oil
5 garlic cloves
100ml pomegranate molasses
1 tablespoon dried mint
1 teaspoon ground coriander
1 teaspoon ground cumin
1 teaspoon mixed spice
2 teaspoon sumac
salt and pepper

Prepare the lamb the day before. Slash the meat across on both sides as deep as you can and place the peeled garlic cloves inside the nooks. Mix all the remaining ingredients together and rub the marinade into the lamb, taking time to massage it into all the nooks and crannies. Cover and place in the fridge to marinate overnight. The next morning take the lamb out of the fridge 30 minutes before you want to cook it so that it reaches room temperature.

Preheat the oven to 160C/fan140/Gas mark 3.
Place the lamb in a large roasting dish with all the marinade juices and add a cup of boiling water.

Cover and cook for about 3 hours until the lamb is tender. Make sure you baste the meat every hour.

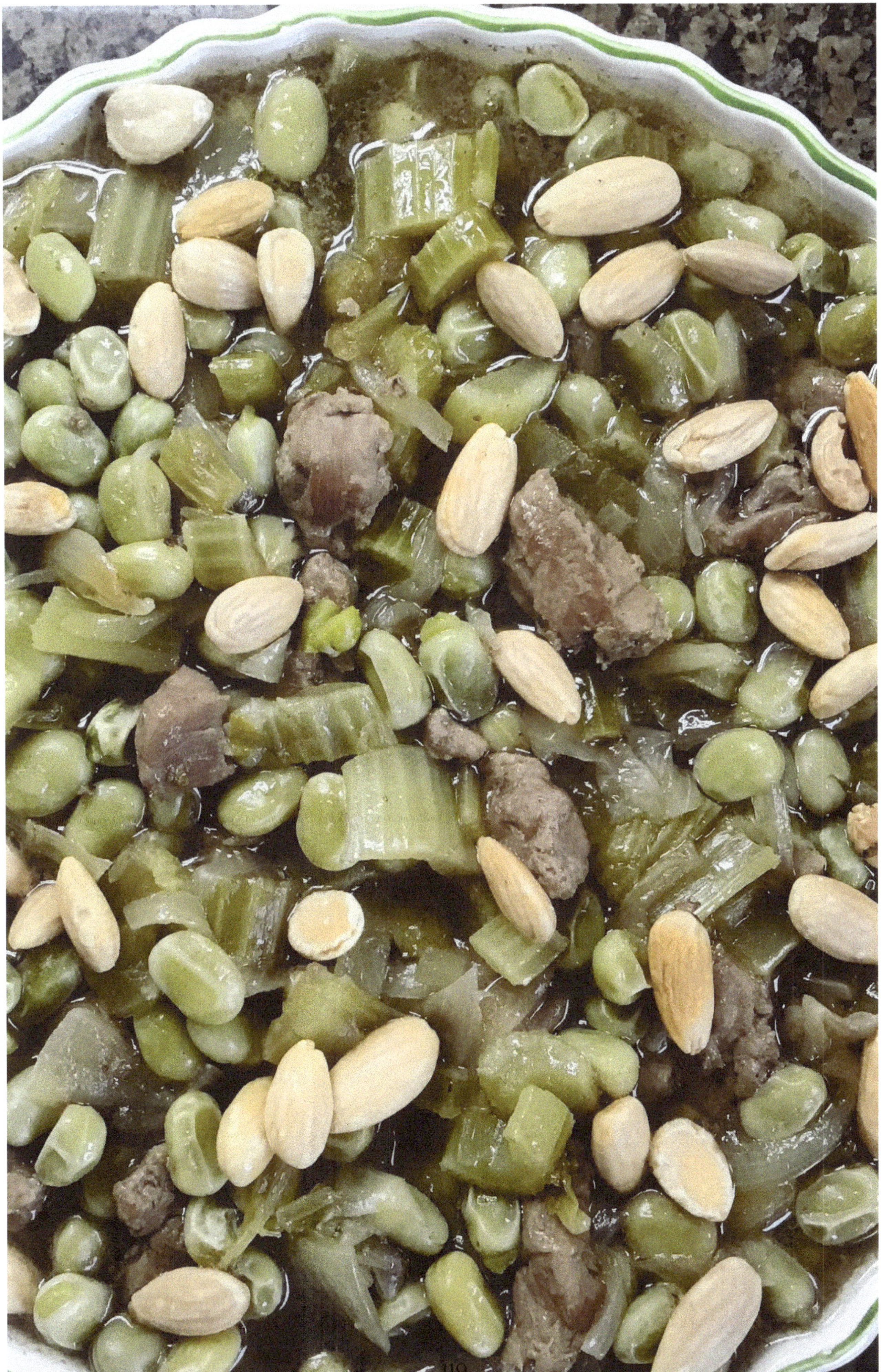

Lah'meh b'ajeen

(Syrian meat pizzas)

Makes 16

These meat pies were very popular amongst the Jews of Aleppo and were always served at parties and celebrations, straight out of the oven and hot. They were so good, they were gone within a few minutes! They are also a traditional fast-food snack sold in the streets in the Middle East.

For the dough
- 2½ teaspoons (1 packet) active dry yeast
- 1½ teaspoon sugar
- 250ml lukewarm water
- 510g strong white bread flour
- 4 tablespoons sunflower oil

For the topping
- 2 medium onions, chopped
- 4 tablespoons sunflower oil
- 800g minced lamb
- 4 tablespoons tamarind paste
- 2 generous teaspoons sugar
- 110ml tomato paste
- salt and cayenne pepper
- 1 teaspoon ground cumin

Preheat the oven at 240C/Gas Mark 9.

Prepare the dough – in a large bowl, mix the yeast and ½ teaspoon sugar with about half the lukewarm water and leave for about 10 minutes, until frothy.

Add the flour, 1 teaspoon sugar, salt and 3 tablespoons oil and mix well, then gradually add the rest of the water – enough to make a firm dough that holds together. Knead vigorously for at least 10 minutes until very soft and elastic. Pour the remaining tablespoon of oil into the bowl and turn the dough to oil it all over. Cover with clingfilm and leave in a warm place for 2 hours, or until doubled in bulk.

Prepare the topping – fry the onions in oil until soft and just beginning to colour. Put in a bowl with the minced lamb and the rest of the topping ingredients and work very well with your hands until you have a soft, well blended paste.

Make the pies – punch down the risen dough and knead for a few minutes Divide into 16 egg sized balls. On a floured surface and with a floured rolling pin, roll each ball out as thinly as possible, less than ¼ cm (1/8 inch) thick. Make round or oval shapes. Each pie should be about 18cm (7 inch) round.

Place the pies on an oiled tray or a tray lined with baking parchment. Spread the filling thickly and evenly, almost to the edge of the dough.

Bake in the preheated oven for 10 minutes. The breads should be well done, but still soft and pliable enough to roll up - that's how some people like to eat them. Serve hot.

Note: instead of tamarind, you can use pomegranate molasses with ½ teaspoon of allspice or lemon juice. You can halve the quantity of ingredients to make 8 pizzas.

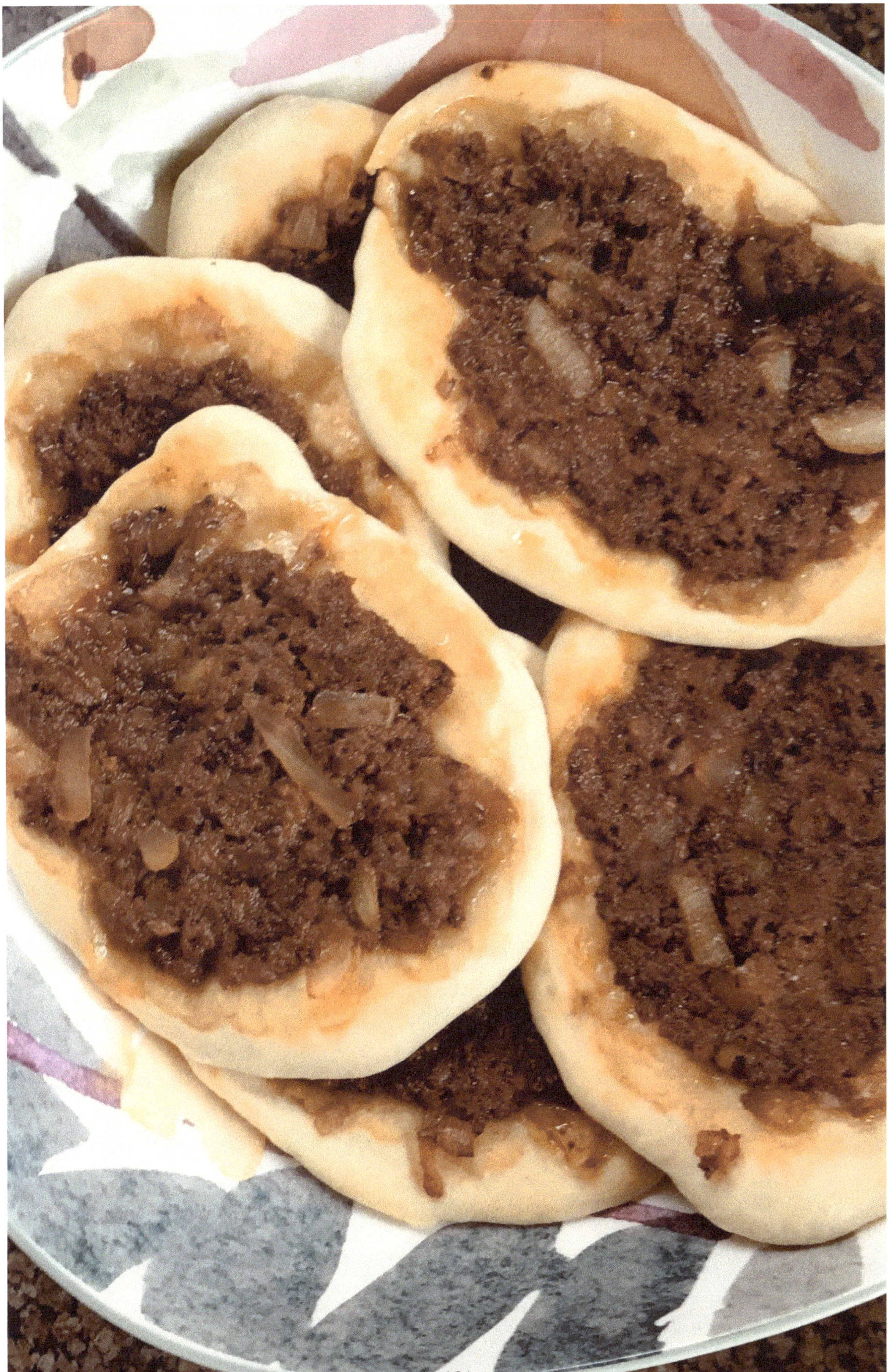

Mah'shi basal
(Stuffed caramelised onions)

The onion is a favourite vegetable throughout North Africa and the Middle East and there are many versions of this dish. In Egypt, it was said that a cook's expertise could be discerned by the tightness of her rolled stuffed onions. This particular recipe results in deliciously caramelised stuffed onions, regardless of how tight they are rolled.

3 large onions, weighing about 300g each

For the filing
1 medium onion, finely chopped
1 tablespoon sunflower or vegetable oil
400g beef mince
100g long grain rice
1 tablespoon tomato paste
200ml water
½ teaspoon cinnamon
½ teaspoon allspice
salt and pepper
30g pine nuts (optional)
1 teaspoon pomegranate molasses

For the sauce
250ml water
1 tablespoon tomato paste
1 tablespoon pomegranate molasses
2 teaspoons tamarind paste
2 teaspoons sugar
1 teaspoon ground cinnamon
½ teaspoon allspice
juice of 1 lemon
salt and pepper

Prepare the onions - cut a vertical slit down the side of each onion and remove the outer skin. Put the onions in a large saucepan, cover with water and bring to a boil. Reduce the heat and simmer for 20 minutes, or until the onion layers begin to soften and come apart. Drain and remove from the pan. When cool, separate the individual layers of each onion.

Prepare the filling – wash the rice well, drain and place in a medium saucepan, cover with water and boil for 10 minutes, until the rice has softened. Drain again, rinse with cold water and place in a bowl. (Some people like add the rice uncooked to the filling, but I prefer it slightly cooked beforehand)

Heat the oil in a large frying pan and cook the onion until soft, about 5 minutes. Add the beef mince and cook for 10 minutes, all the time breaking it down with a wooden spoon. When the meat has browned, add the tomato paste, cinnamon, all spice, salt and pepper, pomegranate molasses and pine nuts, if using. Add the water, cover and simmer for 10-15 minutes, until all the water has been absorbed. Cool, add the rice and mix well.

Prepare the stuffed onions - spoon a teaspoon of the filling into each onion layer and roll tightly. Cover the bottom of a medium/ large ovenproof saucepan with sunflower or vegetable oil. Carefully place the stuffed onions in the saucepan, keeping them close to each other.

Prepare the sauce – in a medium saucepan, add the water, tomato paste, tamarind paste, pomegranate molasses, lemon juice, sugar, cinnamon and allspice, salt and pepper.

Bring to the boil , turn off the heat and immediately pour the sauce over the onions. Top with an ovenproof plate to stop the onions from opening. Bring to the boil, lower the heat, cover and simmer for 30 minutes until the juices have thickened.

Preheat the oven to 180C/ Gas Mark 4.
Transfer the saucepan to the preheated oven and cook for a further 1- 1 ½ hour until the sauce has caramelised.

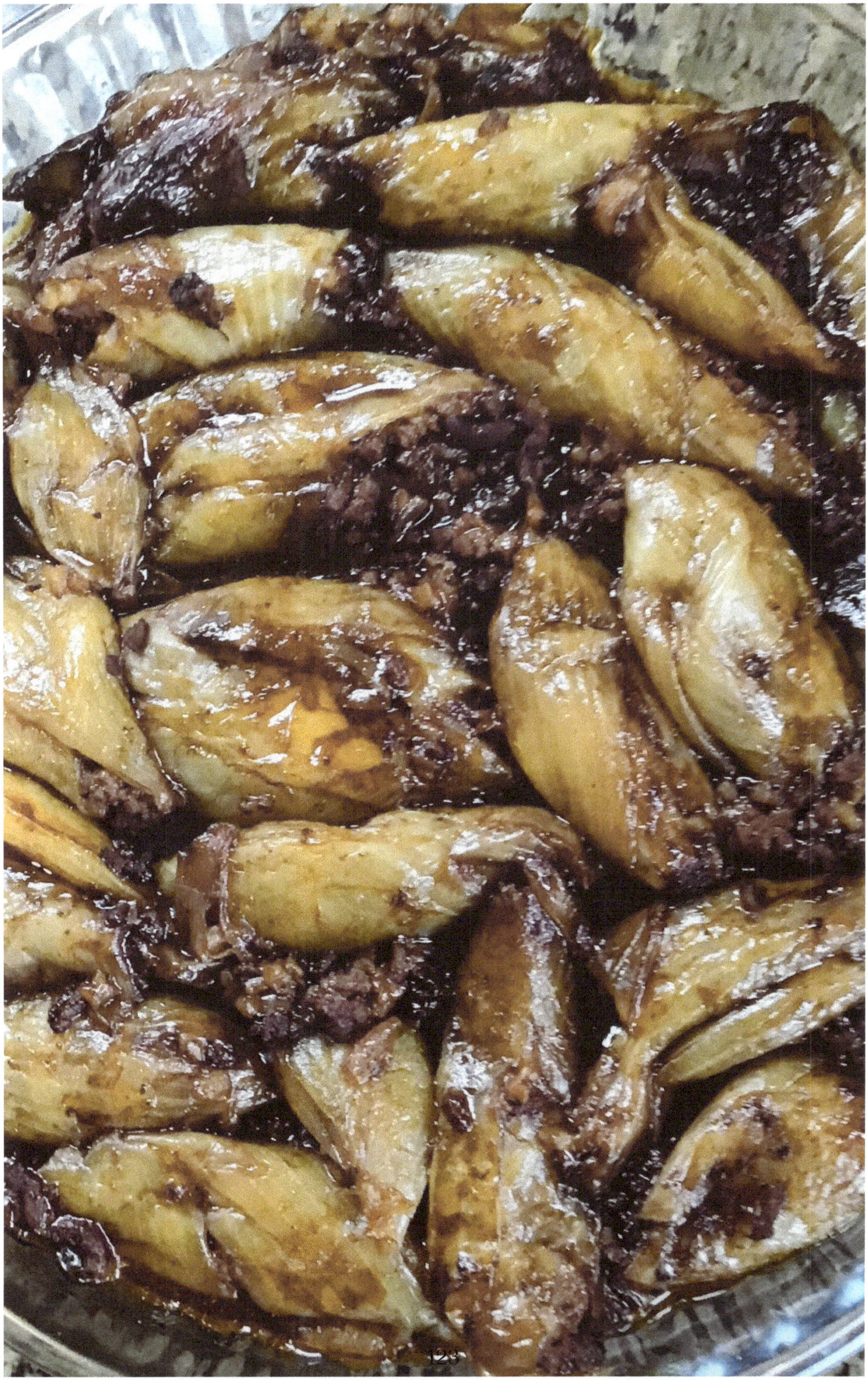

Mah'shi
(Stuffed vegetables)

In Egypt, fresh vegetables were available in abundance throughout the year. A favourite way of cooking was to stuff them, either with minced meat and rice or just rice on its own. This dish is a quintessential part of my childhood and always brings back one particular memory. My father had an elderly relative we called uncle Charles, who lived on his own. He was a lovely quiet man and my parents used to invite him for lunch once a week I was only 7 or 8 years old at the time, but I remember that his favourite dish was these stuffed vegetables. They were served on a large tray and looked impressive. He sat at the head of the table and the tray was always presented to him first.

This dish is a little time consuming, but well worth the effort, and quite therapeutic once you get into the swing of it.

Vegetables
   2 large aubergines
   3 bell peppers (or 6 elongated small peppers, the kind you find in Middle Eastern supermarkets)
   2 large courgettes or 4 medium ones

For the filling
   500g minced beef
   250g basmati rice
   1 medium onion, finely chopped
   generous bunch of flat leaf parsley, chopped
   juice of ½ lemon
   3 tablespoons tomato purée
   few drops of olive oil
   1 teaspoon coriander
   1 teaspoon cinnamon
   1 tablespoon honey

For the sauce
   ½ carton tomato passata
   ¼ cup brown sugar
   2 tablespoons pomegranate molasses
   1 tablespoon tamarind paste
   juice of ½ lemon
   1 generous cup water

Prepare the rice - wash it thoroughly and leave it in water for 20 minutes. Rinse and drain.

Prepare the vegetables - cut the courgettes in half and using an apple corer carefully scoop out the flesh, taking care not to pierce the skin. Discard the flesh. Cut the aubergines across in half (not lengthwise) and scoop out as much of the flesh as you can, discarding this. Cut the top of the peppers and remove any seeds.

Prepare the filling - mix the drained rice with the minced beef, add the chopped onions and all the remaining ingredients. Use this mixture to fill the inside of all the vegetables. Do not fill right to the top as rice expands when cooking.

Assemble the dish - pour a few drops of oil in a heavy ovenproof dish and swirl it round to make sure all the bottom is covered with oil. Arrange the filled vegetables tightly in the dish.

To make the sauce - mix all the ingredients and pour over the vegetables, making sure they are well covered, adding some water if necessary. Cover the vegetables with a heavy ovenproof plate to prevent them spreading.

Preheat the oven to 180C/Gas mark 4.

Cook on the hob over a low heat for 30 minutes, then transfer the pan to the preheated oven and cook for a further 1 hour or until the vegetables are tender and the sauce is reduced.

125

Mah'shi batatas
(Stuffed potatoes)

Stuffed vegetables were a big favourite and this is another example, though it appeared less often at the dinner table, probably because potatoes are quite filling. They are delicious served on their own, with a vegetable such as green beans. This is the way we prepared stuffed potatoes at home, as opposed to the Libyan version called mafrum.

6 medium potatoes
4 tablespoons sunflower or vegetable oil

For the filling
   1 large onion, chopped
   1 tablespoon sunflower or vegetable oil
   300g minced beef
   1 tablespoon tomato paste
   1 teaspoon cinnamon
   ½ teaspoon allspice
   salt and pepper
   200ml water

For the sauce
   300ml water
   2 tablespoons pomegranate molasses
   2 tablespoons tomato paste
   juice of 1 lemon
   1 teaspoon allspice
   ½ teaspoon ground turmeric
   salt to taste

Prepare the potatoes - flatten the top of each potato by cutting the rounded top part. Core them, leaving about 1cm (½ inch) of the outer shell Reserve the interior flesh.

Prepare the filling – heat the oil in a frying pan and fry the onion until soft, about 5 minutes. Add the beef mince and cook for 10 minutes until the meat is browned, all the time breaking it with a wooden spoon. Add the tomato paste, cinnamon, allspice, salt and pepper and 200ml water. Cover, lower the heat and cook for about 10 minutes until the water is absorbed. Remove the meat mixture and place it in a bowl.

In the same frying pan, heat 4 tablespoons sunflower or vegetable oil. When the oil is hot, fry the potato shells well on each side until they begin to turn golden. Drain them upside down on paper towels. Squeeze the reserved interior flesh of the potatoes to remove any excess water and in the same frying pan, fry it for a few minutes until golden brown and drain.

Prepare the stuffed potatoes - stuff each potato shell with the beef filling. Cover the bottom of a heavy, ovenproof saucepan with a light coat of oil and place the stuffed potatoes in the pan, close to each other. Add the fried interior flesh to the saucepan.

Prepare the sauce - in a small saucepan, heat 300ml of water and add the pomegranate molasses, tomato paste, lemon juice, allspice, ground turmeric and salt. Pour the sauce over the stuffed potatoes and potato flesh. Bring to the boil, lower the heat, cover and simmer for 1 hour.

Meanwhile, preheat the oven to 180C/ Gas Mark 4.
Transfer the saucepan to the preheated oven and cook uncovered for 30 minutes or more, until the sauce has reduced and the potatoes are golden brown.

Sephardic brisket

Traditionally, brisket is a cheap cut of meat and can turn out tough if cooked incorrectly. However, it contains a lot of fat which, combined with low-and-slow cooking techniques, can transform the tough meat into a tender and juicy dish. The technique of searing the meat enhances its flavour.

Brisket joint, weighing about 1kg
salt and pepper
flour for coating
¼ cup olive oil
1 medium onion, chopped
1 tablespoons peeled and grated fresh ginger
½ cup fresh orange juice

2 cups chicken stock, vegetable stock or water
1 cinnamon stick
2 tea bags
10 dried pitted prunes
10 dried apricots

Preheat the oven to 180c/Gas mark 4.

Heat the oil in a frying pan Season the brisket with salt and pepper, coat with flour and fry on both sides, about 5-7 minutes each side. Remove the brisket and place it in an ovenproof saucepan.

In the same oil, fry the onions until translucent, about 5 minutes. Add the ginger and orange juice and cook until the liquid has reduced by half. Pour the liquid over the brisket in the pan and add the cinnamon stick and 2 cups of stock or water, enough to cover the brisket.

Cook in the preheated oven for 2 hours or until the brisket is tender, basting and turning at 30 minutes interval. When the brisket is cooked, remove from the pan and transfer to a serving plate. Cool and refrigerate overnight.

Remove the cinnamon stick and purée the sauce in a food processor until smooth - you may have to reduce it in a saucepan over a medium heat if it's too thin. Refrigerate overnight separately from the brisket.

When ready to serve, preheat the oven to 180C/ Gas mark 4. Bring 1 cup of water to the boil and soak the tea bags to make a strong tea. Discard them and put the apricots and prunes in the liquid to plump for 30 minutes, then drain them.

Remove any congealed fat, cut the brisket in slices and place in a baking dish. Warm the sauce which has been refrigerated and pour over the brisket. Add the fruit to the sauce, cover with foil and heat in a preheated oven until hot, about 20 minutes.

Kofta mishmisheya

(Meatballs in apricot sauce)

Makes about 20 meatballs

Recipes using meatballs are as varied as the country and cooking style they originate from. In Egypt, they were usually cooked with a simple tomato sauce and spices such as coriander and cumin. The following recipe is the way my grandmother cooked it, with the addition of a tangy apricot sauce. The end result is quite unusual and very flavoursome.

For the apricot sauce
- 200g amardeen (apricot paste)
- 200ml boiling water

For the meatballs
- 1 tablespoon sunflower or vegetable oil
- 1 small onion finely chopped
- 500g minced lamb
- 1 egg, lightly beaten
- 2 small slices or 1 large slice of bread, crusts removed, softened with a little water, then water squeezed out
- 1 tablespoon tomato paste
- 1 teaspoon allspice
- ½ teaspoon cinnamon
- 20g flat leaf parsley, finely chopped
- salt and pepper to taste

For shallow frying
- 3 tablespoons flour
- 3 tablespoons sunflower or vegetable oil

For the sauce
- 120ml Italian passata or any tomato sauce
- 1 tablespoon pomegranate molasses
- 1 teaspoon tamarind paste
- 1 teaspoon sugar
- 50ml warm water

Apricot paste sheets (amardeen)) can be found in most Middle Eastern shops. They are ideal for this dish, because of their slightly sour taste. Alternatively, you can replace with 100g dried apricots soaked in water, cooked until soft and puréed. However, the sweet/sour combination that is particular to this dish may be lost.

Make the apricot sauce - tear 200g apricot sheets, place in a bowl, cover with 200ml boiling water and soak overnight. You may have to add a little more water.

To make the apricot sauce, transfer the soaked apricots sheets and water to a medium saucepan and cook over a low heat until the sauce is smooth. Set aside.

Make the meatballs – heat 1 tablespoon sunflower or vegetable oil and fry the onion until soft and translucent, about 8 minutes. Place the fried onion in a large bowl and add the minced lamb, beaten egg, bread, cinnamon, allspice, tomato paste, parsley and salt and pepper. Mix well with your hands and shape into meatballs. Roll each one into some flour.

Heat about 2 tablespoons of oil in a frying pan and fry the meatballs until brown, turning them over to make sure they don't stick. Carefully transfer them to a large non stick saucepan and cover with half the apricot sauce, tomato passata or tomato sauce, pomegranate molasses, tamarind paste and sugar.

Add the water and mix well, cover and simmer for 15 minutes. Check half way through to make sure that the meatballs are not sticking to the pan. Remove the lid and cook uncovered for a further 5 minutes or until the sauce has thickened.

Transfer to a serving dish and cover with the remaining apricot sauce. Serve hot with white plain rice.

Note - the sauce will thicken when it cools, so add a little water to the meatballs if reheating.

Mafrum
(Meat stuffed potatoes)

Mafrum is a dish from the Libyan cuisine. A mixture of ground beef and spices is sandwiched inside a potato and cooked in tomato sauce.

Potatoes
　5 large potatoes
　1 cup flour
　2 eggs
　vegetable oil for frying

Meat filling
　500g minced beef
　3 tablespoons flat-leaf parsley, finely chopped
　2 eggs
　½ medium onion, chopped
　1/3 cup breadcrumbs
　½ teaspoon cinnamon
　½ teaspoon cumin
　2 teaspoons paprika
　salt and pepper

Sauce
　1 tablespoon vegetable oil
　2 garlic cloves, minced
　2 teaspoons paprika
　3 tablespoons tomato paste
　2 cups water
　3 fresh tomatoes, sliced or 400g can chopped tomatoes
　1 small onion, chopped
　1 teaspoon salt
　1 teaspoon pepper

Place the meat with all the filling ingredients in a bowl and mix well.

Peel and wash the potatoes. Cut them lengthwise into 1¼cm (1 inch) thick wedges. Cut into each wedge to make a V shaped potato – slicing almost all the way through, as you only want to create an opening and not slice them in half. Take a golf ball size of meat and stuff into the potatoes.

Roll the stuffed potatoes in flour first, then in egg. Heat enough vegetable oil in a large frying pan for shallow frying. Fry the potato wedges on both sides until golden brown. Set aside.

Prepare the sauce – add a little oil to the frying pan used for frying the potatoes. Heat and fry the garlic and paprika quickly so as not to burn them. Add the tomato paste and water, the fresh or tinned tomatoes, salt and pepper and stir.

Arrange the potatoes in a large, heavy bottom saucepan and pour the sauce over. Cover, lower the heat and simmer for 45 minutes until the potatoes are tender.

Serve on a bed of couscous.

Sweet and sour beef stew

900g stewing beef
2½ teaspoons salt
¼ teaspoon black pepper
½ teaspoon cinnamon
1½ teaspoon allspice
3 tablespoons vegetable oil
2 medium sized onions, cut into wedges and separated into layers
2 medium potatoes, peeled and cut into medium chunks
2 medium sweet potatoes, peeled and cut into medium chunks
¾ cup pitted prunes
1 large aubergine, cut into 2cm (1 inch) chunks
400g can chopped tomatoes

Sauce
3 generous tablespoons tomato paste
Juice of 2 lemons, plus 3 tablespoons
2 tablespoons Worcestershire sauce or pomegranate molasses
1 tablespoon tamarind paste
¼ cup firmly packed dark brown sugar
¼ teaspoon salt
2½ cups water

My mother's family originates from Aleppo in Syria. My grandparents left in 1910 for economic reasons and settled in Egypt, which was the new Eldorado, mainly due to the opening of the Suez Canal in 1869. The Jews of Aleppo had developed an elite cooking style which featured fine ingredients, such as cinnamon and allspice and exotic flavours such as tamarind paste and pomegranate molasses. Dried fruits were commonly available in the markets of Aleppo and were added to all sorts of vegetable and meat dishes. This remained very much my grandmother's style of cooking and she taught my mother everything she knew. I have tried to keep the tradition in my own way.

This recipe is from Jennifer Abadi's book A Fistful of Lentils. This is another Syrian Jewish dish which favours the sweet and sour combination of ingredients. It's a very easy dish to prepare, as it's all cooked in one pot. The flavour will improve if prepared a day ahead and reheated in the oven before serving. Depending on the dimensions of the casserole dish you are using, the layers may not completely cover each other. I have used a large 26cm (10 inch) casserole dish, so have spread the vegetables in one layer at a time.

Prepare the layers – combine the meat with the salt, pepper, cinnamon and allspice in a bowl, mixing well with your hands.

Pour 3 tablespoons vegetable oil in a heatproof casserole dish. Spread half the onions in a single layer over the oil and place half the meat over the onions, pressing down firmly. If using a large saucepan, you may have to use all the onions in one layer and then one layer of meat.

Proceed to layer the vegetables- first the potatoes, followed by the sweet potatoes, the prunes and the aubergines, in that order. Press firmly and pour the can of chopped tomatoes over the vegetables.

Prepare the sauce – in a medium saucepan, combine the water, tomato paste, lemons, Worcestershire sauce (or pomegranate molasses), tamarind paste, dark brown sugar and salt. Bring to the boil, turn off the heat and pour the sauce over the layers. Cover, lower the heat and simmer for 1 hour. Correct the seasoning to taste – you may have to add more brown sugar. The sauce should have a sweet-tart taste.

In the meantime, preheat the oven to 180C/Gas Mark 4. Transfer the casserole dish to the preheated oven and bake for 1½ - 2 hours until the potatoes and aubergines are soft. If necessary, cook uncovered for a further 15 minutes if the sauce needs to be reduced.

Serve with white rice.

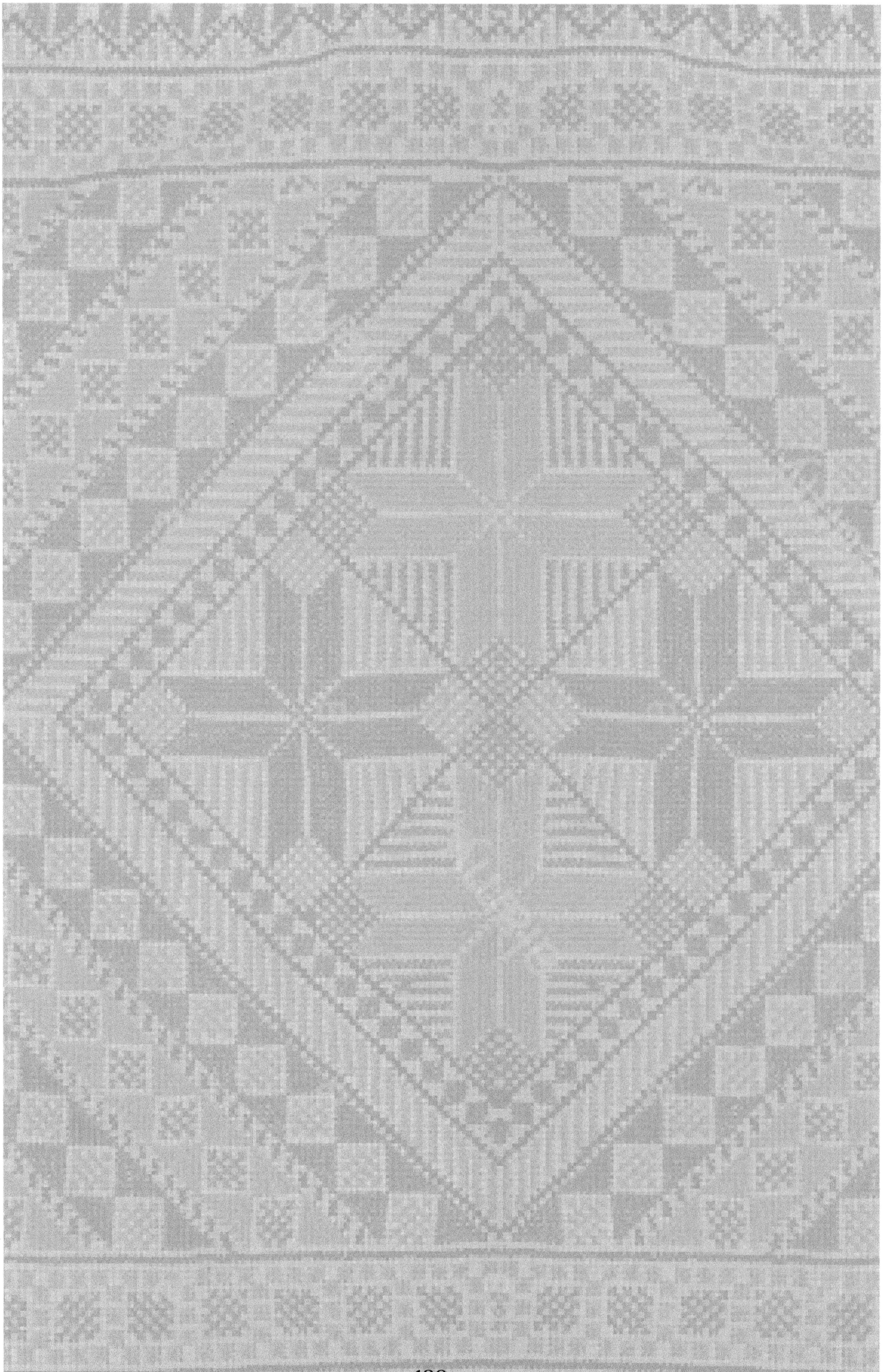

POULTRY DISHES

Poyo
Ferakh

Braised Chicken with quince, almonds and pomegranates

The quince fruit is not edible raw, but cooked it turns into a wonderful dark pink and is very versatile. It has a short season, so my family used to make the most of it — quince jam was the favourite and could be stored for months, but we also used to add the fruit to many savoury dishes. This chicken recipe was one of them.

For the chicken
  1 kg chicken thighs and drumsticks – approximately 5 of each
  vegetable or sunflower oil for shallow frying

For the quince
  3 large quinces
  1 tablespoon vegetable oil
  juice of ½ lemon
  2 tablespoons honey

For the sauce
  2 tablespoons vegetable oil
  1 onion, chopped finely
  2 tablespoons pomegranate molasses
  2 tablespoons tamarind paste
  ¼ cup brown sugar
  1 teaspoon cinnamon
  1 cup chicken stock
  salt and pepper

  seeds of 1 pomegranate
  100g almonds, roasted and chopped

Preheat the over to 180C/Gas Mark 4.

Roast the almonds, chop them up in a food processor and set aside. Cut the pomegranate in half, take out the seeds and place them in a bowl. Set aside.

Steam or boil the quinces for 10 minutes. When cool slice into quarters, peel and cut into medium pieces. Drizzle a little vegetable oil into a large ovenproof casserole dish. Arrange the quince slices around the bottom of the dish. Squeeze the juice of ½ lemon and 2 tablespoons honey over the slices.

Heat some oil in a large frying pan and fry the chicken thighs and drumsticks until browned, about 5 minutes each side. Remove and place them tightly over the quince in the casserole dish.

In the same frying pan, fry the chopped onion and add all the remaining ingredients and chicken stock. When the sauce has boiled, pour it over the chicken and quince slices in the casserole dish. Cover and cook over the hob on a low heat for 30 minutes.

Transfer to the preheated oven and cook for 1 hour or until the chicken is tender.

Sprinkle with the chopped almonds and pomegranate seeds.

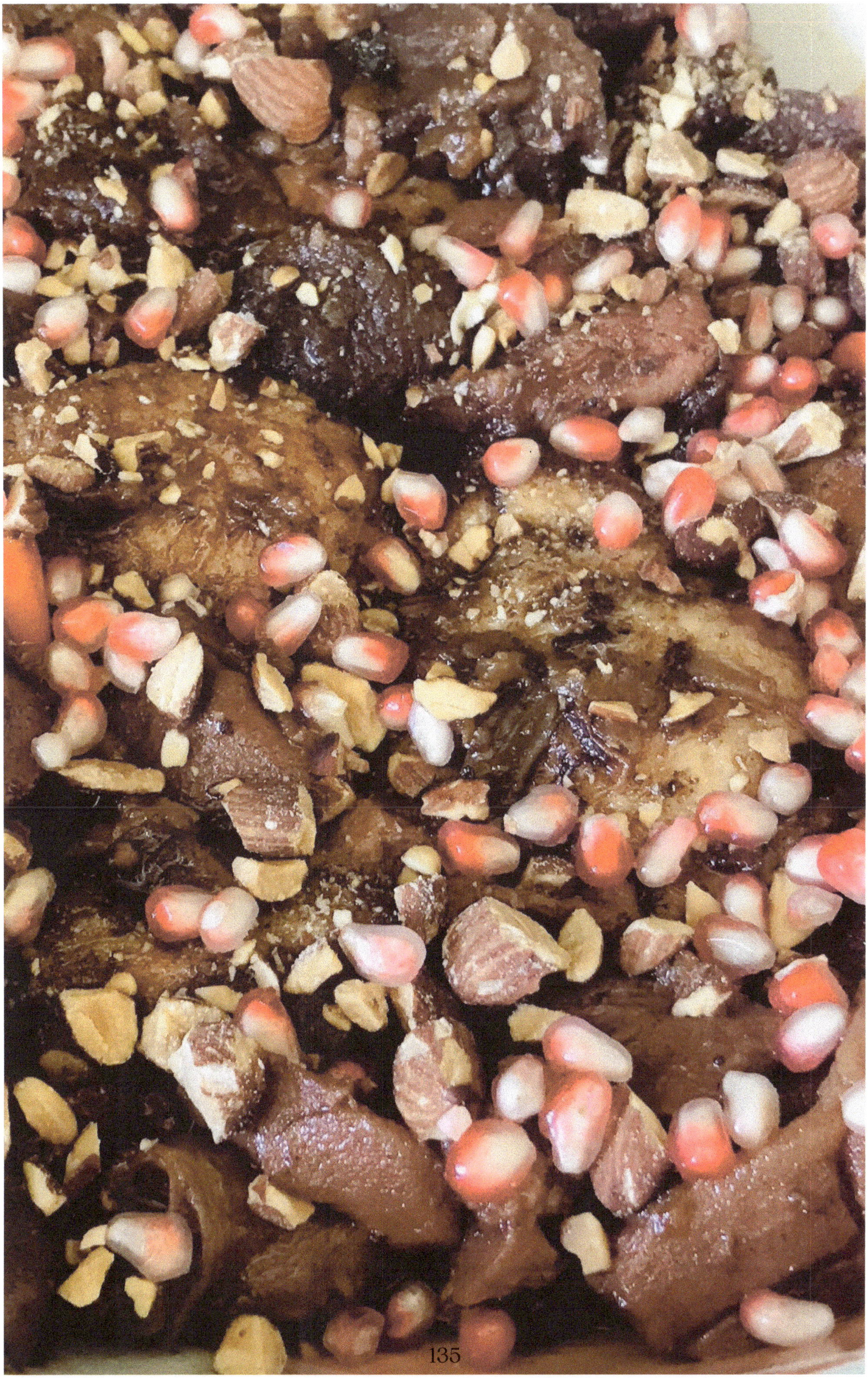

Chicken and potatoes sofrito

Sofrito is a method of cooking slowly in a mixture of oil and very little water, adding water gradually as the sauce reduces. Ground turmeric and lemon juice are also an essential part of a sofrito dish. This was the favourite way of cooking poultry and meat in the Sephardic community in Egypt, with the potatoes fried first before being added to the chicken. The result was quite special and, whenever I smell and taste sofrito, I am immediately reminded of my mother and her cooking. I have added sweet potatoes to the recipe, but this is optional. If not using them, double the quantity of potatoes.

6 chicken thighs (about 1kg)
4 tablespoons sunflower oil
juice of ½ lemon
1 teaspoon ground turmeric
1 teaspoon salt
260ml water
300g potatoes, sliced into 3cm (1½ inch) pieces
300g sweet potatoes, sliced into 3cm (1½ inch) pieces
1 large onion, cut lengthwise and into large strips

Preheat the oven to 180C/Gas Mark 4.

Heat 3 tablespoons oil in a large frying pan and fry the chicken thighs on both sides until brown, about 6 minutes each side. Lift and transfer to a heavy based large saucepan (reserve the frying pan and remaining oil).

Place the chicken thighs skin side up in the saucepan. Add salt, ground turmeric, lemon juice and 250ml water. Cover, lower the heat and simmer for about 30 minutes, turning the chicken frequently and adding a little water if necessary, until the chicken is just tender.

In the meantime, wash the potatoes, peel them and cut into 3cm (1½ inch) cubes. Reheat the remaining oil in the frying pan and fry the potatoes in batches until golden brown. Drain on kitchen paper. Add 1 tablespoon of oil and fry the onion strips until translucent, about 5 minutes.

Add the potatoes and onions to the chicken in the saucepan. Add a little water if necessary, cover and cook on medium heat for a further 15 minutes. The sauce should have reduced by then. If not, cook uncovered for a few more minutes until the potatoes have absorbed most of the juice.

Chicken in a coconut sauce and ginger sauce

2 medium onions, cut lengthwise and thinly sliced
3 tablespoons sunflower or vegetable oil
2 teaspoons fresh grated ginger
1 teaspoon ground turmeric
600g chicken thighs
salt and pepper to taste
350g baby potatoes
400g unsweetened coconut milk
50-100ml water
1 teaspoon sugar
100g cashew nuts
2 tablespoons raisins

The ingredients in this recipe are more reminiscent of India than the Middle East. I have included it because chicken and coconut go wonderfully well together, especially when served over a bed of saffron rice.

In a large saucepan, heat the oil and fry the onions until soft and translucent, about 8 minutes. Add the ginger and turmeric and stir well. Season the chicken thighs with salt and pepper and continue frying, 5 minutes on each side.

Add the potatoes, coconut milk, water and sugar and adjust the seasoning.

Lower the heat, cover and cook for 40 minutes or until the chicken and potatoes are very tender.

Uncover, add the raisins and cashew nuts and cook for a further 5 minutes.

Chicken with rice, chickpeas and vermicelli

This dish was very popular amongst the Jews of Aleppo. The combination of chicken, rice, vermicelli and chickpeas makes it an ideal one-pot meal.

700g chicken thighs or mixture of thighs and breasts
2 onions, diced
3 garlic cloves, chopped
1 tablespoon vegetable or sunflower oil
125g vermicelli, shredded
250g long-grain or basmati rice
1 x 400g can chickpeas, drained
1 teaspoon allspice
¼ teaspoon pepper
1 teaspoon salt

In a large saucepan, cover the chicken with water. Bring to a boil over high heat, then reduce the heat to medium low. Simmer for 1 hour, or until the chicken is fork tender.

Remove and let it stand for 15 minutes. Reserve 2 cups of the broth and store the rest for another use. Cut the chicken into small chunks

In a large frying pan, sauté the onions and garlic until soft, about 6 minutes. Add the vermicelli and rice and sauté for 1 minute. Add the chicken chunks, chickpeas, 2 cups chicken broth, allspice, salt and pepper.

Bring to a boil over a medium heat, then reduce the heat to low. Cover and simmer for 20 minutes, or until the rice is fluffy.

Lemon chicken with sweet potatoes

Chicken breasts can dry very quickly in the oven, so adding plenty of lemon juice, olive oil and chicken bouillon to the pan ensure they remain moist throughout the cooking process.

4 medium sweet potatoes, weighing around 800g
4 chicken breasts, skinless
120ml lemon juice (2 large lemons)
60ml olive oil
3 garlic cloves, minced
15g (1 tablespoon) Dijon mustard
2 teaspoons dried oregano
2 teaspoons ground turmeric
250ml water
2 chicken stock cubes
½ teaspoon salt
½ teaspoon pepper

Preheat the oven to 180C/Gas mark 4.

Wash and peel the sweet potatoes. Cut them into 2cm (1 inch) pieces. Arrange them in a casserole dish and place the chicken breasts on top.

Prepare the lemon mixture - in a large bowl mix the lemon juice, olive oil, Dijon mustard, minced garlic, dried oregano, ground turmeric salt and pepper.

Prepare the bouillon by mixing two stock cubes with 250ml boiling water, add to the lemon mixture and slowly pour over the chicken breasts and sweet potatoes.

Cover and cook in the preheated oven for 50 minutes or until the chicken is tender.

If there is still too much liquid, carefully remove the chicken breasts and sweet potatoes and cook the lemon mixture for a further 10 minutes uncovered, until it has reduced a little.

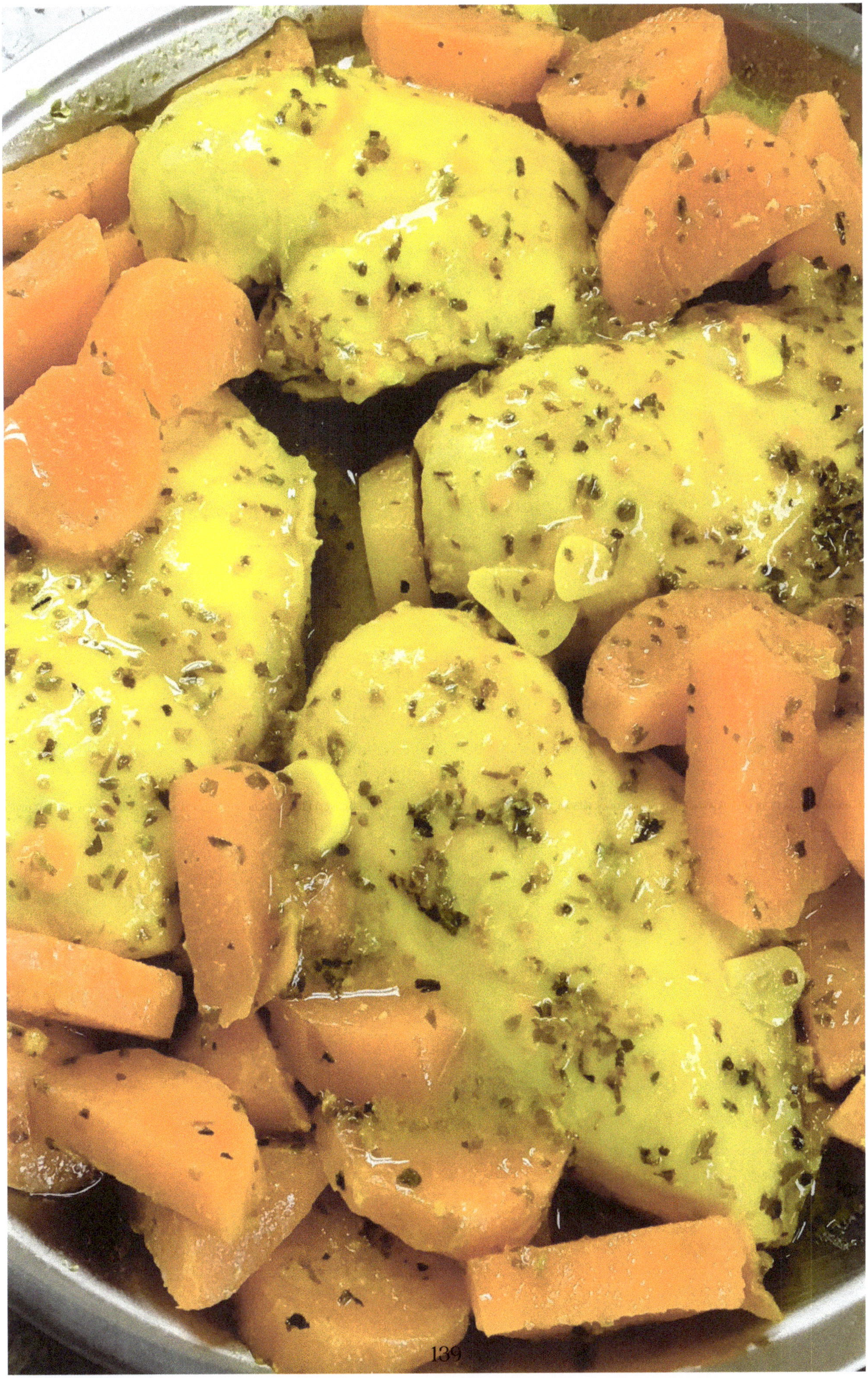

Chicken with dates

Chicken reminds me of the live ones we had in Cairo as special guests in our bathroom once a year, before Yom Kippur, the Jewish Day of Atonement. This was in order to perform the old Jewish custom known as Kapparot, which was to offer a chicken for girls and a rooster for boys, to atone for one's sins. In the Judeo Egyptian culture, the sacrifice of a chicken, which was then given to needy people, was considered a blessing and thought to bring good fortune to the person in honour of whom it was made. There was no time to get attached to the chicken in our bathroom, as they were killed ritually the next day.

4 chicken legs
3 tablespoons sunflower oil
2 large onions, coarsely chopped
2 teaspoons cinnamon
½ teaspoon nutmeg
1 tablespoon honey
400ml water
1 red pepper, thinly sliced
1 medium courgette, chopped
200g pitted dates
juice of 1 lemon
salt and pepper
60g toasted flaked almonds

In a large pan, heat the oil and sauté the chicken legs for a few minutes, turning them once.
Remove and set aside.

Fry the onions in the same oil until soft. Add the cinnamon, nutmeg and honey and mix well. Return the chicken to the pan, add the water, courgette, sliced pepper and salt.

Bring to the boil, cover and cook on medium heat for 45 minutes, until the chicken is tender.

Add the dates and lemon juice and cook for another 10 minutes. Uncover and quickly reduce the sauce if necessary - it should be fairly thick.

Serve sprinkled with the toasted almonds.

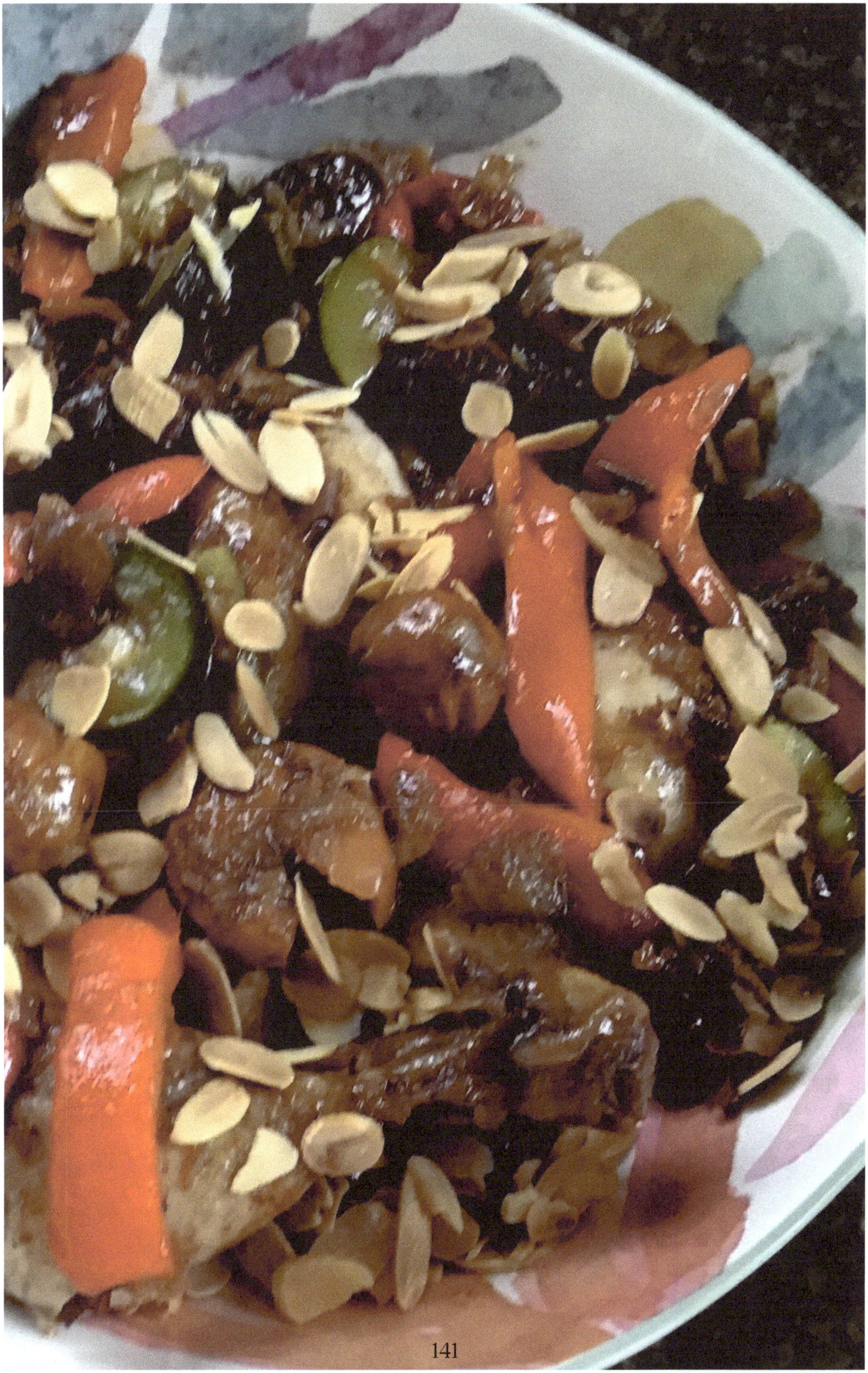

Chicken, aubergine and sweet potato stew

My mother would have cooked this dish with small white potatoes, rather than the sweet variety. Both give an equally tasty result, but I prefer the sweet potatoes because they blend well with fried aubergines..

3 medium aubergines, weighing about 200g each
1 tablespoon coarse salt
1 teaspoon lemon juice
2 medium sweet potatoes, weighing about 300g each
1 large carrot (optional)
1kg chicken thighs and drumsticks
3 tablespoons olive oil
1 large onion, sliced lengthways
2 garlic cloves, minced
1 cup tomato passata sauce or 400g can chopped tomatoes
1 cup water
½ teaspoon sugar
1 teaspoon dried oregano
½ teaspoon ground turmeric
salt and pepper to taste

1 tablespoon lemon juice
½ cup hot water

For shallow frying
  Vegetable or sunflower oil

Prepare the aubergines- cut off the stems and using a sharp knife, peel off strips at intervals along the length of the aubergines, leaving them striped with some peel. Cut each aubergine into slices about 2cm (1 inch) thick. Wash them, sprinkle with coarse salt and place in a colander for 30 minutes. Rinse again and squeeze out the bitter juices. Set aside.

Peel the sweet potatoes and carrot, if using. Wash and cut them into 2cm (1 inch) chunks.

Prepare the chicken – wash and pat dry. Heat 3 tablespoons olive oil and quickly fry the chicken on both sides, turning once. Transfer the chicken pieces to a large casserole pan.

In the same oil, fry the onion until translucent, about 5 minutes. Add the minced garlic and continue frying for 2 minutes. Add the onion and garlic to the chicken in the casserole pan, along with the tomato passata or chopped tomatoes, sugar, dried oregano, turmeric, salt and pepper and enough hot water to cover the chicken, about 1 cup. Cover, lower the heat and simmer for 30 minutes or until the chicken is tender.

Cook the aubergines- heat enough oil in a large frying pan for shallow frying and fry the aubergine slices in batches, 3-5 minutes each side, until tender and golden. Lift out with a slotted spoon and drain on paper towels. Cover with more paper towels and press lightly to soak up the excess oil.

Arrange the aubergine slices, sweet potatoes and carrot, if using, between the partly cooked chicken pieces. Add 1 tablespoon of lemon juice and ½ cup of hot water. Baste the aubergines and sweet potatoes with the cooking liquid so that they absorb the flavour.

Cover and simmer for 20 minutes, shaking the pan occasionally.

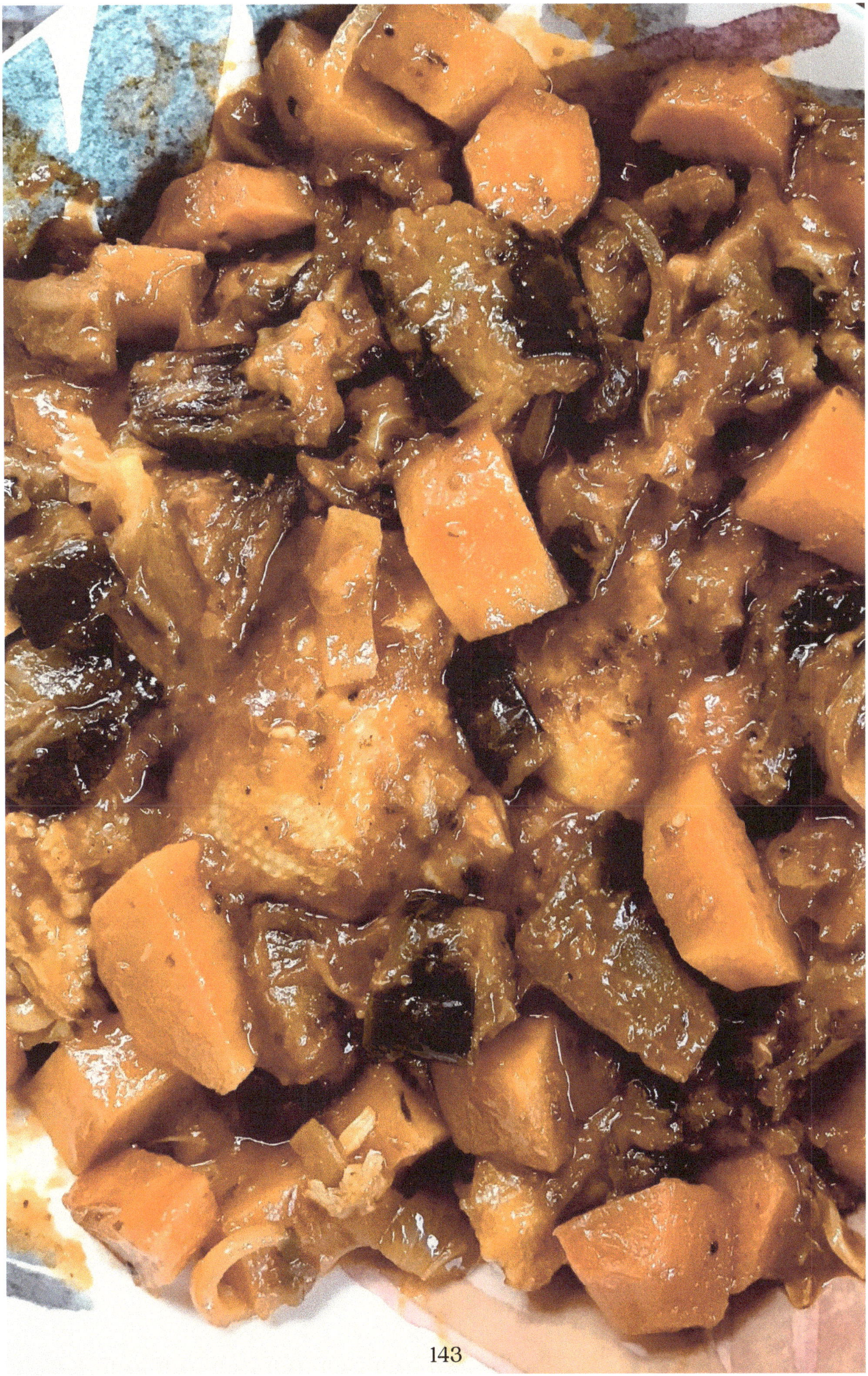

Riz aux abattis
(Rice with chicken livers and giblets)

I have called this dish by its French name, because my mother made it regularly and that is how I think of it. In London in the 1960's, kosher butchers used to sell chicken with a bag of giblets inside. My mother use to make a wonderful rice with these.

50g butter
250g chicken livers
300g chicken giblets
1 large onion, finely chopped
200g basmati rice, washed and rinsed
200ml water
50g raisins
1 tablespoon tomato purée
salt and pepper

In a large non stick saucepan, fry the chicken livers in 25g butter for 5 minutes, turning them constantly. Remove from the pan and set aside. Add the remaining 25g butter and fry the chicken giblets for 6-8 minutes. Remove and set aside.

There should be some butter left in the pan, if not, add a small knob. Fry the onion until translucent, about 5 minutes. Add the rice and water (the amount of water should be the same as that of dry rice), the raisins, tomato purée, salt and pepper. Cover, lower the heat and cook for 15 minutes until all the water has been absorbed and the rice is cooked.

In the meantime, chop the chicken livers and giblets into small pieces. Add them to the rice in the pan as soon as the rice is cooked. Mix well.

Chicken breasts on a bed of green vegetables

I like making this chicken dish in summer. It's ideal when the weather is hot and the sauce is a simple blend of olive oil, lemon juice and garlic.

4 chicken breasts, weighing about 800g in total
6 tablespoons olive oil
4 large celery sticks, cut into 3cm (1½ inch) pieces
2 large leeks, cut into 3cm (1½ inch) pieces
2 Granny Smiths apples, peeled, cored and sliced
juice of 1 lemon
1 teaspoon minced garlic
1 generous teaspoon ground turmeric
handful of basil leaves, torn
1 cup water
salt and pepper

Preheat the oven to 180C/Gas mark 4.

Heat 2 tablespoons oil in a large frying pan. Fry the chicken breasts on both sides, about 3 minutes each Remove and set asid.

Add 2 tablespoons oil to the frying pan and stir fry the celery pieces for 2 minutes, until they are coated. Add the celery and continue to stir fry for another 2 minutes.

Arrange the celery and leeks around the bottom of a large, ovenproof casserole dish (I use one with a 26cm (10 inch) diameter). Place the chicken breasts on top of the vegetables and scatter the sliced apples.

Prepare the sauce – in a small bowl, mix 1 cup water with the remaining 2 tablespoons olive oil, ground turmeric, minced garlic and lemon juice. Add salt and pepper to taste. Carefully pour the sauce over the chicken and vegetables in the casserole dish and scatter a few basil leaves.

Cook in the preheated oven for 1¼ hour or until the chicken and vegetables are tender.

Serve over plain rice and with some yoghurt on the side.

Sweet and sour chicken with apricots

This recipe is from Jennifer Abadi's book A Fistful of lentils. The use of apricots in sweet and savoury dishes is common in many parts of the Middle East, but especially with Syrian Jews. When in season, fresh apricots were used and added to just about everything and I tend to follow this tradition whenever I can. In this dish, the use of tangy dried apricots mixed with a tomato base produces an aromatic sweet and sour result. This dish is inspired by a recipe in Jennifer Abadi's book, 'A fistful of Lentils'.

For the base
- 4 large chicken thighs (about 1 kg)
- 2 tablespoons vegetable or sunflower oil
- 1 red pepper, deseeded and cut into strips
- 2 celery sticks, chopped into 2 cm pieces
- A few celery leaves (optional)
- 1 large leek
- Salt and pepper to taste

For the sauce
- 1 tablespoon vegetable or sunflower oil
- 1 large onion, cut lengthwise and into strips
- 2 teaspoons minced garlic
- 170g tomato paste
- 1 cup cold water
- 2 teaspoons Worcestershire sauce
- 3 tablespoons firmly packed brown sugar
- 6 tablespoons fresh lemon juice (1/2 lemon)
- 1 tablespoon tamarind paste
- 200g dried apricots

Preheat the oven to 180C/Gas Mark 4.

Prepare the chicken- rinse the chicken thighs under cold running water, pat dry with paper towels and sprinkle with salt and pepper.

Heat the oil in a large frying pan, add the chicken pieces and cook for a few minutes on each side until browned. Remove from the pan and set aside.

Prepare the sauce – heat the oil in the same frying pan over medium heat and cook the onions, stirring until golden and soft, about 3 to 4 minutes. Add the garlic and cook for a further 1 minute.

In a medium size bowl, combine the remaining sauce ingredients, except the apricots and pour into the frying pan with the onions and garlic. Bring the sauce to a boil over a high heat. Turn off the heat and set aside.

Arrange one layer of chicken over a large, shallow ovenproof casserole dish (it is better if the chicken thighs fit snugly, so that the sauce will not dry out). Arrange the celery, pepper and celery leaves, if using, around the chicken.

Place the apricots over the chicken. Pour half the sauce, reserving the rest for later. Cover with a tight fitting lid or foil and bake for 1 hour.

After 1 hour, pour the remaining sauce and continue to bake, covered, until the chicken is very tender, about 30 minutes.

Serve hot with plain rice, with the sauce spooned over the rice.

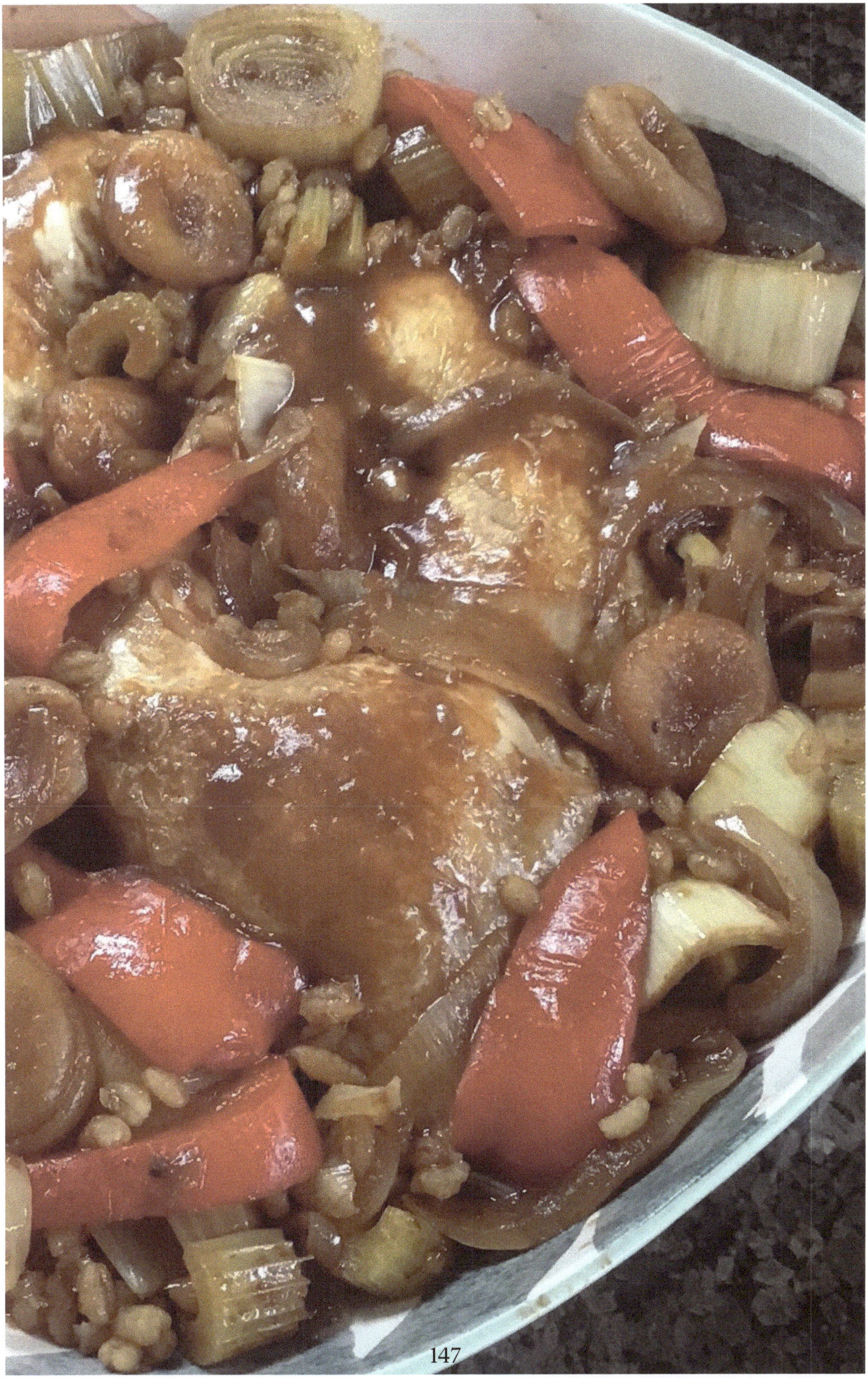

Saffron chicken and potato casserole

Saffron is expensive, but a few strands go a long way and add a special flavour. Together with ground turmeric, they also give great colour to a dish. This is a one pot casserole which can be prepared in advance. Small potatoes work better than larger ones, as they are less likely to disintegrate. I like to start cooking the casserole on the hob for 40 minutes, then carry on in a preheated oven.

a few strands of saffron, infused in hot water
1 large onion
5 tablespoons olive oil
600g chicken thighs
400g white potatoes
400g sweet potatoes
1 teaspoon ground turmeric
juice of ½ lemon
1 teaspoon sugar
1 teaspoon minced garlic
300ml water
salt and pepper to taste

Begin by infusing a few strands of saffron in a little warm wate.

Pour around 1 tablespoon olive oil in a large ovenproof casserole dish and swirl it around so that the base is well coated.

Peel the onion and cut into quarters and then into crescents. Arrange the slices around the bottom of the casserole pan.

Wash and peel the white and sweet potatoes and cut into small chunks or slices. Arrange them carefully on top of the onions in the pan. Place the chicken thighs on top.

Prepare the sauce – in a jug, mix 300ml water with 4 tablespoons olive oil, ground turmeric, minced garlic, sugar, lemon juice and salt and pepper. Add the infused saffron. Pour the sauce over the chicken and potatoes in the casserole pan.

Slowly bring to the boil, lower the heat, cover and simmer for 40 minutes.

Preheat the oven to 180C/ Gas Mark 4.

Transfer to the preheated oven and cook for a further 1 hour or until the chicken and potatoes are tender. The sauce should have reduced, if not continue to cook uncovered for a further 10-15 minutes.

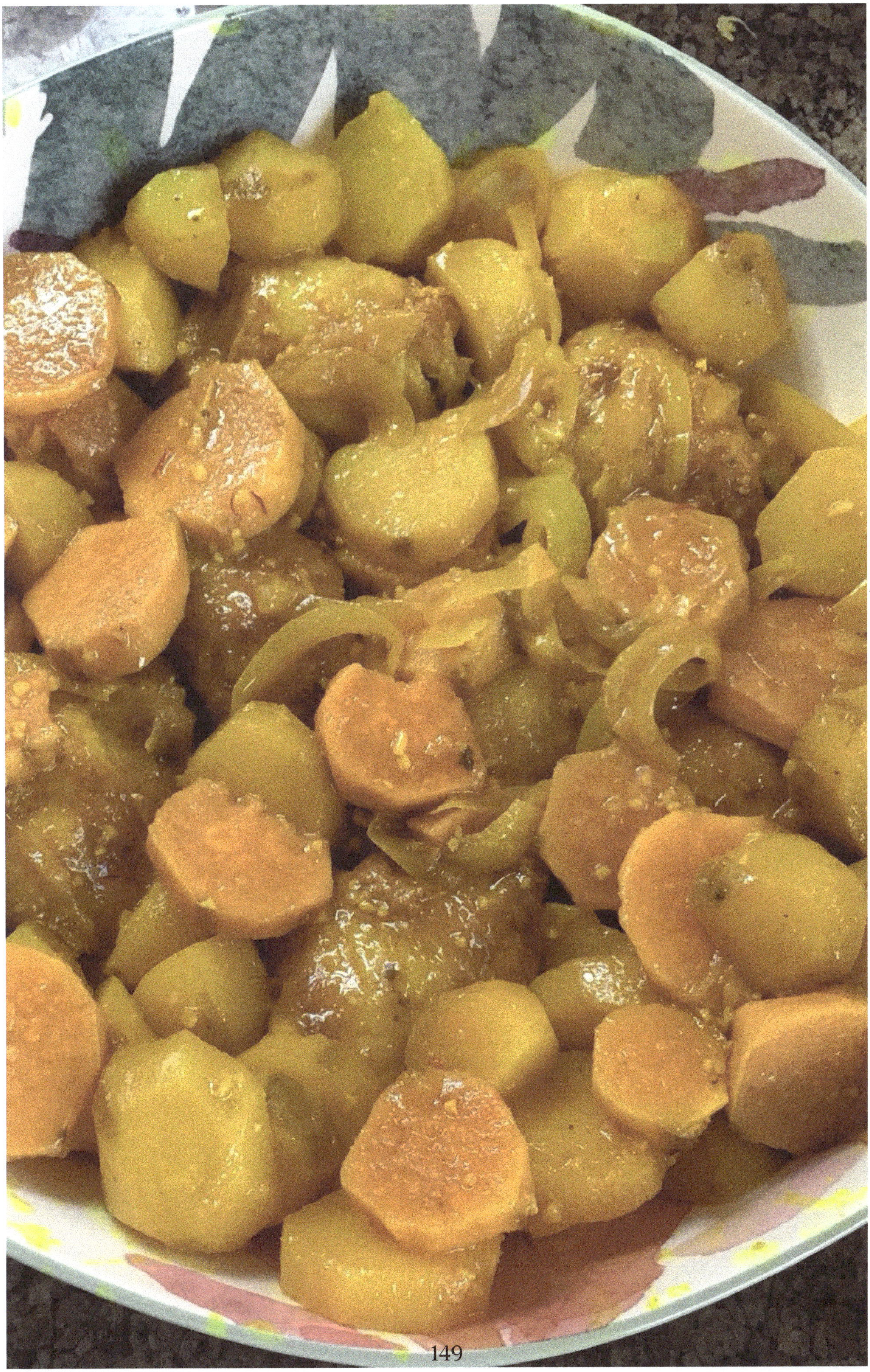

Moroccan chicken Qdra

This dish is based on a Claudia Roden recipe, which I have adapted. What gives it its special taste is the prolonged cooking of the onions. One onion is cooked first, until it melts into the chicken broth and the remainder are added later to give body to the sauce. As dried beans are used, it is important not to add the salt until later, as they would keep hard otherwise.

1 whole chicken, weighing about 1½kg
40g butter
500g onions, finely chopped
1 teaspoon ground turmeric
1½ teaspoon ground cinnamon
150g chickpeas, soaked overnight
100g yellow split peas, soaked overnight
100g blanched almonds, roasted
20g flat leaf parsley, finely chopped
juice of ½ lemon
salt and pepper

Wash and drain the soaked chickpeas and yellow split pas.

Put the chicken, butter and 1 onion, finely chopped, in a large saucepan, cover with water and bring to the boil. Add the turmeric, cinnamon, chickpeas and yellow split peas. Cover, lower the heat and simmer for about 1½ hours, until the chickpeas are soft and the chicken is well cooked, adding more water if necessary.

Remove the chicken, cut it into joints as soon as it is cool enough to handle and set aside. Add the rest of the onions, finely chopped parsley and almonds to the pan. Add salt and pepper to taste and simmer until the onions are soft and the sauce has considerably reduced.

Arrange the chicken pieces on a serving dish. Cover with the chickpeas, split peas and almonds and spoon over the sauce. Squeeze ½ lemon over the dish.

Orange chicken with fresh figs and golden raisins

I try to make the most of the fresh fig season, as it's so short. Apart from the obvious fig jam, I try to include them in savoury dishes and this recipe is an example. I have added raisins to make it more special.

1kg chicken thighs, skin removed
1 large onions peeled, cut into half then lengthwise
2 tablespoons sunflower or vegetable oil
600g potatoes, any variety, peeled and cut into small cubes
300g carrots, peeled and cut into small slices
10 small fresh figs or 6 large ones
100g golden raisins
1 teaspoon mixed spice
1 teaspoon paprika
salt and pepper

For the sauce
  ½ cup fresh orange juice
  1 large tomato, peeled and cut into very small pieces
  4½ teaspoons Worcestershire sauce
  ½ teaspoon soy sauce
  1 tablespoon pomegranate molasses
  1 tablespoon brown sugar
  ½ cup water

Fry the onion in 2 tablespoons oil for 5 minutes until translucent and transfer to a large ovenproof casserole dish. Add a little more oil to the frying pan if necessary and fry the chicken thighs in two batches. Remove when brown on both sides and place over the onions in the casserole dish. Sprinkle with mixed spice, paprika, salt and pepper.

Peel the potatoes, cut into small cubes and do the same with the carrots. Arrange the potatoes and carrots over the chicken thighs. Remove the tops of the figs, wash, cut in half (or quarters if using large figs) and place them unpeeled cut side down around the potatoes and carrots. Sprinkle the golden raisins.

In a separate saucepan, mix all the sauce ingredients, bring to the boil and turn off the heat. Pour the sauce over the chicken and vegetables.

Preheat the oven to 180C/Gas Mark 4.

Cook initially over the hob on a low heat for 40 minutes, then transfer to the preheated oven and cook for a further 1½ hours, until most of the sauce has been absorbed.

Chicken with pomegranate and walnut sauce

Pomegranate molasses are now widely used in Middle Eastern cooking as an ingredient and not just a glaze. If you like a sweeter result, you can replace the walnuts with dried prunes or dates, in which case leave out the sugar.

2 tablespoons sunflower or light vegetable oil
750g -1kg chicken thighs
1 large onion, chopped lengthwise
4 tablespoons pomegranate molasses or pomegranate concentrate
2 teaspoons sugar
100g walnuts
100ml water

Preheat the oven to 180C/Gas Mark 4.

Chop the onion in half and cut into thin strips lengthwise. In a large frying pan, heat 1 tablespoon oil and fry the onion until soft. Transfer to a large, shallow ovenproof casserole dish.

In the same frying pan, heat 1 tablespoon oil and fry the chicken thighs on both sides until browned- you may have to do this in two batches. Place the chicken thighs on top of the onions in the casserole dish, skin side up. Add salt and pepper to taste.

In a small saucepan, mix the water with the pomegranate molasses (or pomegranate concentrate), the walnuts and sugar. Bring to the boil, turn off the heat and cover the chicken thighs with the sauce.

Transfer to the preheated oven and bake for 1 hour until the chicken is tender and the sauce has reduced. Baste the chicken halfway through.

Chicken tagine with apples

A friend of Moroccan origin made this dish, called touajen, a while ago. I had never cooked chicken with apples and I was surprised how tasty it was. It is important to use apples that are firm and crisp, otherwise they will disintegrate. Granny Smiths are probably the best variety.

1kg chicken thighs
2 onions, cut into crescents
3 tablespoons finely chopped flat-parsley
30-40g butter
¼ teaspoon ginger
½ teaspoon ground turmeric
salt and pepper
500g sharp eating apples, peeled, cored and sliced
20g raisins

Place the chicken in a large saucepan with the sliced onions and parsley. Cover with water and add the butter, ginger, turmeric, salt and pepper. Bring to the boil, cover and simmer for about 1 hour, until the chicken is tender and the onions have nearly disintegrated. Reduce the sauce if necessary.

Add the sliced apples and raisins and continue to simmer until the apples are tender, about 10 minutes.

Serve with rice or couscous.

Note – this dish can also be made with pears, quinces or prunes.

Chicken with quince

This dish was often served at Rosh Hashanah (the Jewish New Year). The festival is associated with 'apples and honey' and the quince is a nice break from tradition, while the honey retains the celebratory sweetness.

2 large onions, coarsely chopped
4 tablespoons sunflower or vegetable oil
1 teaspoon cinnamon
1 teaspoon ginger
1 tablespoon pomegranate molasses
1kg chicken thighs
1 teaspoon turmeric powder
½ cup water
2 large quinces
juice of 2 lemons
2 tablespoons honey
salt and pepper

Heat the oil in a large casserole pan and fry the onions for 5 minutes. Add the cinnamon and ginger, pomegranate molasses and the juice of ½ lemon. Lay the chicken pieces on top and sprinkle with salt and turmeric powder. Add ½ cup water, cover and cook on a very low heat for 40 minutes or until tender, turning the chicken once.

Cut the quinces into quarters (no need to peel or core them) and immediately throw them into a saucepan of boiling water. Add the juice of ½ lemon and cook for 15 minutes, until they have softened but are not too soft. Rinse under cold water, remove the cores, cut them in half and set aside.

When the chicken has cooked, remove from the pan and place on a serving dish.
There should be some onion juice left in the pan, if not add a little water. Add the quinces, honey and the juice of 1 lemon to the pan. Cook uncovered for 10 minutes, until the quinces have absorbed most of the juice.

Pour the quinces and remaining juice over the chicken pieces.

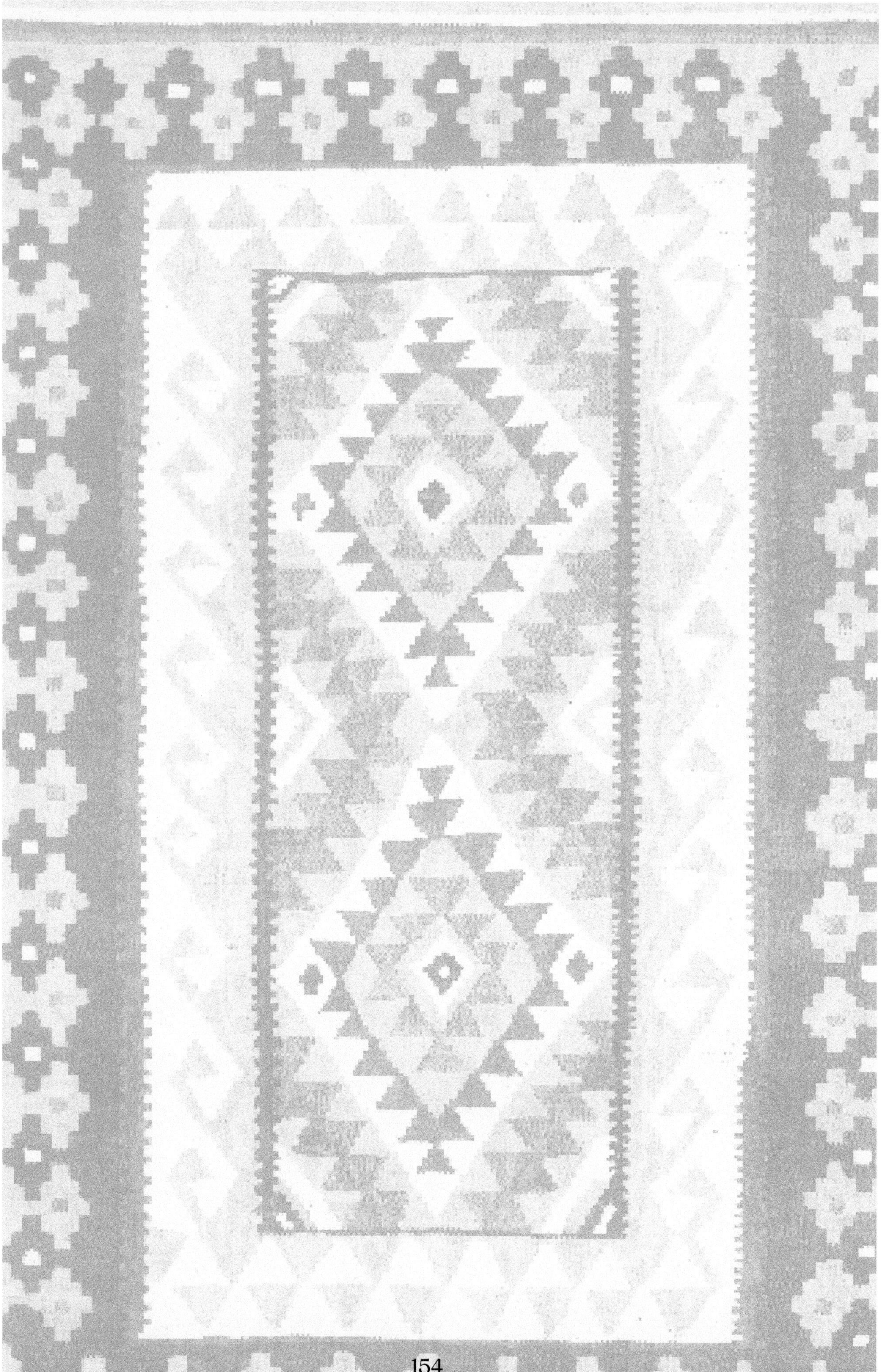

VEGETERIAN DISHES
Komidas sin carne
Atbakh nabatiah

Leek and shallots with cinnamon and prunes

My father would have probably found this dish rather strange, as he liked his leeks cooked with olive oil and lemon or in an omelette, so the addition of dried fruit to vegetables did not appeal to him. However, I think cinnamon and prunes go well with leeks.

3 tablespoons olive oil
4 medium leeks
4 shallots
½ fennel bulb (optional)
300ml tomato juice or 300g can chopped tomatoes
1 teaspoon salt
juice of ½ lemon
½ teaspoon ground turmeric
½ teaspoon cinnamon
50g pitted prunes

Wash the leeks thoroughly and cut into 3cm (1½ inch) pieces, keeping only the white and light green parts.

Peel the shallots and cut lengthwise into 4-6 pieces, depending on size. Keep only the white flesh of the fennel, if using, and cut into small strips.

Heat the oil in a large saucepan and add the leeks and shallots. Fry on medium heat for 10 minutes, until soft. Add the fennel if using and fry for another 2 minutes, until all the vegetables are coated in oil.

Add the tomato juice or chopped tomatoes, salt, ground turmeric, cinnamon and lemon juice.

Lower the heat, cover and simmer for 20 minutes until the vegetables are soft. Add the prunes and cook covered for another 5 minutes.

Serve as an accompaniment to meat or as a vegetarian side dish.

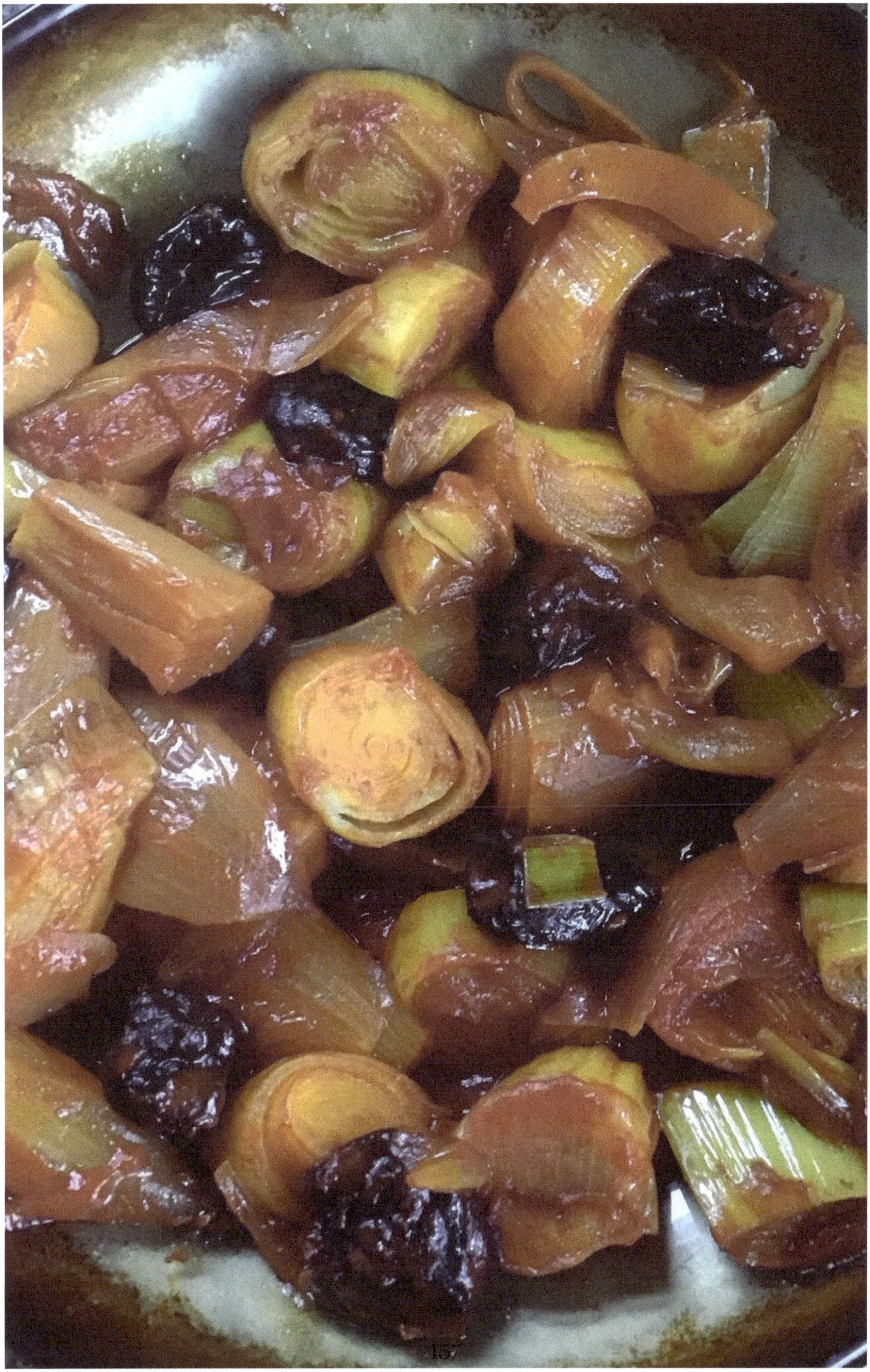

Aubergine and feta kofta

About 20 medium koftas or 12 large ones

This is a simple dish where the koftas are baked, rather than fried, which is a healthier option. It can be served on its own or with a tomato sauce or yoghurt on the side, accompanied by pita bread.

600g aubergines (about 2 large ones) cut into 2cm (1 inch) pieces
3 tablespoons olive oil
175g bulgur wheat
800ml water
1 teaspoon coriander seeds
½ teaspoon ground cumin
2 teaspoons dried mint
15g flat parsley, finely chopped
200g feta cheese
2 large eggs, lightly beaten
2 tablespoons matzo meal or breadcrumbs

Preheat the oven to 180C/Gas Mark 4.

Cut the aubergines in 2cm (1 inch) pieces, sprinkle with salt and place in a colander. Leave for 30 minutes, then squeeze out all the bitter juices.

Place the aubergines on a baking tray, coat with the oil and mix them thoroughly with your hand. Bake for 30 minutes until the aubergines are soft. When cool, quickly blitz in a food processor for a few seconds.

Bring a saucepan with 800ml water to the boil. Cook the bulgur wheat for 15 minutes. Drain, rinse with cold water and drain again.

Toast the coriander and cumin seeds by stirring them in a dry pan until the aromas are released, then grind them in a pestle and mortar.

Place the aubergines and bulgur wheat in a large bowl Add the eggs, feta cheese, chopped parsley, dried mint, coriander and cumin. Add 2 tablespoons of matzo meal or breadcrumbs, salt and pepper to taste and mix thoroughly. Using your hands, mould the balls.

Place on an oiled baking tray and bake in a preheated oven 200C/Gas Mark 5 for 25 minutes or until the koftas are cooked.

Aubergine and leek casserole

In a popular Ladino folk song Si savesh la buena djente (Dear people do you know of the Battle of the Vegetables), the eggplant and tomato argue over which is the superior food. The short answer is that both vegetables are best when married with each other. It is preferable to use fresh tomatoes for this recipe and I have added leeks, though other vegetables, such as peppers or courgettes, will also work.

1 large aubergine, weighing about 300g
2 medium leeks, chopped into 2cm (1 inch) pieces
4 tablespoons sunflower oil
2 medium onions, chopped
3 garlic cloves, minced
2 large tomatoes, chopped
2 tablespoons tomato purée
1 teaspoon ground turmeric
2 teaspoons ground cumin
salt and pepper
150ml water

Preheat the oven to 180C/Gas Mark 4.

Cut the aubergine in 2cm (1 inch) pieces, wash, sprinkle with salt and leave in a colander for 30 minutes. Rinse again and squeeze out all the bitter juices.

Heat 2 tablespoons of oil and fry the chopped onions for 5 minutes, until soft and translucent. Add the garlic cloves and continue frying for a couple of minutes. Remove the onions and garlic and set aside.

Return the pan to the heat, add 2 tablespoons of oil and quickly fry the aubergines and leeks. Add the chopped tomatoes, tomato purée, turmeric, cumin salt and pepper.

Add the fried onions and garlic to the pan and 150ml water, just enough to cover the vegetables.

Transfer to a shallow ovenproof dish, cover and cook in the preheated for 30 minutes.

Aubergine and tomato bake

This dish originates from Syria, but it is also very popular in Turkey. We often had it while on holiday in summer, accompanied by a side salad. In winter, it can be served as a vegetable dish, accompanied by roast chicken or meat.

2 medium aubergines, weighing about 250g each
100ml sunflower or vegetable oil
6 medium ripe tomatoes, sliced
4 tablespoons flat leaf parsley, chopped
1 large onion, finely chopped
150g grated cheddar cheese

For the sauce
　200ml tomato passata or any tomato sauce
　50ml water
　juice of ½ lemon
　1 teaspoon dried oregano
　2 tablespoons tomato purée
　½ teaspoon salt

Preheat the oven to 180C/Gas Mark 4.
Lightly grease a 20 x 20cm (8 x 8 inch) casserole dish.

Wash the aubergines and cut them crossways into 2cm (1 inch) slices Place them in a colander, sprinkle with salt and leave for at least 30 minutes. Rinse and squeeze out the bitter juices.

Heat the oil in a large pan and fry the aubergines slices on both sides until golden. Remove and drain on kitchen paper.

In the same pan, fry the chopped onion until soft, about 5 minutes.

To prepare the sauce, mix all the ingredients together in a bowl. Arrange half the aubergines slices over the base of the baking dish and cover with half the sliced tomatoes and half the fried onions. Sprinkle half the grated cheese and chopped parsley and spread half the sauce over the surface.

Repeat this process with the remaining aubergines, tomatoes, onions, parsley and cheese. Pour the remaining sauce over the surface of the dish.

Cook in the oven for 45 minutes or until the vegetables are well cooked. Remove and leave to cool for 5 minutes.

Roz we hamud

(Rice with a vegetable and lemon sauce)

about 1 litre of chicken or vegetable stock
2 large leeks cut into medium pieces
2 large potatoes cut into medium pieces
2 large carrots or 3 small ones, chopped into small chunks
4 celery stalks with leaves, cut into pieces
3 large garlic cloves, chopped
juice of 2-3 lemons, according to taste
2 teaspoons sugar
salt and pepper
3 courgettes cut into small slices (optional)
6 artichokes hearts, frozen or tinned (optional)
2 tablespoons dried mint

Hamud means sour in Arabic and this dish owes its name to the tartness of the lemons. My family called it ham'd and it was a favourite when something quick and last minute was needed. Whenever I cook it, I have a very vivid memory of my aunt's dining room in Cairo, with its sideboard in dark wood and large dining table. The children used to play around the table, whilst my mother and aunt disappeared into the kitchen and hey presto an hour later reappeared with this wonderfully fragrant dish. I have to confess however that as a child, I didn't particularly appreciate it, probably because the lemony sauce didn't suit my taste buds but I love it now, as well as the memories it brings back and the nostalgia.

Put the celery, carrots, potatoes and leeks in a saucepan, together with the vegetable stock or water. Add salt, pepper, lemon juice and sugar. Bring to the boil, cover and simmer for about 35 minutes or until the vegetables are cooked.

Add the optional vegetables such as courgettes and artichoke hearts and simmer for a further 20 minutes.

Blend in the dried mint and cook for a further 5-10 minutes. Taste and adjust the flavourings, adding more lemon juice if you like the tartness.

Serve over a bowl of hot rice.

Aubergine and walnut ragu

The quantities for this recipe are quite large, so it serves about 10 people. You can leave out the lentils if you prefer a less substantial dish and you can also experiment with other vegetables, so long as you keep the aubergines and walnuts.

200g baby tomatoes
400g aubergines (about 2 medium ones) cut into 3cm (1½ inch) chunks
50g walnuts, roughly chopped
2 tablespoons olive oil
100g celery, chopped into 2cm (1 inch) chunks
2 small carrots, cut into thin strips
1 shallot, finely chopped
1 red pepper, cut into thin strips (optional)
100g red or brown lentils
400g tin of chopped tomatoes
1 teaspoon tomato paste
20g fresh leaf parsley, finely chopped
5-6 sun dried tomatoes, sliced (optional)
400ml boiling water

For the marinade
  30ml olive oil
  20ml balsamic vinegar
  6 garlic cloves, roughly chopped
  ½ teaspoon dried chilli flakes (optional)

Preheat the oven to 220C/Gas Mark 7.

Mix the marinade ingredients in a bowl and season with salt and pepper.

Scatter the aubergines, walnuts and baby tomatoes in an oven dish and pour over the marinade. Mix everything together and bake for 30-35 minutes until the aubergines have softened and the walnuts have browned, tossing the mixture so that it cooks evenly. Set aside.

Meanwhile, heat the olive oil in a large saucepan over medium heat. Add the carrots, celery, shallot and red pepper, if using. Season with salt and pepper and simmer for 10 minutes until softened.

Add the lentils and cook for a further 2 minutes to allow the flavours to infuse. Blend in the tinned tomatoes, tomato paste, chopped parsley, sun-dried tomatoes if using and boiling water.

Bring to a simmer and cook covered for a further 20-25 minutes until the liquid has reduced to a thicker consistency - you may have to continue to cook uncovered for a further few minutes if the sauce has not reduced sufficiently.

Finally, add the roast aubergines, baby tomatoes and walnuts and simmer for a further 10 minutes.

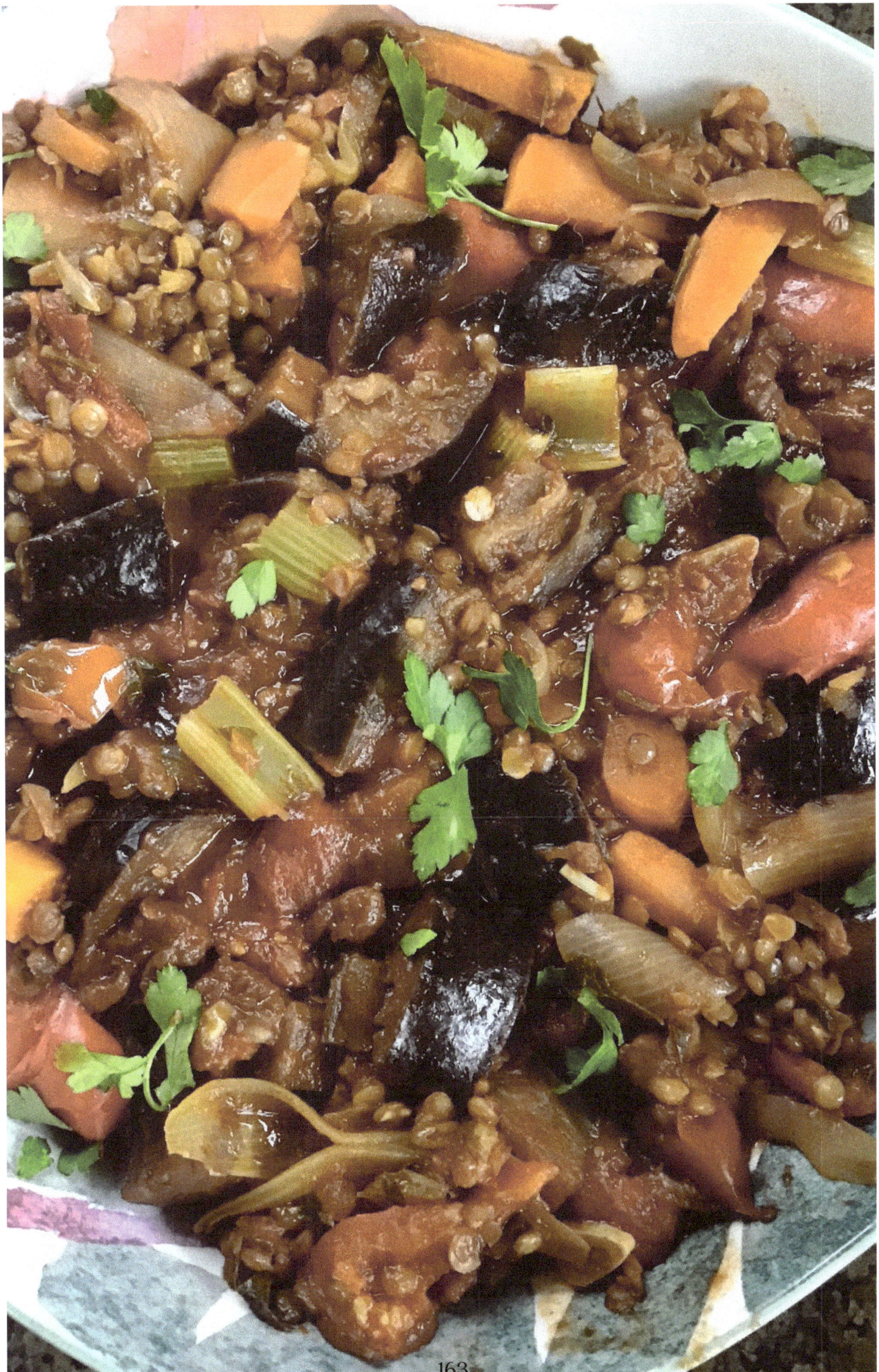

Berendjenas rellenas de keso
(Sephardic stuffed aubergines)

There are numerous versions of stuffed eggplant in Sephardic cooking, depending on what ingredients you have available. My favourite one is this simple cheese-filled version which is a healthier option, as the aubergines are baked rather than fried.

2 large aubergines, cut in half lengthwise
4 tablespoons sunflower or vegetable oil
1 medium onion, chopped
2 garlic cloves, minced
2 tablespoons chopped fresh parsley
80g breadcrumbs
1 teaspoon dried oregano
½ teaspoon salt
150g crumbled feta cheese
125g grated cheddar cheese or 250g ricotta cheese
1 large egg, lightly beaten
1-2 tablespoons olive oil for drizzling

Preheat the oven to 180C/Gas Mark 4.

With a melon baller or a grapefruit knife, scoop out the cores of the aubergines, leaving a 1 cm (½ inch) shell Reserve the pulp. In a large pot of salted boiling water, cook the shells for 3 minutes, until tender but not soft, and drain.

Coarsely chop the reserved aubergine pulp. Heat 2 tablespoons oil over medium heat, add the onion and garlic and sauté until soft, about 5 minutes. Add the remaining 2 tablespoons oil, the aubergine pulp and chopped parsley. Sauté until softened, about 10 minutes.

Remove from the heat and stir in the breadcrumbs, dried oregano, salt, cheeses and egg.

Oil a large baking pan. Lightly salt the inside of the aubergine shells and stuff with the pulp mixture. Arrange on the base of the pan and drizzle with a little oil.

Cover with foil and bake for 20 minutes. Uncover and bake for a further 10 minutes until golden. Serve warm.

Keftes de espinaka con muez
(Spinach patties with walnuts)

Spinach has a delicate flavour which provides an excellent base for many other foods. It has a particular affinity to eggs, cheese, lemon and fresh herbs such as dill, basil and oregano. These patties are nice as a starter or served in summer with a salad. The addition of walnuts gives them an extra bite.

400g fresh spinach
3 tablespoons olive or sunflower oil
1 large onion, chopped
2 garlic cloves, minced
50g walnuts, finely chopped
80g matzo meal or breadcrumbs
3 large eggs, lightly beaten
½ teaspoon nutmeg
¾ teaspoon salt
small bunch chopped dill
vegetable or sunflower oil for frying

Wash the spinach, drain and chop. Cook in 1 tablespoon oil until tender, about 4-5 minutes. Set aside and when cool, squeeze out all the excess water.

Heat the remaining 2 tablespoons of oil and fry the onion and garlic until translucent, about 5 minutes.

In a large bowl combine the eggs, spinach, matzo meal, walnuts, chopped dill, fried onion and garlic. Add the nutmeg and salt and shape the mixture into patties.

In a large skillet or frying pan, heat a layer of oil over medium heat. Fry the patties in batches, turning them once, until golden brown, about 3 minutes per side.

Drain on paper towels Serve warm with lemon wedges.

Baked sweet potatoes with fried shallots

I had some sweet potatoes and shallots which had to be used up and thought, why not try combining the two. The result was surprisingly good, especially when served with Greek yoghurt on the side. I think the tastiest way of cooking sweet potatoes is to simply cut them in half and bake them with their skin.

600/800g sweet potatoes
4 banana shallots (about 400g), finely chopped
yoghurt to serve

Preheat the oven to 180C/Gas Mark 4.

Peel the sweet potatoes and cut them in half lengthwise and again, if using large sweet potatoes. Each slice should be about 8-10cm (3-4 inch) long.

Place in a baking tray, cut side up and drizzle a little olive oil over each potato. Add the chopped shallots. Cover with foil and bake in the preheated oven for 45 minutes or until the potatoes are soft. Remove from the oven and cool.

Shakshouka

(Fried peppers and tomatoes with eggs)

Shakshuka was very often cooked at home, long before it became fashionable in England. It was another one of those light meatless dishes which could be put together quickly and suited the heat of Egyptian summers.

2 medium onions
3 tablespoons vegetable or sunflower oil
2 large peppers seeded and cut into thin strips
4 large tomatoes
4 eggs
juice of ½ lemon
1 tablespoon tomato purée
1 tablespoon sugar
salt and pepper

Peel the onions, cut into thin slices and fry them in a large shallow frying pan in hot oil for 10 minutes, until translucent.

Add the peppers and continue frying for another 5 minutes. Chop the tomatoes and add to the pan.

Add the lemon juice, tomato purée, sugar and salt and pepper to taste. Lower the heat, cover and simmer for 15 minutes.

Make 4 wells and crack the eggs open on top. Cook for a further 4-5 minutes until the eggs are set.

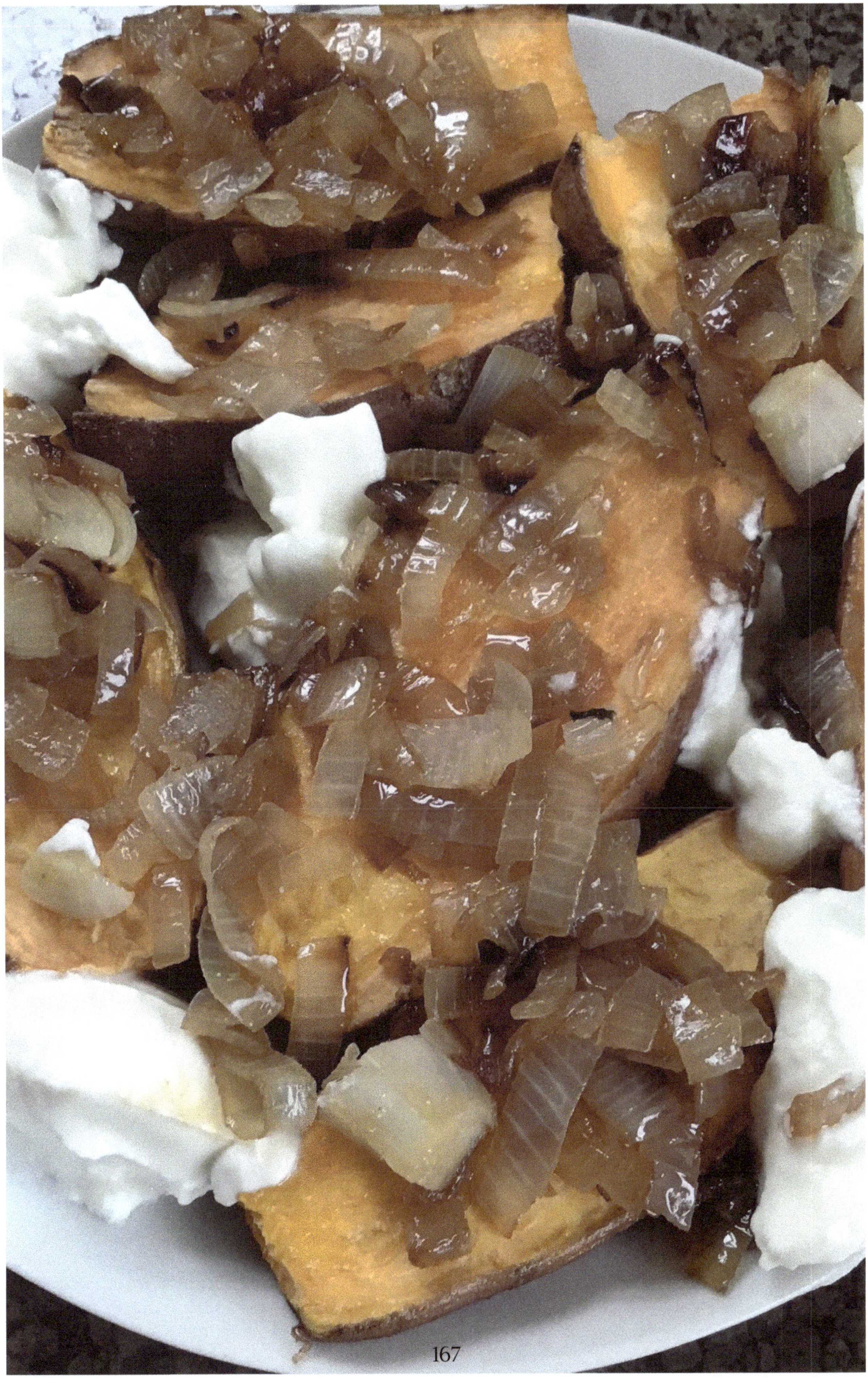

Stuffed courgettes with lemon mint sauce

This dish was often served as part of an elaborate meal provided after a Shabbat service to honour a Barmitzvah or Batmitzvah ceremony, an engagement or any other special occasion. It was accompanied by a salad or a meat or chicken dish. I have adapted Jennifer Abadi's recipe in her book A Fistful of lentils.

Filling
    400g can chickpeas, drained and rinsed
    100g long grain rice
    ½ large onion, chopped
    1 tablespoon olive oil
    juice of ½ lemon
    10g flat leaf parsley, finely chopped
    1 teaspoon tomato paste
    ¼ teaspoon ground cinnamon
    ½ ground allspice
    2 tablespoons unsalted butter, melted
    ½ teaspoon salt

Courgettes
    6 medium courgettes
    2 cups cold water

Sauce
    juice of 1 lemon
    ½ teaspoon salt
    2 teaspoons minced garlic
    60g unsalted butter, melted
    2 teaspoons dried mint

Prepare the filling – wash the rice, drain, place in a saucepan, cover with water and boil for 10 minutes until the rice has softened. Drain and rinse again.

In a large bowl, mix the rice, drained chickpeas, chopped onion, parsley, lemon juice, olive oil, tomato paste, melted butter, salt and spices. Combine with your hands and set aside.

Prepare the courgettes – cut each courgette in half crosswise (not lengthwise, you don't want to create a boat shape). Using a vegetable corer, scoop out all the flesh from each courgette half, leaving a shell of skin about ½cm (1/8 inch) thick. Discard the pulp.

Rinse the courgette shells in cold water and pat dry. Stuff each squash to within 2cm (1 inch) of the cut end – the filling will expand while cooking.

Coat the bottom of a large ovenproof casserole with oil. Place the stuffed courgettes side by side, very close together If you have extra filling, use it to fill the gaps between the stuffed courgette.

Pour 2 cups cold water over the courgettes and place an ovenproof plate on top (this will help to pack the filling inside the shells as the rice expands). Cover the casserole dish with a tight fitting lid and steam over a medium heat for 30 minutes.

Prepare the sauce – in a small bowl, combine the lemon juice, garlic, salt and melted butter Add the dried mint and mix well. Remove the plate on top of the courgettes and pour the sauce over. Cover and continue to simmer on a low heat for 1 hour. This can also be completed in a preheated oven at 180C/Gas Mark 4.

The dish is ready when the rice is tender and the sauce is reduced to a third of its original volume. It may be refrigerated for 1 day after cooking. Add water, a tablespoon at a time, if the sauce appears too thick when reheating.

Serve hot.

Burghul bi kousa

(Burgul with courgettes)

50ml olive oil
1 large onion, chopped
1 teaspoon salt or to taste
1 teaspoon pepper
4 teaspoons tomato purée
juice of ½ lemon
1 tomato thinly sliced
4 medium courgettes, cut into medium slices
1-1½ cup water
250g fine burgul
olive oil to drizzle

Bulgur is a cereal food made from the cracked parboiled groats of several different wheat species, most of them from durum wheat. It was a staple in ancient Mesopotamia and has even been found in Egyptian tombs. It is now widely available in supermarkets, but in Middle Eastern stores it comes in two granulations, fine and coarse. Fine bulgur is generally used in salads and vegetable dishes, whereas the coarser variety is preferred for making the Syrian kibbe.

Heat the olive oil in a large shallow pan and fry the chopped onion for 5 minutes, until soft and translucent. Add the salt and pepper, tomato purée and lemon juice. Mix well for 2 minutes and add the sliced tomato, courgettes and 1 cup water. Cover, lower the heat and cook for 10 minutes.

Add the burgul and a little more water if necessary - not too much or the burgul will become soggy. Cook covered for a further 10 minutes until the water has evaporated. Mix with a fork and drizzle with a little olive oil.

Betingan mah'shi bi'safargel
(Stuffed aubergines with quince)

This is another favourite with Syrian Jews and the combination of aubergines and quince cooked in a sweet and sour sauce is lovely. The recipe works much better with baby aubergines, which are sold in Turkish and Middle Eastern grocery stores.

15 baby aubergines
150g basmati rice
150ml water
4 tablespoons olive oil
1 large onion, finely minced
1 tablespoon tomato purée
juice of ½ lemon
1 teaspoon cinnamon
1 teaspoon all spice
20g fresh coriander, chopped
50g raisins (optional)
2 quinces
salt and pepper

For the sauce
   250ml water
   1 tablespoon tamarind paste
   1 tablespoon pomegranate molasses
   juice of 1 lemon
   1 tablespoon brown sugar
   2 tablespoons tomato purée

Cut the top of the aubergines and gently scoop out the flesh inside - you can use a vegetable peeler, rotating all the time until the flesh is released, but be careful not to tear the aubergines. Discard the flesh.

Wash the rice and place it in a saucepan with 150ml water, bring to the boil and cook covered on medium heat until all the water is absorbed. Chop the onion and fry in 2 tablespoons of olive until translucent.

Transfer the cooked rice and onion to a large bowl. Add the lemon juice, tomato purée, remaining 2 tablespoons olive oil, cinnamon, all spice, coriander and raisins, if using. Add salt and pepper and mix well.

Stuff the aubergines with the rice mixture and place them in an ovenproof casserole dish, sprinkled with a little oil at the bottom.

Peel the quinces, cut them into halves, then quarters. Cut each quarter into 2cm (1 inch) pieces. Arrange the quinces around the aubergines in the casserole dish.

Prepare the sauce – in a saucepan, mix the water, tamarind paste, pomegranate molasses, lemon juice, brown sugar and tomato purée Bring to the boil, remove from the heat and pour over the aubergines and quince pieces. They should be just covered with the sauce.

Place a heavy plate on top of the vegetables – this will prevent the stuffed aubergines from opening while cooking.

Cover, lower the heat and cook for 1 hour. Remove the cover and the plate and cook uncovered in a preheated over 180C/Gas Mark 4 for a further 30 minutes until the sauce has reduced.

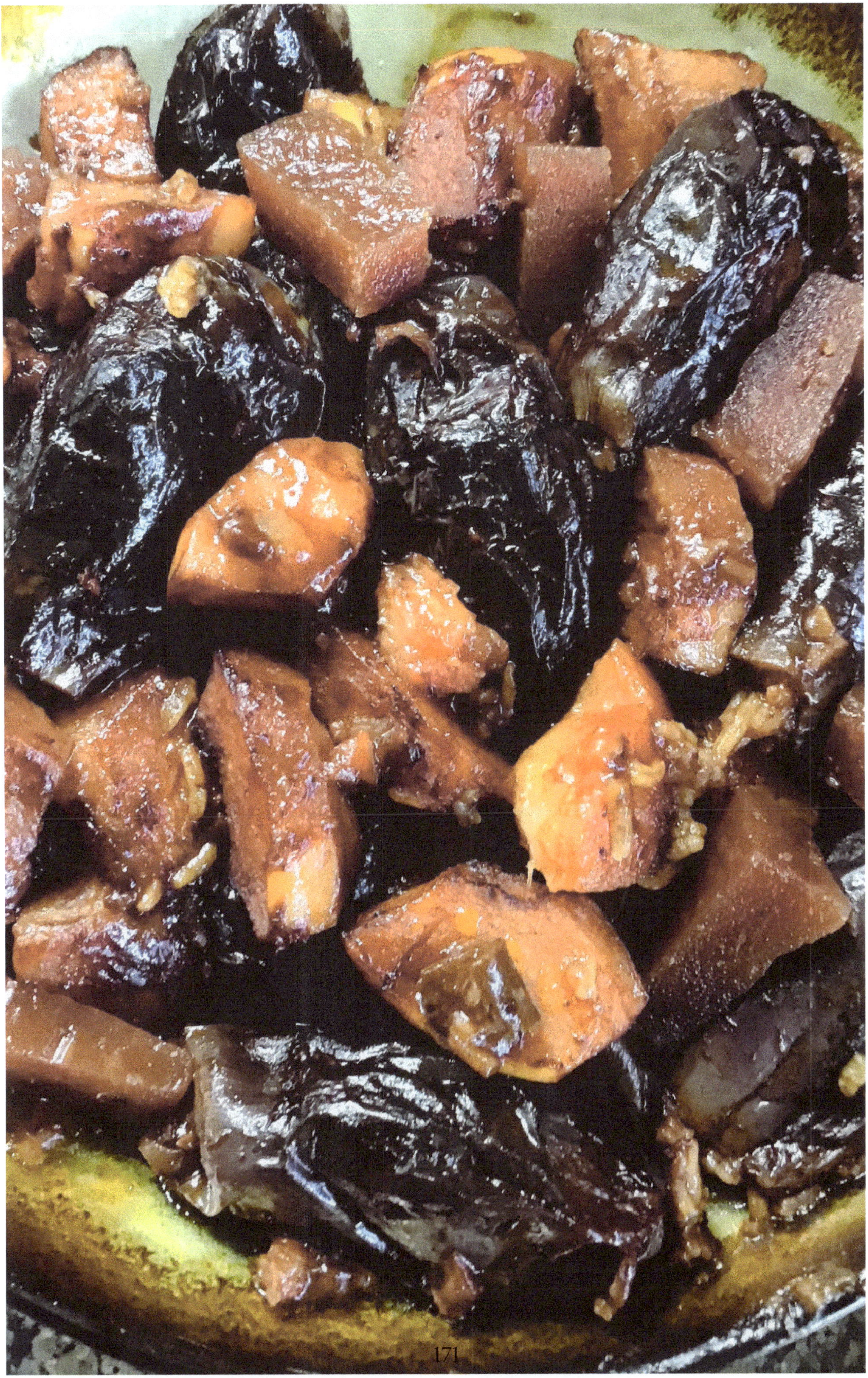

Fasoulia
(Green beans with tomatoes)

Fasoulia is the Arabic word for green beans. It was often served at lunchtime to accompany rice and a meat stew and the traditional way of cooking it was with olive oil and tomatoes. In Egypt we used fresh tomatoes, but tinned ones also work. You can use fresh green beans or frozen sliced ones.

3 tablespoons olive oil
1 medium onion, sliced into crescents
3 garlic cloves, minced
3 large tomatoes, sliced or 1x 400g tin peeled tomatoes
½ cup water
1 teaspoon sugar
1 teaspoon turmeric powder (optional)
juice of 1 lemon
800g fresh beans, washed and trimmed or 900g bag frozen sliced green beans
salt and pepper to taste

Heat the oil in a large frying pan or casserole dish. Cut the onion into small crescents, mince the garlic and fry them until translucent, about 5 minutes.

Add the fresh or tinned tomatoes, water, lemon juice, sugar and turmeric powder, if using. Add salt and pepper and slowly bring to the boil.

Add the green beans - if using frozen beans, take them straight out of the freezer and quickly run them over cold water first to remove any excess water.

Bring to the boil, lower the heat, cover and cook for 20 minutes. The secret is to let the beans braise slowly in the tomato sauce, allowing them to become very tender.

Fil fil mahshi bi fireek
(Peppers stuffed with freekeh)

Freekeh is an ancient dish derived from Levantine and North African cuisines. It is used in the Middle East in many dishes because of its versatility. In Egypt, freekeh was prepared with onions and tomatoes and was also served as pigeon stuffed with freekeh. I have included it as the main ingredient in the stuffing instead of rice, which was far more commonly used in our house.

4 peppers, halved lengthways and deseeded
2 medium onions
50ml olive oil
2 tomatoes thinly sliced
2 tablespoons tomato purée
250ml tomato sauce
100g freekeh
1 teaspoon ground cumin
1 teaspoon ground coriander
salt and pepper
juice of 1 lemon
½ cup water
1 tablespoon pomegranate molasses
1 teaspoon sugar

Preheat the oven to 180C/Gas Mark 4.

Cook the freekeh in boiling water for 10 minutes. Drain and rinse. Wash the peppers, cut them lengthwise and remove all the seeds.

Heat the oil and fry the onions until translucent, about 5 minutes. Add the sliced tomatoes, tomato purée and sauce, the juice of ½ lemon, ground coriander, cumin, salt and pepper. Cook the mixture for 5 minutes and add the freekeh.

Fill the peppers with the mixture and place them in an oiled ovenproof dish. Drizzle a little olive oil over them.

In a small bowl, mix the juice of ½ lemon, 1 tablespoon pomegranate molasses, 1 teaspoon sugar and ½ cup of water and pour over the peppers.

Cook in a preheated oven for 1 hour until the peppers are tender.

Jerusalem artichokes with carrots and potatoes

Despite its name, the Jerusalem artichoke has no relationship to Jerusalem and it is not a type of artichoke. It looks a bit like a knobbly, pink-skinned ginger root and has a sweet, nutty flavour. Although not widely used, perhaps because of its awkward appearance, it is a versatile food, which can be used raw in salads or cooked. There is no need to peel it and you can cook it as you would potatoes - roast, sauté, bake, boil or steam.

**500g Jerusalem artichokes
2 large potatoes, peeled and cut into medium chunks
3 large carrots, peeled and cut in medium slices
3 tablespoons sunflower or vegetable oil
1 tablespoon flour
2 cups vegetable stock
juice of 1 large lemon
1 teaspoon ground turmeric
salt and pepper**

Wash the Jerusalem artichokes and cut them into medium sized chunks (there is no need to peel them, just cut off the end bits).

Wash the potatoes, peel and cut into chunks. Peel and cut the carrots into slices.

Heat the oil in a casserole dish. When hot, gradually add the Jerusalem artichokes, potatoes and carrots. Add 1 tablespoon flour or enough to coat all the vegetables. Stir well and continue cooking for about 5 minutes.

Add the vegetable stock, lemon juice, ground turmeric, salt and pepper.

Cover and simmer until the water is absorbed, the vegetables are cooked and you are left with a thick sauce. Add more lemon juice to taste.

Layered aubergines and potatoes with a coconut sauce

This dish takes time to prepare but the result is well worth it. It will also keep in the fridge for a few days.

For the sauce
 90g coconut milk powder mixed with 180ml water or 400g can of coconut milk
 50g fresh ginger, grated
 large bunch flat leaf parsley, chopped
 4 garlic cloves, crushed
 1 teaspoon cinnamon
 ½ teaspoon nutmeg
 ¼ teaspoon ground cloves
 150ml single cream
 2 tablespoons yoghurt
 2 teaspoons honey
 salt and pepper

For the vegetables
 500g onions, cut into 1cm (½ inch) pieces
 600g potatoes, cut into 1cm (½ inch) pieces
 500g aubergines (2 large aubergines) cut into 1cm (½ inch) pieces
 500g tomatoes (or 2 beef tomatoes) cut into 1cm (½ inch) pieces
 3 tablespoons olive oil

Blitz all the sauce ingredients in a food processor and set aside.

Cut the aubergines, sprinkle some salt and leave them in a colander for 30 minutes Squeeze out all the bitter juices. Cut the onions, potatoes and tomatoes in 1cm (½ inch) pieces.

Cover the bottom of a large casserole dish with the oil and start layering the vegetables – first the onions, then the potatoes, the aubergines and finally the tomatoes. Pour some of the coconut sauce between each layer and press gently to make sure it covers all the vegetables.

Cover and simmer on a very low heat for 1½ hours. Lift the lid and continue cooking uncovered for about 15 minutes or until all the sauce has been absorbed.

Baked cauliflower with potatoes

Although available all year round, cauliflower is at its best from September to November. Sephardic Jews are very partial to this vegetable and prepare it in many forms, including cooked in a tomato sauce or fried. This recipe combines both methods. Soak the cauliflower first, head down, in cold water for 30 minutes to refresh and, for extra crispness, mix 1 teaspoon vinegar and 1 teaspoon salt into the soaking water.

1 cauliflower head
500g small potatoes
2 eggs
150g flour
vegetable or sunflower oil for shallow frying
1 onion, cut into slices

For the sauce
   1 cup vegetable stock
   3 teaspoons tomato purée
   juice of ½ lemon
   1 teaspoon turmeric powder
   ½ teaspoon pepper
   1 teaspoon salt
   a handful fresh parsley, chopped (optional)

Preheat the oven to 180C/Gas Mark 4.

Cut the cauliflower into florets. Throw into a saucepan of boiling water and boil for 6 minutes – it's important not to overcook it or allow it to get mushy. Remove from the water and set aside. Peel the potatoes, wash and par boil for 5 minutes.

Place the lightly beaten eggs and 150g flour on two separate plates.

Heat enough vegetable or sunflower oil for shallow frying. Coat the cauliflower florets first with the flour, then the beaten egg and again with the flour. Fry in hot oil until they are brown on both sides, remove and drain on paper towels.

Fry the potato slices in the same oil.

Arrange the cauliflower florets and the potato slices in a large ovenproof dish. Fry the onion and arrange the slices over the cauliflower and potatoes.

Prepare the sauce - place all the ingredients in a saucepan, heat quickly and remove from the hob. Pour the sauce over the casserole dish, making sure all the vegetables are covered.

Bake in a preheated over 180C/Gas Mark 4 for 1 hour or until all the vegetables are cooked.

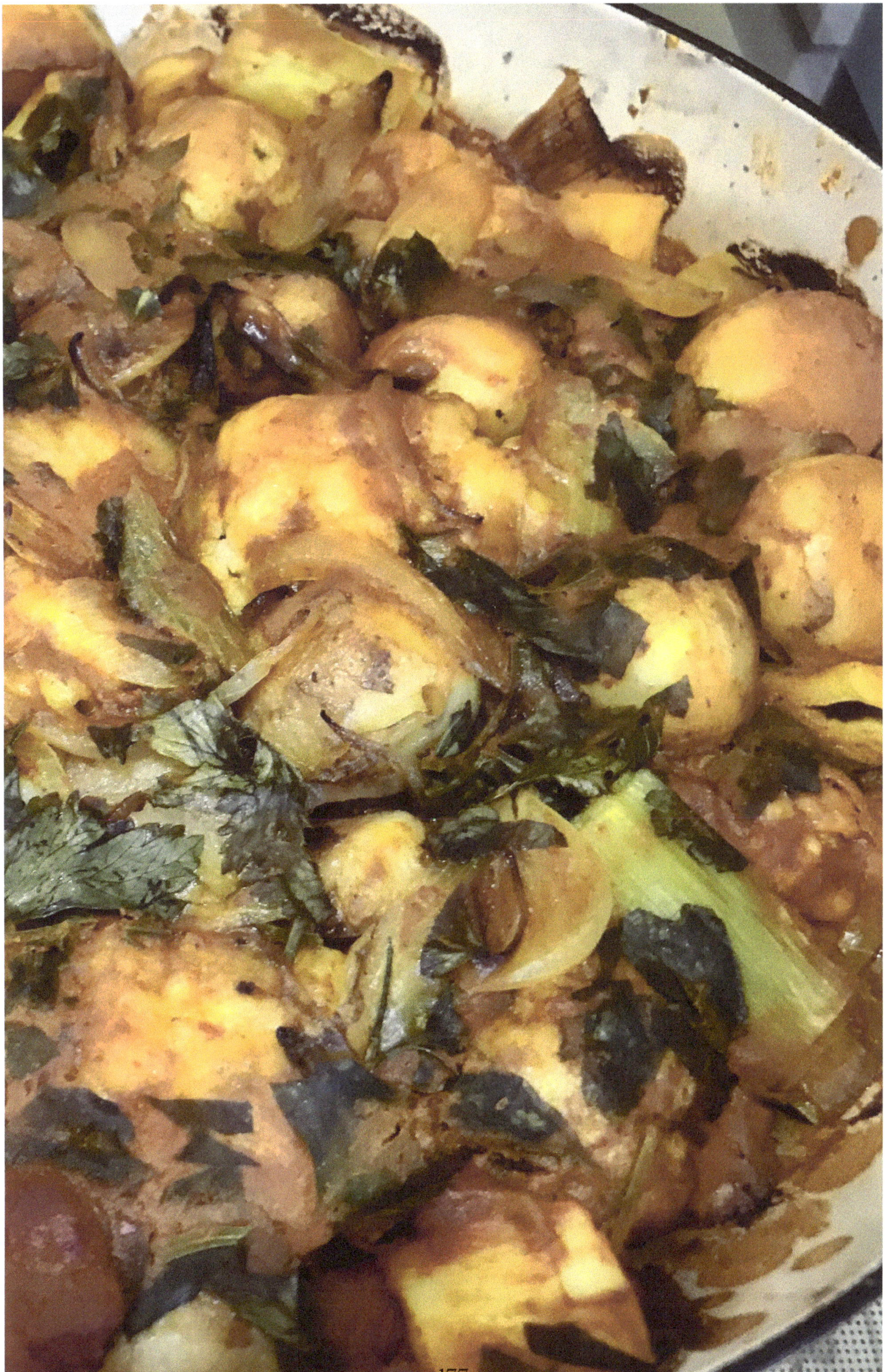

Malfoof
(Stuffed cabbage)

Malfoof means wrapped in Arabic. This is a vegetarian dish using chickpeas and rice, instead of minced beef. It's different from the European version of stuffed cabbage, because this recipe uses chickpeas and the sauce is a blend of sweet and sour.

1 large Savoy cabbage

Filling
    400g can chickpeas, drained and rinsed
    1 cup long grain or basmati rice
    2 cups cold water
    1 onion, finely chopped
    1 bunch flat leaf parsley, chopped
    2 tablespoons tomato purée
    1 tomato, skin removed and chopped
    2 tablespoons pomegranate molasses
    juice of ½ lemon
    1 teaspoon cinnamon
    1 teaspoon salt
    1 tablespoon olive oil
    1 cup raisins or sultanas
    1 teaspoon honey

Sauce
    2 tablespoons olive oil
    2 tablespoons pomegranate molasses
    1 tablespoon tamarind
    2 tablespoons tomato purée
    250ml tomato passata sauce (half a carton)
    1 teaspoon honey
    1 teaspoon cinnamon
    juice of ½ lemon
    3 cups cold water

Preheat the oven to 180C/Gas Mark 4.

Prepare the cabbage - fill a large saucepan with water and bring to the boil. Cut and discard the core of the cabbage and peel off the leaves. Blanch a few at a time in the boiling water, 3 minutes per batch. Remove each batch and immediately rinse in cold water. Place in a colander and continue blanching until all the leaves have been done.

Prepare the rice - wash and rinse and add two cups of water. Bring to the boil, lower the heat, cover and cook until the water has been absorbed – the rice should be al dente.

Prepare the filling by mixing all the ingredients together in a bowl.

Prepare the sauce - mix all the sauce ingredients in a small saucepan, bring to the boil and turn off the heat. Cover the bottom of a heavy casserole dish with half the sauce.

Make the stuffed cabbage - dry the cabbage leaves by pressing gently to remove any excess water. Cut the larger leaves in half and remove the stalk in the middle. With the smaller leaves remove the stalk at the top. Stuff the leaves one at a time - put some filling in the middle of the leaf (1 tablespoon, or less for the smaller leaves) and roll each filled leaf as tightly as you can without breaking it.

Place each stuffed leaf seam side down in the casserole dish, packing them tightly side by side. If you have more than one layer, spread some of the sauce over the first layer. If you have any of the filling left, squeeze the stuffed leaves further and place the remaining filling in the middle.

Pour any remaining sauce over the stuffed leaves. Place a large ovenproof plate on top – the weight of the plate will keep them from unrolling.

Cover and bake in the preheated oven for 1½ hours until the sauce has been absorbed and the stuffed leaves are tender.

Note - you can speed up the process by cooking on the hob first on a low heat for 30 minutes, then transferring to the oven for a further 1 hour.

Rice with raisins and pine nuts

Rice is the preferred grain of Sephardic Jews. It was introduced to Spain by the Moors in the 8th century and has remained a constant in their cuisine ever since. Rice traditionally symbolises fertility, prosperity and abundance.

1 large onion, finely chopped
4 tablespoons oil
2 tablespoons pine nuts
200g uncooked basmati rice
3 tablespoons raisins
1 teaspoon sugar
1 teaspoon cinnamon
1 teaspoon each salt and pepper
600ml boiling water

Sauté the onion in the oil until golden. Add the pine nuts and cook until they turn lightly brown. Remove the onion and pine nuts and set aside. In the same pan sauté the rice, stirring constantly until it becomes golden brown, about 10 minutes.

Return the onions and pine nuts to the pan. Add the raisins, sugar, cinnamon, salt and pepper. Pour in the boiling water, stir well, cover and cook over a low heat until all the water is absorbed, about 20 minutes.

Note - to reheat cooked rice, sprinkle about 1 tablespoon hot water and place over a low heat. Cook until piping hot, to make sure any bacteria is killed.

Okra with tomatoes

Okra, known as bamia in Arabic was a very popular vegetable in Egypt. No self respecting Egyptian cook served it unless it had been cooked as a stew with meat and this also applied to my family. However, this vegetarian version is just as nice. Frozen baby okra which can be bought from Middle Eastern groceries works well and is much cheaper than the fresh variety.

500g fresh or frozen okra
3 tablespoons oil
2 fresh tomatoes
2 teaspoons tomato purée
juice of 1 lemon
1 teaspoon ground turmeric
1 teaspoon ground coriander
1 cup water

If using fresh okra, trim both ends and rinse well under cold water. If using frozen, use straight from the freezer.

Fry the okra for 5 minutes in a saucepan with 3 tablespoons oil, stirring constantly. Add 1 cup water, tomato purée, lemon juice, ground turmeric, coriander and salt and pepper to taste. Cut the tomatoes into slices and place them over the okra.

Cover and cook for 30 minutes until the okra is tender and the sauce has thickened. Add more lemon juice to taste.

Serve over a bed of rice.

Note - ground turmeric adds a lovely yellow colour.

Aubergine parmigiana

This dish reminds me of three happy years I spent in Milan. I lived with my mother's sister, Marie who was an excellent cook. Italian markets were always bursting with beautiful looking aubergines and fresh tomatoes, especially in midsummer. My aunt often made melanzane alla parmigiana and I always chose it as a main course in a restaurant. The dish is welcome on a bleak winter evening, when it is a cheerful reminder of warmer days.

2 medium aubergines
6 tablespoons vegetable or sunflower oil
150g mozzarella cheese
200g tomato passata sauce or
200g fresh tomato and basil sauce
3 medium tomatoes
½ teaspoon dried oregano
a few basil leaves, torn

Wash the aubergines and cut lengthwise in 1cm (½ inch) slices. Place in a colander, sprinkle with salt and leave for 30 minutes. Squeeze out the bitter juices.

Preheat the oven to 180C/ Gas Mark 4.

Heat the oil in a large frying pan and fry the aubergines in batches on a gentle heat until golden. Turn the aubergines so that both sides are coloured and they are soft. Remove with a slotted spoon and drain well on kitchen paper.

Arrange the aubergine slices in an ovenproof dish to cover the base evenly. Slice the tomatoes and place on top. Cut the mozzarella in thin slices or chop and completely cover the tomatoes to form another layer.

Pour over the tomato sauce and sprinkle ½ teaspoon dried oregano.

Bake in the preheated oven for 15-20 minutes until the dish is sizzling.

Serve with a few torn basil leaves on top.

Tomatoes stuffed with cheese, Sephardic style

Tomatoes are usually stuffed with a mixture of minced beef and rice, added to other stuffed vegetables, such as courgettes and peppers and cooked in a sauce. This is much easier to make and is ideal served in spring or summer.

6 large tomatoes or 8 medium ones
125g grated cheese
125g feta cheese, crumbled
2 large eggs, beaten
salt and pepper
3 tablespoons olive oil
300ml water
1 tablespoon tomato paste
juice of ½ lemon
¼ teaspoon ground turmeric (optional)

Prepare the tomatoes – cut the stem ends and carefully scoop out the seeds and pulp – you can either discard this or add them to the water when cooking the tomatoes. Sprinkle the insides of the tomatoes with salt and invert on paper towels to drain for about 30 minutes.

Make the stuffing – in a medium bowl, combine the cheeses and eggs and add salt and pepper. Stir to blend and spoon the stuffing into the tomatoes.

In a large heavy saucepan, heat 3 tablespoons oil over medium heat. Place the tomatoes, filling-side down, in the pan and fry until browned, about 3 minutes. Invert the tomatoes and pour in 300ml water. Add the tomato paste, lemon juice and ground turmeric, if using.

Bring to the boil, cover, lower the heat and simmer for about 20 minutes, until the tomatoes are tender but not mushy.

Khodar b'meshmesh
(Sweet and sour vegetable stew)

This dish reminds me of my maternal grandmother, who was born and brought up in Aleppo. She and her husband moved to Egypt around 1910 seeking a better life, as the opening of Egypt's Suez Canal in 1869 had drastically affected the major caravan route that had sustained centuries of trade in Aleppo. My grandparents settled in Cairo, where my grandmother kept the Syrian-Jewish style of cooking, characterised by a predilection for the combination of sweet and sour ingredients. Dried fruits were widely used in meat and vegetables dishes and I grew up with many of them ending with b'meshmesh — with apricots.

Layers
¼ cup vegetable oil
3 coarsely chopped onions
2 large sweet potatoes, peeled and cut into small cubes
2 large white baking potatoes, peeled and cubed
1 aubergine, chopped into 2cm (1 inch) pieces
3 vine tomatoes
12 each dried apricots and dried prunes

Sauce
400g tomato sauce such as passata
1 generous cup cold water
½ cup lemon juice
2 teaspoons pomegranate molasses or Worcestershire sauce
1 tablespoon tamarind paste
1 tablespoon honey
¼ cup dark brown sugar
¼ teaspoon cinnamon
2 teaspoons ground allspice
salt and pepper to taste

This is a layered vegetable dish, so use a large heatproof and ovenproof casserole dish.

Cover the base with the vegetable oil, tilting it to spread it evenly along the bottom.

Proceed to layer the vegetables, using only half the ingredients at a time : onions, sweet and white potatoes (together), aubergine, tomatoes, dried apricots and prunes. Make sure they are packed tightly in the dish, then continue with the second layer, always packing tightly.

Prepare the sauce - put all the ingredients in a pan and bring to the boil. Remove the sauce from the heat and pour it over the vegetables, making sure they are well covered.

Cover and simmer over a low heat for 30-45 minutes. Adjust the taste if necessary.

Preheat the oven to 180C/Gas Mark 4.

Transfer the dish to the oven and cook for a further 1½-2 hours.

Serve over rice.

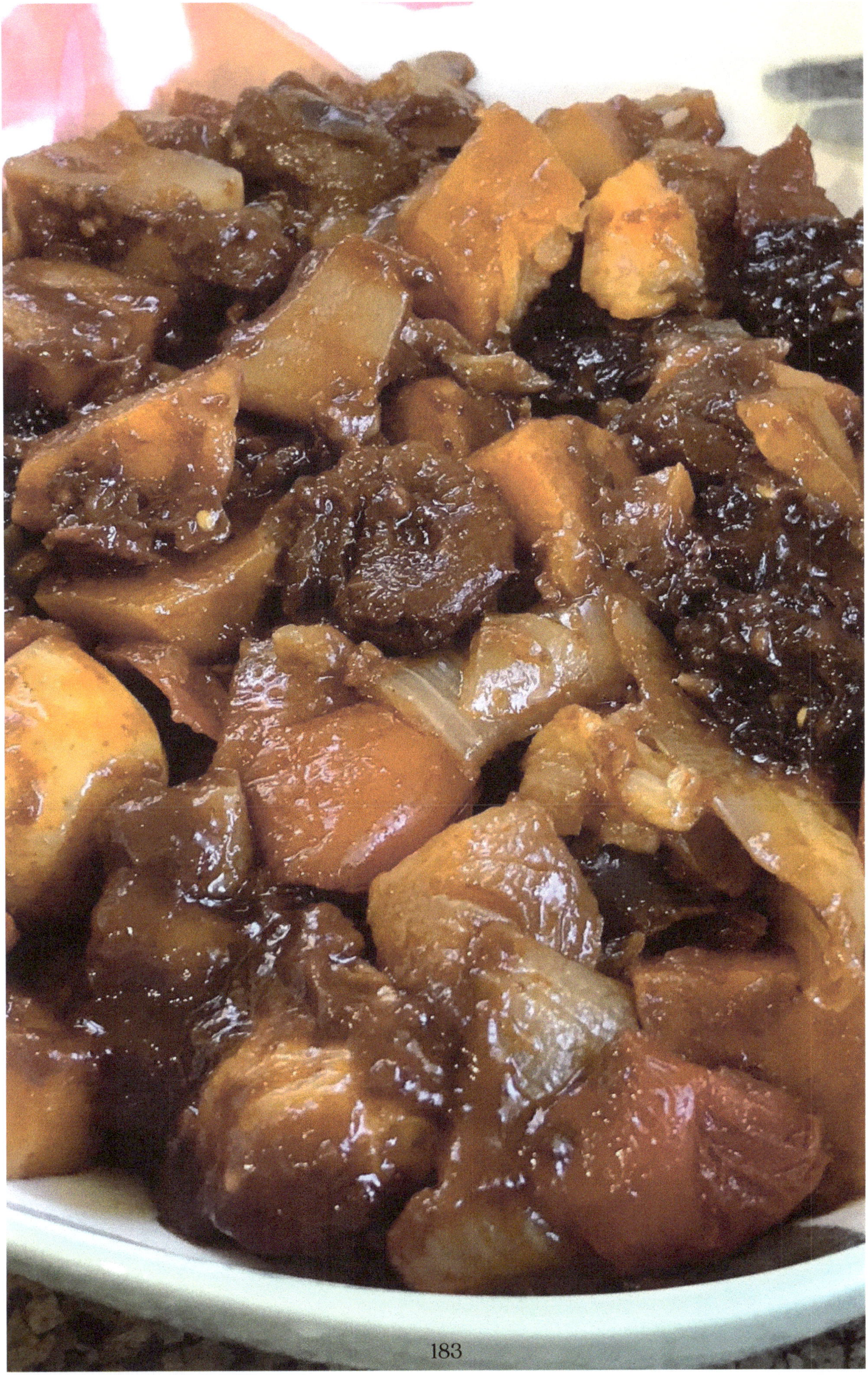

Arroz pilaf con berendjenas y pinyones

(Aubergine pilaf with pine nuts)

Pilaf is a rice dish whose recipe usually involves cooking in stock or broth, adding spices and other ingredients such as vegetables or meat. The technique is achieving cooked grains that do not stick. This pilaf makes a tasty change from basic plain rice and is great served with roast chicken or beef.

2 aubergines, weighing about 450g
sunflower or vegetable oil for shallow frying

For the rice
  2 tablespoons olive oil
  1 large onion, chopped
  2 garlic cloves, grated
  1 teaspoon sugar
  ½ teaspoon ground cumin
  ½ teaspoon ground coriander
  1 cinnamon stick
  200g long grain or basmati rice
  1 teaspoon tomato paste
  400g can peeled tomatoes
  ½ chicken or vegetable stock cube
  400ml boiling water
  1 teaspoon salt
  20g toasted pine nuts

Prepare the aubergines- cut the stem off and, using a sharp knife, peel 1¼cm (½ inch) strips at intervals along the length of the aubergines, leaving them striped with some peel. Cut them into slices or cubes about 1¼cm (½ inch) thick. Place in a colander and sprinkle with salt. Leave for 1 hour, then squeeze out the bitter juices.

Heat enough oil to in a frying pan for shallow frying. Fry the aubergines in batches until tender and lightly golden on both sides. Lift out with a slotted spoon and drain on a plate lined with paper towels. Press lightly with paper towels to soak up the excess oil.

Make the rice – wash it well, drain and rinse again. Cover with warm water and leave to soak for about 15 minutes. Drain and set aside.

Heat the olive oil in a large heavy based saucepan and fry the onion until soft and translucent, about 10 minutes. Add the garlic and stir in the sugar, coriander, cumin and cinnamon stick and mix well. Add the rice, stirring constantly for 1 minute until the grains are well coated and blend in the tomato paste, peeled tomatoes and salt.

Crumble ½ chicken or vegetable stock cube in 400ml boiling water, pour the stock over the rice and stir once. Bring to a boil, cover with a tight fitting lid, reduce the heat to medium and simmer undisturbed for about 15 minutes or until the rice has absorbed all the liquid.

Turn off the heat, stretch a clean folded tea towel over the top of the pan and press the lid tightly. Leave the pilaf to stand for 10 minutes. Discard the cinnamon stick, toss in the aubergines and pine nuts and fluff up with a fork.

Lentil, aubergine and pomegranate stew

Pomegranates have been cultivated throughout the Middle East and the Mediterranean region for several millennia. In England, the fruit is typically in season from March to May. Pomegranate seeds are used in salads, cooking and meal garnishes. They add colour to the dish, but also a tangy crunchiness, which blends well when mixed with al dente brown lentils.

1½ teaspoon cumin seeds
1 teaspoon coriander seeds
175g brown lentils
1 medium onion, chopped
2 tablespoons olive oil
2 large aubergines, weighing around 600g in total
80ml pomegranate molasses
2 teaspoons sumac
1 tablespoon tomato purée
1 teaspoon sugar
900ml cold water
salt and pepper to taste
2 banana shallots, finely chopped and fried in a little extra virgin oil
10g mint leaves or 2 teaspoons dried mint
10g fresh flat parsley, chopped
seeds of ½ pomegranate to serve

Cut the aubergines in 2cm (1 inch) pieces, sprinkle with some salt and leave in a colander for 30 minutes. Rinse and squeeze out the bitter juices. Rinse the lentils and cook for 15 minutes until they begin to soften. Drain them.

Toast the cumin and coriander seeds in a dry pan over a low heat for 1 minute. Grind them in a mortar and pestle or spice grinder. Fry the banana shallots in a little extra virgin oil and set aside.

Fry the chopped onion in 2 tablespoons olive oil for 5 minutes, until translucent. Add the aubergines and continue to fry for another 10 minutes, then add the drained lentils, pomegranate molasses, sumac, tomato purée, sugar, the toasted coriander and cumin, salt and pepper.

Pour 900ml cold water, cover and simmer for 45 minutes or until all the water has been absorbed. Gently mash everything with the back of a wooden spoon and finally add the fried shallots, fresh parsley and mint and cook for a further 5 minutes.

To serve, scatter with pomegranate seeds.

Karnabit frita

(Cauliflower florets stew)

Arnabit is the Arabic word for cauliflower. In the Ladino community, it was included in many stews and vegetable dishes. Fried cauliflower was the traditional way of cooking it, with the florets dipped in egg and flour first and then fried. It was then smothered in a tangy tomato and vegetable sauce and always served with rice.

1 large cauliflower - about 1 kg

For coating
 ¼ cup plain flour
 2 large eggs

For shallow frying
 sunflower or vegetable oil

For the vegetable base
 ¼ cup olive oil
 1 large onion, roughly chopped
 reserved cauliflower leaves and stalks
 1 large carrot, diced
 1 large potato, diced
 400g can chopped tomatoes
 ½ teaspoon sugar
 1 cup hot vegetable stock
 salt and pepper
 2 tablespoons fresh lemon juice
 ½ cup hot water

Preheat the oven to 180C/Gas Mark 4.

Prepare the cauliflower- cut off the green leaves and stalks from the cauliflower and reserve them for the vegetable base. Break the cauliflower florets from the stem and clean thoroughly by soaking in cold salted water for 15 minutes. Rinse well and drain.

Steam the florets over boiling salted water for about 7 minutes or until just tender - be careful not to overcook them. Refresh with cold water and drain in a colander.

Coat the cauliflower florets with flour and then with beaten egg. Heat about 2½cm (1 inch) oil in a deep frying pan over a medium heat. Cook the florets in batches until they are crisp and golden in both sides. Lift out with a slotted spoon and drain on paper towels.

Make the vegetable base – heat the olive oil in a large ovenproof casserole dish over medium heat. Toss in the onion, reserved cauliflower leaves and stalks, carrot and potato and cook stirring for 5 minutes. Add the salt, pepper, sugar and canned tomatoes, pour in the hot stock and bring to a boil. Cover, reduce the heat and simmer for 30 minutes, stirring occasionally.

Pour in the lemon juice and hot water. Arrange the cauliflower over the vegetable base, cover and continue to simmer for 10 minutes.

Preheat the oven to 180C/Gas Mark 4.

Transfer to the preheated oven and bake for 15 minutes or until the cauliflower tops are crisp.

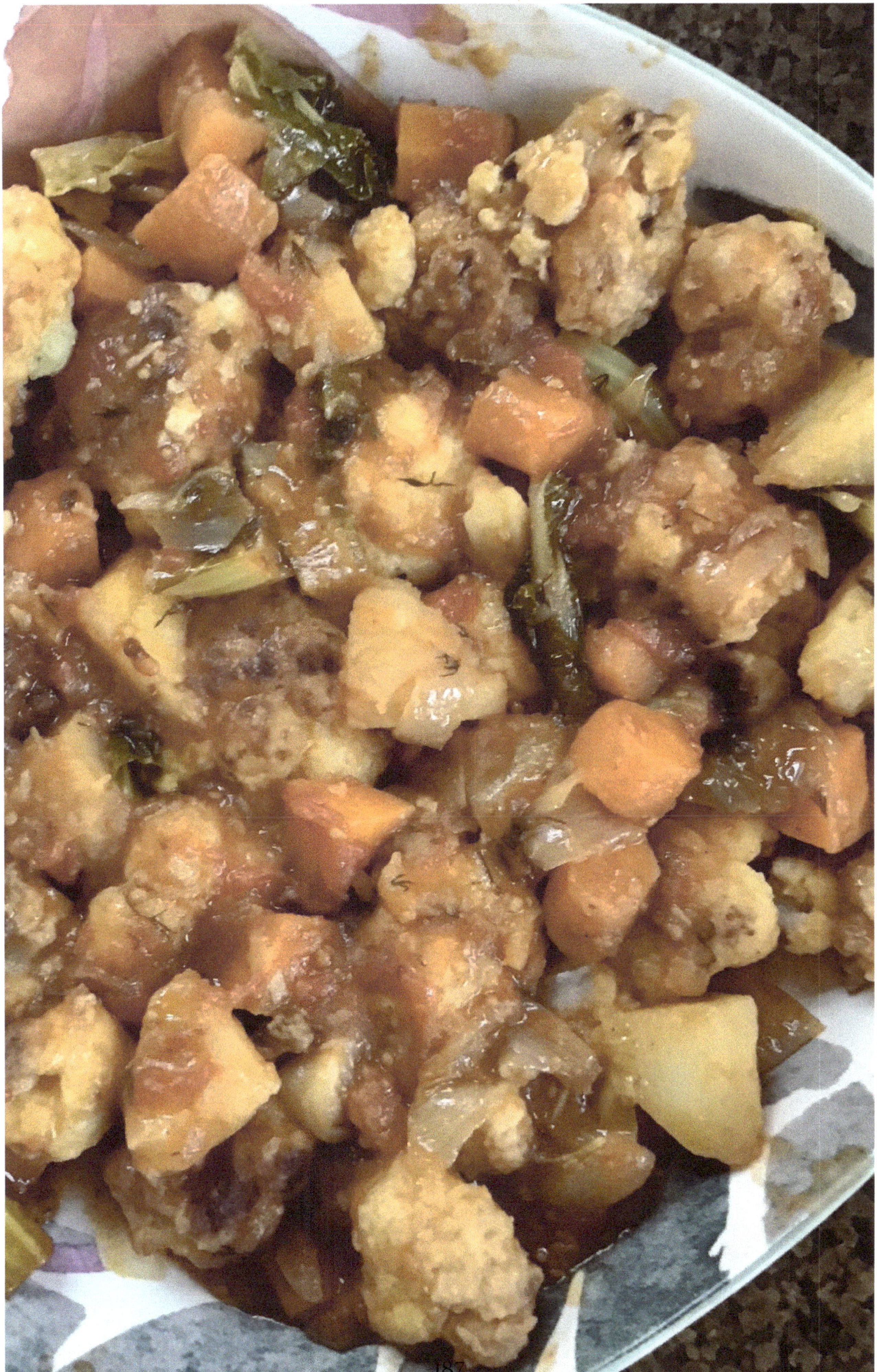

Bamia b'mishmosh

(Okra with prunes and apricots)

Okra is an extremely popular vegetable in the Middle East and is also known as ladies's fingers because of its dainty shape. It's very glutinous, but this can be lessened considerably by soaking it in a mixture of salt water and lemon juice before cooking. This recipe is inspired by my maternal grandmother, who often added dried fruit to her cooking.

500g fresh okra, stems trimmed or 400g pack of frozen baby okra
2 tablespoons vegetable oil
3 garlic cloves, finely chopped
1 tablespoon tomato paste
1 tablespoon tamarind paste
1 teaspoon sugar
½ teaspoon ground turmeric
juice of 1 lemon
1 teaspoon salt
1 cup water
½ cup dried apricots
½ cup pitted prunes

Heat the oil in a medium saucepan. Gently sauté the okra, shaking the pan occasionally rather than stirring with a spoon. Add the garlic and continue sautéing until the okra is lightly browned.

Add the tomato and tamarind paste, sugar, lemon juice, ground turmeric, salt and water.

Cover and simmer over a low heat for 30 minutes, then add the apricots and prunes - you may have to add a little more water.

Cook for a further 30 minutes until the okra is crisp and tender. Keep an eye on it while cooking, as the okra should not become mushy.

Serve over white rice.

EGYPTIAN DISHES
Atbakh masria

Baclawa
(Nut-filled filo pastry)

Baclawa was associated with celebrations in all the Jewish communities throughout the Middle East. In Egypt, we called it ba'alawa and it was present at all the festivals. Muslims prepared it during Ramadan and family members offered it as a gesture of affection. It is still the pastry of choice for a dinner party or afternoon tea.

Makes about 40 pieces

For the filling
500g walnuts, almonds or hazelnuts or a mixture of three
3 tablespoons caster sugar

For the pastry
175g unsalted butter
100ml sunflower oil
500g filo pastry

For the syrup
400g sugar
200ml water
juice of ½ lemon
2 tablespoons orange blossom water

Preheat the oven to 180C/Gas Mark 4.

Prepare the filling – grind the nuts medium fine and blend with 3 tablespoons sugar. You can use a food processor, but be careful not to pulse for too long, a few seconds are enough.

Melt the butter with the oil over a low heat and pour about 4 tablespoons over the nuts. Mix well and set aside.

Grease a 30cm (12 inch) baking dish or tin. Fit half the pastry sheets in the dish, one at a time, brushing each generously with the butter and oil mixture. Ease the filo pastry into the corners, folding and overlapping as required and trimming the edges if necessary.

Work with one sheet at a time and keep the rest wrapped in a clean tea towel, as filo pastry dries very quickly.

Spread the nut mixture evenly over the sheets. Cover with the remaining sheets of filo, one at a time, brushing each, including the top, with the melted butter and oil mixture.

With a sharp-pointed knife, cut parallel lines right through all the layers to the bottom, making small diamond or rectangular shapes.

Bake in the oven for about 1 hour. If it is not browned, raise the heat slightly for a few minutes until the pastry is golden.

Make the syrup while the pastry is in the oven. Simmer the sugar and water with the lemon juice for 10 minutes, then add the orange blossom water. Let it cool.

Take the baclawa out of the oven, cool for 5 minutes and pour the syrup all over. Some people like to put the pastry back in the oven for a further 5 minutes at the same heat.

Note - the best filo pastry is the one sold in Middle Eastern and Turkish supermarkets, as the sheets are very fine, which is ideal for baklawa. The added bonus is that it is sold in packs of 500g and it's also much cheaper than the filo pastry sold in standard supermarkets.

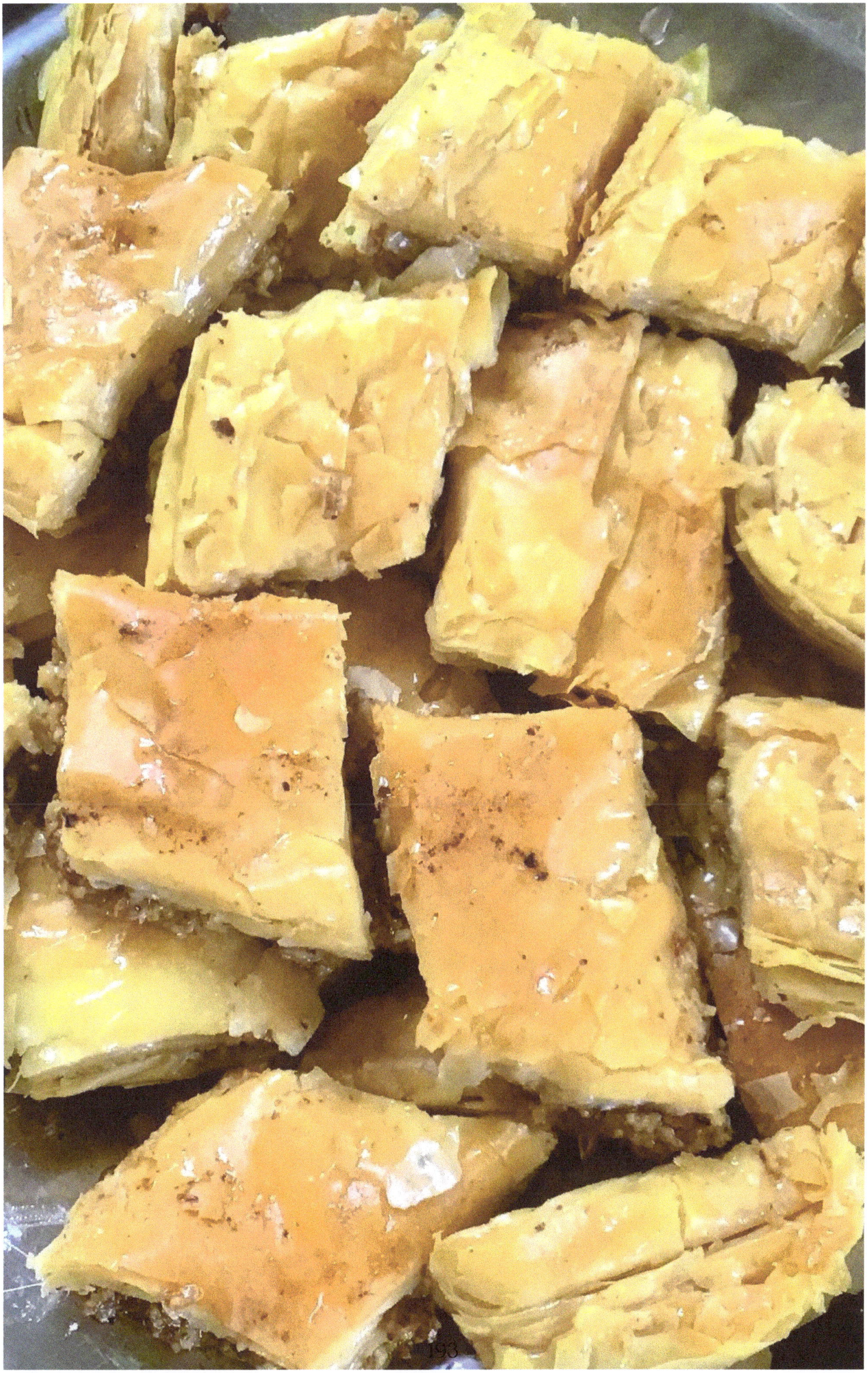

Aish el saraya
(The palace bread)

Makes 25 pieces

This is a traditional Egyptian dessert which is simple to make. It is more like a bread pudding with a fragrant cream on top and you get that Middle Eastern feel because of the rose water used to flavour the dish. You can also use orange blossom water.

10 slices white bread, crusts removed and toasted
2½ cups milk
1/3 cup caster sugar
600ml double cream
1/3 cup cornflour
2 teaspoons rosewater
1 cup chopped pistachios

For the rosewater syrup
2/3 cup caster sugar
2/3 cup water
3 teaspoons lemon juice
3 teaspoons rose water

Make the rosewater syrup – mix the sugar, water and lemon juice in a medium saucepan. Stir on a low heat for 3 minutes until the sugar dissolves. Increase the heat to high and simmer for a couple more minutes. Remove from heat and stir in the rosewater. Cool for 10 minutes.

Prepare the base - place half the toasted bread on a lightly greased baking dish about 17 x 26cm (7 x 10 inch), cutting to size. Pour half the syrup over the bread, top with the remaining bread and drizzle with the remaining syrup.

Make the cornflour - mix the cornflour with a little milk to make a smooth paste.

Place the remaining milk in a saucepan, together with the cream and sugar. Heat for a couple of minutes, then add the cornflour paste. Cook, stirring constantly for 6-8 minutes until the mixture boils and thickens. Stir in 2 teaspoons of rosewater.

Pour the cornflour mixture over the bread in the dish and sprinkle with the chopped pistachios. Refrigerate overnight or until set.

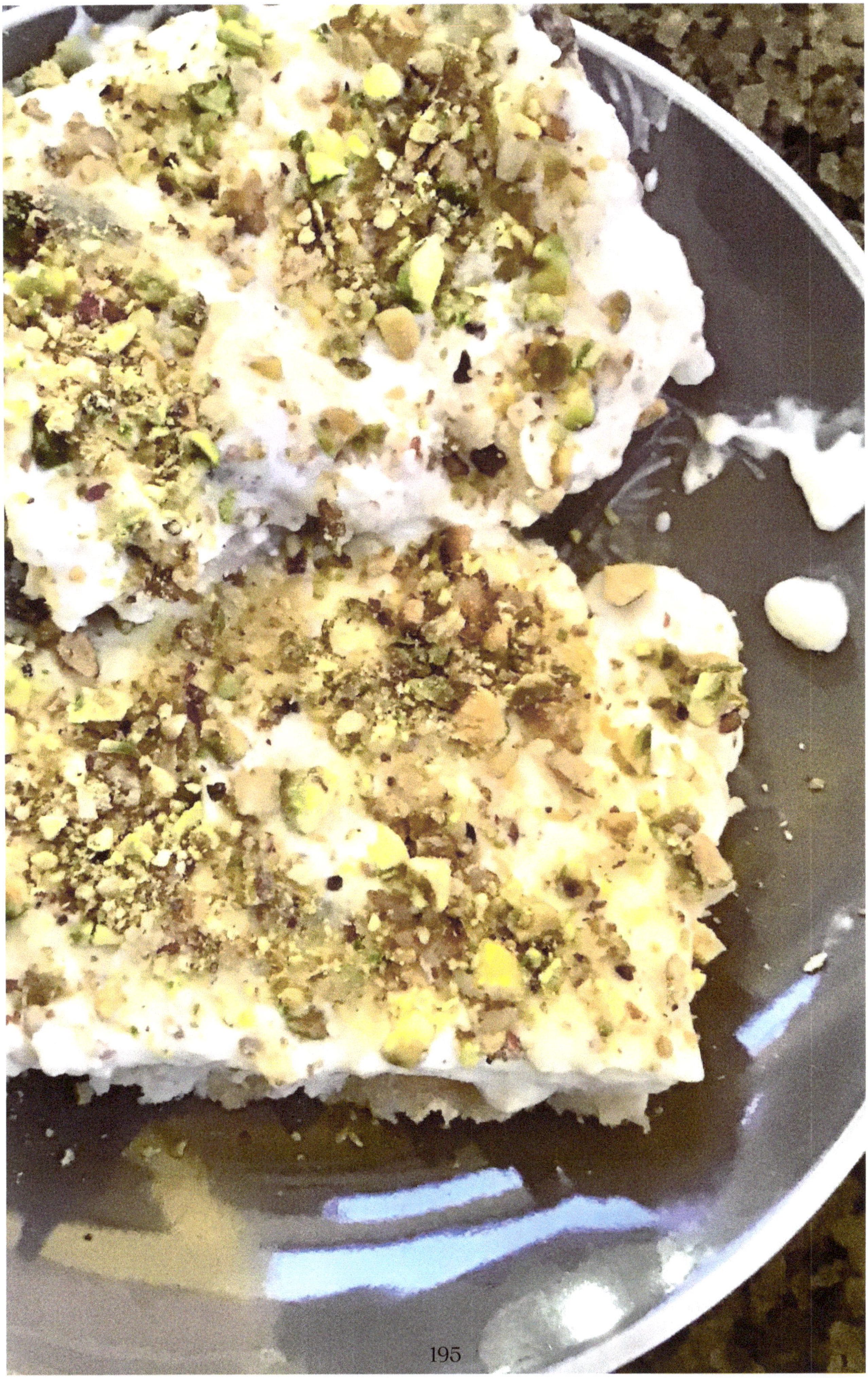

Basbousa cake with cream

This recipe is slightly different from the traditional basbousa because it has eggs and is baked with cream in the middle, giving the cake a moist and spongy texture. It can also be served as a dessert.

Cake ingredients
- 170g semolina, fine or coarse
- 100g granulated sugar
- 25g coconut flakes or desiccated coconut
- 3 large eggs
- 2 teaspoons baking powder
- 180g sunflower oil
- 250ml full fat yoghurt

Filling
- 500ml milk
- 40g (4 tablespoons) cornflour
- 2 tablespoons cream (optional)
- 1 tablespoon sugar
- ½ teaspoon vanilla extract

For later
- 1 tablespoon water

Sugar syrup
- 200g granulated sugar
- 180ml water
- 1 tablespoon honey
- 1 teaspoon lemon juice

Preheat the oven to 180C/Gas Mark 4.
Grease a 22cm (9 inch) cake pan.

Make the syrup - stir all the ingredients together in a medium saucepan, bring to a boil, reduce the heat and simmer for 10 minutes. Remove from heat and cool.

Make the cake - in a deep bowl, combine all the cake ingredients and mix well.

Pour half the mixture in the prepared pan and bake for 15 minutes in the preheated oven.

Make the filling - mix the cornflour with 100ml milk in a saucepan until you have a smooth paste. Stir in the sugar, vanilla extract and the rest of the milk. Transfer the pan to the stove and cook over medium heat, stirring constantly until the mixture thickens, about 5-8 minutes. Add the cream, if using.

Take the cake pan out of the oven, spread the filling on top and level the surface. Add a tablespoon of water to the remaining semolina mixture and mix well. Spread the mixture over the filling in the cake and level.

Bake for a further 40-45 minutes. Remove from the oven and immediately pour the cooled syrup. Cover and let stand for 15 minutes to let the syrup soak and cool down. Garnish with nuts or leave plain.

Bessara

(Egyptian fava beans and herb dip)

This fava bean dip is rooted in Egyptian history and is believed to date back to the Pharaonic era. The word beesara is derived from the hieroglyphic bees- oro, (bees meaning cooked and oro which means beans).

250g fava beans, soaked overnight
1 medium onion, chopped
3 garlic cloves
½ bunch fresh flat leaf parsley, chopped
½ bunch fresh coriander, chopped
½ teaspoon black pepper
salt to taste

For the onion topping
   1 medium onion, cut into strips
   1 garlic clove, minced
   ½ teaspoon caraway seeds
   ½ teaspoon coriander seeds
   2 tablespoons olive oil

Soak the fava beans overnight. Rinse and drain.

Place the beans in a large pot, cover with water and bring to a simmer. When froth appears on the surface, drain the water and add new water to cover the beans. Simmer for 25 minutes, then add the herbs, onion and garlic and cook until the beans are completely soft, drain, reserving some of the water.

Purée the beans in a food processor and add a little of the reserved water.

Return the beans to the saucepan, add salt and pepper and cook over a low heat until the consistency thickens enough to allow you to scoop it with a piece of bread.

Prepare the onion topping - using a pestle and mortar, grind the garlic, caraway and coriander seeds. Heat the oil in a skillet and fry the onion until golden, about 5 minutes. Add the garlic and spices and fry for a further 2 minutes. Remove and drain over paper towels.

Pour 2 tablespoons olive oil over the cooked beans. Transfer to a serving dish and garnish the surface with the fried onions.

Serve at room temperature with bread, spring onions, olives or pickles.

Dukka

(Egyptian nut, seed and spice blend)

Dukka is an old Egyptian specialty, a mixture of nuts and spices in a dry, crushed but not powdered form. It is eaten as a snack, sprinkled over bread, toast or crackers and can also be served as an appetiser, with olive oil on the side and the bread dipped in the oil first.

250g sesame seeds
125g coriander seeds
100g hazelnuts
60g ground cumin
½ teaspoon salt

Roast all the ingredients separately in a preheated oven 180C/Gas mark 4.

Pound them together until they are finely crushed, but not pulverised. This can be done in small batches in a spice grinder or electric blender for a few seconds only, otherwise the mixture will become a paste.

Dukka should look like a fine mixture, but not a paste. It is lovely even eaten on its own.

Egyptian Kishk

(Rice with yoghurt and caramelised onions)

Kishk is a famous Middle Eastern dish which is prepared differently according to each country, and Egyptian kishk is not the same as its Lebanese and Palestinian counterparts. One of my Syrian friends makes a similar dish called labaneya, which involves cooking the rice with garlic and dried mint separately and replacing the caramelised onions on top with chicken pieces.

1 litre (1000ml) chicken broth
25g short grain rice
80ml sunflower or vegetable oil
2 medium onions, chopped
200ml full fat yoghurt, preferably Greek
30g flour
20ml lemon juice
salt to taste
1 tablespoon roasted pine nuts (optional)

Heat the chicken broth in a medium saucepan, add the rice and simmer until the rice is tender, about 20 minutes.

Heat the oil in a separate pan and fry the onions until caramelised, stirring constantly, about 15 minutes. Reserve 1 tablespoon of the onions for the garnish and spoon the rest into the simmering broth.

Mix the yoghurt with the salt, lemon juice and flour until smooth and blend with 80ml of chicken broth.

Pour the yoghurt mixture into the hot broth and bring to the boil. Reduce the heat and simmer until the flavours have blended, about 2-3 minutes.

Garnish with the reserved caramelised onion and toasted pine nuts.

Note – The dish can be served hot or at room temperature, accompanied by chicken or a salad.

Egyptian lamb fattah

In Egypt, this dish is traditionally served during Eid, the festival that marks the end of Ramadan. It's also a favourite dish to celebrate any occasion, such as weddings, gatherings and the birth of a child .Fattah is very popular in the Middle East, where it is known under different names.

For the lamb
   45ml (3 tablespoons) vegetable or sunflower oil
   2 medium onions, roughly chopped
   900g diced lamb, cut into 2½cm (1 inch) pieces
   8 cardamom pods, crushed
   2 bay leaves
   1 litre (1000ml) chicken stock, vegetable stock or water
   salt and pepper

For the rice
   30ml (2 tablespoons) oil
   300g long grain rice
   450ml water
   3 pitta breads

For the sauce
   30ml (2 tablespoons) oil
   1 tablespoon crushed garlic
   5 tablespoons tomato purée
   ½ teaspoon ground cumin
   1 tablespoon white wine vinegar
   400ml water
   salt and pepper

Make the lamb - heat 45ml (3 tablespoons) oil in a large sauté pan and fry the onions until soft, but not golden, about 5 minutes. Add the lamb and fry until lightly browned, about 10 minutes. Stir in the cardamom and bay leaves, followed by the stock. Season with salt and pepper, bring to the boil and skim off the foam on the surface. Lower the heat, cover and simmer for about 1-1½ hours until tender.

Make the rice - wash it well until the water runs clear and drain. Heat 30ml (2 tablespoons) oil in a heavy based saucepan on medium heat. Add the rice and stir until all the grains are coated. Add 450ml water and bring to the boil. Turn the heat to the lowest setting, cover and cook for 20-25 minutes until the water has been absorbed and the rice is tender.

For the pitta bread - preheat the oven to 200C/Gas Mark 5 and line a large baking sheet with baking parchment. Split the pitta bread horizontally into two thin halves, then tear or cut them into bite-sized pieces. Spread on the baking sheet and bake for 10-12 minutes, turning them halfway though, until golden brown and crisp.

Make the sauce - heat 30ml (2 tablespoons) oil in a pan on a medium heat. Fry the garlic until lightly golden. Add the tomato purée and mix for 2-3 minutes, followed by the ground cumin and wine vinegar and stir for a few seconds. Add 400ml water, mix well until blended, season with salt and pepper and simmer for 15 minutes, until the sauce has reduced and thickened.

To assemble – spread the baked pitta bread on a large serving dish, top with the rice, then add the lamb and some stock from the pan. Drizzle some tomato sauce over the top. Serve with extra stock and tomato sauce on the side.

Ful Medames
(Cooked fava beans)

This is undoubtedly one of the national dishes of Egypt. Ful is the Egyptian word for broad beans and medames means buried - referring to the original cooking method of burying a pot of beans and water under hot coals. The traditional way is to soak dried fava beans overnight, then cook them in a slow cooker. However, nowadays Middle Eastern supermarkets stock a large variety of canned fava beans and this is what I have used because it's quicker and just as nice.

3 x 400g cans of ful medames
6 tablespoons extra virgin oil
juice of 2 lemons
2 teaspoons cumin powder
salt and pepper
3 garlic cloves, crushed
4 hard boiled eggs

Drain the canned fava beans in a colander and rinse them thoroughly. Transfer to a saucepan, cover with water, bring to the boil and cook for 10 minutes. Drain, reserving some of the water.

Transfer the beans to a large plate and roughly mash them. Add a little of the reserved water to give them a smooth consistency and mix in 3 tablespoons extra virgin oil, salt, pepper, ground cumin and lemon juice.

In a small frying pan, fry the crushed garlic with 1 tablespoon of extra virgin oil and add this to the fava beans mixture.

Roughly chop the hard boiled eggs and scatter over the beans. Drizzle with the remaining 2 tablespoons oil and adjust the taste – you may have to add more salt and lemon juice.

Serve with flatbread or pita bread.

Kahk
(savoury small bracelets)

Makes about 60

These are found all over the Middle East. They were a staple in our house, as we didn't have the choice of crackers and savoury biscuits available in supermarkets nowadays and almost everything was home baked. These savoury dry bracelets were eaten as a snack and my mother continued to make them regularly in England. They are great with a cup of tea.

1 sachet dry yeast (7g)
125ml warm water
 pinch of sugar
500g strong white bread flour
1 teaspoon salt
2 teaspoons ground cumin
1 teaspoon ground coriander
180g unsalted butter
1 whole egg, lightly beaten
sesame seeds (about 6 tablespoons)

Pour half the water (it must be warm) in a small bowl and sprinkle the yeast, add the sugar and 2 tablespoons of the flour. Stir vigorously and leave aside for about 10 minutes until the mixture froths.

Put the remaining flour in a large bowl. Mix in the salt, cumin and coriander. Add the butter or margarine and 1 tablespoon oil. Add the yeast mixture and the remaining water, just enough to make a dough that sticks together in a ball, adding more water if necessary.

Knead for 10 minutes. Pour a little oil in the bowl and roll the dough around to grease it all over. Cover with clingfilm and leave for about 1½ hours until the dough haas risen and almost doubled in siz.e

Preheat the oven to 190C/Gas Mark 5.
Line two large baking trays with baking parchment or greaseproof paper.

Punch down the dough. Take some small lumps and roll them between your palms into long thin rolls about 10cm (4 inch) long. Make little bracelets by bringing in the ends together and pinching. Brush the tops with the beaten egg and dip them upside down into a bowl of sesame seeds.

Place the bracelets a little apart on the baking sheets. Let them rise for 20 minutes.

Preheat the oven at 190C/Gas mark 5.

 Bake the bracelets for 6 minutes, then lower the heat to 100C/ Gas mark ¼ and bake for a further 20 minutes, until they are golden on top.

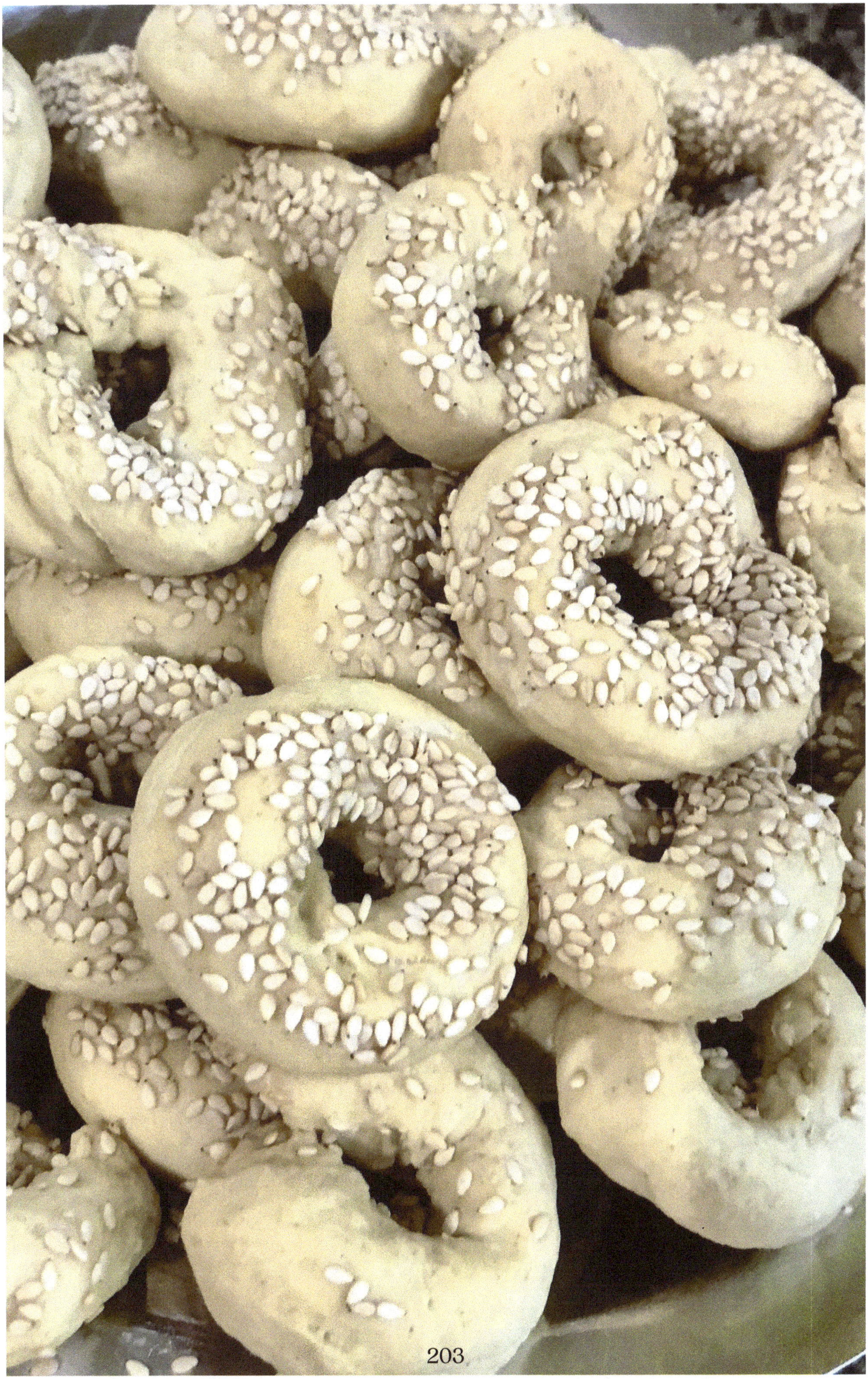

Kar'assaly

(Egyptian pumpkin milk pudding)

Kar'assaly is a classic Egyptian dessert which consists of cooked pumpkin mixed with sugar, butter, nuts and raisins. It exists in many variations and is typically made with a layer of pumpkin chunks cooked in a little water and granulated sugar until the pumpkin softens. I prefer to have a thinner layer of sauce on top, but a different version is a thick milk pudding layer, using 900ml milk and 16g cornflour.

For the pumpkin layer
- 1 kg pumpkin, peeled, cubed and deseeded
- 100g granulate sugar
- 1 teaspoon allspice
- 2 tablespoons orange juice (optional)
- 50ml water
- 15g butter

For the filling
- 75g raisins
- 50g desiccated coconut
- 85g flaked almonds (toasted)
- ½ teaspoon ground cinnamon
- ½ ground cardamom

For the béchamel layer
- 500g milk
- 10g cornflour
- ½ teaspoon vanilla extract
- demerera sugar for sprinkling

Preheat the oven to 180C/Gas Mark 4.
Lightly grease a 22 x 22cm (9 x 9 inch) square baking dish.

Prepare the pumpkin – place the pumpkin, sugar, all spice, orange juice (if using), water and butter in a heavy bottom pan. Cook uncovered over medium heat for 20-30 minutes until the pumpkin softens. Stop cooking as soon as the pumpkin is fork tender.

Prepare the filling – mix all the filling ingredients in a bowl.

Make the béchamel layer – place 425ml milk in a saucepan. Whisk the remaining 75ml with the cornflour and add to the milk in the saucepan. Cook over a medium heat, stirring continuously, until the mixture thickens, adding more milk or water if too thick.

Assemble the dish – layer the pumpkin mix at the bottom of the dish. Cover with the nut, raisin and spice mixture and spread the béchamel layer on top Sprinkle with some demerera sugar.

Bake for 20 minutes until golden on top.

Khoshaf

(Egyptian dried fruit salad)

Khoshaf is an Egyptian dessert of dried fruit. We always had this at the end of the Passover meal and sometimes just as a special dessert. It's very versatile, as any dried fruit can be used, but a combination of apricots and prunes works well. Serve with ice cream to make it extra special.

1 cup dried apricots, chopped or halved
½ cup dried prunes, halved
½ cup raisins
1 cup orange juice
1 ¼ cup water
1 ¼ cup sugar
2 tablespoons rose water or orange blossom water

To serve - vanilla ice cream

Some roasted coconut flakes, chopped hazelnuts or chopped pistachios.

Soak the dried fruit overnight with 1¼ cup water. Drain and keep the water.

Put the drained water in a saucepan and add enough to make up to 1¼ cup. Add the orange juice, sugar and dried fruit and bring to the boil. Lower the heat and cook uncovered for 10 minutes.

When the fruit mixture has cooled, add 2 tablespoons of rose water or orange blossom water.

Serve with a scoop of vanilla or some greek yoghurt.

Kahk bi sukar
(Icing sugar shortbread cookies)

Makes 45

Kahk are said to have originated in Ancient Egypt during Pharaonic times. Today, these cookies are an essential component of the Muslim Eid-el-Fitr, the feast after Ramadan. The fillings can vary and include pistachios, almonds and walnuts.

250g unsalted butter
45g icing sugar
1 egg yolk
¼ teaspoon vanilla extract
1 teaspoon baking powder
75g self raising flour
160g plain flour, plus extra
70g walnuts or almonds, crushed

Preheat the oven to 180C/Gas Mark 4.
Lightly grease two baking trays and line with baking parchment or greaseproof paper.

Beat the butter and sugar in an electric mixer until light and fluffy. Add the egg yolk and vanilla extract and beat well to combine.

Sift the baking powder and flours. Gradually add these to the butter mixture, along with the nuts and mix well. You may have to add a little more flour - the mixture is ready when it comes together as a ball. Wrap it in clingfilm and place in the fridge for 30 minutes.

Place the dough on a floured board. Mould it into little sausages about 10cm (4 inch) long and 1cm (½ inch) wide and bring the ends together to form a small bracelet. Place the bracelets on the trays and bake for approximately 12 minutes, until the cookies are slightly browned on the base.

Remove from the oven and sift a little icing sugar on top after 5 minutes. Place on a cooking rack to cool completely, then dredge with more icing sugar so that they are well coated. Store in an airtight container.

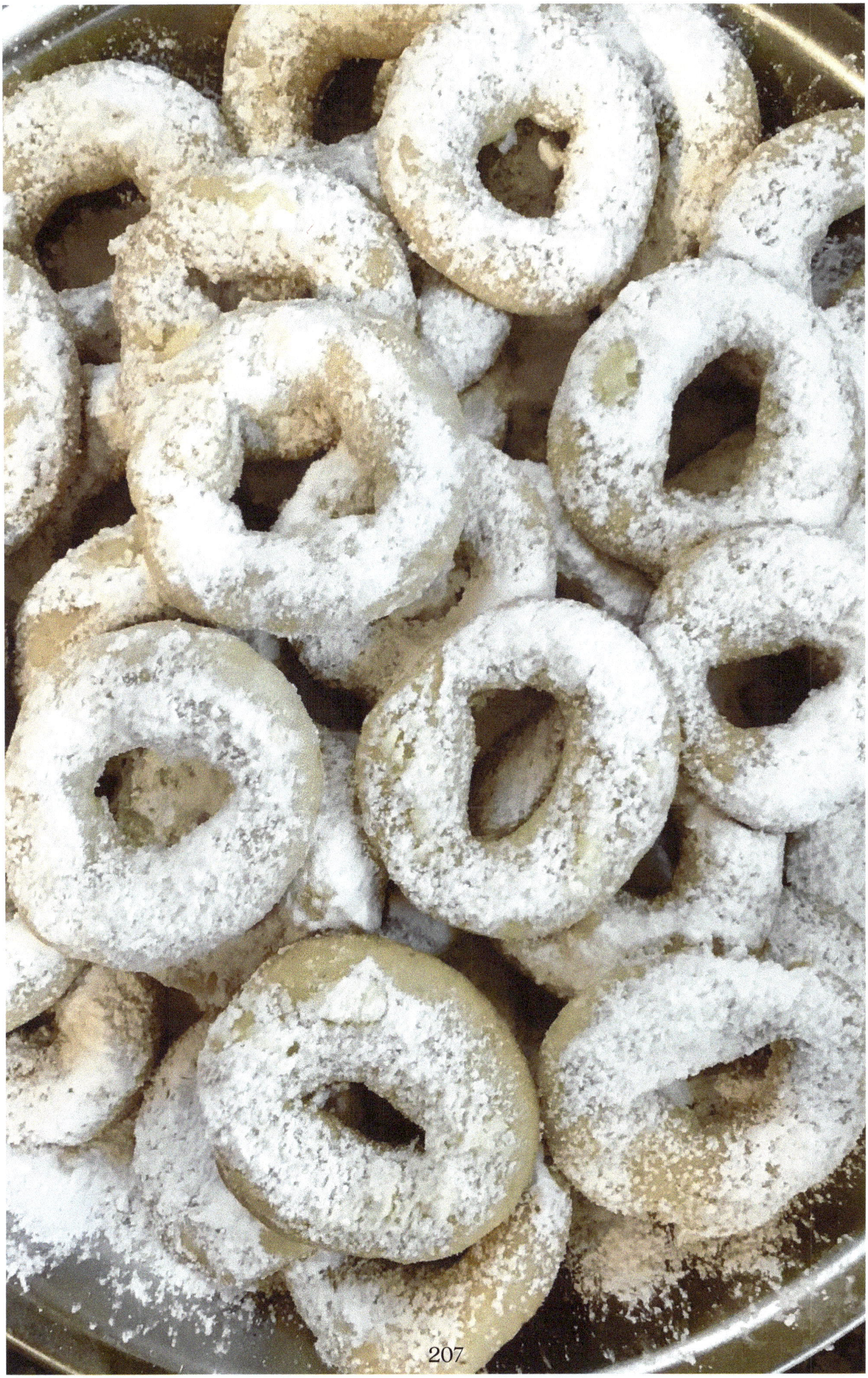

Konafa bil mikassarat

(Konafa nests with mixed nuts)

Makes 14 nests

Konafa, also known as angel hair, is a shredded filo dough available from Middle Eastern and Turkish grocery shops, where it is usually sold as kataifi. The traditional way of making it is in a deep round dish, about 25cm (10 inch) in diameter. I have shaped the pastry into nests, using a bun tray with 12 deep cups.

400g pack konafa (shredded kataifi dough)
250g unsalted butter, melted

For the syrup
  225g sugar
  250ml water
  juice of ½ lemon
  1 tablespoon rose water or orange blossom water

For the filling
  350g pistachios, walnuts or almonds or any combination of those
  2 tablespoons sugar

Begin by making the syrup – combine the sugar, water and lemon juice in a pan. Bring to the boil, lower the heat and simmer for 10 minutes until the syrup had reduced and is thick enough to coat a spoon. Leave a few minutes to cool, then add 1 tablespoon of rose water or orange blossom water.

Preheat the oven to 180C/Gas Mark 4.

For the filling - blitz the nuts and sugar for 10 seconds in a food processor - no longer, as the nuts must retain some consistency. Mix with 4 tablespoons of the melted butter.

Make the konafa - place it in a large bowl and carefully pull all the strands apart to loosen them. Pour the melted butter and work with your hands until all the strands are thoroughly coated with the butter.

Lightly grease each cup in the bun tray. Take one small lump of the pastry and shape it firmly into and around each of the cups. Put one spoonful of the nut filling over the pastry, then top with another lump of pastry and press firmly again. Brush each filled cup with a little melted butter.

Bake for 20 minutes in the preheated oven or until the pastries are golden brown. Remove from the oven, immediately pour the syrup over each of the pastry nests and sprinkle with a few nuts.

Note - alternatively, use a round pie dish (diameter 25cm/10 inch) and spread half the pastry on the bottom of the pie plate. Flatten it with the palm of your hands, spread the nut mixture evenly over the surface and cover with the remaining pastry. Flatten the top again.

Bake for 55-60 minutes or until golden. Pour the cold syrup over the hot pastry as soon as you take it out of the oven. When cool, run a sharp knife around the pie so as to loosen the sides and turn out, inverting it onto a large serving dish.

Konafa with cream

Konafa is a shredded filo dough which is also known as angel hair. It was often offered at parties and celebrations and every family had their own individual twist on the recipe. It can be made with cream, cheese or nuts and my aunt Sophie's konafa with nuts was by far the best. I remember that she always made it especially for me when I visited her in Paris.

For the syrup
- 400g sugar
- 250ml water
- 1 tablespoon lemon juice
- 1 tablespoon orange blossom water

For the cream filling
- 140g ground rice
- 1 litre whole milk
- 3 tablespoons sugar
- 140ml double cream (optional)

For the pastry
- 500g konafa (kataifi) pastry
- 250g unsalted butter, melted
- 100g pistachios, coarsely chopped, to garnish

Alternative version
Nut filling
- 350g walnuts
- 350g almonds
- 200g ground almonds
- 2 tablespoons sugar
- 4 tablespoons butter, melted

Preheat the oven to 180C/Gas Mark 4.
Lightly grease a 30cm (12 inch) round pie plate.

Make the syrup first - boil the sugar, water and lemon juice for 10-15 minutes, then add the orange blossom water. Cool and chill in the refrigerator.

For the filling, mix the rice flour with enough milk to form a smooth creamy paste. Bring the rest of the milk to the boil and add the ground rice paste. Stir vigorously with a wooden spoon, lower the heat and continue stirring for 15 minutes until the mixture thickens. Add the sugar and stir. Let it cool before adding the cream, if using.

Prepare the konafa pastry - place it in a large bowl and carefully pull all the strands apart to loosen them. Pour the melted butter and work with your hands until all the strands are thoroughly coated.

Spread half the pastry on the bottom of the pie plate. Cover evenly with the cream, then with the rest of the pastry. Press down and flatten gently with the palm of your hands.

Bake in the preheated oven for about 1 hour, then turn the oven higher for a further 10 minutes until the pastry colours. Pour the cold syrup over the hot pastry as soon as you take it out of the oven.

When cool, run a sharp knife around the pie so as to loosen the sides and turn out, inverting it onto a large serving dish. Sprinkle with the chopped pistachios.

Alternative version

Quickly blitz the walnuts and almonds in a food processor for a few seconds, being careful not to do this for too long or the mixture will turn into a paste. Add the ground almonds, sugar and melted butter. Spread half the pastry over the pie dish, cover with the nut mixture and finally with the remaining pastry. Bake as with the cream filling. Pour the cold syrup over the hot pastry as soon as you take it out of the oven.

Megadarra

(Rice with brown lentils)

This dish is popular throughout the Arab world and amongst Jewish communities of Middle Eastern origin, in particular those of Syrian and Egyptian background— my grandmother pronounced it mujadarra. It is made using brown lentils and rice, seasoned with coriander or cumin, topped with fried onions and generally served with yoghurt, among other vegetables and side dishes. We had it regularly while growing up, especially in summer as it is light and can also be eaten at room temperature. The dish is sometimes nicknamed 'Esau's favourite.'

4 large onions cut in half and sliced
100ml olive oil
230g brown lentils
250g basmati rice
1 teaspoon ground cumin
salt and pepper
yoghurt to serve

Fry the onions in the hot oil for about 10 minutes, stirring often, until they turn a rich golden brown.

Rinse the lentils and cook them in 1 litre water for 20 minutes. Wash the rice, drain and add to the lentils, together with the ground cumin and half the fried onions. Add salt and pepper to taste.

Cover and cook on a low heat for about 20 minutes or until the rice and lentils are tender.

Serve with the remaining onions sprinkled on top and yoghurt on the side.

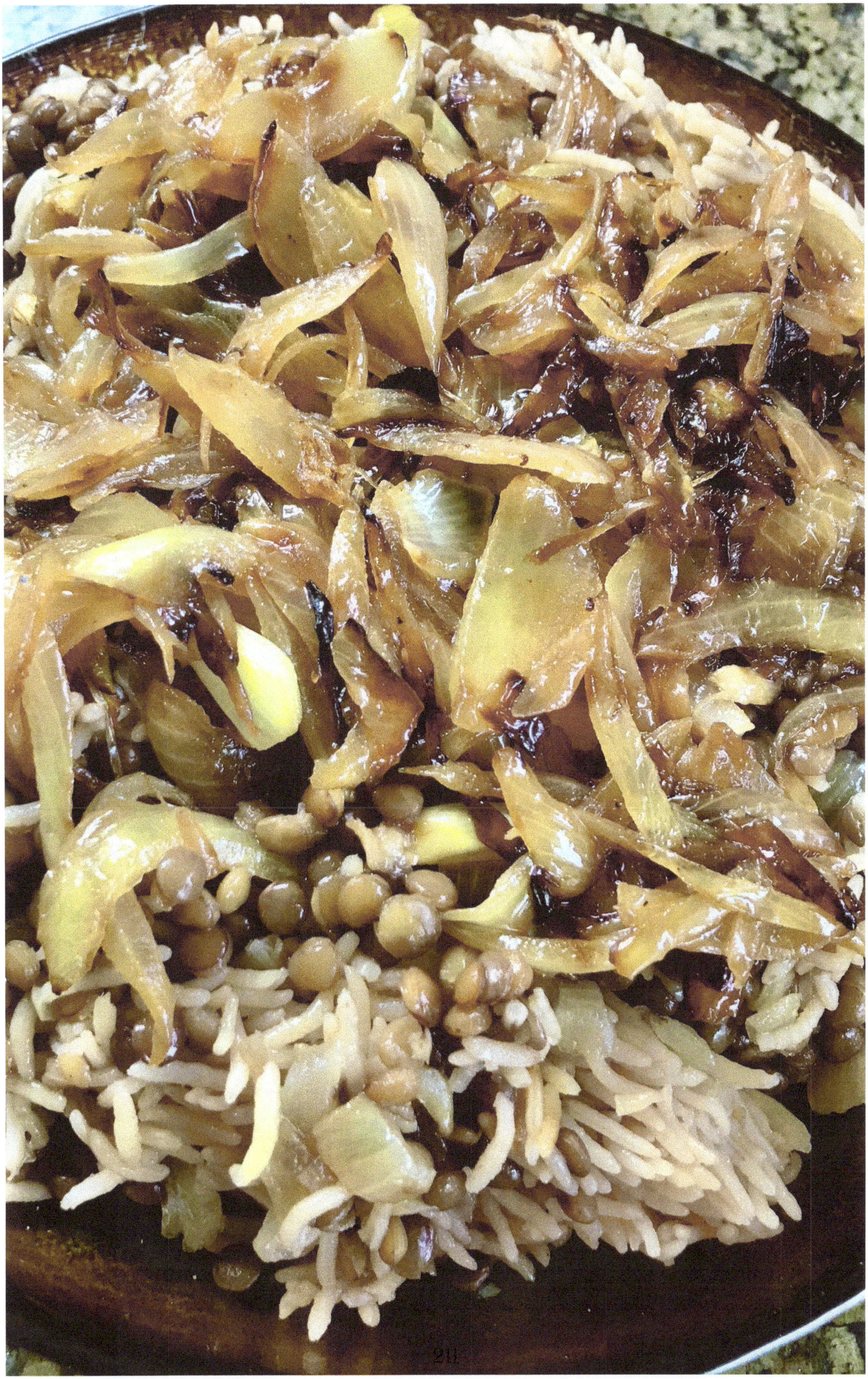

Koshari

(Egyptian rice, lentils and macaroni)

This is one of Egypt's most popular dishes, served in many restaurants, cafés and take aways. It's an unusual combination of rice, pasta and lentils and is simple to make because each component can be prepared separately. The dish is then assembled just before serving.

Ingredients
- 120g brown lentils, washed and drained
- 200g white long-grain rice or basmati rice
- 500ml water
- 120g canned chickpeas (optional)
- 1 cup raw macaroni pasta

Tomato sauce
- 1 tablespoon olive oil
- 1 medium onion, finely chopped
- 2 garlic cloves, crushed
- 375ml tomato sauce
- ½ teaspoon ground cumin
- ¼ teaspoon salt and pepper
- 250ml water

Onion garnish
- 60ml vegetable or sunflower oil
- 2 large onions, sliced

Cook the lentils - wash the rice and lentils well and drain. Place them in a pan and add 500ml water. Cover, bring to the boil and simmer for 20 minutes or until the rice is soft and the water has been absorbed.

Prepare the tomato sauce - heat the oil in a pan and fry the onion and garlic until golden brown. Add the tomato sauce, cumin, salt and pepper and water. Bring to the boil, lower the heat and simmer for 20-25 minutes until the sauce has reduced and thickened.

Prepare the onion garnish – heat the oil in a frying pan over medium heat and add the sliced onions. Fry for about 15 minutes or until the onion is soft and caramelised. Set aside.

Cook the macaroni at around the same time that you cook the rice. Fill a separate pan with water, add a sprinkle of salt and bring to a boil. Add the macaroni to the boiling water and cook until tender and drain.

Assemble the dish - combine the lentils and rice, macaroni and tomato sauce as follows:
1st layer – rice and lentils
2nd layer - macaroni
3rd layer – chickpeas, if using
4th layer – tomato sauce
5th layer – onion garnish

Note – the dish can be assembled and kept in a warm oven for 10-15 minutes until required.

Molokheya

(also known as the green soup)

Molokheya is one of Egypt's most famous dishes and derives its name from the leaf which gives it its distinctive taste. It looks like spinach because of its colour, but is nothing like it. Instead, it has a glutinous texture which some people may not like. It's impossible to find fresh molokheya in Europe, but it is now widely available dried and frozen (the latter is better) in all Middle Eastern and Turkish stores. It is served with rice and chicken, though Egyptians prefer rabbit. Molokheya is without doubt my favourite comfort food and I have it regularly in winter. I like it with rice and chicken in a bowl, topped with the soup.

1 kg chicken legs, or a mixture of chicken thighs and legs
2½ litres water
1 onion
salt and pepper
2 x 400g packs of frozen molokheya
(use straight from the freezer)

Garlic and coriander mixture (ta'aliya)
    6 garlic cloves, finely chopped
    3 tablespoons oil
    1 tablespoon ground coriander

Put the chicken in a large pot, cover with 2½ litres water and bring to the boil. Remove the scum, add the onion, salt and pepper, cover and cook for 1 hour until the chicken is tender. Remove the chicken from the pan, cool and shred it into pieces.

Make the oil, garlic and coriander mixture, known as ta'aliya in Arabic. Heat the oil in the frying pan over medium heat and add the garlic. Cook until lightly browned and add the coriander. Stir and remove from the heat.

Strain the chicken stock and return to the pot. Just before you are ready to serve, bring the broth to the boil, add 2 packs of frozen molokheya and simmer for about 5 minutes until the molokheya has thawed. Leave the pan uncovered and do not stir - just allow the liquid to heat gently until it reaches boiling point, then remove from the heat. Be careful not to overcook, as this can result in separation and a two-layered soup.

Add the garlic and coriander mix and stir to combine. If necessary, add some water to achieve the desired consistency and adjust the seasoning to taste.

Serve in bowls with rice or pita bread. The bread can be broken into pieces and then used to scoop the molokheya, or it can be added to the bowl of soup and eaten with a spoon.

Muhallabieh
(Almond custard)

Every Middle Eastern community has its own flavourings and presentation for this rice flour pudding, known as muhallabeya. It was traditionally served by Egyptian Jews during the festival of Shavuot. A Turkish version uses vanilla or lemon zest, whereas Iranians prefer cardamom. Egyptians generally use orange blossom water or rose water, with a sprinkling or almonds or pistachios.

**3 tablespoons rice flour
2 tablespoons cornflour
1 litre (1000ml) milk
120g sugar
110g ground almonds
2 tablespoons rose water
chopped pistachios to decorate**

Combine the rice flour and cornflour with 60ml milk to make a smooth paste. Add the sugar to the remaining milk, place in a pan and bring to the boil over medium heat.

Reduce the heat and add the flour paste gradually, stirring constantly with a wooden spoon so that it does not boil over - be careful not to burn the bottom of the pan.

Continue stirring for 10-15 minutes until the mixture thickens - it should coat the back of the spoon. Add the rose water and cook for a further 2 minutes. Remove from the heat and stir in the ground almonds.

Cool a little before dividing into individual ramekins. Refrigerate for 3-4 hours and serve decorated with chopped pistachios.

Muhallabieh bil amardeen
(Apricot pudding)

Amardeen is a fruit leather, which can be made with different fresh fruits, such as apricots, peaches, apples or pears. The most popular is a thick and sticky apricot paste that can be bought from Middle Eastern grocery shops. The packet looks like a folded letter inside a bright orange cellophane.

350g amardeen (apricot paste)
500ml water

3 tablespoons cornflour
60ml water
1 tablespoon sugar

Cut the amardeen sheets into small pieces and place in a large bowl. Cover with 500ml water. Leave to dissolve for several hours or overnight, stirring occasionally, until the apricot leather becomes a thick liquid.

In a cup, mix the cornflour with 60ml water to form a smooth paste. Place the apricot paste with its liquid in a pan and bring to the boil over medium heat. Add the cornflour paste, reduce the heat to a simmer and add the sugar. Stir continuously until the mixture has thickened, about 5 minutes.

Serve with cream, crème fraîche, or vanilla yogurt.

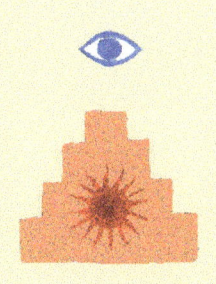

Ta'ameya

(Egyptian falafel)

About 16 -18 pieces

The Arabic word t'aameya translates as 'tasty little bits'. Falafel are generally made with chickpeas throughout the Middle East, but the Egyptian recipe, known as ta'ameya, uses fava beans instead, resulting in a lighter and moister texture. It is thought by some to be the original falafel and they are also shaped differently, looking more like small discs than balls. Ta'ameya, together with ful medames (a stew of cooked fava beans) are the most popular and well known street foods of Egypt.
We often had them in summer while on holiday with warm, freshly baked flatbread. A Sudanese friend made me some ta'ameya, which was delicious and looked and tasted exactly the same as the ones we had in Egypt.

Ta'ameya
   250g fava beans covered in cold water and soaked overnight
   3 garlic cloves, crushed
   ½ leek, finely chopped
   5 spring onions, finely chopped
   ½ teaspoon bicarbonate of soda
   2 teaspoons chickpea flour
   bunch of fresh leaf parsley, chopped
   bunch of fresh coriander, chopped
   1 teaspoon ground cumin
   salt and black pepper
   sunflower oil to deep fry

Yoghurt sauce
   250ml plain yoghurt
   4 tablespoons tahini
   juice of ½ lemon
   salt and pepper

Drain the fava beans well in a colander. Tip them into the food processor, along with all the other ingredients, Blitz for a couples of minutes until you have a rough paste. Tip into a bowl and refrigerate for 1 hour.

Divide the mixture into 16-18 pieces about the size of a golf ball. Press them down with your fingers to make small patties. Heat the oil and when it begins to sizzle fry the falafel in batches. Cook each side for 2-3 minutes until golden brown, then flip over and cook the other side.

Whisk all the ingredients for the sauce together and, if required, add a little cold water to obtain a smooth consistency. Serve with the tahini/yoghurt sauce and flatbread.

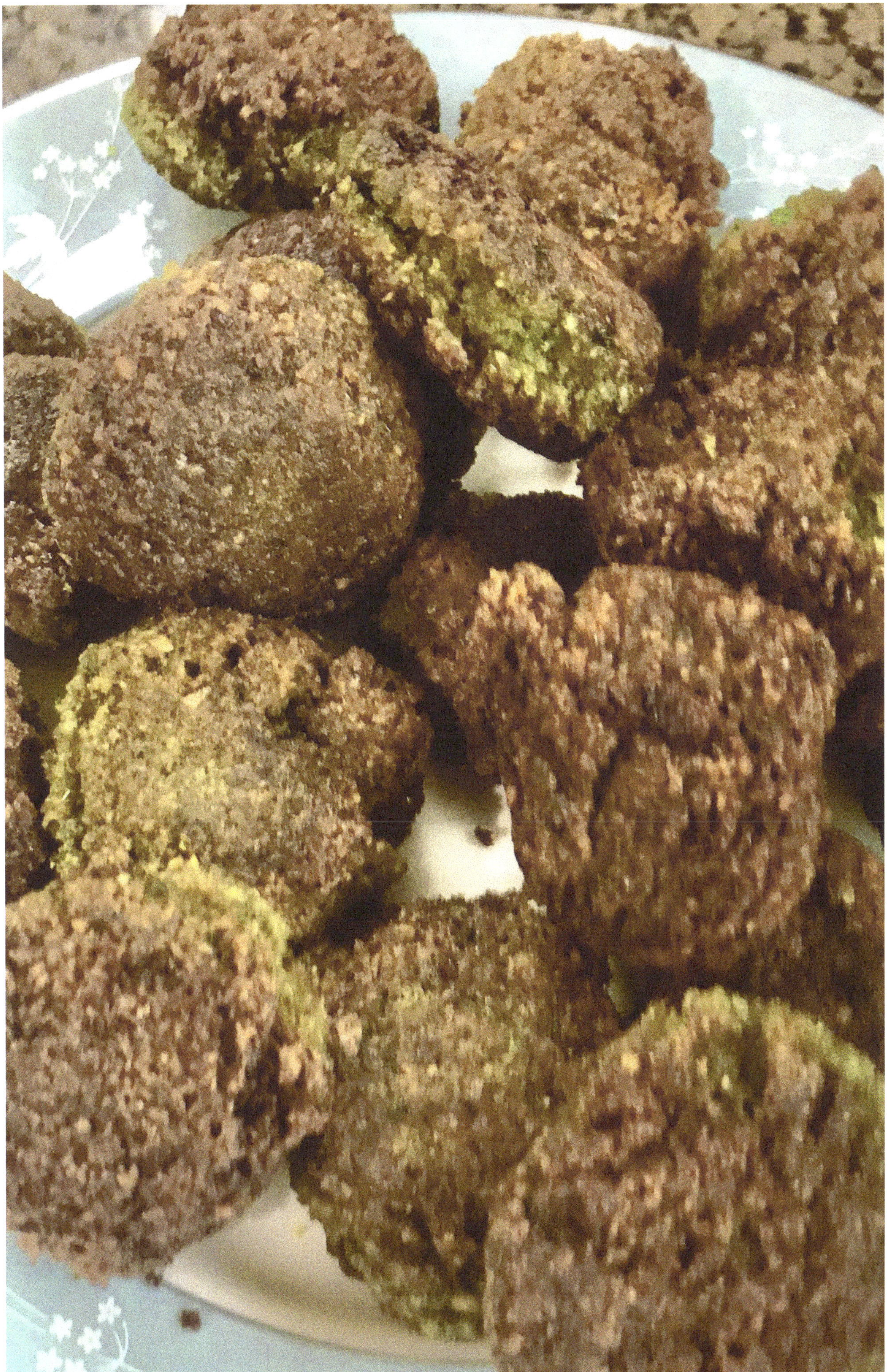

Om Ali

(Egyptian bread pudding)

This is an old Egyptian classic. Legend has it that Om Ali was the first wife of the sultan Ezz El Din Aybeck. When the sultan died, his second wife had a dispute with Om Ali, resulting in the second wife's death. To celebrate, Om Ali made this dessert and distributed it among the people of the land. Another version is that the name is thought to originate from a bread pudding which the Irish mistress of the Khedive Ismail, a Miss O'Malley, made for him. This dish can also be made with bread fried in butter.

120g filo pastry
140g raisins or sultanas
175g mixed flaked almonds, hazelnuts and almonds
1 litre (1000ml) milk
320ml double cream
100g sugar
2 teaspoons cinnamon

Preheat the oven to 160C/Gas Mark 2.

Break up the filo pastry sheets and cook them in the preheated oven for about 15 minutes until crisp and brown.

Crumble into a baking dish and sprinkle the raisins and nuts in between the layers. Bring the milk, cream and sugar to the boil and pour over the pastry. Sprinkle with cinnamon.

Return to the oven and bake at 220C/Gas Mark 8 for about 20 minutes or until the top is browned. Serve very hot.

Sharkaseya

(Walnut sauce for chicken)

Sharkaseya is typically served from the kitchens of Egyptian families with Turkish ties or ancestors. It is a rich and creamy sauce served on top of boiled chicken, accompanied by white rice.

Walnut sauce
  2 large slices white bread, crusts removed and cut into small pieces
  2 cups walnuts, finely chopped
  3 cups chicken broth

Garlic butter
  60g butter
  6 garlic cloves, crushed and minced
  2 teaspoons ground coriander
  ½ teaspoon salt
  paprika for decoration

To make the walnut sauce - remove the crusts from the bread, cut into small chunks and soak in a little water for 30 minutes. Squeeze out any water.

Finely chop the walnuts in a food processor. Add the bread and 1 cup of the chicken broth. Pulse again until the ingredients are well mixed. Transfer to a large saucepan and add the remaining 2 cups of broth.

Mix well over medium heat, lower the heat and simmer for 25-30 minutes until the mixture reaches a thick consistency - it should be like a thick creamy sauce, so you may have to add more broth.

To make the garlic butter – in a small pan, melt the butter and add the garlic and coriander.

Stir fry for 3 minutes. Add the garlic butter to the sauce, mix well and add salt to taste.

Sprinkle some paprika over the top to give the mixture some colour.

Zalabia

(Egyptian syrup drenched doughnuts)

Makes around 40

This is an Egyptian sweet which is made by deep frying dough and then, as with so many Middle Eastern pastries, soaking it in a thick sugar syrup. It reminds me of a very similar sweet, which we called loukomadis. We had it as a special breakfast treat whilst on holiday. We sometimes stayed in a seaside resort called Ras el Bar, which was pretty basic, but my parents and their group of friends found the rustic charm quite appealing. Every morning without fail, the vendor would make his appearance and we were treated to the hot loukomadis, dripping with sugar syrup Loukomadis, like zalabia, should be crispy and crunchy on the outside and chewy on the inside and should only be eaten when hot.

For the dough
- 2 teaspoons dried yeast
- 1 teaspoon sugar
- 2 tablespoons warm water
- 475g plain flour, sifted
- 2 cups warm water
- vegetable or sunflower oil for deep frying

For the syrup
- 400g sugar
- 300ml water
- juice of ½ lemon
- 4 drops vanilla essence

Begin by making the syrup – combine the sugar, water and lemon juice in a pan and place over medium heat to dissolve the sugar. Bring the syrup just to the boil and simmer for 10 minutes. Turn off the heat and leave to cool.

Place 2 tablespoons warm water in a cup. Sprinkle the yeast and sugar. Stir and leave in a warm place for 10 minutes until bubbles form.

Sift the flour in a large bowl, make a well in the centre and add the yeast liquid. Gradually add 2 cups warm water and mix together to form a sticky consistency. Cover the batter with a tea towel and leave to rise in a warm place for 2 hours or until the dough doubles in size.

Heat enough oil for deep frying over a high heat. When the oil is just starting to smoke, drop a teaspoonful of batter into the hot oil. It should expand immediately. Add several spoonfuls so that you are cooking the doughnuts in batches. Turn them over when they are golden on one side.

As soon as each batch is cooked, remove the doughnuts and place them directly into the sugar syrup, turning them over to make sure they are fully coated. Leave for a few minutes, then remove from the syrup and drain in a colander. Repeat for each batch.
Serve immediately.

Note - For a healthier alternative, omit the sugar syrup and coat with honey or roll in caster sugar.

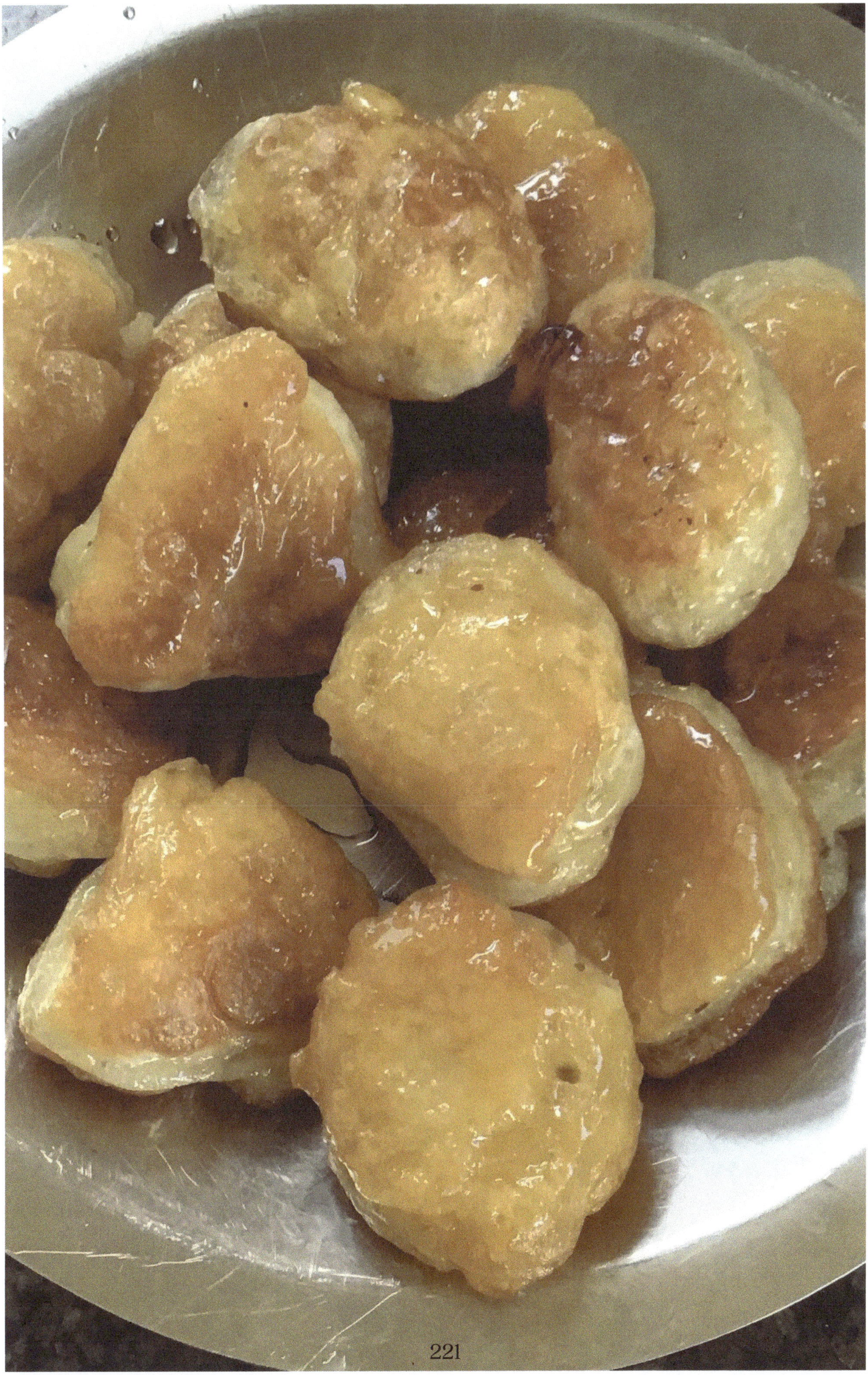

Ghorayebah
(Egyptian butter biscuits)

Makes 25 pieces

Every household always had a tin of these crumbly, melt in the mouth biscuits, along with menenas (our version of ma'amoul), to welcome visitors. This involved an amusing ritual, which was part of a certain etiquette. When the lady of the house offered the guest more pastries, it was considered polite to refuse initially. The host would insist and would continue to do so for a short while, until the guest was 'persuaded' to have more. My mother continued to do this with her Egyptian friends, even when we lived in London.

250g unsalted butter, softened
80g icing sugar
½ teaspoon vanilla
1 tablespoon vegetable oil
275- 300g plain flour, sifted
½ teaspoon baking powder
25 whole blanched almonds (optional)
icing sugar for dredging

Preheat the oven to 180C/Gas Mark.
Line two large trays with baking parchment or greaseproof paper.

In a mixing bowl, beat the butter, icing sugar and vanilla. Add 1 tablespoon oil and baking powder, then gradually add the flour until the dough forms a ball that comes away from the bowl.

Shape the mixture into small balls the size of a walnut. Arrange them on the baking sheet about 2½cm (1 inch) apart – this is important, as they spread. If using, place a whole blanched almond in the middle of each one.

Bake for 15 minutes. They should still be white and soft and will firm up when they cool.

Dredge with icing sugar when they have hardened.

Basbousa bil laban zabadi

(Semolina cake with yoghurt)

Makes 24 squares

Basbousa was a pastry traditionally served with tea or coffee in Egypt. It is one of the many Middle Eastern cakes which relies on a final coating of cooled sugar syrup to soften and sweeten it. There are many ways of making it, the most popular being with yoghurt, coconut or almonds. I have used a mixture of yoghurt and coconut.

For the syrup
250/300g sugar
500ml (2 cups) water
juice of ½ lemon
3- 4 drops vanilla essence

For the basbousa
125g fine semolina
100g coarse semolina
150ml yoghurt
25g desiccated coconut, mixed with 2 tablespoons of milk
225g sugar
1 teaspoon baking powder
110g unsalted butter, melted plus extra for greasing

Start by making the syrup – combine the sugar, water and lemon juice in a pan. Bring to the boil, lower the heat and simmer for 10 minutes until the syrup has reduced and thickened. Add the vanilla essence, let the syrup cool and place it in the fridge until the basbousa is ready to come out of the oven.

Preheat the oven to 180C/Gas Mark 4.
Grease and line a 15 x 25cm (6 x 10 inch) cake pan.

Make the basbousa - combine the two semolinas, coconut mixture, sugar, yoghurt and baking powder. Add the melted butter and mix thoroughly.

Put the mixture in the cake pan and press firmly into place. Place in the centre of the oven for 50- 60 minutes or until golden brown. When cooked, remove the cake from the oven and cut into diamonds or squares. Immediately pour the cold sugar syrup over the hot basbousa.

Note - this dessert tastes even better the day after it has been made, when the syrup has been fully absorbed.

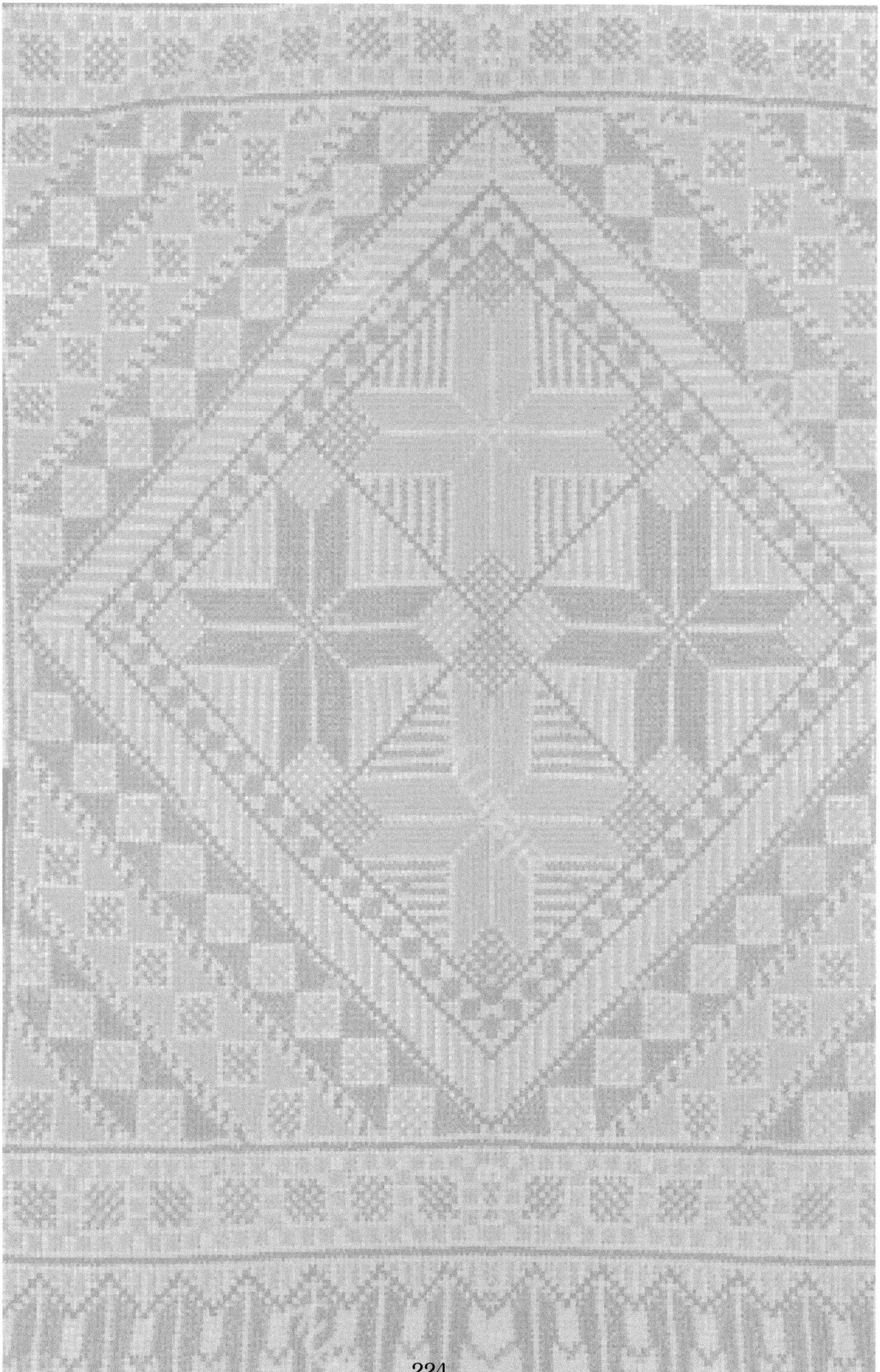

PASSOVER DISHES
Pessah

Passover orange cake

This is a Judeo-Spanish cake which can be made for Passover, as it does not have any flour. Sephardic Jews like using oranges in cakes and the addition of orange blossom water gives it a Middle Eastern touch. Baking powder can be substituted with a kosher brand.

3 medium oranges
6 large eggs
240g caster sugar
2 tablespoon orange blossom water
1 teaspoon baking powder
260g ground almonds

Preheat the oven to 180C/Gas Mark 4.
Grease a 22cm (9 inch) springform cake tin and line with baking parchment.

Wash the oranges, cover with water and boil for 1½ hours or until they are very soft. Drain, allow to cool, remove the seeds and purée them in a food processor.

Beat the eggs with the sugar until pale and fluffy. Add the orange blossom water, baking powder and almond mixture. Lastly, fold in the puréed oranges and mix thoroughly. Transfer to the prepared cake tin.

Bake in the preheated oven for 1 hour or until a skewer inserted in the middle comes out clean.

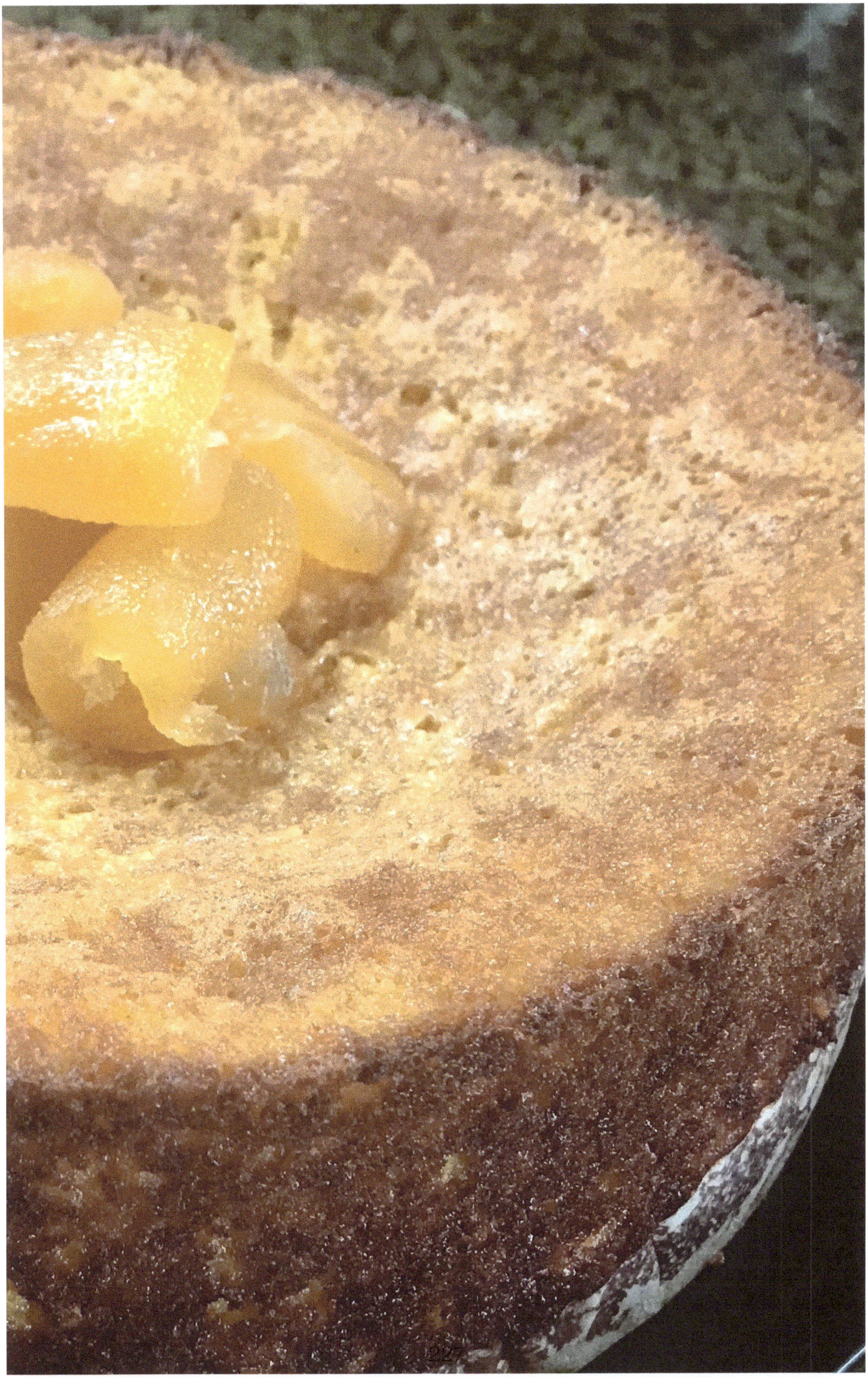

Beignets de Pâques

(Matzo fritters in syrup)

Along with haroset, coconut jam and special biscuits, these matzo fritters were our quintessential Passover treat when I was growing up. Everyone had a recipe for these, but of course, the ones I remember best are my mother's. These beignets are similar to the Spanish bimuelos and very different from matzo brei, as matzo meal is used instead of matzah sheets.

4 eggs, separated
2 tablespoons sugar
pinch of salt
grated zest of 1 lemon
80-90g medium matzo meal
vegetable or sunflower oil for frying

For the syrup
150g sugar
300ml water
125ml honey
juice of ½ lemon

Make the syrup first – place the sugar, water, honey and lemon juice in a medium pan and bring to the boil. Simmer for about 10 minutes or until the syrup has thickened.

Make the fritters – beat the egg whites until foaming, add 2 tablespoons sugar and continue beating until they form stiff peaks. In a separate bowl, beat the egg yolks with the salt and lemon zest and fold in the egg whites. Fold in the matzo meal and mix carefully to incorporate it.

Heat enough oil in a large frying pan to deep fry. When it begins to sizzle, drop in heaped tablespoons of the egg and matzo meal mixture. Fry over medium heat, turning the fritters to make sure they are brown all over. Drain on kitchen paper

While the fritters are still hot, dip them in the sugar syrup, let them soak for about 10 minutes, and lift out with a slotted spoon.

Serve hot or cold.

Chocolate, almond and pear cake

The classic recipe for this cake is chocolate and almonds, which is how I remember having it. I have added the pears because it makes a change from a plain sponge and I like the combination of pears and almonds. The pears must not be overripe and can be substituted with apples.

240g dark chocolate
175g unsalted butter, softened, plus extra for greasing
125g caster sugar
210g ground almonds
4 large eggs, separated
2 large or 3 medium pears, peeled, cored and sliced
pinch of salt

Preheat the oven to 180C/Gas Mark 4.
Line the base of a 22cm (9 inch) springform cake tin with baking parchment and grease with a little butter.

Melt 175g chocolate in a bowl over a pan of simmering water.

Cream 125g of the butter with the sugar in a bowl until fluffy and mousse-like. Stir in the ground almonds, followed by the egg yolks, one at a time, mixing well after each addition. Fold in the diced pears and melted chocolate and stir to combine.

In a separate clean bowl, whisk the egg whites with a pinch of salt until stiff but not dry. Fold gently into the chocolate mixture until there are no white streaks. Pour the cake batter into the tin.

Bake for 50 minutes, until firm to the touch. Cool for a few minutes in the tin, then turn onto a wire rack to finish cooling. Don't worry if the cake sinks slightly and cracks appear, as you are going to cover the surface anyway.

Put the remaining 50g butter and 75g chocolate in a bowl over a pan of simmering water. Once melted, stir and spread over the top of the cake, allowing the mixture to run down the sides.

Serve with crème fraîche or ice cream, if you wish.

My mother's Passover biscuits

My mother baked these biscuits for Passover every year without fail and I always looked forward to them. They are easy to make, but it's difficult to get the right crunchiness, as this depends on your oven and the size of the baking tray. My mother's were just right, not too hard but crunchy enough to dunk in your tea — the thinner the biscuits are, the crunchier they will be.

5 large eggs
230g sugar
100ml sunflower or vegetable oil
215g matzo meal

Preheat the oven to 160C/Gas Mark 3.
Grease and line a 30 x 20cm (12 x 8 inch) baking tray.

Beat the eggs with the sugar for 5-8 minutes, until the mixture is light and fluffy. Add the oil and mix for a couple more minutes. Fold in the matzo meal and combine through. Pour into the baking tray.

Bake for 45 minutes initially. Take the biscuits out of the oven while their colour is still light.

Cut them through in small squares and return to the oven for another 30 minutes, until they are darker and feel crunchy.

Turn off the heat and leave the tray in the hot oven for 15 minutes.

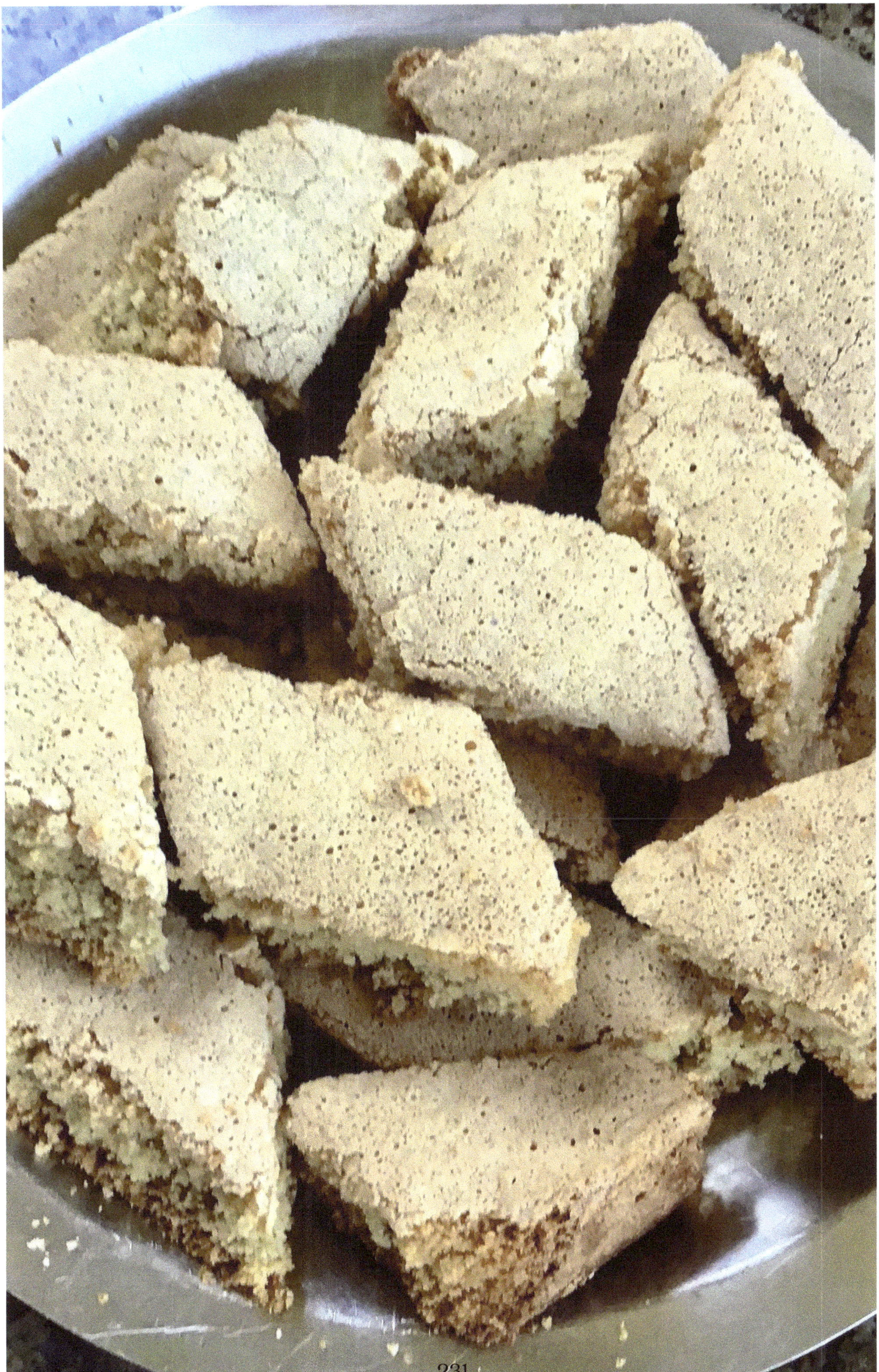

Chocolate and macaroon cake

This recipe is adapted from one in Denise Phillips' book New Flavours on the Jewish Table. It's a Passover cake, as the macaroon-style biscuit contains no flour and it uses egg white as a leavening agent. It can also be enjoyed all year round.

200g unsalted butter, plus extra for greasing
140g medium matzo meal or breadcrumbs
160g amaretti biscuits
120g dark chocolate, broken into chunks
200g caster sugar
1 teaspoon almond essence
5 eggs, separated
180g toasted flaked almonds
icing sugar, for dusting

Preheat the oven to 180C/ Gas Mark 4.
Line a 22cm (9 inch) cake tin with baking parchment and grease with butter. Dust with matzo meal and shake off any excess.

Put the amaretti biscuits in a food processor and whiz to form crumbs. Reserve 3 tablespoons for the topping.
Place the chocolate in a bowl with 1 tablespoon water and heat over a pan of simmering water, stirring, until melted.

Cream the butter with all but 2 tablespoons of the sugar and the almond essence. Add the egg yolks one at a time, followed by the matzo meal and amaretti biscuits crumble. Stir in the melted chocolate and toasted almonds.

In a clean, grease-free bowl whisk the egg whites until stiff but not dry. Add the 2 tablespoons sugar and whisk again. Fold 1 tablespoon of the egg whites into the chocolate mixture, then fold in the remaining whites.

Spoon the mixture into the prepared cake tin, sprinkle with the reserved biscuit crumbs and bake for about 40 minutes or until a skewer inserted in the centre comes out clean.

Allow the cake to cool for 10 minutes, then invert it on to a serving plate and remove the paper. To serve, dust with icing sugar.

Clementine cake

The use of boiled clementines produces a very moist and citrus-flavoured result. This is a very easy cake to make all year round and it is also suitable for Passover, as it uses ground almonds instead of flour — just replace the baking powder with a kosher brand.

4 clementines, skin on, weighing about 375g
6 large eggs
225g sugar
250g ground almonds
1 heaped teaspoon baking powder
100g dark chocolate, grated

Put the clementines into a saucepan, cover with cold water, bring to the boil and simmer for about 1½ hours. Drain and set aside. When cool, cut the clementines in half and remove the pips. Pulp everything, including skins and pith, in a food processor.

Preheat the oven to 190C/Gas Mark 5.
Grease and line a 20cm (8 inch) springform cake tin.

Beat the eggs with the sugar. Add the ground almonds and baking powder, mix well and fold in the pulped clementines. Stir well.

Pour the cake mixture into the cake tin and bake for 1 hour or until a skewer inserted into the centre of the cake comes out clean. Cover the cake with foil after about 40 minutes to prevent the top from burning.

Remove from the oven and immediately grate the chocolate over the top while still in the tin. Leave to cool completely.

Note - the cake can be stored in an airtight container for 3 days. It is best served the day after it is made , so that the flavours of the clementines and ground almonds have had a chance to blend.

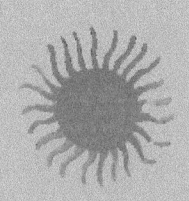

Citrus lavender cake

This cake makes a delicious dessert, especially if served with some crème fraîche. The combination of the citrus fruit and lavender works great and the lavender is not overpowering.

200g unsalted butter softened
200g caster sugar
3 eggs, separated
1 teaspoon vanilla extract
2 teaspoons baking powder
grated zest of 1 orange
grated zest of 2 lemons
2 teaspoons lavender
300g ground almonds
100ml natural yoghurt

For the syrup
90g caster sugar
juice of 1 orange
juice of 2 lemons
1 teaspoon dried lavender

Preheat the oven to 180C/Gas Mark 4.
Grease a 22cm (9 inch) cake tin and line the bottom with baking parchment.

Cream together the butter and sugar in an electric mixer until light and fluffy. Add the egg yolks, one at a time, mixing well between each addition. Add the baking powder, orange and lemon zest, dried lavender and ground almonds. Mix well, then stir in the yoghurt.

In a separate bowl, whisk the egg whites until they hold stiff peaks, then fold them gently into the cake batter. Pour the batter into the cake tin. Bake for 50 minutes, or until a skewer inserted into the centre comes out clean. Cover the top with foil after 20 minutes if it starts browning too much.

To make the syrup, put the sugar, orange and lemon juices and dried lavender into a saucepan. Bring to the boil and simmer until you have a thick syrup.

When the cake comes out of the oven, pierce it all over with a skewer or cocktail stick. Drizzle the syrup when the cake is still warm.

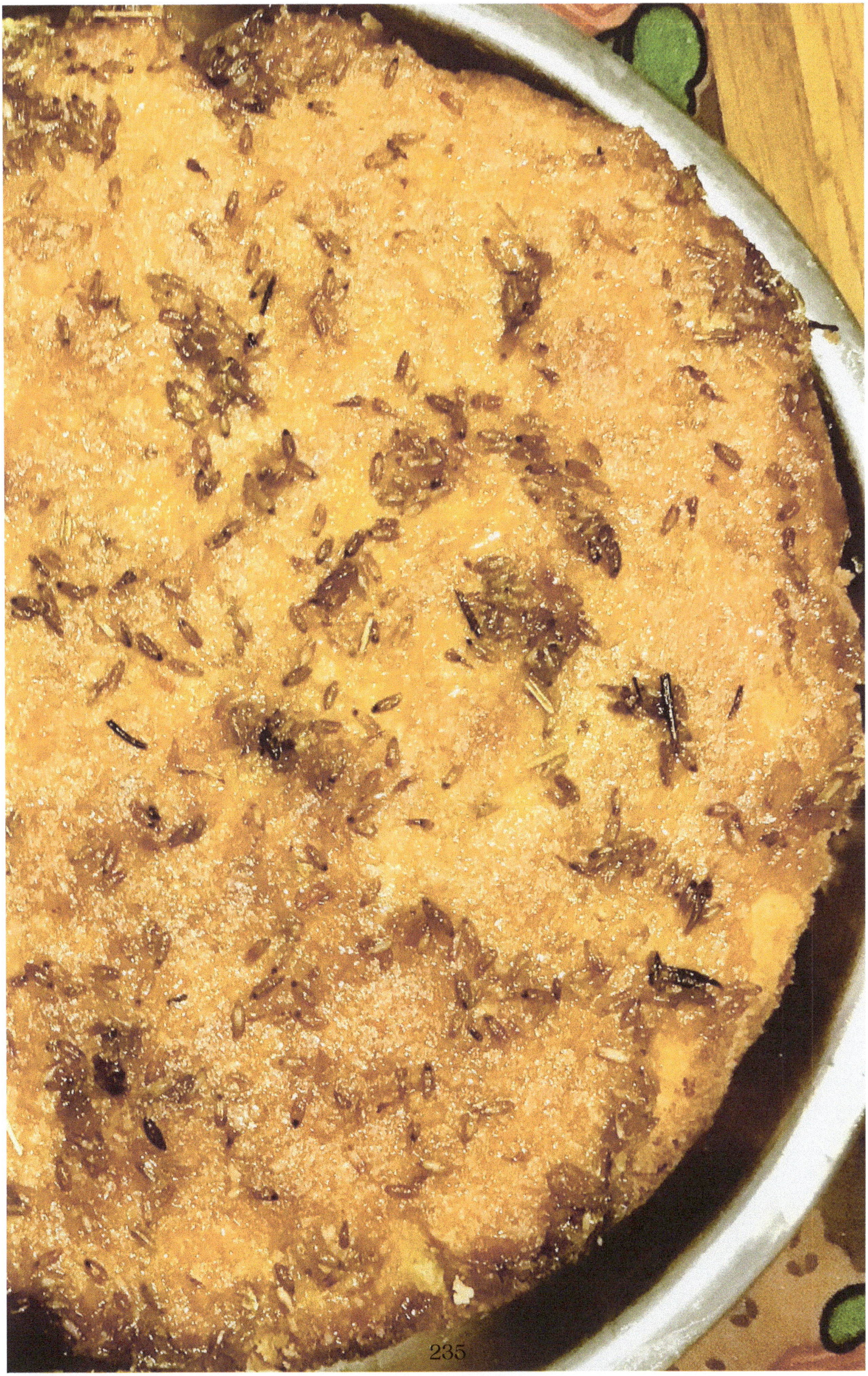

Haroset
(Date and raisin preserve)

Haroset is the traditional date and raisin paste eaten at Passover. It is symbolic of the mortar used by the Israelite slaves when they lay bricks for Pharaoh's monuments. There are numerous versions for this recipe, depending where you originally come from and every family had its own favourite. Ashkenazi Jews favour an apple-walnut mixture, whereas the classic Sephardic recipe uses dates and raisins and sometimes walnuts and apples.

In Egypt, the preparation of the haroset was a laborious task. Dates had to be pitted and raisins thoroughly washed several times. These were then put into a large pot and left to simmer on a very low heat for twenty four hours. Sugar and vinegar were added and the result was a thick, reddish brown, delicious haroseth – I used to look forward to the jam all year. The recipe below is my family's and the one which was usually made by Egyptian Jews. No sugar is required, as the fruit is already sweet enough.

250g pitted dates
250g large sultanas or flame raisins
1-2 cups water
120ml sweet red Passover wine (optional)

Chop the dates Put them in a bowl with about 1 cup water, or enough to cover and leave them to soak overnight. The following day, bring the mixture to a boil in the same water and simmer over a very low heat, stirring constantly with a wooden spoon to prevent the fruit from burning. Squash to a smooth paste against the sides of the pan. Just before using, add the wine, if using and stir well.

Note – you can make the paste even smoother by puréeing it in a food processor. If you prefer to keep the preserve longer than a few weeks, cook it with about 200g sugar.

A variation includes adding 2 sweet apples, peeled and grated, 30g ground almonds, 1 teaspoon ground cinnamon and ½ teaspoon ground mixed spice to the soaked fruit before cooking.

Hazelnut Passover cake

Passover cakes are different because they are light and airy, being made with nuts and no flour. We look forward to them all year and every year, without fail, we promise ourselves that we will continue to make them on a regular basis. Somehow, this never happens and perhaps this is just as well - they are special, as is Passover, so they should be reserved for the festival. This is a classic Passover cake and any ground nuts can be used.

6 large eggs, separated
170g caster sugar
200g ground hazelnuts
30g fine matzo meal
juice of 1 orange

Preheat the oven to 180C/Gas Mark 4.
Grease a 20cm (8 inch) cake tin and line with parchment paper.

Separate the eggs. Beat the egg yolks with half the sugar until light and fluffy, about 5 minutes.

Fold in the ground hazelnuts and matzo meal.

Beat the egg whites with the remaining sugar until soft peaks form. Add the sugar 1 tablespoon at a time and continue to beat until you have stiff peaks and the mixture holds when the bowl is turned upside down.

Gently fold the egg whites into the egg and nut mixture.

Spoon the batter into the cake tin and level off. Bake in the preheated oven for 25 minutes or until a skewer instead in the middle of the cake comes out clean.

Cool and use a skewer to pierce the top of the cake here and there. Drizzle with a little orange juice to moisten.

Note – you can split the cake in half and fill with whipped cream, or you can serve it plain or with cream on the side.

Sablés de Pâques
(Passover biscuits)

Makes around 45 sandwiched biscuits

My mother used to make these every year for Passover and called them sablés de Paques. Strictly speaking they are not as crumbly as authentic French sablés, as they are made with matzo meal. She added an extra touch by sandwiching them together with either jam or chocolate.

For the biscuits
- 170g unsalted butter
- 340g sugar
- 3 large eggs
- 340g potato flour
- 340g fine matzo meal

30g cocoa powder

For the filling
- apricot or strawberry jam
- or chocolate ganache made with 100ml double cream and 100g dark chocolate

Cream the butter and sugar until fluffy. Add the eggs, one at a time, followed by the potato flour and matzo meal. Mix well until all the ingredients are blended.

Divide the mixture into two equal parts. Add 30g cocoa powder to one part and work with your hands until it is well blended. Wrap both mixtures with cling film and refrigerate for 30 minutes.

Prepare the chocolate ganache – break the chocolate into small pieces. Heat the cream in a pan until it's very hot and blend well with the chocolate until you have a smooth consistency. Refrigerate for 15 minutes, no more as the ganache will harden and make it difficult to spread.

Preheat the oven to 170C/Gas Mark 3.
Line two baking trays with baking parchment.

Take the biscuit mixture out of the fridge and make the biscuits, using biscuit cutters of your choice. The easiest way is to flatten small lumps of the mixture on a board and cut into the desired shape.

Bake in the preheated oven for 10-12 minutes. The biscuits will harden once they cool.

Sandwich the biscuits when they have cooled. Microwave the jam for a few seconds to make it easier to spread and use the ganache to sandwich the chocolate biscuits.

Note – you can halve the recipe if you don't want a large quantity of biscuits. The ganache can be substituted with any ready-made chocolate spread.

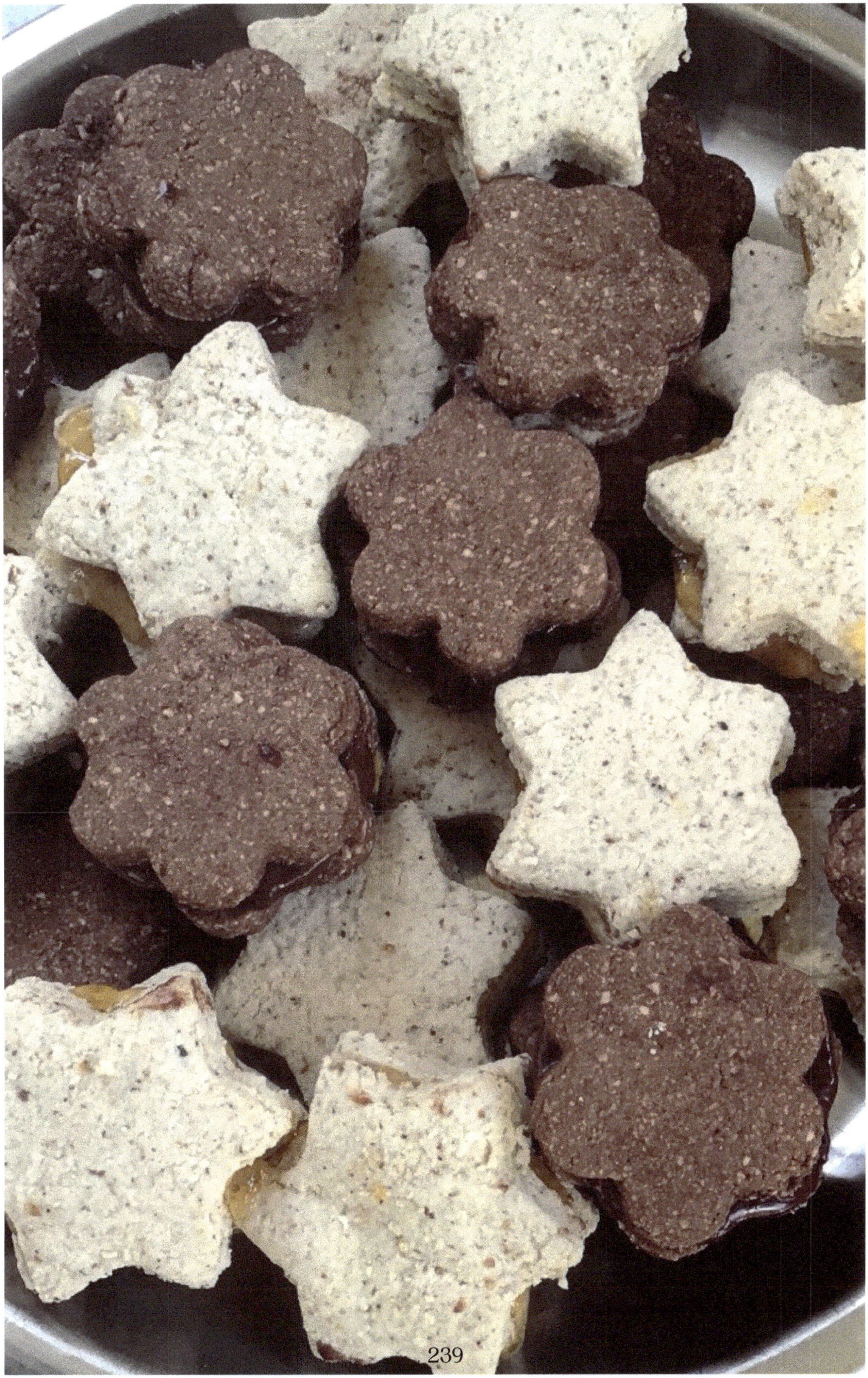

Matzah pudding

Serves 9

4 matzah sheets
2 apples
150g soft brown sugar
120g mixed dried fruit
2 tablespoons ground almonds
2 teaspoons mixed spice
75g unsalted butter or margarine, melted, plus extra for greasing
4 large eggs, beaten

This is the Passover equivalent of bread pudding and it's also a good way of using any leftover matzah.

Preheat the oven to 180C/Gas Mark 4.
Grease a 22 x 22cm (9 x 9 inch) baking dish with butter.

Soak the mixed fruit in 200ml apple juice for 15 minutes, then drain.

Break up the matzah sheets into bite-sized pieces and soak them in cold water until soft, about 10 minutes. Squeeze the liquid out of the matzah and discard the water. Set aside.

Peel, core and roughly chop the apples. Place the apple pieces in a large bowl with 125g of the sugar, the drained mixed dried fruit, ground almonds, mixed spice, melted butter or margarine and eggs and mix well. Add the matzah and stir to combine.

Pour the batter into the baking dish and top with the remaining 25g sugar. Bake for 50 minutes or until set.

Serve warm at room temperature, cut into squares.

Passover coconut cake

250g desiccated coconut
240ml fresh orange juice
290g sugar
5 tablespoons sunflower oil
6 eggs, separated

This is my favourite Passover cake. I love the taste of coconut anyway, but what makes it unusual is the creamy mixture you get when the cake is inverted. It's a great dessert to serve after the Passover meal.

Preheat the oven to 180C/Gas Mark 4.
Grease and line a 22cm (9 inch) cake tin.

In a bowl, mix the coconut and orange juice. Leave for about 20 minutes until the coconut is soft.

Separate the eggs. Beat the egg yolks with the sugar until light and fluffy. Add the sunflower oil and the coconut and orange juice mixture and mix well.

In a clean bowl, beat the egg whites with a hand held mixer until stiff and fold into the egg mixture.

Transfer the mixture to the cake tin and bake in the preheated oven for 45 minutes or until a skewer inserted in the middle comes out clean.

Turn upside down on a plate while the cake is still warm. The creamy egg mixture, which will have sunk to the bottom, will come out on top.

Raisin streusel cake

This cake takes a little longer to make than the classic Passover ones, mainly because of the addition of the streusel. The result is worth it though.

For the streusel
- 60g unsalted butter
- 135g sugar
- 3 teaspoons ground cardamom
- 1½ teaspoons cinnamon
- 60g matzo meal

For the cake
- 60g matzo meal
- 90g potato flour
- ½ teaspoon salt
- ½ teaspoon ground ginger
- 5 large egg whites
- 200g + 60g sugar
- 5 large egg yolks
- 60g unsalted butter, melted
- 2 tablespoons lemon zest
- 1½ tablespoons lemon juice
- 100g raisins

Preheat the oven to 180c/Gas Mark 4.
Grease a 22cm (9 inch) cake tin and line with baking parchment.

For the streusel - mix together the butter, sugar and spices in a medium bowl. Gradually add the matzo meal and mix until crumbly. Divide the mixture in two.

Spread half the streusel on a baking sheet and bake for 10 minutes until the top is golden. Cool and break into bits.

For the cake - combine the first 4 dry ingredients in a bowl and set aside.

Using an electric mixer, beat the egg whites in a small bowl until soft peaks form. Gradually add 200g sugar and beat until stiff, but not dry. Set aside.

Beat the egg yolks and 60g sugar in another bowl until the mixture is thick and slowly dissolving ribbons form when the beaters are lifted. At a low speed, add the melted butter, lemon zest and juice. Fold in the dry ingredients first, followed by the egg whites in 2 additions.

Pour half the batter in the prepared cake tin and sprinkle with the baked streusel and half the raisins. Spread the remaining cake batter over and sprinkle with the unbaked streusel and remaining raisins.

Bake in the preheated oven until a tester inserted in the middle of the cake comes out dry, about 40 minutes.

Cool on a rack. Cover with foil and let the cake stand for 1 hour to soften the topping.

Passover apple cake

Any sweet red apple variety is good for this recipe. The apples can be substituted with pears, as long as they are not too ripe. Any nuts can be used for the topping, but I prefer roasted hazelnuts.

For the cake
- 3 large eggs
- 175g caster sugar
- 60ml vegetable oil
- 175g fine matzo meal
- 4 apples, peeled and finely diced

For the topping
- 85g mixed nuts, finely chopped
- 100g caster sugar
- 1½ teaspoon ground cinnamon

Preheat the oven to 180C/ Gas Mark 4.
Grease a 20cm (8 inch) cake tin and line with baking parchment.

Prepare the topping – in a small bowl, mix the chopped nuts with the sugar and cinnamon (you can use a food processor to pulse the nuts for a few seconds). Set aside.

Wash and peel the apples, then dice them finely.

In an electric mixer or a hand held one, beat the eggs, sugar and oil until the mixture is light and airy. Using a large metal spoon, fold in the matzah meal and mix well into the batter.

At the last moment, drop in the finely diced apples and blend smoothly.

Pour the mixture into the cake tin. Sprinkle the topping mixture over the batter mix.

Bake in the preheated oven for approximately 1 hour, until a skewer inserted in the middle comes out clean.

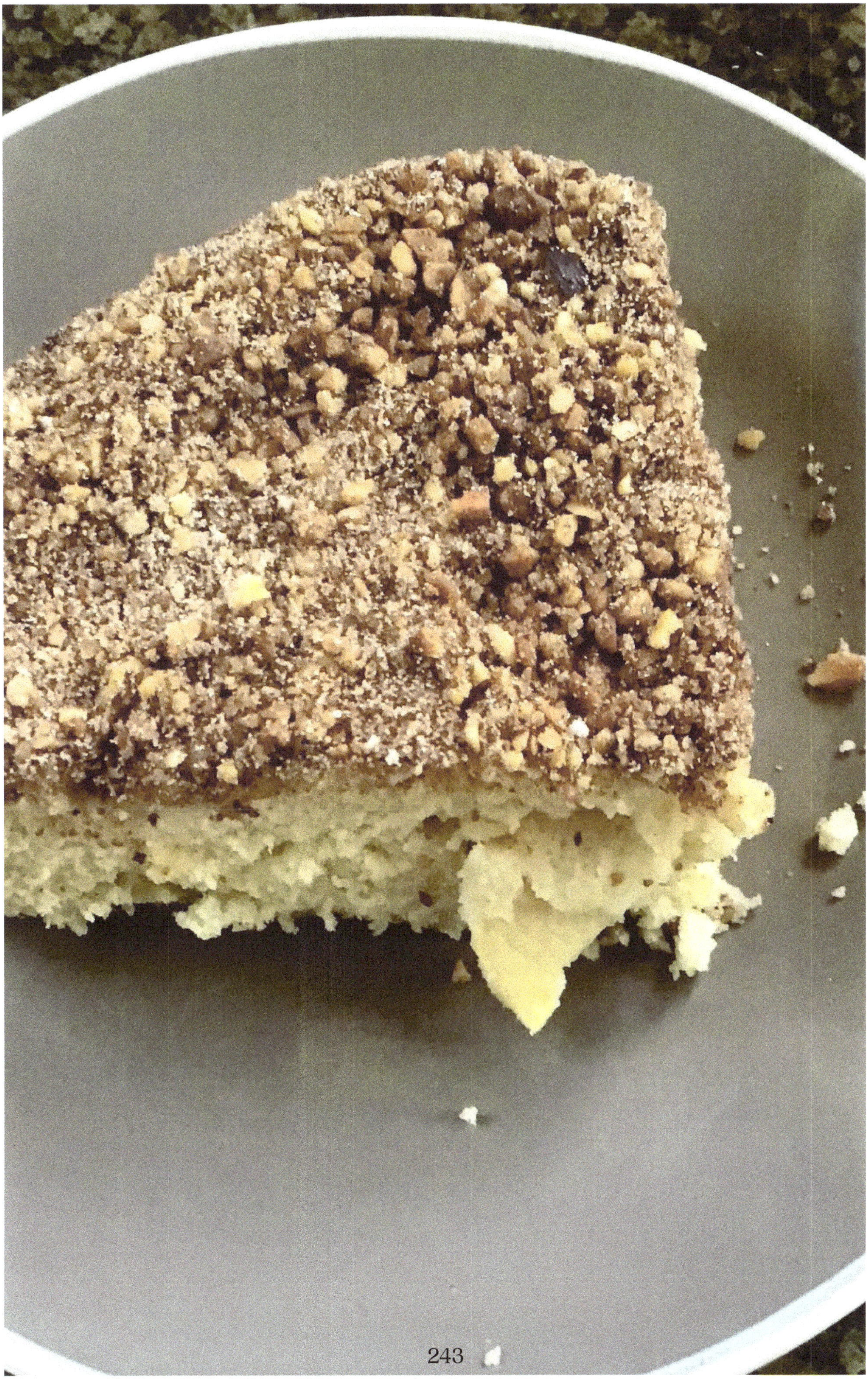

SAVOURY & SWEET PASTRIES

*Cosas de orno
Almoajanat
&
Cosas de masa
Moajanat
helwa*

Borek with aubergine filling

Makes 35

Borek is a Turkish version of the Arabic sambusak and the Sephardic borekas. The difference is that the dough is made with butter only, as opposed to oil or a mixture of butter and oil. The dough is adapted from a recipe I found in Claudia Roden's Book of Middle Eastern Food..

For the dough
    450g plain flour, sifted
    ½ teaspoon salt
    225g unsalted butter
    2 eggs, beaten
    about 2 tablespoons water

For the filling
    500g aubergines
    150g feta cheese, crumbled
    100g grated cheese, gruyère or cheddar

Preheat the oven to 170C/Gas Mark 3.

Prepare the filling – wash the aubergines, prick them all over with a fork and roast them in a preheated oven until they are soft, about 40 minutes. When cool, peel the aubergines, squeeze out all the bitter juices and mash them with a fork.

Add the crumbled feta cheese and grated cheese and mix well.

Prepare the dough – sift the flour and salt into a large mixing bowl. Work the butter into the flour, first with your fingers, then by rubbing the mixture lightly between the palms of your hands - the mixture should have the texture of breadcrumbs. Alternatively, you can quickly blitz the ingredients in a food processor.

Add the eggs and work them in lightly. Add the water gradually, working it gently until the dough forms a soft ball which comes away from the bowl. Stop as soon as this happens, as the dough should be worked as little as possible. Cover the bowl with a damp cloth and leave in a cool place for at least 1 hour.

Roll the dough out on a lightly floured board with a lightly floured rolling pin. Roll out as thinly as possible and cut rounds of about 8cm (3 inch) in diameter with a pastry cutter. Alternatively, take walnut sized lumps of dough, roll into a round ball and flatten out as thinly as possible between the palms of your hands.

Put a heaped teaspoon of filling in the centre of each circle. Fold the pastry over to make a half moon shape and pinch the edges together to seal them. Pinch and fold over all round the edges to make a festoon effect. Keep the dough wrapped in clingfilm while working, as it dries very quickly.

Arrange on ungreased baking trays. Brush the tops with the egg yolk, sprinkle with sesame seeds and bake in a preheated oven for about 45 minutes, until golden.

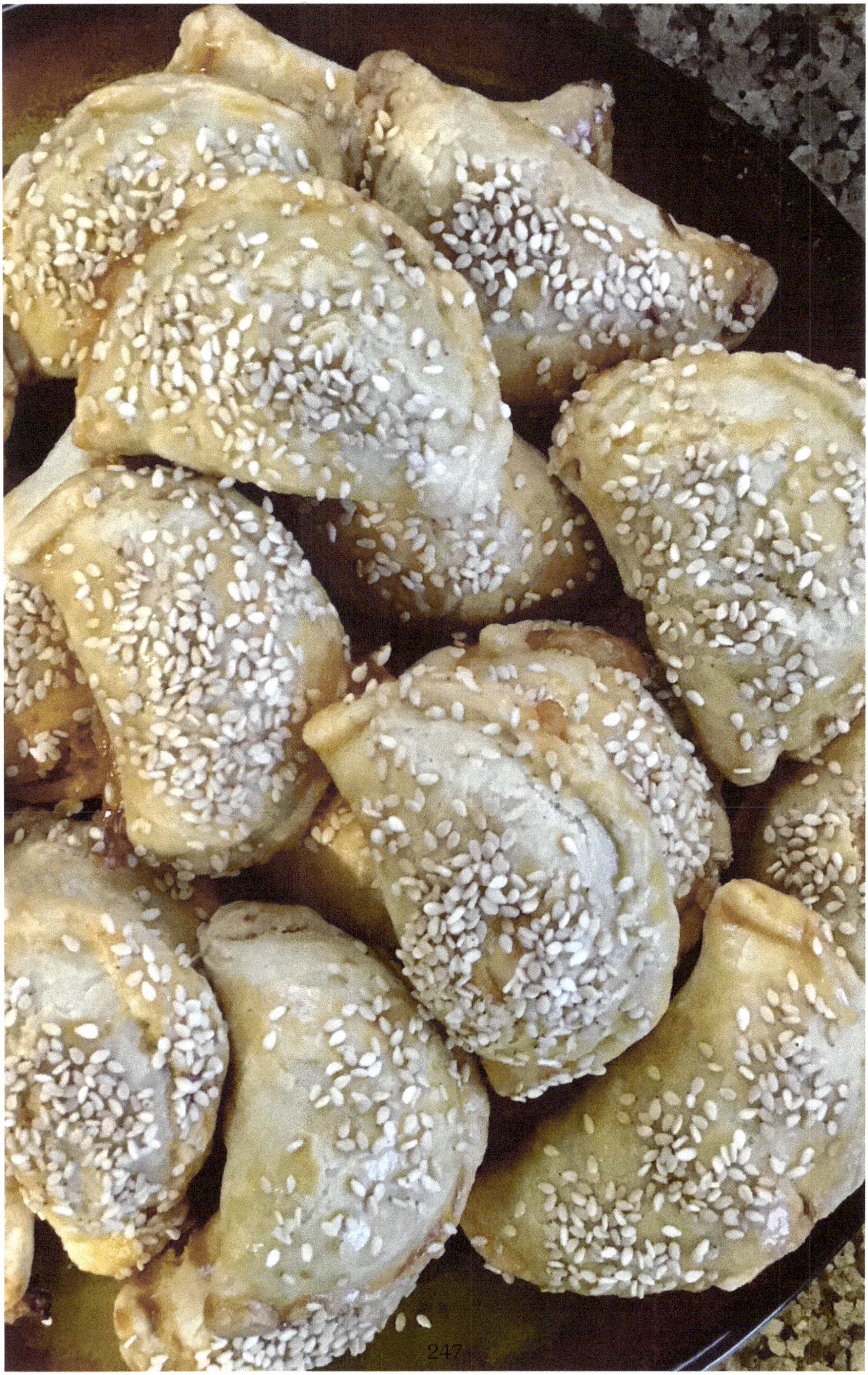

Tapada

(Large Sephardic pie)

This pie is made with the same dough and filling as borekas, but is easier, as you are only rolling out one large pastry dough.

For the dough
  125g sunflower oil
  125g unsalted butter
  125ml warm water
  ½ teaspoon salt
  about 550g flour

For the filling
  500g frozen spinach, thawed
  2 eggs, lightly beaten
  250g feta cheese, crumbled
  50g grated cheddar or emmental
  4 tablespoons grated parmesan
  pinch of salt if necessary

Prepare the filling – drain the spinach in a colander and press all the water out. Mix with the rest of the filling ingredients, leaving out the parmesan. You can use any combination of cheese. I have replaced the feta cheese with a mixture of 150g goat's cheese, 50g mozzarella cheese and 100g grated cheddar.

Make the dough – heat the oil and butter in a pan over a low heat until the butter melts.

Add the water and salt and mix well. Add the flour gradually, enough to make a soft, greasy dough which holds together in a ball – stirring with a fork to begin with, then working with your hands. The dough should be handled as little as possible, so stop mixing as soon as it holds together.

Cover with clingfilm and leave to rest for 20 minutes at room temperature. Do not refrigerate, as the dough will become unworkable.

Preheat the oven to 180C/Gas Mark 4.

Make the pie – with the palm of your hands, press out the dough into a greased 22cm (10 inch) pie dish. Spread the filling over the surface and sprinkle the top with parmesan cheese. The dough base should be thin, so you may have some dough left over.

Bake in the preheated oven for 35 minutes or until the top is golden.

An alternative way is to use 2/3 of the dough for the base, spread the filling and cover with the rest of the rolled out pastry. Trim the edges, pinch together to seal the pie and brush the top with 1 egg yolk mixed with 1 teaspoon of water.

Borekas de espinaka

(Spinach pies)

Makes 24

A mixture of oil, butter and water in equal measures is the traditional dough for the Sephardic borekas. It is also the easiest to work with and always produces excellent results. I try to follow the family tradition by making them as often as I can and keeping some on standby in the freezer.

For the dough
- 125ml sunflower oil
- 125ml unsalted butter
- 125ml water
- ½ teaspoon salt
- about 550g plain flour

For the filling
- 2 packets frozen spinach (400g each)
- 250g feta cheese, crumbled
- 70g grated cheese, cheddar or gruyère
- 2 eggs, lightly beaten
- salt and pepper

1 egg yolk mixed with a drop of water, for glazing

Preheat the oven to 180C/Gas Mark 4.
Lightly grease 2 large baking trays or line with parchment paper.

Prepare the filling – thaw the spinach overnight. Drain well in a colander and squeeze out the excess water. You will be left with about 300g of spinach.

Put the drained spinach in a large bowl. Add the cheeses, eggs and a little salt. Mix well.

Prepare the dough – melt the oil and butter over a low heat. Transfer to a mixing bowl and add the water and salt. Add the flour gradually, using a fork or spoon. When all the flour has been added, mix well with your hands until you have a soft, greasy dough that hold together in a ball which does not stick - you may have to add a little more flour. Stop mixing as soon as the dough holds together, as it should be handled as little as possible.

Take walnut sized lumps of dough and roll each into a ball. Press and squash between your palms until you have a 10cm (4 inch) round. Alternatively, you can flatten it over a lightly floured board.

Put 1 heaped teaspoon of filling in the middle of each round and fold the dough over the filling in a half moon shape. Pinch the edges firmly together to seal the pies, then gently fold and twist the edges.

Place the pies on the baking trays. Brush with the egg yolk mixed with a drop of water.

Bake in a preheated oven about 30 minutes, until slightly golden. Eat hot or cold.

Cheese and basil bulemas

Makes 18/20

From boyos to borekas, Sephardic cuisine is not short of savoury pastries. These are the lesser known bulemas, coils of dough most often filled with cheese, spinach or eggplant.

For the dough
- 1½ teaspoon active dry yeast
- 1 teaspoon granulated sugar
- 1 cup warm water (about 110°F)
- 375g bread flour, plus more as needed
- 1½ teaspoon kosher salt
- 100ml vegetable oil, divided
- 1 egg, beaten, for egg wash

For the filling
- 40ml vegetable oil
- 2 large shallots, halved through the root and thinly sliced
- salt and pepper
- 310g ricotta cheese
- 20 basil leaves, roughly torn
- ½ teaspoon (tightly packed) finely grated lemon zest
- 115g crumbled feta cheese
- 30g finely grated parmesan cheese

Stir together the yeast, sugar and water in a medium bowl. Let sit until foaming, 5–10 minutes.

Prepare the dough - in a large bowl, stir together the flour and salt. Add 20ml oil to the yeast mixture, then pour into the flour. Stir until the dough starts to come together, then turn out onto a lightly floured surface and knead, adding a little more flour, if needed, until it is smooth and elastic, but not sticky, about 8-10 minutes. (You can also knead it in a mixer fitted with a dough hook on medium speed, 5-8 minutes)

Pour the remaining 80ml oil into a large, shallow baking dish. Divide the dough into equal-size pieces (typically 18–20 out of a batch) and roll into balls. Place the balls in the oil, and turn to coat. Cover the baking dish and let stand about 30 minutes.

Make the filling - heat 40ml oil in a medium saucepan over a low heat. Add the shallots, a little salt and pepper and cook, stirring occasionally, until softened and lightly browned, 5–6 minutes. Remove from the heat and cool.

Mix the ricotta cheese with the lemon zest and basil leaves. Blitz in a food processor for a few seconds until blended and add the shallots, crumbled feta cheese and grated parmesan.

Preheat the oven to 180C/Gas Mark 4.

Line two large baking sheets with parchment paper.

Assemble the bulemas - lay another piece of parchment paper on a flat surface. Working with one ball of dough at a time, place it on top of the parchment and using your fingertips and a rolling pin, stretch and roll into thin, 18cm (7 inch) diameter rounds.

Spread 2 rounded tablespoons of filling in a line along the edge of one side of the dough round. Roll up the dough tightly like a jelly roll, starting with the filled side; gently stretch the roll with your finger tips to lengthen slightly. Starting from one end of the roll, coil it onto itself, tucking the end underneath.

Place the coils on the prepared baking sheets and brush with the egg wash.

Bake until golden brown, 30–40 minutes. Serve warm or at room temperature.

Store leftovers in an airtight container in the fridge for up to a week (or freeze for up to 3 months). Reheat in a preheated oven until warmed through, about 10 minutes.

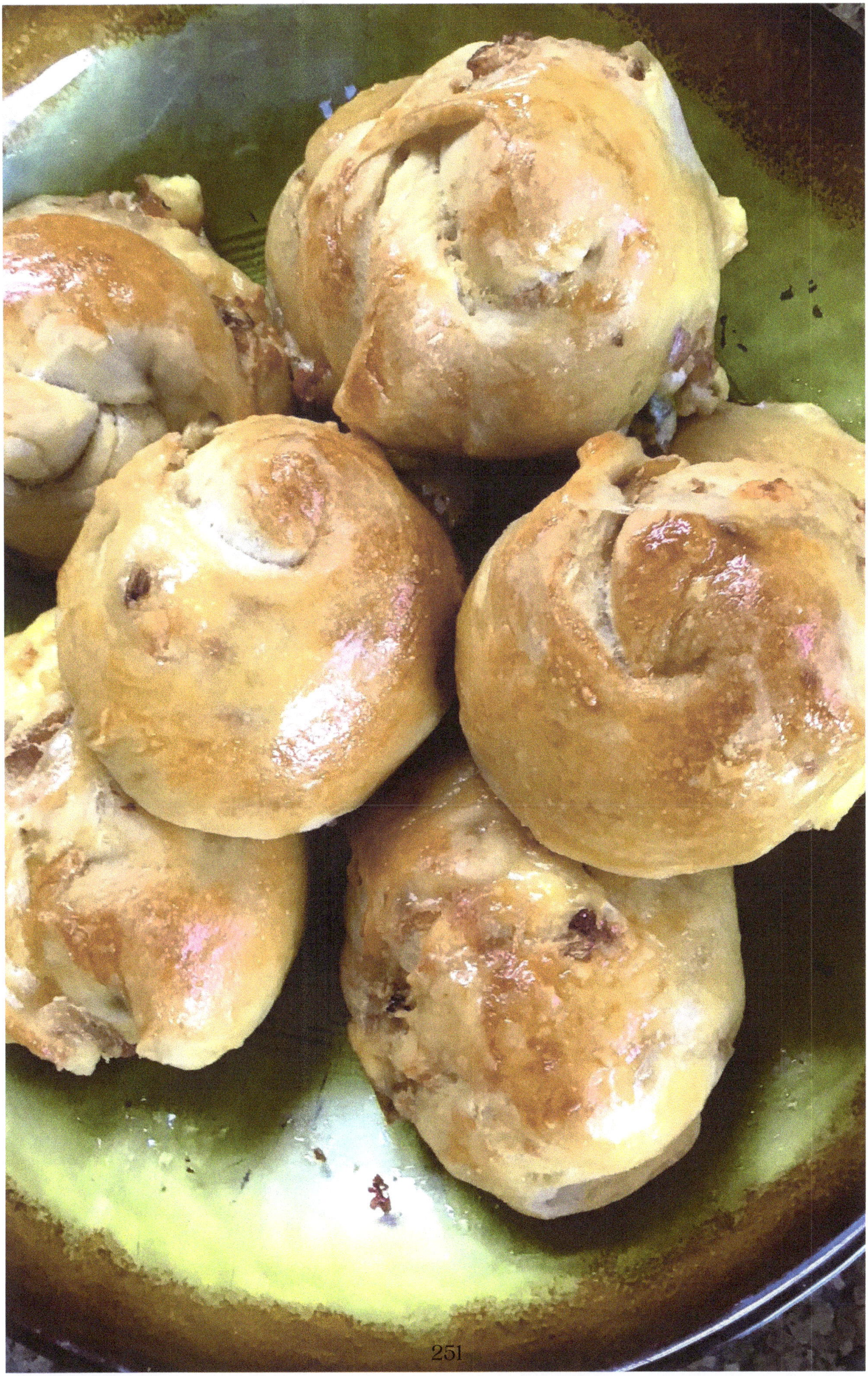

Boyos with a cheese or aubergine filling

Makes 24

Boyos comes from the Spanish word for balls and these round pastries originate from Spain and Portugal. They can also be found in Turkey and Greece, with different shapes and fillings. The texture is more like a bread dough.

For the dough
- 750g plain flour, plus extra for dusting
- 7g quick yeast (1 sachet)
- 3 tablespoons parmesan cheese
- ½ teaspoon salt
- ½ teaspoon caster sugar
- 400ml warm water
- olive oil

For the cheese filling
- 150g feta cheese
- 150g cream cheese
- 50g grated cheese, medium strength
- 1 large egg

For the aubergine filling
- 3 medium aubergines
- 200g feta cheese

1 egg yolk + 1 egg yolk mixed with a drop of water

Preheat the oven to 200C/Gas Mark 6.
Lightly brush two baking sheets with a little olive oil or line with parchment paper.

First prepare the dough - mix the flour, yeast, salt and sugar together in a bowl. Add the water and mix well to form a slightly sticky dough - you might need to add a little extra flour or water to reach the desired consistency. Bring the dough into a ball and place in a well oiled bowl. Cover with cling film for an hour, until risen and doubled in size.

For the cheese filling, crumble the feta cheese and mix with the other cheeses and egg in a bowl.

Make the aubergine filling - wash the aubergines, cut the stems and ends and prick all over with a fork. Grill in a preheated oven for 45 minutes or until the skin is soft. Cool, peel them and squeeze out the bitter juices. Blitz in a food processor with the feta cheese.

Make the boyos - divide the dough into 24 balls. Use the cheese filling for 12 balls and the aubergine filling for the remaining 12.

Work with small chunks of the dough Roll it out on a floured board with a rolling pin and using the bottom of a large glass, cut a circle. Place a tablespoon of filling in the middle of the circle, then using your finger, rub the border of the pastry with a little of the egg yolk. Fold in each side of the circle to the middle, covering the filling, then pinch and press down with your thumb to seal it. Repeat with the remaining pastry and fillings until you have 24 boyos.

Place them on the baking sheets. Mix the remaining egg yolk with a teaspoon of cold water and brush this over the pastries.

Bake for 25-30 minutes in the preheated oven until golden brown.

Serve when still hot.

Filo triangles with cheese

Makes 30

Filo pastry, which we called fila in Egypt, is a legacy of the Ottoman world and was used to make all kinds of pies in different shapes and with a variety of traditional fillings. Filo pastries were always present on the buffet tables of Egyptian Jews, such as small pies for finger foods and large pies, cut into squares, for sit down meals. You can use any combination of cheeses and I like a mixture containing cottage cheese, as the texture is softer.

250g filo pastry
90g butter, melted
2 tablespoons sunflower oil

For the filling
200g cottage cheese
180g cream cheese, such as Philadelphia
120g grated cheese, such as cheddar
2 eggs, lightly beaten

1 egg yolk mixed with 1 teaspoon water to glaze

Preheat the oven to 180C/Gas Mark 4.
Line two large baking trays with baking parchment.

Prepare the filling by mixing the cheeses with the eggs.

Melt the butter and oil in a saucepan.

Work with 2 filo sheets at a time and cover the rest with a clean tea towel – this is important, as filo pastry dries very quickly and then becomes unworkable.

Cut each sheet of filo into 4 rectangle strips about 30 x 10cm (12 x 4 inch). Work with 1 strip at a time. Brush the whole of each strip with the melted butter. Take a heaped teaspoon of filling and place it at one short end of the filo strip, about 3cm (1¼ inch) from the edge. Fold that end over the filling. Pick up a corner, lift it up with the filling and fold diagonally, making a triangle.

Continue folding, picking up one corner after another, until the whole strip has been folded into a triangular shape. Make sure any holes are closed so that the filling does not ooze out.

Place the pastries on the baking tray and brush lightly with melted butter or with an egg yolk mixed with a drop of water.

Bake for 30 minutes or until crisp and golden.

Pastelles
(Sephardic meat and rice pies)

This is another Sephardic staple. Pastelles and their smaller version, pastelicos, are usually made with minced beef or a mixture of minced beef and rice. Some people have them for Saturday morning Shabbat lunch, but we had them as part of a light snack, with a leek omelette or salad.

For the dough
- 250ml + 75ml water
- 110ml vegetable, sunflower or olive oil + 1 tablespoon
- 1 teaspoon salt
- 420g plain flour

For the filling
- 1/2 medium onion, finely chopped 250g minced beef
- 50g uncooked long grain rice
- 1/2 teaspoon salt
- 1 teaspoon tomato paste
- 1 teaspoon dried oregano
- 1/2 teaspoon cinnamon
- 75ml water
- 1 hard boiled egg

For the egg wash
- 1 egg yolk mixed with 1 tablespoon water
- sesame seeds for sprinkling

Preheat the oven to 190C/Gas Mark 5.
Line 1 large baking tray with parchment paper.

Prepare the filling - cook the egg in boiling water for 10 minutes. Cool and chop into small pieces.

Rinse the rice well under water and drain.
Heat 1 tablespoon oil in a large frying pan and add the chopped onion. Cook for 5 minutes, stirring, until translucent. Add the beef mince and continue cooking, breaking up the meat with a wooden spoon, until brown – about 10 minutes.

Add the rice, salt, tomato paste, dried oregano and cinnamon. Stir and add 75ml water, making sure that the mixture is well covered. Cover, lower the heat and simmer for 12 minutes until the meat is cooked, the rice is al dente and all the water has evaporated. Add the chopped egg and mix well.

Prepare the dough - in a large saucepan, bring 250ml water, oil and salt to a boil. Remove from the heat and quickly stir in the flour, using a wooden spoon, until a soft dough forms.

Scrape onto a lightly floured surface and knead, using more flour if necessary, until the mixture is soft and pliable. Form into 12 balls about 5cm (2 inch) in diameter and 12 smaller balls about 4cm (1 1/2 inch) in diameter. Place on parchment lined baking tray, cover with clingfilm and set aside at room temperature for 20 minutes.

Make the pastelles - using floured hands, shape 12 larger dough balls into cups about 6 -8 cm (2 1/2 -3 inch) wide and 2cm (1 inch) deep. Place them on the baking tray, about 2cm (1 inch) apart.

Divide the mixture evenly between the cups, filling up to the top.

On a lightly floured surface and using a floured rolling pin, roll the 12 smaller dough balls into 5cm (2 inch) rounds. Cover each filled pastelles with a round, pinching the edges together in an upward motion to make a raised lip.

Brush the top and sides with egg wash and sprinkle with sesame seeds.

Bake in a preheated oven for 35-40 minutes until golden brown.

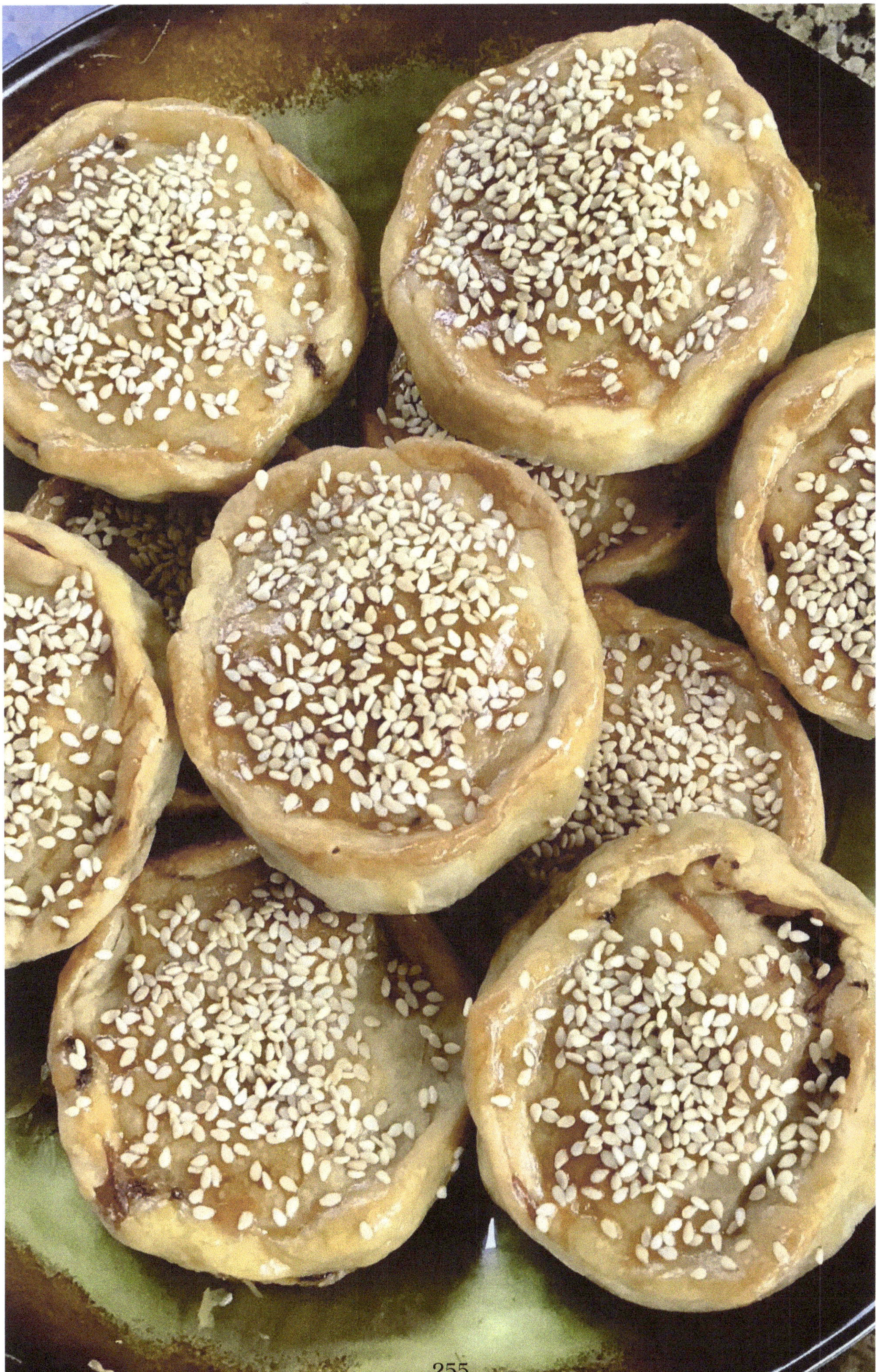

Pastelicos

(Small pastries filled with beef and pine nuts)

Pastelicos are small pies made with a thin dough that is crimped at the edges. This Sephardic savoury pastry can be served at lunch with some tahini sauce or eaten as a snack.

Makes 24

For the filling
- 30ml sunflower oil
- 1 medium onion, finely chopped
- 250g beef mince
- 115ml water
- 15g pine nuts, toasted
- ½ teaspoon ras-el-hanout spice
- ½ tablespoon salt
- ½ teaspoon pepper

For the dough
- 290ml water
- 150g butter
- 25ml sunflower oil
- ½ teaspoon salt
- 350g all purpose flour
- ¼ cup sesame seeds, for sprinkling

Prepare the filling – in a large frying pan, heat the oil over medium heat. Add the onion and sauté until golden, about 5 minutes. Add the beef mince and sauté, breaking the meat into small pieces with a wooden spoon until cooked through, about 5 minutes. Add the water and cook until the water evaporates, about 5 minutes.

Meanwhile, toast the pine nuts over medium heat in a dry skillet until golden.

Add the pine nuts, ras-el-hanout spice, salt and pepper to the meat and onion mixture. Set aside to cool for at least 30 minutes – the filling is easier to handle if done a day ahead and placed in the refrigerator to cool.

Preheat the oven to 180C/Gas Mark 4.
Line two baking trays with parchment paper.

Make the dough – place the water, salt, oil and butter in a large saucepan. Heat over medium heat until the water starts to boil. Remove from the heat and immediately stir in the flour with a wooden spoon until well combined.

Allow the dough to cool for a few minutes until it can be easily handled.

Shape and stuff the pastelicos – pinch of a small amount of dough, about the size of a cherry tomato. Roll into a ball shape and press down on the centre of the dough forming a 2cm (1 inch) pocket for the filling. Fill the pocket with 1 teaspoon of the filling to the top edges of the dough pocket.

Take a smaller piece of dough and press it into a disc shape that fits over the top of the pocket. Pinch around the edges to connect the top to the bottom. Create a crimping design around the edge of the pocket.

Place the finished pastelicos on the prepared baking sheet – they can be placed close together, as they will not rise or expand while baking. Continue with the rest of the dough and filling. Sprinkle some sesame seeds evenly over the top.

Place in the oven and bake until golden brown, about 45 minutes.

Serve hot or at room temperature.

Sambusek
(Middle Eastern pies)

This is the classic recipe for sambusek, essentially a bread dough enriched with oil. The traditional filling is cheese, but spinach, chickpea or meat fillings are also popular. There is an alternative version, which we called Syrian sambusek. It uses semolina and butter, but no yeast and the result is a crumbly pastry, which I prefer.

For the dough

Dough using yeast
- 2¼ teaspoons dry yeast
- 230ml water
- 1 teaspoon sugar
- 60ml sunflower, vegetable or olive oil
- 2 teaspoons salt
- 480g plain flour

Dough using semolina
- 250g plain flour
- 110g semolina
- 225g unsalted butter
- 1 teaspoon salt
- 50ml cold water

For the filling
- 120 grated cheddar
- 120g feta cheese
- 1 large egg, beaten
- 1/8 teaspoon baking powder
- pinch of salt

1 egg yolk mixed with a drop of water to glaze

You can use any combination of cheeses for the filling and goat's cheese also works well. If using a creamier cheese like ricotta, change the proportions to 100g ricotta and 140 grated cheese.

For the yeast version - in a large bowl, dissolve the yeast in ¼ cup of the water (about 55ml). Stir in the sugar and let the yeast mixture stand for 10 minutes until foamy. Add the remaining water, oil, salt and half the flour. Gradually add enough of the remaining flour for the mixture to hold together. On a lightly floured surface, knead the dough until smooth and elastic, 10-15 minutes.

If using an electric mixer with a dough hook, combine the flour, oil and salt in the bowl and add the yeast mixture. With the machine on, gradually add enough warm water to form a ball, then process around the bowl 25 times.

Place the dough in a large bowl, cover and leave in a warm place until doubled in bulk, about 2 hours.

For the semolina version - combine the flour and semolina and add salt and butter. Work until the mixture is crumbly and gradually add the water until you have a soft dough. Form into a ball and use straightaway.

Prepare the filling - combine all the ingredients and stir to blend.

Preheat the oven to 180C/Gas Mark 4.
Line 2 large baking trays with parchment paper.

Make the sambusek - divide the dough into 25 walnut sized lumps and roll each into a ball. Press and squash between your palms and pull into a 7cm (2½ inch) round. Alternatively, flatten the dough ball on a lightly floured surface and cut a round using an upturned drinking glass. Work in small batches and keep the rest of the dough covered, as it dries very quickly.

Spoon 1 heaped teaspoon of filling into the centre of each dough round. Fold the dough over the filling into a half moon shape. Pinch the edges firmly together to seal the pies. You can also pinch, fold and twist all around the edges.

Place the sambusek 5cm (2 inch) apart on the prepared baking trays. Brush the tops with the egg yolk and, if you wish, sprinkle with sesame seeds.

Bake until lightly golden but not browned, about 20 minutes.

Serve warm or at room temperature.

Roasted aubergine and goat's cheese tart

Ready made shortcrust pastry can be very handy, especially if you are pushed for time. Try to use an all butter one, as it makes a difference to the taste. This tart can be eaten warm or at room temperature and it's great for picnics.

320g pack all butter shortcrust pastry
flour, for dusting

For the filling
2 small aubergines
1 yellow pepper
1 red onion, thinly sliced
2 large garlic cloves, unpeeled
3 tablespoons olive oil
150g cherry plum tomatoes
175ml double cream
2 eggs
100g goat's cheese
salt and pepper to taste

Preheat the oven to 180C/Gas Mark 4.

Wash the aubergines and cut them into 2½cm (1 inch) cubes. Wash and deseed the pepper and cut into strips. Toss the aubergines, peppers and onion together with the garlic, olive oil and some seasoning. Tip onto a large baking tray and roast for 20 minutes.

Toss through the tomatoes and roast for a further 15-20 minutes until the vegetables are tender and beginning to caramelise. Remove from the oven and cool.

Meanwhile, lightly grease a 18cm (7 inch) loose bottomed tart tin. Roll out the pastry on a lightly floured board and line the tart tin with the pastry. Chill for 30 minutes.

Prick the base of the tart tin with a fork, line with baking parchment and fill with baking beans. Bake for 15 minutes, then remove the beans and parchment and bake for 10-15 minutes until the pastry is lightly golden.

Squeeze the garlic from their skins and mix with the cream, followed by the eggs and some seasoning.

Tip the vegetables in the pastry case, spreading out to an even layer. Crumble the goat's cheese, then pour over the cream mix.

Bake for 35-40 minutes until the tart is just set, with a slight wobble in the centre.

Note – you can substitute the goat's cheese with feta cheese.

Boyikos de rayo
(Cheese scones)

Makes 24

The name boyikos de rayo, derived from rayo in Ladino (grater), refers to the decorative imprint that was traditionally made on the scones with a grater. These savoury small scones were usually served for the Jewish festival of Shavuot. They are best eaten warm for brunch or as a teatime treat.

200g flour
1 tablespoon baking powder
large pinch of salt
115g feta cheese, crumbled
150 grated cheese, any
115ml full fat milk or cream
1 egg, lightly beaten
80ml vegetable oil

For the egg wash
1 egg yolk, mixed with
1 tablespoon milk

For the topping
4 tablespoons grated cheese

Preheat the oven to 200C/ Gas Mark 6.
Line two large baking trays with baking parchment.

In a large bowl, sift together the flour, baking powder and salt and stir in the cheeses. Make a well in the centre of the dry ingredients and pour in the milk or cream, egg and oil. Mix the ingredients well with a spatula until well combined.

Turn onto a lightly floured board and knead briefly. Do not overwork the dough. Roll into about 20 balls and flatten slightly.

Arrange the scones on the baking trays 2½cm (1 inch) apart. Brush the tops with the egg wash and sprinkle with grated cheese.

Bake for 20-25 minutes until lightly golden.

Spinach filo triangles

Makes 30

My mother often served these when she hosted one of her cards games and the spinach filling was her favourite. In Greece, they are called spanakopita and the flaky layers of dough work well with the slightly salty filling of spinach and feta. They are very quick to prepare, as ready made filo pastry is now widely available

250g filo pastry
90g unsalted butter, melted

For the filling
  500g fresh spinach or
  frozen leaf spinach
  100g feta cheese, mashed
  100g gruyère cheese
  50g ricotta cheese
  1 egg
  salt and pepper
  a good pinch of nutmeg

Preheat the oven to 180C/ Gas Mark 4.
Line 2 baking trays with parchment paper or grease the baking trays.

Prepare the filling - wash the spinach, remove only the rough stems and drain the leaves well. Cook by putting the spinach in a saucepan on a low heat with the lid on for a few minutes only, until it crumples into a soft mass. Drain in a colander and when cool enough, press as mush of the water out as you can. If using frozen spinach, simply thaw and squeeze all the water out with your hands.

Mix the spinach with the rest of the filling ingredients.

Melt the butter in a saucepan.

Work with 2 sheets of filo at a time and keep the rest covered with a tea towel as filo dries very quickly and then becomes unworkable.

Cut each sheet of filo into 4 long strips and put them in a pile on top of each other.

Brush the top strip lightly with the melted butter. Take a heaped teaspoon of filling and place it at one end of the short strip of filo, about 3cm (1¼ inch) from the edge. Fold that end over the filling. Pick up a corner and, lifting it up with the filling, fold diagonally, making a triangle. Continue to fold, picking up one corner after another, until the whole strip has been folded into a triangular shape. Make sure that any holes are closed that that the filling does not ooze out.

Place the filo triangles close to each other on the prepared baking trays and brush the tops with melted butter.

Bake for 30 minutes, or until crisp and golden.

Note - you can use any combination of cheeses.

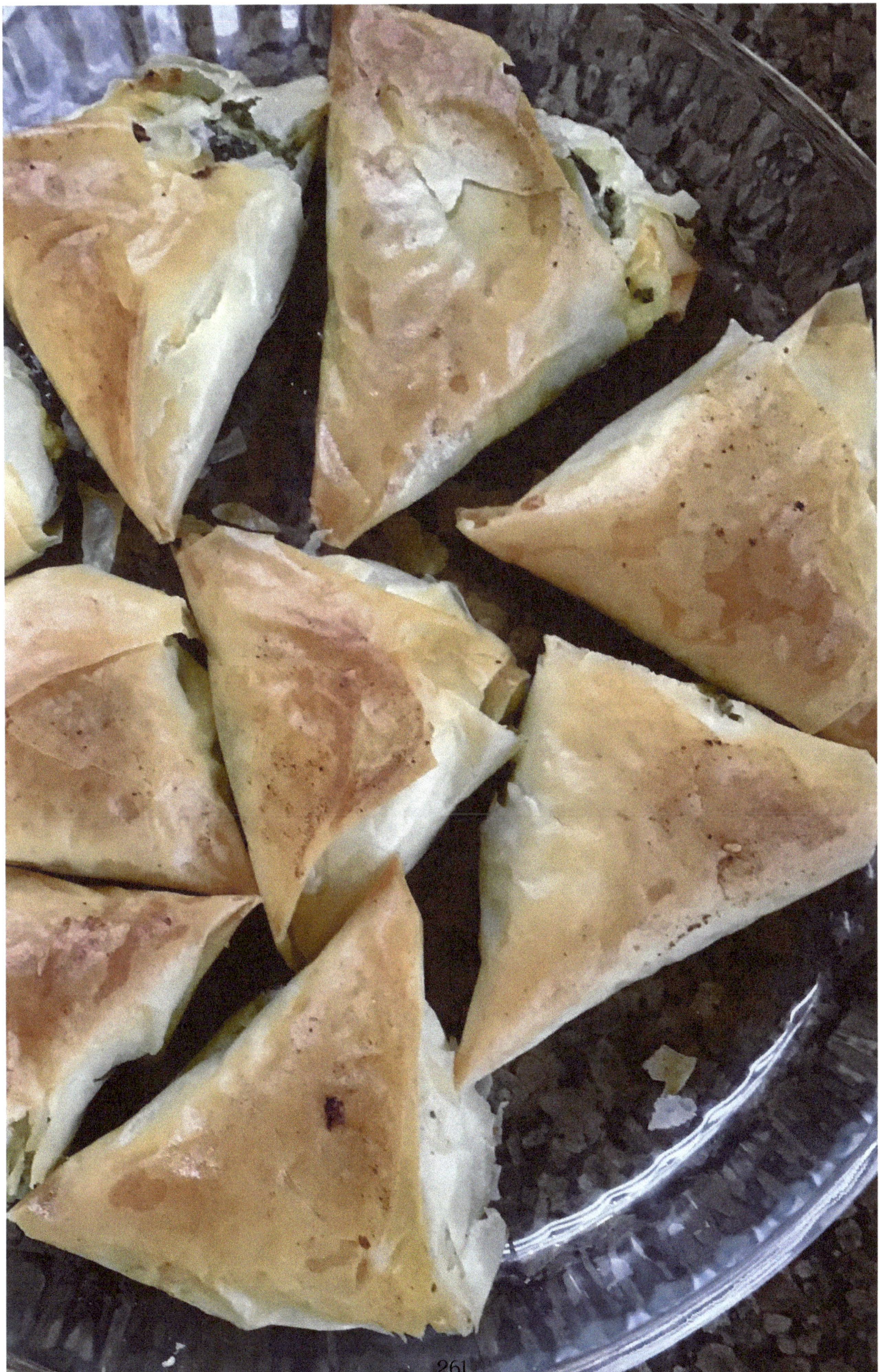

Borekas

(Small cheese pies)

Makes 25

These little pies are the trademark and pride of Jews of Spanish descent. They were a staple in my family and an essential part of my childhood. Every housewife had her own variation and prided herself that hers were the best, but the ones I remember most fondly are my aunt Sophie's, as her pastry just melted in the mouth. There is another reason why these pies are special for me, as they remind me of my late sister Claudine. I used to visit her in West Yorkshire as often as I could when she fell ill. Towards the end she could eat very little, but she still loved these borekas and always asked me to bring some with me.

For the dough
  125ml sunflower oil
  125ml unsalted butter
  125ml water
  ½ teaspoon salt
  about 550g plain flour

For the filling
  450g grated cheese
  (any mixture such as feta, grated cheddar, gruyère or emmental)
  1 egg, lightly beaten

  1 egg yolk mixed with a drop of water for glazing

Preheat the oven to 180C/Gas Mark 4.
Oil 2 large baking trays or line with baking parchment.

Prepare the dough - heat the oil and butter in a pan over a low heat until the butter melts. Add the water and salt and mix well.

Add the flour gradually, starting with around 250g. Mix first with a fork, then start working with your hand. Continue adding the flour until you have a soft dough that holds together in a ball. Stop mixing as soon as the dough holds together. Cover with cling film and leave to rest at room temperature for about 20 minutes. Do not refrigerate.

Make the filling by mixing the cheeses and egg – the filling should hold together. If runny, add some more grated cheese.

The half moon pastry is the traditional shape for borekas. Take walnut sized lumps and roll each into a ball. Press and squash between your palms until you have a 10cm (4 inch) round. Place a heaped teaspoon of filling in the middle of each round. Fold the dough over the filling into a half moon shape, then pinch the edges firmly together to seal the pies. Pinch, fold and twist all around the edges - you can also use a fork to seal the edges. You should have about 25 pies.

Place the pies on the baking trays a few centimetres apart. Brush with the eggs wash and sprinkle some sesame seeds (optional).

Bake in the preheated oven for about 30 minutes, until slightly golden.

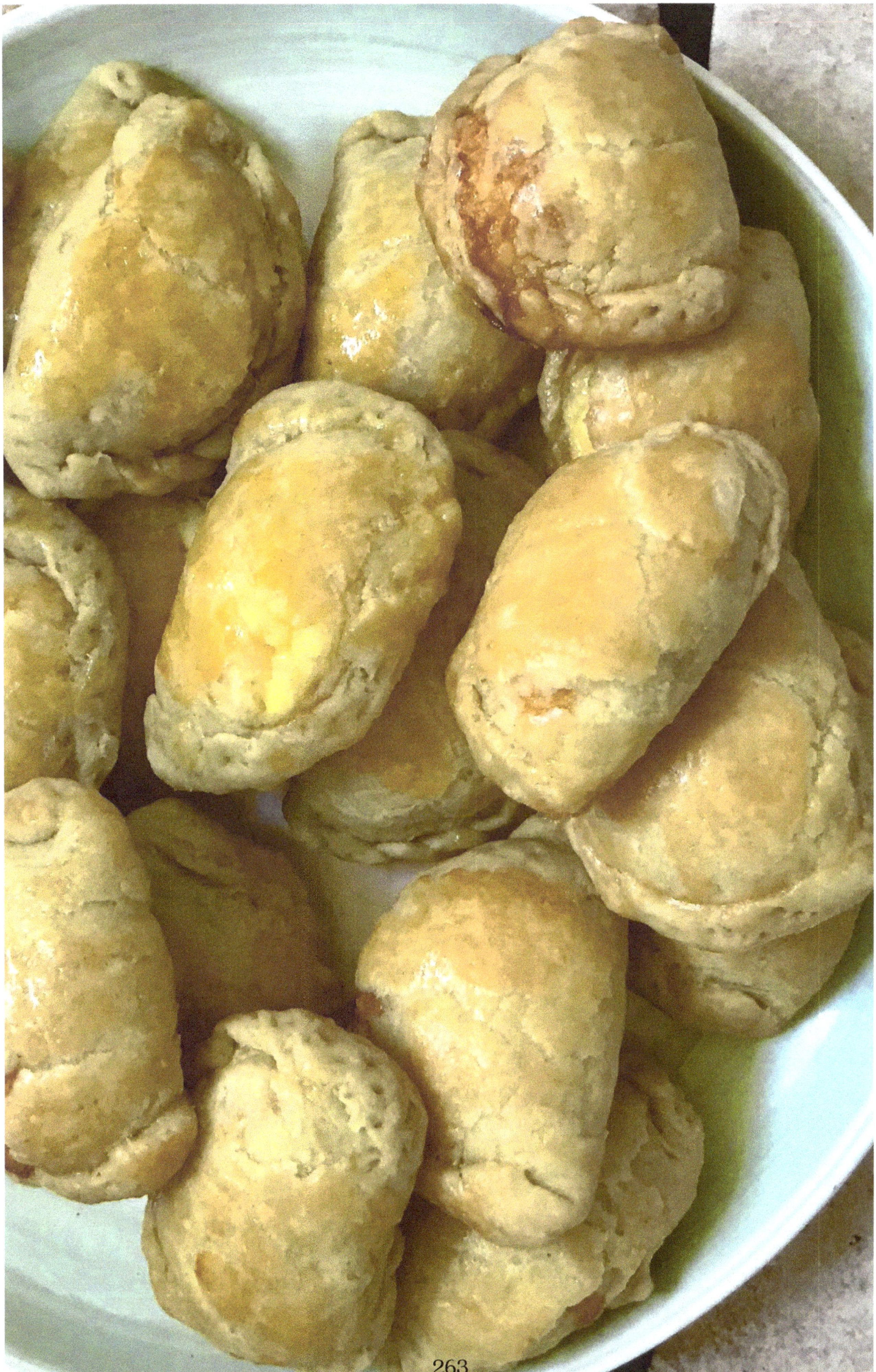

Borekitas

(Sephardic potato and cheese pies)

Borekitas are small pies that are well known in any Sephardic household. They are the smaller version of borekas and have a potato and cheese filling, instead of a mixture of cheeses. My aunt Sophie's were the best, perhaps because she always made them with so much love.

Makes about 40

For the dough
- 110ml olive oil
- 115g butter
- 200ml water
- 3 tablespoons vinegar
- 1 teaspoon salt
- 525g plain flour

For the filling
- 2 medium potatoes, boiled and mashed
- 70g feta cheese
- 25g grated mild cheddar or gruyère cheese
- 2 tablespoons parmesan cheese
- 60g thick yoghurt, ricotta cheese or quark
- 1 large egg + 1 egg white (reserve the yolk for glazing)

For the topping
- 1 egg yolk mixed with 2 teaspoons water
- sesame seeds

Preheat the oven to 180C/Gas Mark 4.
Line two baking trays with parchment paper.

Prepare the dough – in a medium saucepan, mix the butter, oil and water. Bring to the boil and remove from the heat Cool for 2 minutes and add the vinegar and salt.

Add the flour and mix until the dough separates from the sides of the pot. Wrap in clingfilm and refrigerate for 1 hour.

For the filling – wash and peel the potatoes. Place in a small saucepan and cover with water. Bring to the boil, cover and cook for 20 minutes or until soft. Drain any water and mash coarsely with a fork. Bring to room temperature and add the rest of the ingredients for the filling. Mix well.

Make the borekitas - divide the dough into 6 portions. On a lightly floured board, roll one portion into about 1cm (½ inch) thickness. Using a 7cm (3 inch) glass or cookie cutter, cut out dough circles. Place 1 teaspoon of the filling in the middle of each circle and fold. Twist the ends together with your fingers and place on a baking tray. Repeat with the rest of the dough and scraps.

Brush the pastries with egg wash and sprinkle with sesame seeds on top.

Bake for 25-30 minutes or until the pastries are golden brown. Serve warm.

Note - the baked borekitas freeze well in an airtight container for up to one month. For best results, reheat them in an oven, NOT in the microwave.

Assabih bil loz
(almond filo cigars)

Makes about 26

Assabih means fingers in Arabic and this is what we called these pastries in Egypt, though in Turkey and North Africa they are called cigars. They are slim rolls of filo pastry stuffed with ground almonds (or a mixture of nuts), baked and sprinkled with icing sugar. Some people prefer to soak them in a sugar syrup, in the same way as baklava. They were served at parties and celebrations and it was also a tradition for the bride's mother to bring some to a mikveh (ritual bath), to offer to the women relatives and friends who accompanied the bride.

250g ground almonds
125g caster sugar, or to taste
3 tablespoons orange blossom water
250g filo pastry
100g unsalted butter, melted
icing sugar to dust with

Preheat the oven to 180C/Gas Mark 4.
Line a large baking tray with parchment paper.
Prepare the filling – mix the ground almonds, sugar and orange blossom water with 10g melted butter. Work with your hands until the mixture, combined with the oil in the almonds, binds slightly together.

Cut each sheet of filo into 4 rectangle strips, about 10cm (4 inch) long. Work with 2 sheets of filo at a time and keep the rest wrapped in a tea towel, so that the filo does not dry out.

Brush each strip lightly with melted butter. Put 1 heaped teaspoon of filling along one short end of the rectangle and roll up like a cigarette. A third of the way, tuck in the ends to trap the filling and continue to roll so that the roll looks like an open cigar.

Arrange on the prepared baking sheet and brush the tops with butter.

Bake for 30-40 minutes, until crisp and golden.

Cool and dust with icing sugar.

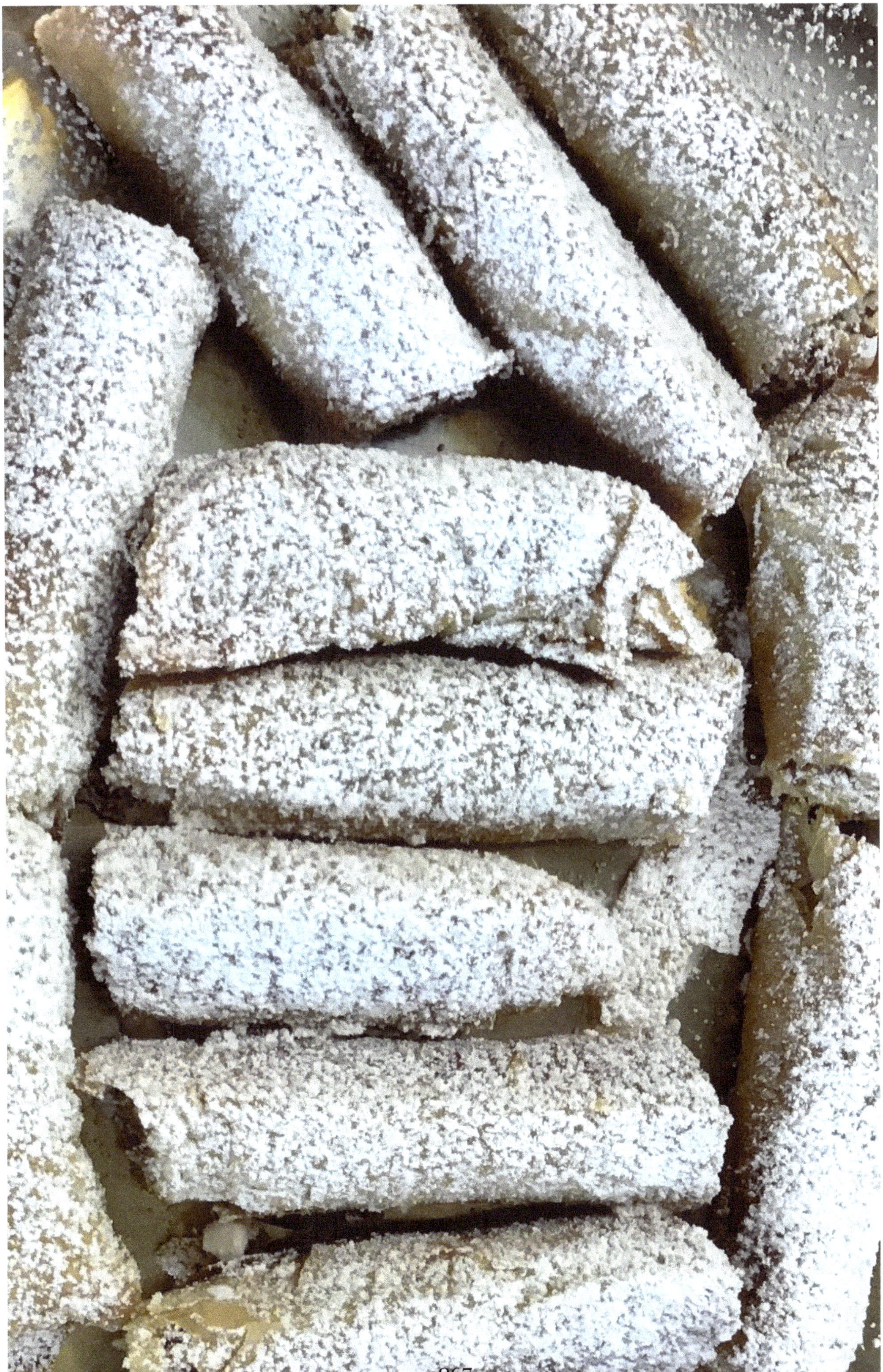

Barazeh shami
(Damascus sesame biscuits)

Makes about 25

These biscuits are unusual because they are brushed with melted butter and sesame seeds on both sides before baking.

450g plain flour
225g caster sugar
175g butter
¼ teaspoon dried yeast
1 teaspoon sugar
180ml warm water
50g melted butter
200g sesame seeds

Sift the flour in a large bowl and stir in the sugar. Add the butter, cut into small pieces and rub in until the mixture resembles fine breadcrumbs.

Dissolve the yeast and 1 teaspoon of sugar in a little of the water. Let it stand for 10 minutes until it foams and add to the flour mixture. Gradually add the remaining water and knead for about 5 minutes until the dough is soft and easy to handle. If necessary, add a little more flour or water.

Cover the bowl with a cloth and leave in a warm place for about 1 hour or until the dough has risen to about twice its size.

Preheat the oven to 170C/Gas Mark 3.

Remove the dough from the bowl and place on a lightly floured working top. Punch the dough down and knead for a further 1-2 minutes. Divide the dough into 2 portions.

Sprinkle the working surface with a little more flour and roll out one portion until it is about 5mm (¼ inch) thick. Using a 6cm (2 inch) biscuit cutter, cut out as many rounds as possible. Repeat with the remaining portion of pastry.

Grease two large baking trays or line with baking parchment.

Spread the sesame seeds out on a plate and melt the butter. Lightly brush both sides of each biscuit with butter and then dip into the sesame seeds, so that both sides are coated.

Arrange on the baking sheets, 2½cm (1 inch) apart and bake in the oven for 20-25 minutes or until the biscuits are golden brown.

Remove from the oven, cool completely and store in an airtight container.

Canella
(cinnamon nut cookies)

These biscuits are very quick to make and I like the lovely aroma of cinnamon while they are cooking. They go perfectly with a cup of tea or coffee.

Makes about 25

- 100g unsalted butter
- 100g caster sugar
- 75g brown sugar
- 1 large egg
- 2 tablespoons double cream
- 1 teaspoon vanilla essence
- 200g plain flour
- 1 teaspoon baking powder
- 1½ teaspoon cinnamon
- 100g ground walnuts
- 25 walnut halves

Preheat the oven to 180C/Gas Mark 4.
Grease two large baking trays or line with parchment paper.

Cream the butter and both sugars in an electric mixer. Add the egg, cream and vanilla. Beat well.

Sift together the flour, baking powder and cinnamon, add to the butter mixture and mix well. Add the ground walnuts and mix again.

Pinch walnut size pieces of dough, roll into balls and put on the prepared trays, 2cm (1 inch) apart. Place a walnut half in each cookie and press gently to flatten.

Bake in the oven for 15-20 minutes until light brown.

Karabij
(Nut filled ma'amoul with naatif cream)

Karabij are nut filled ma'amoul pastries covered with a cream called naatif. They were served during the Jewish festival of Purim, but were also present in all the grand occasions and celebrations. Naatif was made with something called bois de Paname, a pale dry wood It is not available in Europe, but the following recipe for making the cream is a good substitute.

Makes around 30 pastries

Make the ma'amoul pastries following the recipe for nut filled ma'amoul. Allow them to cool and prepare the naatif cream.

Naatif cream
- 450g granulated sugar
- 200g water
- juice of ½ lemon
- 3 egg whites

Make the sugar syrup – place the sugar, water and lemon juice in a saucepan. Bring to the boil, lower the heat and simmer for 10 minutes until the syrup reaches a firm consistency.

Beat the egg whites. When they begin to stiffen, gradually add the hot steaming syrup, then continue beating until the cream is soft and spreadable.

Coat each pastry with the naatif cream and place them on a serving plate.

Ma'amoul stuffed with nuts

Makes around 30 pastries

This is the classic recipe for ma'amoul, using a mixture of flour and semolina. In Egypt, the date filled ma'amoul were round, whereas the nut filled ones had an oblong shape. The only way to achieve this was to use a special ma'amoul mould which nowadays can be purchased online. Alternatively, you can make them round like the date filled ones.

For the dough
  230g plain flour, sifted
  175g fine semolina
  225g unsalted butter
  1 teaspoon rose water (optional)
  ¼ to ½ cup lukewarm water

For the filling
  400g nuts (almonds, walnuts, pistachios or a mixture of those)
  3 tablespoons icing sugar
  40g unsalted butter, melted
  ½ teaspoon orange blossom water

Preheat the oven to 180C/Gas Mark 4.
Line 2 baking tray with parchment paper.

Prepare the filling – chop the nuts very finely or blitz them quickly in a food processor. Add the icing sugar, melted butter and orange blossom water and mix well.

Prepare the dough – in a large bowl, sift the flour and semolina. Add the butter and mix with your hands until you have a crumbly consistency. Add the water slowly, stopping as soon as the dough is soft and malleable.

Divide the dough into 4 portions. Work with 1 portion at a time and cover the rest with clingfilm.

Take a walnut sized ball from the dough and gently press down the centre with your finger until you have a 1cm (½ inch) indentation. Place a teaspoon of the filling in the indentation and close the pastry into a ball.

If using the special ma'amoul mould, lightly dust the mould with a little semolina or icing sugar. Press the top of the pastry firmly against the mould in order to impress the pattern. Lightly tap the mould on a hard surface to remove the pastry.

If making a round shape, make a design by pinching all over the top with dented pincers or by pricking with a fork.

Place the pastries on a baking tray and bake for about 20 minutes - the bottom of the pastries should be lightly browned and the top still pale.

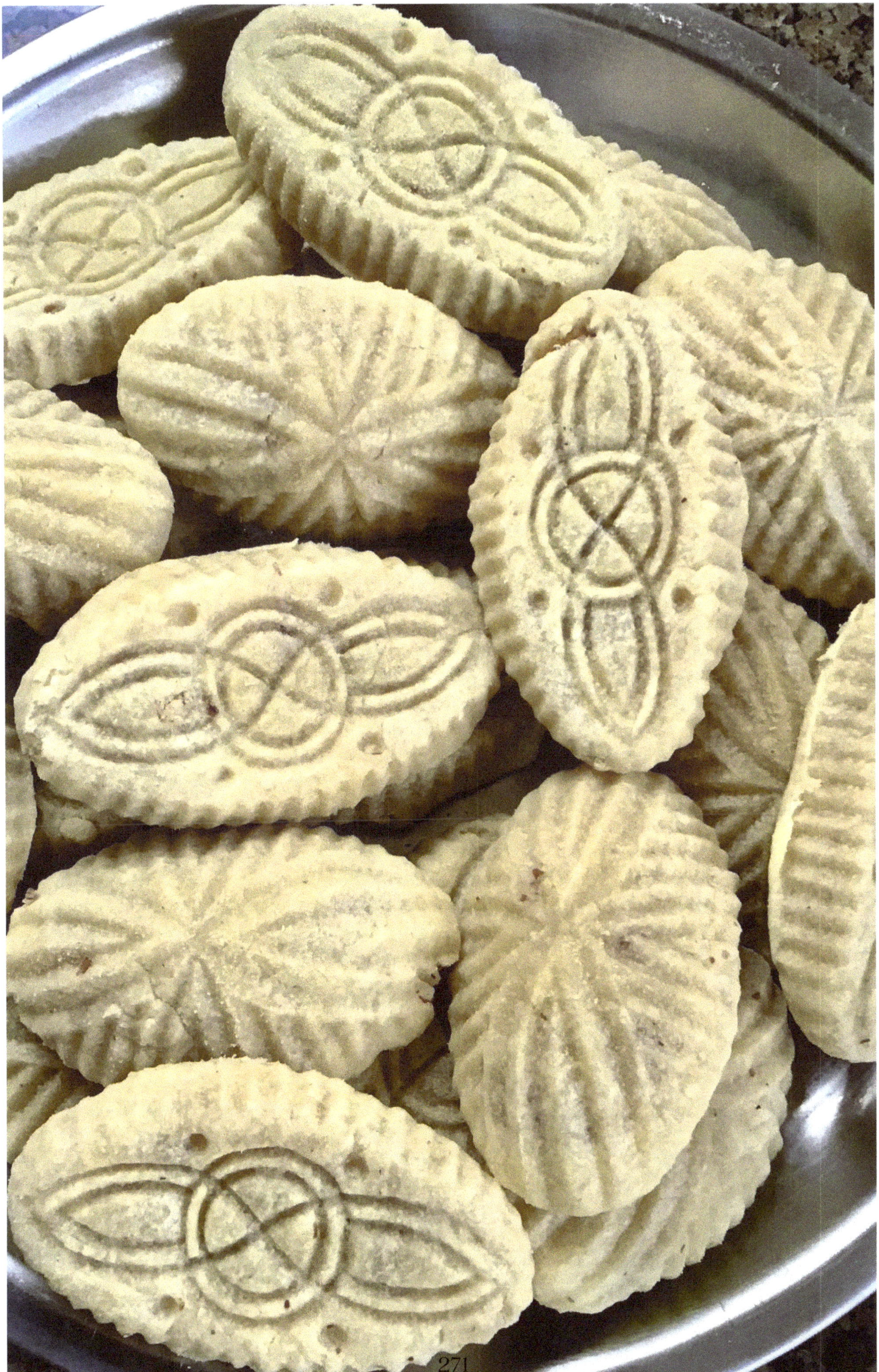

Ma'aroud
(Date and marzipan slices)

Makes 30

Ma'aroud resembles ma'amoul, as they both use a combination of dough and dates. However, ma'amoul are made as individual circle pastries, whereas ma'aroud are rolls that are stuffed with dates and cut into small slices. My mother often used to make them when we came to London, as a quick alternative to ma'amoul. I have mixed some marzipan with the dates as I wanted to add a Sephardic touch to a traditional Middle Eastern pastry – marzipan, or massapan as the Jews from Spain call it, is the favourite basis of many Sephardic sweetmeats and confectionery. Ready made date paste is sold as a block and is available from all Middle Eastern stores.

For the dough
260g plain flour
175g semolina
½ teaspoon baking powder
2 tablespoons sugar
115ml vegetable or sunflower oil
100g unsalted butter
100ml lukewarm water

For the filling
350g dates or date paste
150g marzipan

Preheat the oven to 180C/Gas Mark 4.

Line a large baking tray with baking parchment.

Prepare the dough – mix the flour, semolina, baking powder and sugar. Add the butter, oil and water. Use your hands to make the dough and add more water or flour if necessary - the dough should be soft and manageable. Divide it into 6 pieces.

Prepare the filling - If using dried dates, chop them up, add a drop of oil and soften them in the microwave for 10 seconds. Ready made date paste, if available, is softer and easier to handle. Mix the dates with the marzipan and divide into 6 pieces.

On a lightly floured board, place a piece of dough and roll out into a rectangle.

Place 1 piece of the date and marzipan mixture about 2cm (1 inch) from the edge and carefully fold to make a roll.

Place on a baking sheet and cut into 2cm (1 inch) pieces. Repeat with the other 5 rolls of dough and 5 pieces of date and marzipan mixture, cutting each roll in 2cm (1 inch) pieces.

Bake in a preheated oven for 35-40 minutes until the top is golden.

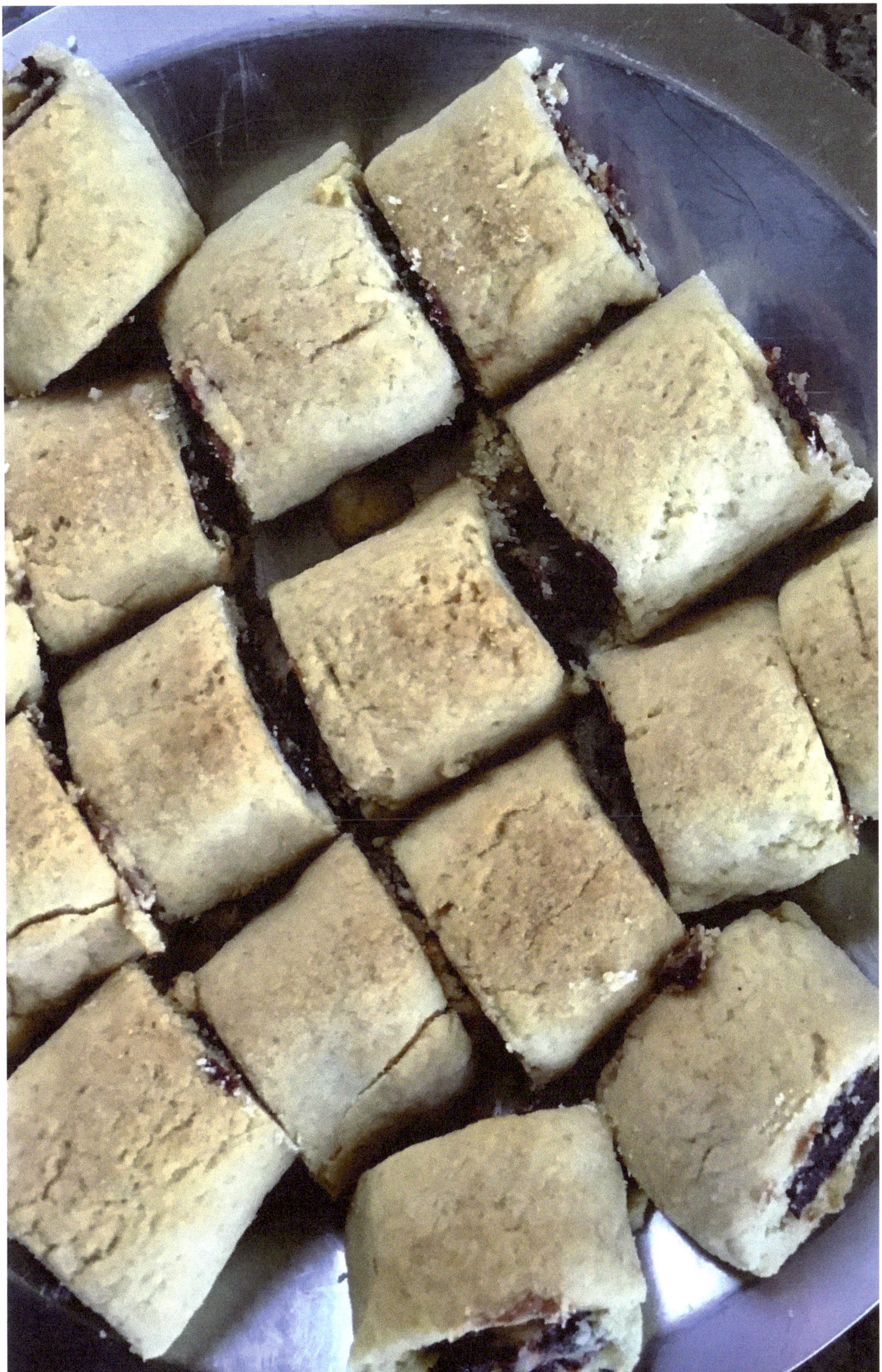

Nut and raisin pastries

These soft pastries are filled with almonds, raisins and candied peel. They were originally an old specialty of Rome, where they were called pizza dolce Romana. I found the recipe in Claudia Roden's Book of Jewish Food and have adapted it slightly.

Makes 24 pastries

500g flour
125g sugar
250g unsalted butter
5-8 tablespoons sweet white wine or water
50g pine nuts
50g almonds, coarsely chopped
60g raisins
70g candied peel

icing sugar to sprinkle on

Preheat the oven to 160C/Gas Mark 3.
Line a large baking tray with baking parchment or waxed paper.

In a large bowl, mix the flour and sugar and work into a soft dough with the butter – you may use a food processor for this - then turn the mixture into a bowl.

Add just enough liquid – a tablespoon at a time – to make the dough hold together.

Work in the almonds, raisins, candied peel and pine nuts. Shape into little round cakes, about 6cm (2½ inch) in diameter, pressing the mixture firmly between your palms.

Place on the baking tray and bake for 25-30 minutes. The pastries will still be soft and hardly coloured, but they will firm up when they cool. Do not try to remove them until they are firm.

Sprinkle with icing sugar when they have cooled completely.

Halva and sumac shortbread

Sumac is a citrus- flavoured spice that comes from the berry of a shrub that grows in the Mediterranean. It is very popular in Middle Eastern cooking and is now available in most super markets. These biscuits are crunchy on the outside and soft on the inside.

Makes around 30

225g unsalted butter, softened
115g caster sugar
100g halva
1 tablespoon rose water
1 tablespoon ground sumac
250g plain flour
pinch of salt
granulated sugar to sprinkle (optional)

Preheat the oven to 170C/Gas Mark 3.
Line 2 baking sheets with baking parchment.

Cream the butter and sugar in a bowl until soft. Crumble in the halva, add the rose water and sumac and mix again until smooth. Add the flour and salt and mix until the dough comes together.

Bring the dough into a ball, knead lightly and briefly until you have a pastry-like consistency. Roll out on a lightly floured surface and cut out biscuit shapes around 5cm (2 inch) in diameter. Prick the surface with a fork and sprinkle with granulated sugar.

Bake for around 12-15 minutes until golden brown.

Cook on a wire rack and store in a tin or airtight container.

Anise biscuits

Makes 40

These anise-scented biscuits are found all over the Middle East, particularly in Lebanon and Syria. They use oil instead of butter and are usually shaped like small bracelets. Anise seeds are available in Middle Eastern stores.

250g plain flour
1½ teaspoon baking powder
a pinch of salt
1 tablespoon anise seeds
2 teaspoons ground anise
½ teaspoon cardamom
½ teaspoon ground cinnamon
180g caster sugar
1 egg, beaten
3 tablespoons warm water
110ml sunflower or rapeseed oil

Line two baking trays with baking parchment.

Mix the flour, baking powder, salt, anise seeds, ground anise, cardamom, cinnamon and sugar together in a large bowl.

Make a well in the centre and pour in the beaten egg and warm water. Gradually add the oil, a tablespoon at a time, until the mixture comes together in a pliable dough. Wrap in clingfilm and leave to rest for 20 minutes.

Break off pieces of dough the size of an olive. Flatten on a lightly floured board and cut into shape, using a biscuit cutter of your choice. Place the biscuits on the baking trays and make little cuts with a knife along each biscuit.

Bake for 15–20 minutes until firm and golden brown.

Note – the biscuits will keep for up to two weeks in an airtight container.

Sablés à la confiture

(Shortbread biscuits with a jam filling)

Makes around 25 jam filled biscuits

My mother used to bake these on a regular basis. They are shortbread biscuits filled with jam and are very easy to make. You can use any jam you like, or even a hazelnut or chocolate spread.

150g unsalted butter, softened
100g sugar
250g plain flour
100g ground almonds
¼ teaspoon cinnamon
20-30ml water
100g apricot or strawberry jam

Preheat the oven to 180C/Gas Mark 4.
Line 2 large baking trays with greaseproof or parchment paper.

Cream the butter with the sugar until fluffy. Add the flour, cinnamon and ground almonds and mix well, adding just enough water to make a soft dough.

Divide the dough into 4 portions. On a lightly floured board, roll out one portion of pastry dough and using biscuit cutters, cut the pastry into different shapes – I have used a variety of small biscuit cutters, but you can use larger ones if you prefer bigger biscuits. Continue with the remaining 3 portions.

Place on the baking tray and bake for 15 minutes. Let them cool.

Warm the jam in the microwave for 1 minute. Take one biscuit, spread a little jam over the top and cover with another biscuit of identical shape. Continue until you have used all the biscuits.

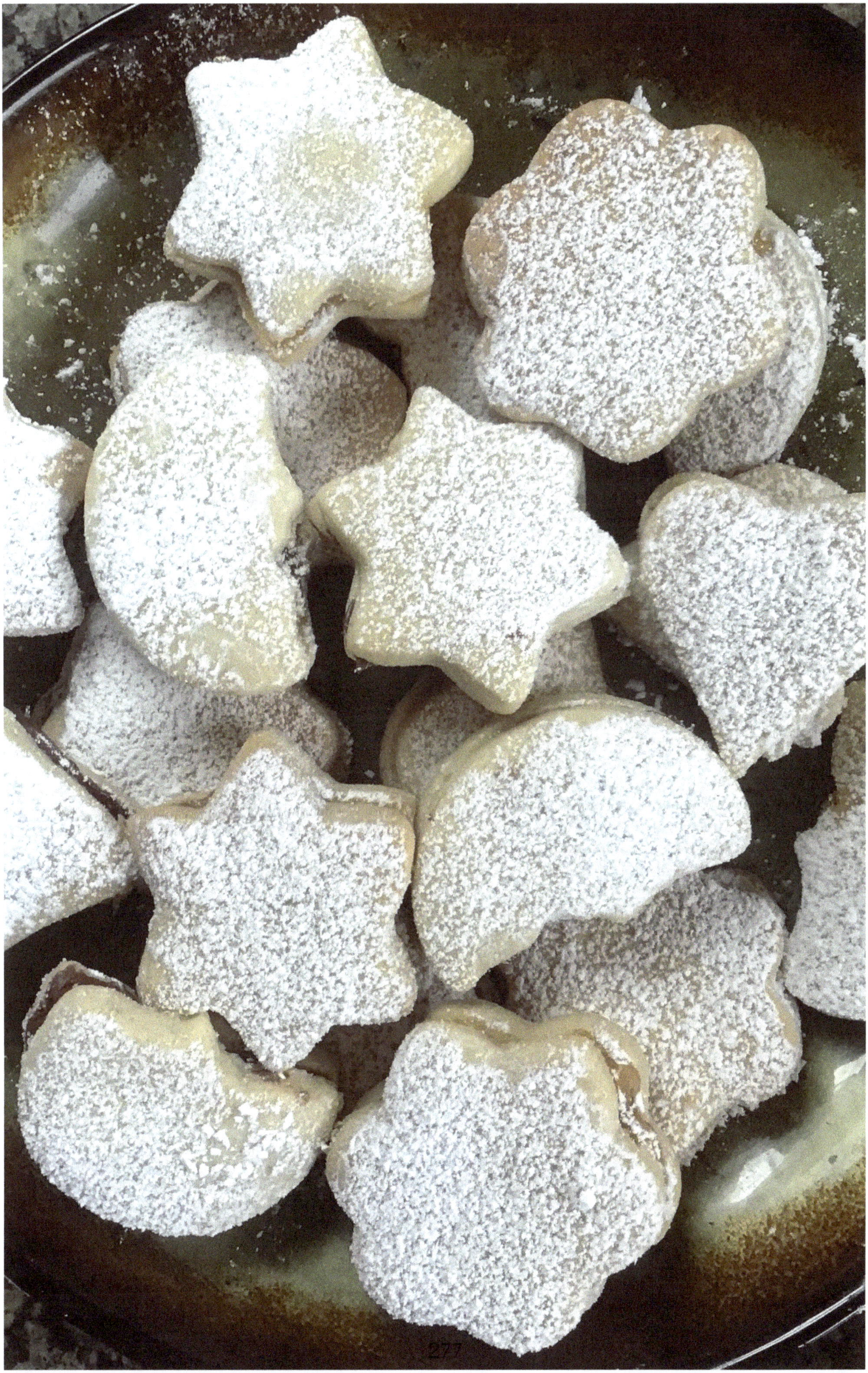

Egg free chocolate cupcakes

Makes 30 cupcakes

These cupcakes take no time to make, as there is very little mixing involved. You can be as creative as you like with regard to the topping. Buttercream frosting is the usual choice, but that is too sweet for my liking, as the cupcakes are very rich anyway. I like using grated chocolate or chocolate sprinkles instead.

100ml milk
1½ teaspoon apple cider vinegar
170g light brown muscovado sugar
110ml sunflower oil
1 teaspoon vanilla extract
90g yoghurt
150g self raising flour
60g cocoa powder
1 teaspoon baking powder
½ teaspoon salt

For the topping
  50-80g dark chocolate, grated sprinkles or chocolate curls

Or
Buttercream icing
  200g unsalted butter, softened
  1 teaspoon vanilla extract
  400g icing sugar
  1-2 tablespoons milk
  100g dark chocolate, melted

Preheat the oven to 180C/Gas Mark 4.
Line a 12-hole muffin tin with muffin cases.

Stir together the milk and vinegar in a mug – the milk should curdle slightly. Set aside.

In a large bowl, whisk together the sugar, oil and vanilla extract, then whisk in the yoghurt, making sure to combine all the sugar. Add the curdled milk and mix.

In another large bowl, sift together the flour, cocoa powder, baking powder and salt. Gradually whisk the wet ingredients into the dry until smooth. Be careful not to over mix.

Divide the batter evenly between the cases and bake in the preheated oven for 15-20 minutes, until well risen and a skewer inserted into the centre of a cake comes out almost clean. It should be slightly paste-like, but not wet and glistening – slightly underbaked makes for a fudgier cake.

Leave the cakes on a wire rack to cool. Sprinkle with grated chocolate or chocolate curls.

Alternatively, make the buttercream frosting – beat the butter and vanilla in a mixer on high speed until pale. Add the sifted icing sugar in two batches, beating well, until light and fluffy. Loosen the frosting with milk and mix again, then pour in the melted chocolate and stir through. Spread the frosting onto the cupcakes with a palette knife or pipe in a circular motion from the outside of the cake inwards, in one continuous motion, to create a whipped top.

Note – the cupcakes will keep in an airtight box for up to 2 days.

Halva and tahini brownies

Makes 16 pieces

These brownies are extra rich, due to the addition of halva, which is very sweet. You can halve the quantity of halva or leave it out altogether. The tahini paste adds an unusual nutty taste.

250g unsalted butter
250g dark chocolate
4 large eggs
260g caster sugar
140g spelt flour
60g cocoa powder
100g tahini paste
200g vanilla halva, broken into 2cm (1 inch) pieces
½ teaspoon sea salt flakes

Preheat the oven to 180c/Gas Mark 4.
Butter and line a 20 x 30cm (8 x 12 inch) baking dish with parchment.

Put a heatproof bowl over a pan of simmering water and add the butter and chocolate. Stir occasionally and remove from the heat when the mixture has completely melted. Set aside to cool.

Whisk the eggs and caster sugar in a bowl until combined. Do not over whisk. Stir the egg mixture into the chocolate mixture.

Sift the flour and cocoa powder and fold everything together.

Pour the mixture into the prepared baking dish.

Stir the tahini well and drizzle this over the brownie mixture. Dot with halva pieces, then gently run a knife through it to give it a marbled effect. Sprinkle with sea salt.

Bake for 25 minutes. The brownies should just be set, but a little wobbly.

Sansaticos

(Almond frangipane-filled filo triangles)

Makes around 30

These are Sephardic triangle-shaped filo pastries filled with chopped nuts and scented with the zest of oranges or orange blossom water. In many communities, they were traditionally served at the ritual Bridal Bath, Banyo de Novia. They are usually dipped in a sugar syrup as soon as they come out of the oven. I prefer a pastry that is less sweet and have opted for a dusting of icing sugar instead. They make a great dessert, served with ice cream and mixed berries.

250g ready-made filo pastry, at room temperature
100g unsalted butter, melted

For the filling
200g walnuts, finely chopped
85g caster sugar
1½ teaspoon ground cinnamon
2 tablespoons unsalted butter, melted
grated zest of 1 orange

icing sugar for dusting

Preheat the oven to 180C/ Gas Mark 4.
Line two large baking trays with baking parchment.

Prepare the filling by combining all the filling ingredients in a bowl.

Make the filo triangles- open a filo sheet on a flat working surface with the narrow end nearest you. Keep the remainder covered with a damp towel – this is important, as the pastry dries very quickly. With a sharp knife, cut the sheet along the length in 3 rectangular strips, approximately 30 x 10cm (12 x 4 inch) each.

Brush each strip with melted butter and put 1 heaped spoonful of filling at the short end, about 3cm (1¼ inch) from the edge. Lift up the bottom corner and fold diagonally to make a triangle- shaped pastry. Continue to fold the triangle over itself until the whole strip is used.

Repeat with the remaining filo sheets and filling. Transfer the pastries onto the prepared baking trays, spaced 1cm (½ inch) apart. Brush the tops with melted butter.

Bake in the preheated oven for 25-30 minutes, until crisp and golden. While the pastry is still warm, sprinkle with sifted icing sugar and serve.

Note – alternatively, the pastries can be dipped in a warm sugar syrup, made of 125g sugar, 75ml water, ½ tablespoon lemon juice and 2 tablespoons liquid honey. Boil the water and sugar with the lemon juice for about 10 minutes, until thick enough to cost the back of a spoon, then add the honey and cook for a minute longer.

The baked pastries can be stored in an airtight container for up to one week – place the triangles between layers of baking paper.

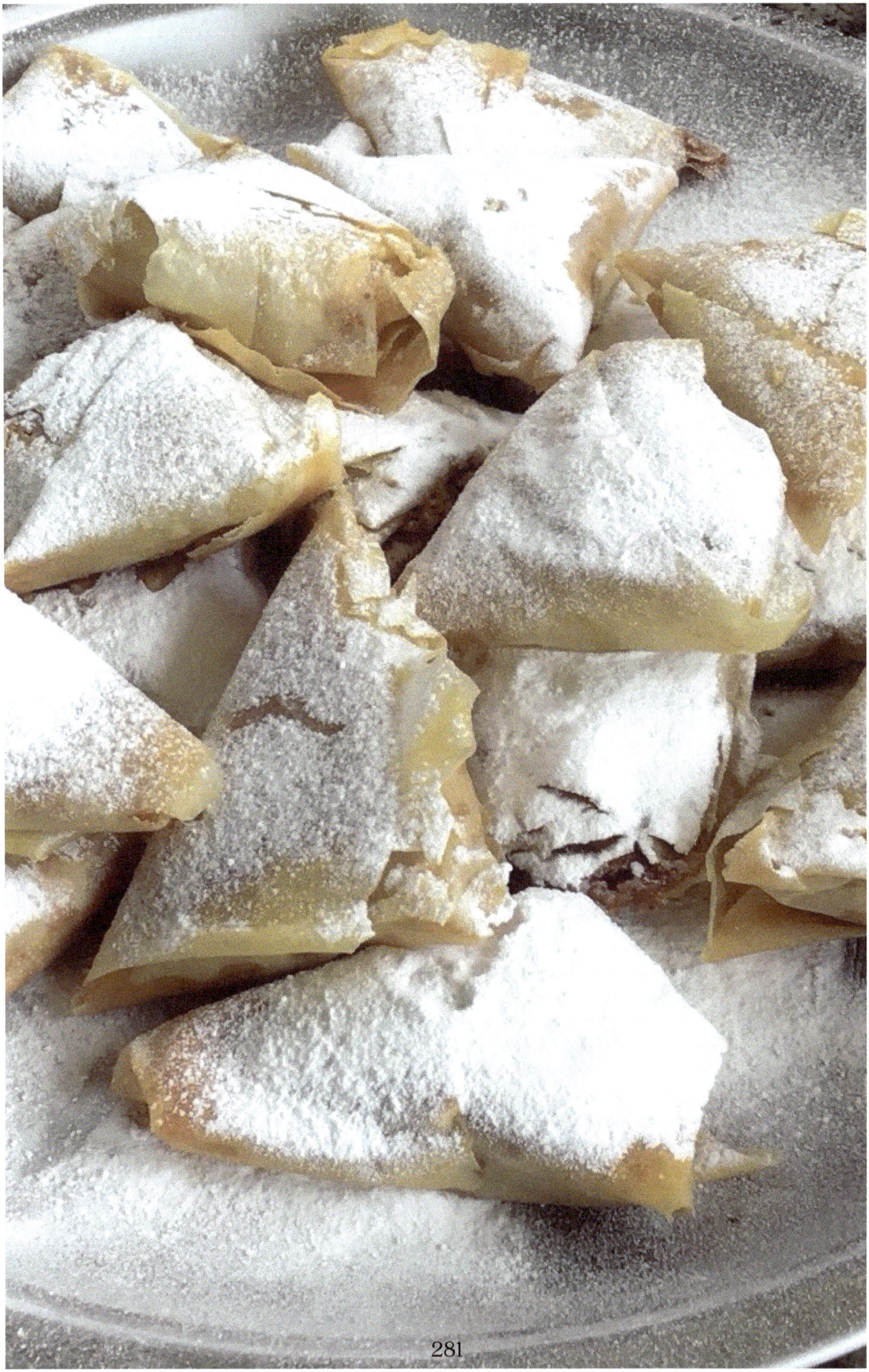

Maamoul aux figues
(Maamoul with figs)

Makes around 25

The recipe for this dough is different from the classic one we used in Egypt and the fig filling is also unusual, as dates are the traditional one for ma'amoul.

125g unsalted butter, softened
50g icing sugar
yolk of 1 egg
200g plain flour
pinch of salt

For the filling
  25 dried figs, chopped
  2 tablespoons orange blossom water

Preheat the oven to 180C/Gas Mark 4.
Line a large tray with baking parchment.

Prepare the filling – cut the dried figs into small pieces and blitz them in a food processor with the orange blossom water. Separate into 25 small balls.

Make the dough - mix the butter with the icing sugar until soft. Add the egg yolk and a pinch of salt and mix well. Gradually add the flour, mixing the dough with your hands, until you have a soft malleable ball which does not stick to your hand.

Separate the dough into 25 pieces. Take one piece of dough and flatten it with your hands. Slowly enlarge the sides and gently press the bottom until you have the shape of a small pot.

Fill the hole with a lump of filling, bring the dough over the filling and close it into a ball.

Repeat this with the rest of the dough pieces and fillings.

Arrange the pastries on the baking tray lined and gently flatten each one. Make a design by pinching all over the top with dented pincers.

Bake in a preheated oven for 20 minutes.

Note - I have used a special ma'amoul mould which can be bought online from a company called Made in Syria.

Travados

(Sephardic nut pastries)

Makes 25 pieces

Travados are Turkish Sephardic pastries served at holiday celebrations, especially the festival of Purim and the Jewish New Year (Rosh Hashanah). They are delicious with a cup of tea or coffee and will keep well for a week in an airtight container.

For the filling
   50g almonds, chopped
   50g walnuts, chopped
   50g hazelnuts, chopped
   1 egg
   6 tablespoons honey
   1 teaspoon cinnamon
   ½ teaspoon ground cloves

For the dough
   230ml vegetable oil
   120ml water
   2 teaspoons baking powder
   430g plain flour, sifted

For the syrup
   150ml water
   150g caster sugar
   100ml honey
   juice of ½ lemon

Preheat the oven to 180C/Gas Mark 4.
Line two large baking trays with parchment paper.

Prepare the filling – blitz the nuts in a food processor for 10 seconds. Combine the rest of the ingredients in a bowl, add the nuts and mix to a soft paste.

Prepare the dough – combine the oil, water and baking powder in a bowl Add the flour, a little at a time. Mix without kneading, to form a soft, pliable dough. Add a little more flour if the dough is too oily, or more oil or water if it's dry and crumbly. Do not overwork the dough. Wrap in foil and refrigerate for 1 hour.

Make the biscuits – pinch off 25 walnut sized pieces of dough and roll into balls. On a lightly floured board, flatten each ball into a circle, using a glass turned upside down. Place 1 teaspoon of the prepared filling in the centre of each circle. Fold over to form a semi circle and press down the edges with your fingers to seal. Repeat until all the dough pieces and filling have been used.

Place the biscuits on the prepared baking trays and bake for 30 minutes or until golden.

To make the syrup, heat the water, sugar, honey and lemon juice in a large saucepan and stir until the sugar has dissolved. Place the lukewarm pastries into the syrup and simmer for 3 minutes. Remove with a slotted spoon and drain.

Note – if you prefer something less sweet, substitute the honey syrup with icing sugar sprinkled over the baked biscuits.

Sephardic biscochos

Makes 36

Biscochos are a Sephardic classic and part of a rich ethnic culture. Together with borekas and other small pastries, they represent a collection of recipes which have been passed on from generation to generation. They are twice baked, like biscotti, but the crumb is much lighter.

3 large eggs
85ml sunflower oil
125g caster sugar
½ teaspoon vanilla extract
415g plain flour, sifted
1 egg yolk for glazing
some sesame seeds

Preheat the oven to 180C/Gas Mark 4.
Line two baking tray with parchment paper.

Beat the eggs until light and foamy for about 10 minutes - it's very important not to be tempted to cut down the time. Add the sugar, oil and vanilla extract and beat well until combined.

Sift the flour in a large bowl and pour the wet ingredients over the flour.

Use your hands to lift the flour over the liquid and continue until the dough is combined. If the dough is too sticky, add some flour, if it's too hard, add a little oil – you want a dough that will roll out without sticking to the table and will not crumble when pressed.

Assemble the dough into a ball, place it on a working surface and cover with a bowl. Let it rest for 10 minutes.

Divide the dough into 36 walnut sized balls. Work with a few balls at a time and keep the rest covered so that the dough does not dry out.

Roll each ball into about 12cm (5 inch) length. When rolling towards the edges, don't flatten your hands to the table, otherwise the ends will be pointy. Use a lifting motion at the ends to maintain the same thickness.

Slice the biscocho at an angle. Run a knife below it to loosen it from the working surface, gently lift and place it on the prepared baking tray in a round shape. The biscuits will puff a little, but they will not spread while baking. Brush lightly with egg wash and sprinkle with sesame seeds.

Bake in a preheated oven for 20 minutes, until golden on top. The biscochos should not be dark. Let them cool.

Place them all in one tray, return to the oven, lower the temperature to 160C/ Gas Mark 3 and bake for another 15 minutes.

Sweet Borekitas

Makes about 40

This is a sweet version of the Judeo Spanish borekas. They are drizzled with a blend of honey and orange blossom or rose water and are traditionally made for Rosh Hashahah, the Jewish New Year.

450g unsifted flour, plus more for dusting
120ml sunflower or vegetable oil
50g caster sugar
250ml hot water

200g unsalted butter, melted
1 egg yolk for glazing

Filling 1
100g ground almonds
grated zest of 1 lemon
1 tablespoon cinnamon
¼ teaspoon ground cloves
100g caster sugar

Filling 2
125g ground walnuts
grated zest of 1 orange
1 tablespoon cinnamon
¼ teaspoon nutmeg
100g caster sugar

To glaze
4-5 tablespoons honey
2 tablespoons orange blossom water or rose water

Preheat the oven to 180C/Gas Mark 4.
Line 2 large baking trays with baking parchment or lightly grease the base.

In a large bowl, place the flour, oil, sugar and hot water. Mix quickly with your hands until the dough is blended and pulls away from the side of the bowl. Add a little more flour is the dough is too sticky. Lightly press the dough into a ball. Cover and allow to rest at room temperature for 1 hour.

Select the filling and combine the ingredients.

Melt the butter in a saucepan.

Pinch pieces of dough the size of an egg. Roll out on a well floured board with a rolling pin and cut a circle with a glass turned upside down. Brush some melted butter on the bottom of the circle and fill the centre with 1 teaspoon of the filling. Sprinkle a little more melted butter over the top. Fold the circle over the filling to form a half moon and gently press down the edges. Using the tines of a fork, seal by pressing and imprinting all around the cut edges. Repeat until all the dough, including the excess, has been used.

Place the pastries on the prepared baking trays and brush over with any remaining melted butter, then with the egg yolk.

Bake in the preheated oven for 25 minutes.

Brush the pastries with the honey and orange blossom mixture when they are still hot.

Menenas
Ma'amoul with date filling

Makes around 30

Menenas are the Jewish Egyptian version of the Arab ma'amoul. The difference is that the only ingredients used are butter and flour, resulting in a pastry that melts in the mouth. The small tartlets are traditionally stuffed with either nuts or a date paste. Every Jewish family kept a supply of these in their cupboard and the custom was to offer them to visitors, along with a cup of Turkish coffee and some homemade jam. I have been told they were my absolute favourite food as a toddler and apparently that was all I wanted to eat, along with bananas.

For the dough
  500g flour
  250g unsalted butter
  2 tablespoons sugar
  1 tablespoon rose water or orange blossom water (optional)
  1 tablespoon milk or more if required
  icing sugar for sprinkling

For the date filling
  500g soft pitted dates
  1 teaspoon sunflower oil

Preheat the oven to 160C/Gas Mark 3.
Line two large trays with baking parchment.

Prepare the date filling - chop the dates, add the oil and microwave for a few seconds until the dates are soft and malleable. Knead into a ball and divide into 30 small lumps.

Prepare the dough - mix the flour and sugar and rub in the butter. Work until the mixture resembles fine breadcrumbs. Add the rose water or orange blossom water, if using and just enough milk to bind the dough into a soft malleable ball. Divide this into 30 walnut sized lumps.

Take a lump of the dough, make a hole in the centre with your thumb then enlarge it slowly by turning and pressing until you have the shape of a small pot. Fill the hole with the date filling and bring the dough up to close into a ball. Any breaks can be easily patched as the dough is very soft. Flatten the filled balls slightly and place on a greased baking sheet. Make a design by pinching all over the top with pincers or a fork.

Bake in a preheated oven for 20-30 minutes - no longer as it's important you don't let them brown. The pastries will be soft and look pale when they come out of the oven, but they will firm up.

Sprinkle with icing sugar when cool.

Note - you will need some special dented pincers to decorate the top, but these are hard to find in England and a fork or angled tweezers will do just as well.

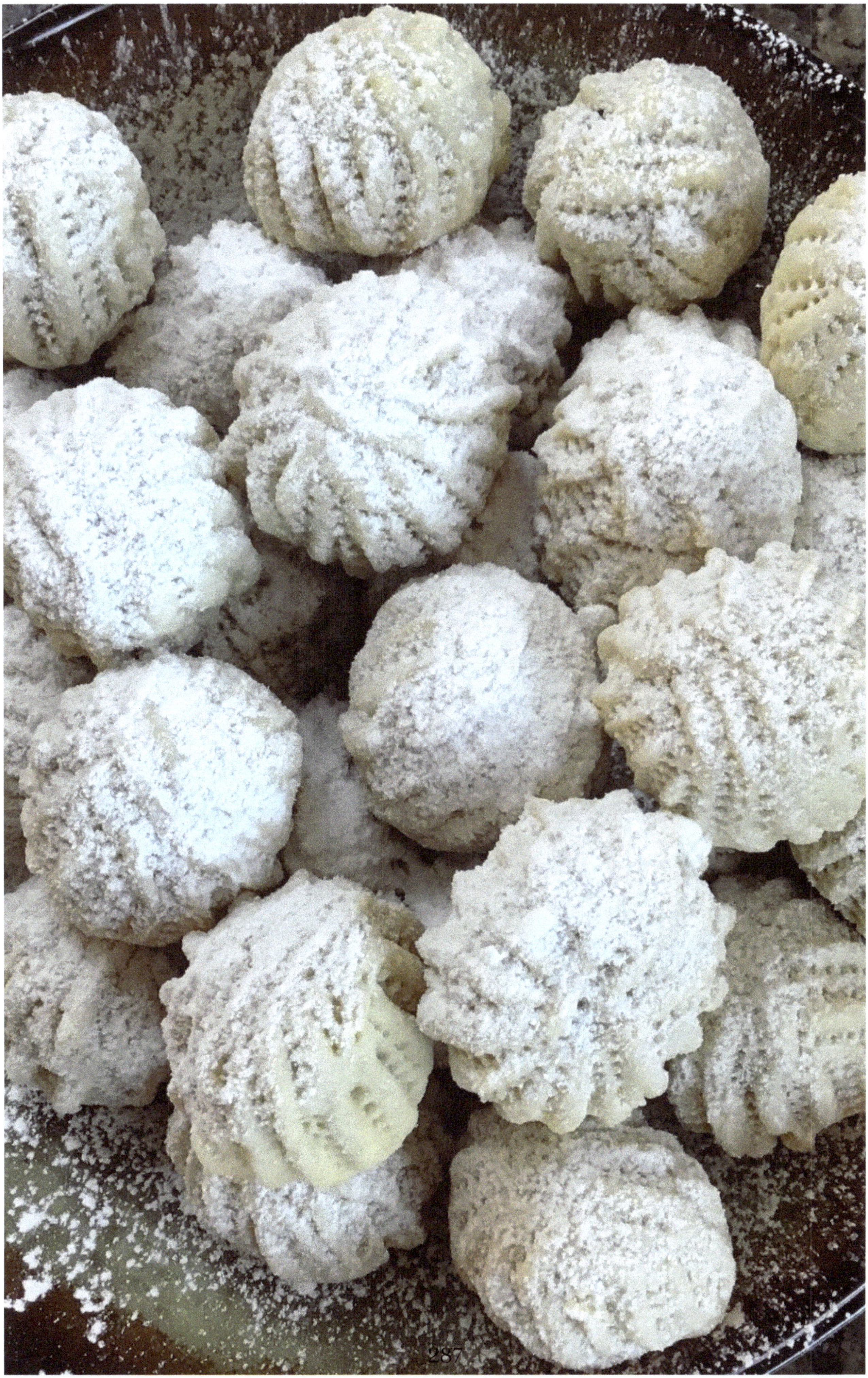

Mankouche au halwa

Makes 30

This is a Moroccan version of ma'amoul. The dough is different and more like a shortcrust pastry and the filling is also unusual, as ma'amoul are usually stuffed with dates or nuts.

For the dough
    250g unsalted butter
    140g icing sugar
    2 large eggs
    450-500g plain flour
    2 tablespoons orange blossom water
    1 tablespoon water

For the filling
    200g plain biscuits
    100g almonds, finely chopped
    200g halva
    150g apricot jam

Preheat the oven to 180C/Gas Mark 4.
Line a large tray with baking parchment.

Prepare the filling – crumble the biscuits in a food processor until you have a fine powder.

Transfer to a bowl. Blitz the almonds in a food processor for a few seconds and add to the biscuit mixture. Crumble the halva on top, then add the apricot jam and work with your hands until the mixture sticks together.

Make 30 small lumps with the filling mixture and set aside.

Prepare the dough - mix the butter and icing sugar with a hand mixer and add the eggs, one at a time. Gradually add 300g of the flour, working it first with a fork and then with your hands. Add the orange blossom water and continue adding the rest of the flour and a drop of water – just enough to bind the dough into a soft, malleable ball

Divide the dough into 30 walnut sized lumps.

Take a lump of dough and flatten it in your hand. Slowly enlarge the sides and gently press the bottom until you have the shape of a small pot (the dough is very soft and malleable, so it's very easy to shape and won't tear). Fill the hole with a lump of filling, then bring the dough over the opening and close it into a ball. Repeat this with the remaining lumps of dough and the filling.

Arrange the filled pastries on the baking tray and flatten gently with your hand. Make a design by pinching them all over the top with dented pincers or with a fork.

Bake in a preheated oven for 18 minutes. The pastries will be very soft and pale when they come out of the oven, but they will firm up when they cool.

290

CAKES
Pasteles
Cake

Pomegranate cake

I made this cake for Rosh Hashanah (the Jewish New Year) because the pomegranate seeds are one of the symbolic foods of the festival. It looked very pretty next to the traditional honey cake and kept well for a few days.

seeds (arils) of 1 pomegranate
90g unsalted butter, softened
150g caster sugar
1 large egg
2 teaspoons vanilla extract
½ teaspoon almond extract
250g plain flour, sifted
1½ teaspoon baking powder
½ teaspoon salt
150ml buttermilk or milk
20g demerera sugar to sprinkle

Preheat the oven to 180C/Gas Mark 4.
Generously grease a 22cm (9 inch) cake pan.

Spread the seeds of the pomegranate on a paper towel to take the moisture out.

Sift the flour, baking powder and salt and set aside.

Beat the butter and sugar until light and fluffy. Add the egg, vanilla and almond extracts. Add the flour mixture and buttermilk alternately, mixing on a low speed until the mixture is combined, no longer.

Scrape the batter into the prepared cake pan and smooth the top Sprinkle the pomegranate seeds on top of the batter, pressing them down slightly. Sprinkle with demerera sugar.

Bake in the preheated oven for 10 minutes, then lower the heat to 160C/Gas mark 3 for a further 50-60 minutes or until a skewer inserted in the middle comes out clean.

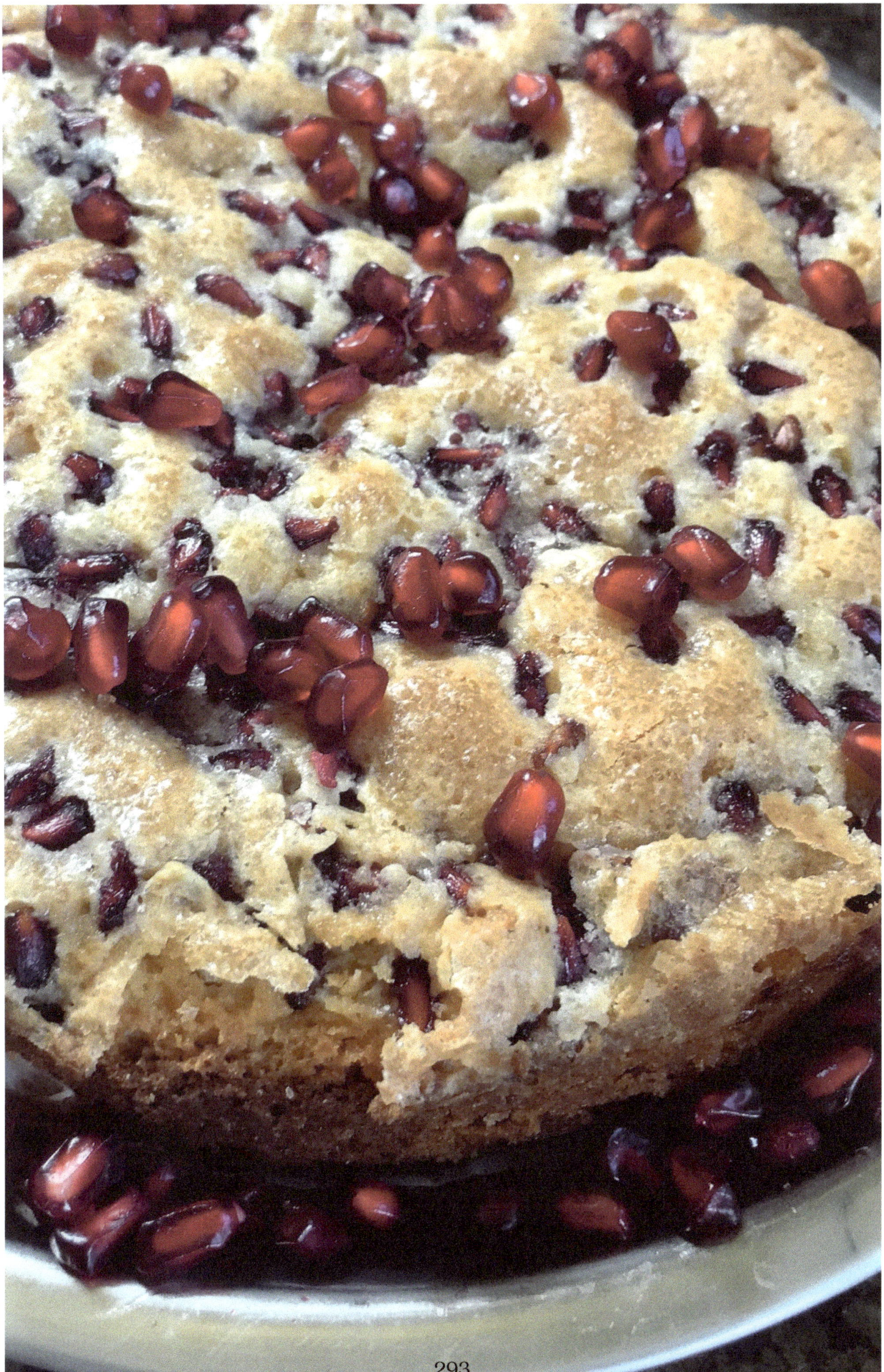

Chestnut and coffee cake with marrons glacés

This cake is very easy to make and is a lovely treat in the cold winter months. My mother used to make a similar version, using meringue shells instead of a cake base. The chestnut cream is extra special, but it can be replaced with a hazelnut spread.

For the cake
- 175g caster sugar
- 6 medium eggs
- 50g unsalted butter, melted
- 175g plain flour, sifted
- 2 teaspoons coffee essence

For the filling
- 450g double cream, lightly whipped
- 150g chestnut cream

For the topping
- 6 marrons glacés, chopped or 50g grated chocolate

Preheat the oven to 180C/Gas Mark 4.
Lightly grease a 22cm (9 inch) cake tin and line with baking parchment.

Whisk the eggs and sugar in a large bowl. Fold in the flour, melted butter and coffee essence. Pour into the prepared tin and bake for 35-40 minutes.

Remove from the oven and cool in the tin for 10 minutes before placing on a rack. When completely cooled, invert the cake onto a serving plate.

Whip the cream and fold in the chestnut purée through the cream.

Spread the mixture evenly over the cake. Decorate with chopped marrons glacés or grated chocolate.

Tunisian pistachio and orange cake

This cake has a coarse texture and nutty flavour. It is seeped with a light orange and sugar syrup, although this can be left out. I have added orange blossom water to the syrup, but again this is optional. You can serve it with a dollop of cream.

4 medium eggs
250g caster sugar
125g unsalted butter, melted
125g olive oil
zest of 2 oranges
250g pistachios, ground
70g polenta
125g plain flour
1½ heaped teaspoons baking powder

For the syrup
juice of 2 oranges
50g caster sugar
1 tablespoon orange blossom water (optional)

Preheat the oven to 150C/Gas Mark 2.
Grease a 22cm (9 inch) spring form cake tin and line with baking parchment.

Beat together the eggs and caster sugar until thickened. Slowly add the melted butter and oil and mix until smooth. Add the orange zest.

Combine the ground pistachios, flour, polenta and baking powder. Slowly fold this into the wet ingredients.

Transfer the mix to the prepared cake tin and bake for 50-60 minutes or until a skewer inserted in the middle comes out clean. The cake should be firm to the touch.

To make the syrup, place the orange juice and 50g caster sugar in a small pan. Heat on a gentle heat and reduce the liquid by one third until just thickening to a syrup.

Using a skewer, make a few fine holes into the cake. Slowly and evenly spoon on the orange syrup until the cake absorbs it all.

Note - the syrup is optional. If you prefer to leave it out, scatter the top with some chopped pistachios while the cake is still warm.

Membrillo, buttermilk and poppy seed traybake

Membrillo, the traditional quince paste eaten at Christmas, can be expensive to buy, so any fruit cheese, such as damson or pears, would work well in its place. There isn't much sugar in the batter, as most of it comes from the quince. I prefer to bake it as a traybake, but you can use a cake tin.

70ml melted butter, plus a little extra
250g white spelt flour, plus a little extra for the tin
1 teaspoon baking powder
50g caster sugar
½ teaspoon fine sea salt
60g poppy seeds
zest of 2 lemons
2 medium eggs
350ml buttermilk or yoghurt
250g membrillo (quince paste) cut into tiny cubes
3 tablespoons demerera sugar

Heat the oven to 220/Gas Mark 7.
Lightly grease and flour a 20 x 30cm (8 x 12 inch) baking dish.

In a large bowl, combine the flour, baking powder, caster sugar, poppy seeds, lemon zest and salt.

In a separate bowl, mix together the eggs and buttermilk or yoghurt, then add the melted butter. Add this to the flour mixture and stir briefly, until just combined. Gently fold in two-thirds of the membrillo cubes until they are evenly distributed.

Transfer the cake mixture to the prepared dish and arrange the remaining membrillo across the top in a pattern. Sprinkle with demerera sugar.

Bake in the preheated oven for 25-30 minutes or until a toothpick inserted in the middle comes out clean.

Serve warm or at room temperature.

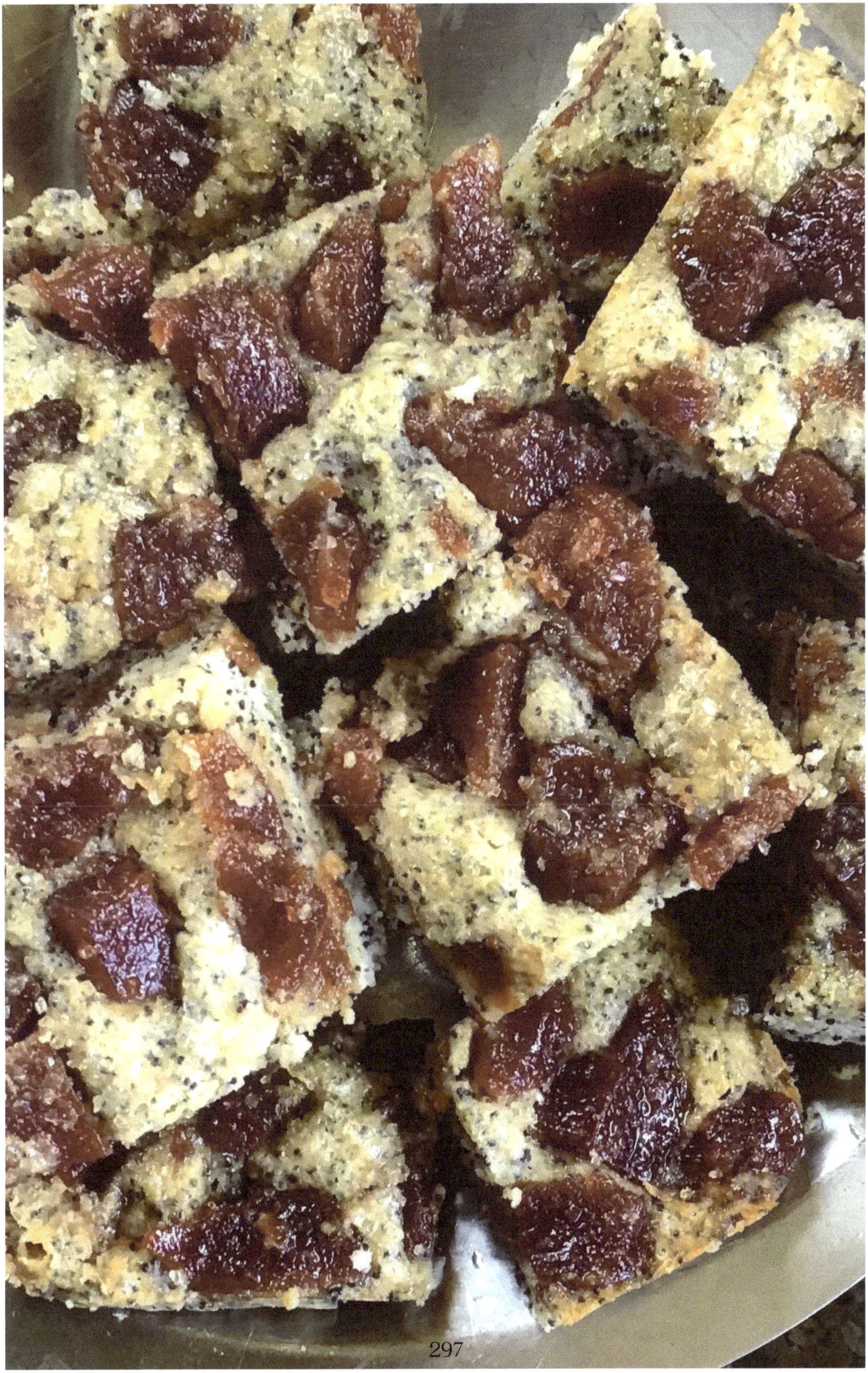

Eggless chocolate cake

Cakes made without eggs can be a little tricky and it's important to find a substitute which works. I have tried many and most have been a disappointment, the result being dense and dry. This is by far the best recipe and the only one I use now. In fact, it is so good that I prefer it to the standard ones with eggs.

325g self raising flour, sifted
½ teaspoon bicarbonate of soda
85g unsweetened cocoa powder
¼ teaspoon salt
115g unsalted butter
400g sugar
120ml sour cream
120ml vegetable or sunflower oil
360ml buttermilk
1 teaspoon coffee
2 teaspoons vanilla extract
1 teaspoon apple cider vinegar

Preheat the oven to 180C/Gas Mark 4.
Grease a 22cm (9 inch) cake pan and line with parchment paper.

In a large bowl combine the flour, bicarbonate of soda, salt and cocoa powder. Set aside.

Mix the butter and sugar in an electric mixer or in a large bowl, using a hand held mixer. When smooth, add the sour cream, oil, buttermilk, coffee, vanilla extract and apple cider vinegar. Mix well. Add the flour and cocoa mixture gradually until you have a smooth batter. Do not over mix.

Pour the batter into the prepared cake pan. Bake for 35-40 minutes or until a skewer inserted in the centre of the cake comes out clean.

Remove the cake from the oven and set on a wire rack. Allow to cool completely and decorate with chocolate frosting or grated chocolate.

Note - this cake is very rich, so instead of chocolate frosting I use either grated chocolate or chocolate buttons.

Fig and almond filo tart

This tart is inspired by the traditional baklava. What differentiates it is the mixture of frangipane, honey and figs which give it a natural sweetness, so there is no need to pour a sugar syrup over the pastry, as is the case with baklava.

8 medium figs
2 tablespoons clear honey

For the filo tart
6 sheets filo pastry
150g unsalted butter, melted
40g walnuts, finely chopped

For the frangipane
50g unsalted butter, softened
150g caster sugar
2 large eggs
140g ground almonds
40g pistachios, finely chopped

Preheat the oven to 180c/Gas Mark 4.
Grease a 23cm (10 inch) round tart tin.

Cut the figs in half and place them cut side up on a roasting tin. Brush them with the honey and bake for 10-20 minutes until soft.

Make the frangipane-: cream the butter and sugar for about 3 minutes, until light and fluffy. Add the eggs one at a time and the ground almonds. Mix well.

Place 1 filo sheet inside the middle of the tin, followed by another sheet, leaving the sides hanging. Brush generously with melted butter. Repeat with the next 4 sheets, brushing each sheet individually with melted butter.

Sprinkle the chopped nuts on the base of the tart, followed by the frangipane.

Place the figs carefully on top of the frangipane and gently fold the hanging pastry, one layer at a time. Brush the top with melted butter and finish by sprinkling the pistachio nuts.

Bake for 35-40 minutes. Remove from the tin and place on a serving plate, drizzle some honey and serve warm.

Seville orange and honey cake

Seville oranges are only available in January and February. Their bitter taste and thick skins are quite unique, so I try to make the most of the season - this means marmalade, but cakes also work well. This is one of my favourite recipes.

Ingredients
- 200g unsalted butter
- 200g caster sugar
- 1 Seville orange, zest and juice
- 2 large eggs
- 300g plain flour, sifted
- 1 teaspoon baking powder
- ½ teaspoon bicarbonate of soda
- 150ml thick yoghurt
- 50ml sunflower oil

Syrup
- 1½ Seville oranges
- 75g caster sugar
- 40g clear honey

Preheat the oven to 180C/Gas Mark 4.
Grease and line a 22cm (9 inch) cake tin.

Using electric beaters, beat the butter, sugar and orange zest until light and creamy. Beat in the eggs, one at a time, until thoroughly combined. Gradually add the sifted flour, baking powder, bicarbonate of soda, sunflower oil, yoghurt and orange juice, until fully incorporated.

Transfer to the prepared cake tin and bake for 1¼ hour or until a skewer inserted in the middle comes out clean. Cover with foil after 40 minutes if browning too quickly.

Remove from the oven and cool in the tin on a wire rack for 10 minutes.

Make the syrup – use a zester to pare thin strips of zest from the oranges. Juice the oranges and put the juice in a pan, together with the zest, sugar and honey.

Bring to the boil, reduce the heat and simmer for 5-6 minutes, stirring frequently, until reduced, thick and syrupy.

Using a skewer, poke holes all over the cake while still in the tin. Pour most of the syrup over the cake, reserving the zest and about 1 tablespoon of the syrup. Set aside to cool completely.

Transfer to a serving plate. Pour over the remaining syrup and arrange the zest on top.
Serve with a spoonful of crème fraîche.

Note - if you can't get Seville oranges, use 1 regular orange for the batter and ½ grapefruit with 1 orange for the syrup.

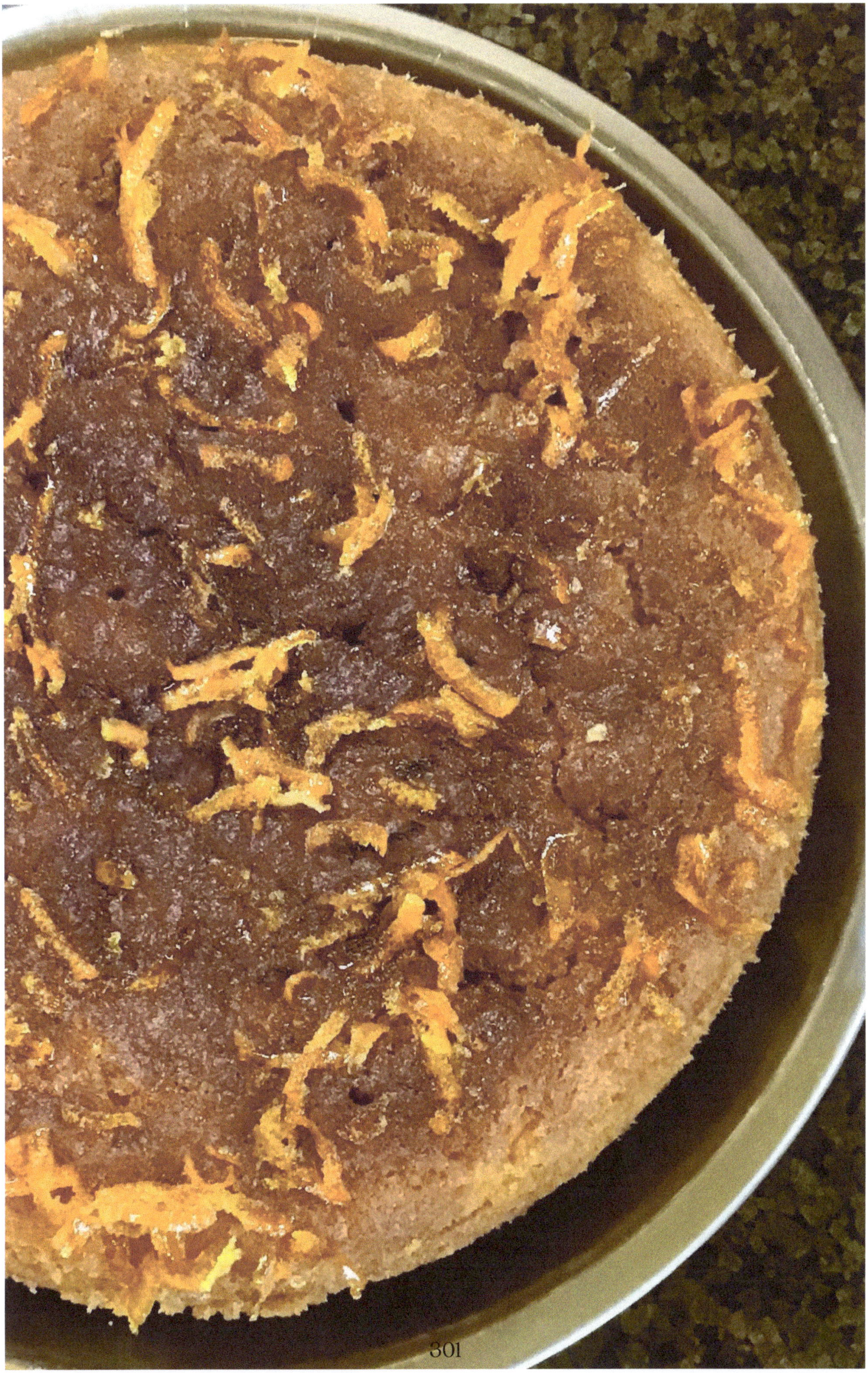

Fig and almond tart

Figs are my favourite fruit and nothing compares to the beautifully ripe ones you could get in any market in France or Spain when in season. In contrast, the ones you get in England are usually underripe and the best way to use them is in savoury or sweet dishes.

For the pastry
- 220g plain flour, sifted, plus more to dust
- 40g icing sugar, sifted
- ¼ teaspoon salt
- 120g unsalted butter, cubed
- zest of ½ orange
- 1 egg yolk
- 2-4 tablespoons cold water

For the filling
- 8 large figs or 12 small ones
- 3 tablespoons honey

- 200g unsalted butter
- 175g sugar
- 200g ground almonds
- 2 large eggs, lightly beaten
- ¼ teaspoon salt
- 1 teaspoon orange blossom water (optional)

Preheat the oven to 180C/Gas Mark 4.
Grease and flour a 23cm (10 inch) tart tin.

Start with the pastry - sift the flour, add the sugar, salt and the cubed butter. Work the mixture until you have a texture resembling fine breadcrumbs. Add the egg yolk, orange zest and just enough water to make a smooth dough – it's important to add the water slowly. Mould the dough into a ball, wrap with cling film and leave in the fridge for at least 30 minutes.

Prepare the figs - wash, chop the stems, cut them in half, place on a baking tray cut side up and drizzle with the honey. Place in the preheated oven and cook for 10 minutes. Remove and cool.

Take the pastry out of the fridge and bring it to room temperature for 15 minutes.

Line the base and sides of the prepared tin with the pastry, making sure you get an even layer. Prick all over with a fork. Cover the top with grease proof paper and fill the surface with baking beans. Bake the tart for 15 minutes.

Take the tart out of the oven and remove the greaseproof and baking beans. Return to the oven and bake for a further 15 minutes until golden on top. Leave to cool.

Prepare the filling - mix the butter and sugar until creamy and pale. Add the eggs, ground almonds, salt and orange blossom water, if using. Spoon the mixture on top of the pastry and press the figs into the almond mixture.

Return the tart to the oven and bake for 45 minutes or until golden all over.

Fig and raspberry crumble cake

There are a lot of ingredients in this cake, but it's worth the effort, especially when fresh figs are in season.

For the cake
- 100g unsalted butter, softened plus extra for greasing
- 150g caster sugar
- 2 large eggs, lightly beaten
- ½ teaspoon vanilla extra
- 125g plain flour
- 1 teaspoon baking powder
- 100g natural yoghurt
- 75g ground almonds
- 7 large figs stem removed and chopped into medium pieces
- 175g raspberries
- 30g flaked almonds

For the crumble topping
- 50g flour
- 25g unsalted cold butter, cut into cubes
- 35g soft light brown sugar

Preheat the oven to 180C/Gas Mark 4.
Grease and line the base of a 20cm (8 inch) springform cake tin.

Prepare the crumble - mix the flour and butter together with your fingertips until you have a crumble mixture. Add the soft brown sugar and mix well.

Make the cake - cream together the butter and sugar until pale and fluffy. Add the eggs one at a time, beating well after each addition. Sift the flour and baking powder and add them to the batter slowly, alternating with the yoghurt. Fold in the ground almonds and half the chopped figs. Pour the mixture into the prepared cake tin.

Add the remaining chopped figs and half the raspberries. Scatter on the crumble, then the remaining raspberries and finally the flaked almonds.

Bake in the oven for 1¼ hour or until a skewer inserted in the centre comes out clean.

When cool transfer onto a serving plate. Serve with crème fraîche.

Fresh fig cake with a crumb topping

Although I have used fresh figs, sliced apples or pears will do well. The advantage of this cake is that it can be made in advance and refrigerated.

For the cake
- 3 large eggs
- 240ml vegetable or sunflower oil
- 100g caster sugar
- 90g light brown sugar
- 120ml water
- 1½ teaspoon vanilla extract
- 240g plain flour
- 2 teaspoons baking powder
- ¾ teaspoon salt
- 1¼ teaspoon ground cinnamon
- 50g crystallised ginger, diced
- 5-10 fresh figs (depending on size), cut vertically

For the crumble
- 60g all purpose flour
- ½ teaspoon baking powder
- pinch of salt
- 2 tablespoons white sugar
- 2 tablespoons brown sugar
- ¼ teaspoon ground cinnamon
- 75g melted butter
- 75g walnuts, chopped

Preheat the oven to 180C/gas Mark 4.
Grease and line a 22cm (9 inch) cake tin.

In a large bowl, combine the eggs, vegetable or sunflower oil, sugars, water and vanilla extract. Whisk and set aside.

In a small bowl, combine the flour, baking powder, salt and cardamom. Whisk to combine. Add the dry ingredients to the wet ones and whisk slowly to blend. Stir in the crystallised ginger.

Pour the cake batter into the pan and arrange the figs cut side up in a circle around the cake. Set aside.

Make the crumble – mix the flour, baking powder, salt, sugars and cinnamon until combined. Add the melted butter and stir with a fork until a crumble forms. Stir in the walnuts. Sprinkle the crumble mixture on top of the figs and cake, evenly distributed.

Bake the cake in the preheated oven for 50-60 minutes or until a skewer inserted in the middle comes out clean. If the top starts to brown too quickly, cover with foil until fully baked through.

Note – this cake reheats beautifully, just wrap tightly in foil and refrigerate. To serve, place in a preheated oven (covered in the foil) and bake for 20 minutes or until warmed through.

Banana, medjool date and chocolate cake

I often serve this cake for dessert, with a dollop of crème fraîche. The taste of bananas is not overpowering, which can sometimes happen. Instead, there is a nice balance between the dates, chocolate and bananas. It's important to use medjool dates, as they are soft and just blend into the cake.

150g salted butter
150g caster sugar
2 eggs
1½ bananas, plus ½ banana sliced, for decoration
6 medjool dates
50g dark or milk chocolate, broken into pieces
175g self raising flour, sifted
½ teaspoon baking powder

Preheat the oven to 160C/Gas Mark 4.
Grease a 18cm (7 inch) round baking tin and line with baking parchment.

Cream the butter and sugar together until pale and fully. Add the eggs and beat again until well combined.

Mash the bananas in a bowl until smooth. Add them to the cake mix with the dates and chocolate and fold in gently. Do not overwork. Fold in the sifted flour and baking powder.

Spoon the batter into the prepared tin and arrange the remaining sliced banana on top for decoration.

Bake for 50-60 minutes or until a skewer inserted into the centre comes out clean.

Glazed mango sponge

Mango is an unusual topping for a cake, but I was curious to give it a try and the result was not disappointing. It is better to use ripe and fragrant mangoes, rather than the underripe varieties you get in supermarkets. These will still work, sprinkled with a little sugar beforehand.

1 ripe mango
2 large eggs, lightly beaten
170g caster sugar
115g plain yoghurt
120ml sunflower oil
finely grated zest of 1 lime or 1 lemon
180g plain flour, sifted
1½ teaspoon baking powder
30g desiccated coconut
2 tablespoons icing sugar, sifted (optional)

Preheat the oven 180C/ Gas Mark 4.
Grease and line a 20cm (8 inch) loose bottom tin.

Peel the mango and cut into thin slices. Arrange over the bottom of the cake tin.

Put the eggs, caster sugar, yoghurt, sunflower oil and lime or lemon zest in a large bowl. Stir until smooth and mixed.

Sift over the flour and baking powder and carefully fold in. Fold in the desiccated coconut. Spoon the mixture over the sliced mango in the prepared cake tin.

Bake for 50 minutes until the top is golden and firm to the touch. Cover with foil after 30 minutes if the cake begins to brown too much.

Leave the cake in the tin for 15 minutes and then turn out onto a dish, mango side up. Peel off the lining paper.

Optional - thickly dust with icing sugar. Place under a preheated hot grill for 3-4 minutes until the sugar has melted and the top is golden.

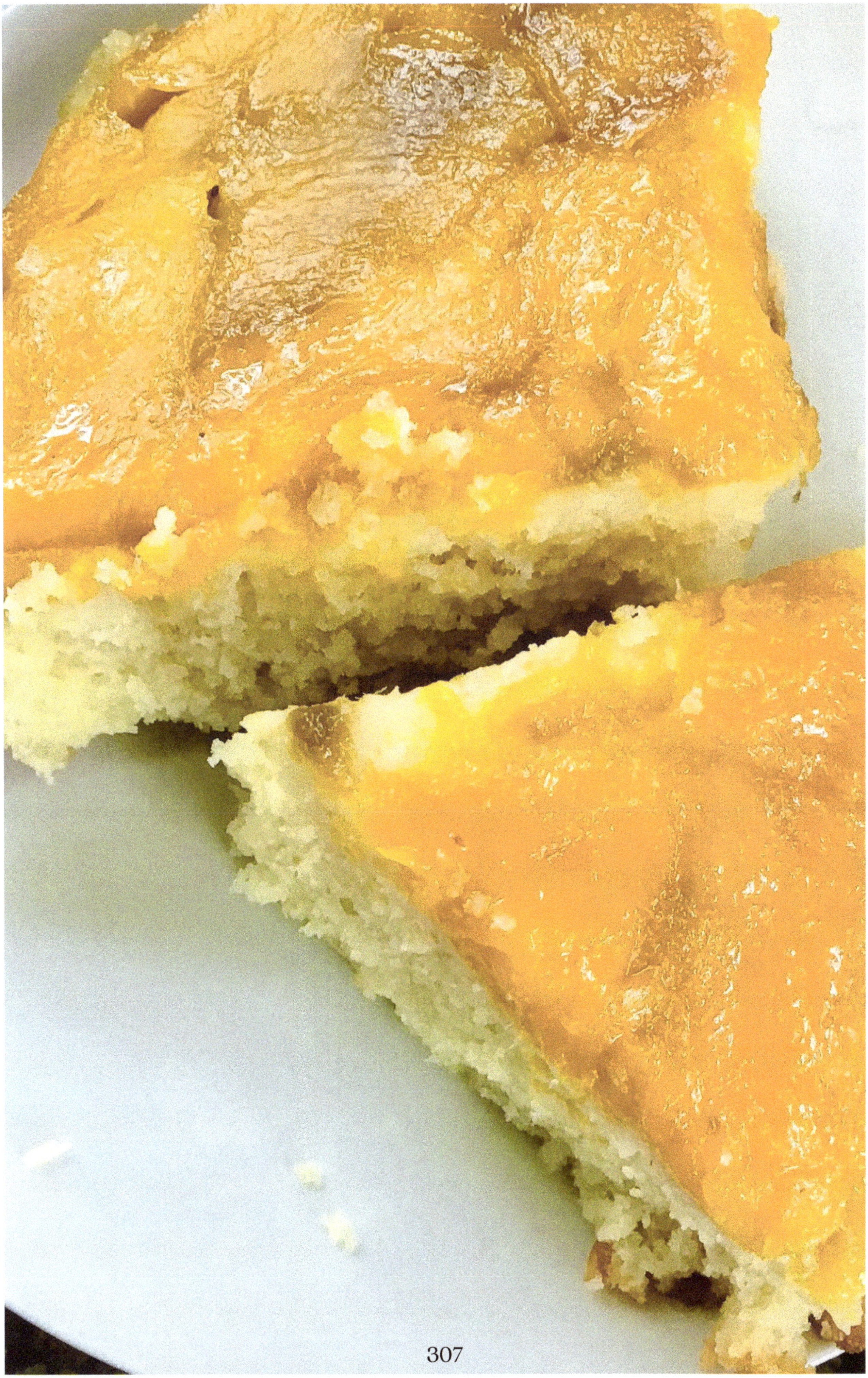

Pan di Spagna

(Spanish sponge cake)

In Egypt, pan di Spania, or rather pain d'Espagne, as we used to call it in French, was a generic term for sponge cakes. However, the classic recipe for this Sephardic cake is a legacy of the Jews of Medieval Spanish origin. No book about Sephardic cooking would be complete without it and we always had it as part of a meal at the breaking of the Yom Kippur (Day of Atonement) fast.

6 eggs, separated
100g caster sugar
zest of 1 orange or 1 lemon
80g self raising flour

Preheat the oven 190C/Gas Mark 6.
Grease and line a 23cm (9 inch) cake tin, preferably spring-form.

Beat the egg yolks with the sugar to a thick, pale cream. Add the orange or lemon zest.

In a separate bowl, beat the egg whites until stiff, then fold them into the egg mixture. Gradually fold in the flour.

Pour into the prepared cake tin and bake in the preheated oven for 40 minutes or until a skewer inserted in the middle of the cake comes out clean.

Note- this cake is featherlight and can be served as a dessert, accompanied by fresh strawberries or berries and whipped cream.

Rosh Hashanah Honey Cake

This is my favourite recipe for the traditional Rosh Hashanah (Jewish New Year) honey cake. It's quite easy to make, despite the long list of ingredients and you may have to be patient as it takes quite a long time to bake in the oven.

Ingredients
- 440g plain flour
- 1 tablespoon baking powder
- 1 teaspoon bicarbonate of soda
- ½ teaspoon salt
- 4 teaspoons ground cinnamon
- ½ teaspoon ground allspice
- 250ml vegetable oil
- 175g honey
- 175g golden syrup
- 150g caster sugar
- 100g soft brown sugar
- 3 large eggs
- 1 tsp vanilla extract
- 180ml orange juice
- 250ml freshly brewed coffee (or strong tea)

Topping
- a handful of flaked almonds (optional)

Honey Glaze
- 60g icing sugar, sifted
- 1 tablespoon honey
- 1-3 teaspoons hot water

Preheat oven to 180°C/Gas Mark 4.

Grease a 22cm (9 inch) cake tin.

In a large bowl whisk the flour, baking powder, bicarbonate soda, salt and spices.

In another bowl, mix together all the wet ingredients, adding coffee last.

Make a well in the centre of the dry ingredients and add the wet ingredients, mixing with a strong whisk or wooden spoon and combine until all the ingredients are fully incorporated. (You can try to mix it in an electric mixer, but it is a very wet batter and mine goes everywhere!)

Pour into the prepared cake tin and sprinkle the top with almonds, if using.

Bake for 40-45 minutes, until the cake springs back when gently pressed. As the batter is liquidy, it may take extra time, depending on your oven.

Allow to cool for at least 15 minutes before removing from the pan. To glaze the cake - mix together the icing sugar, honey and 1-3 teaspoons hot water, depending on how thin you want the glaze. While the cake is still warm, trickle, spoon or brush the glaze over the cake.

Spiced date, prunes and walnut loaf

There are many versions of a date and walnut loaf. This one is a little different because of all the spices and the addition of prunes. Although you can bake it in a 900g loaf tin, I prefer to use a square cake one, as I find it easier to cut.

100g pitted dried dates, halved
100g pitted prunes, halved
1 teaspoon bicarbonate of soda
240ml boiling water
140g muscovado sugar
2 eggs
grated zest of 1 orange
280g plain flour
2 teaspoon baking powder
1 teaspoon ground ginger
1 teaspoon ground cinnamon
½ teaspoon ground nutmeg
pinch of salt
125g walnuts, roughly chopped

Preheat the oven to 180C/ Gas Mark 4.
Grease a 22 x 22cm (8 x 8 inch) square cake tin, line it with baking parchment and grease again.

Place the dates and prunes in a bowl with the bicarbonate of soda and boiling water and set aside to cool.

Beat the sugar and eggs together in a bowl, then add the orange zest and the date and prune mixture. Stir to combine.

In a second bowl, sift together the flour, baking powder, ginger, cinnamon, nutmeg and salt. Add this to the prune mixture and fold through, adding the walnuts last. Pour into the prepared tin.

Bake for about 1 hour, or until the cake is deep brown and springy when you press on it gently. A skewer inserted into the centre should come out clean, but there should still be a little bit of sticky fruit.

Cool in the tin for 10 minutes, then turn out on a wire rack and leave to cool at room temperature. The cake will keep well for a few days if wrapped in foil.

Note – I brush the surface of the cake with a mixture of date syrup and a little water as soon as it comes out of the oven, as it gives it a nice shine – 2 tablespoons date syrup and 1 tablespoon water, mixed well. You can also use agave syrup or honey.

Sponge cake Ottoman style

This sponge cake has desiccated coconut and cardamom, the scent of which is so reminiscent of Middle Eastern markets. The cake is sandwiched with rose petal jam, available in Mediterranean grocery stores.

190g caster sugar
3 eggs, separated
1 teaspoon vanilla extract
240ml sunflower oil
190ml milk
150g plain flour
2 teaspoon baking powder
2 teaspoon cardamom
140g desiccated coconut
pinch of salt
4 tablespoons rose petal jam
icing sugar for dusting

Preheat the oven to 180C/ Gas Mark 4.
Grease two 17cm (7 inch) cake tins and line with baking parchment.

Beat the sugar and egg yolks in a bowl until creamy. Add the vanilla extract, sunflower oil and milk and beat again.

In a separate bowl, combine the flour with the baking powder, ground cardamom and coconut and add this to the wet ingredients, stirring to combine.

In another bowl, whisk the egg whites with the salt until they hold their shape when you remove the whisk. Stir a large dollop of the egg whites into the cake batter, then gently fold in the remainder, trying not to knock too much air out. Pour the batter into the tins.

Bake in the preheated oven for 30 minutes, or until golden brown and a skewer inserted into the middle of the cakes comes out clean.

Cool the cakes on a wire rack, then sandwich together with the jam and dust with icing sugar.

Note – although rose petal jam goes well with the coconut and makes the cake extra special, raspberry or strawberry jam can also be used.

Sponge cake with whipped cream and praline

My mother always made this cake when she had her friends round for a card game. I remember it fondly and for a long time was reluctant to give it a go, as the thought of making the praline was daunting. When I finally tried, I was surprised at how easy it was.

For the cake
- 225g softened butter
- 225g caster sugar
- 4 large eggs
- ½ lemon, zested
- 1 teaspoon vanilla extract
- pinch of salt
- 225g self raising flour, sifted
- splash of milk

For the cream
- 284ml tub whipping cream or double cream,

For the praline
- 100g caster sugar
- 1 tablespoon water
- 50g almonds or hazelnuts or a mixture of both

Prepare the praline in advance.
Roast the almonds or hazelnuts in a preheated oven for 10 minutes. Remove and allow to cool.

Heat the sugar in a heavy-based saucepan on a low heat and add 1 tablespoon water. Allow the sugar to dissolve, then to melt to form a deep golden caramel. Do not stir the sugar as it's cooking, but keep moving the pan to allow it to dissolve evenly. As soon as you reach the desired golden caramel colour, tip in the roasted almonds and remove from the heat.

Immediately pour the mixture onto a non stick baking tray or a tray lined with baking parchment. Cool for a few minutes. Cover the praline with grease proof paper and use a rolling pin to break it. Alternatively, blitz in a food processor for a few seconds. The praline will keep for up to one week in an airtight container.

Make the cake.
Preheat the oven to 180C/gas Mark 4.
Grease and line the base of two 20cm (8 inch) spring- form cake tins with baking parchment.

Using an electric whisk, beat the butter and sugar until smooth. Add the eggs one at a time, scraping the sides of the howl and beating well after each addition. Add the lemon zest, salt and vanilla extract. Add the flour gradually and finally a splash of milk, enough to soften the batter.

Pour into the prepared tins and bake for 25-30 minutes or until a skewer inserted in the centre of the cakes comes out clean. Leave to cool completely on a wire rack.

Whip the cream until you have a smooth consistency. Spread half on top of the first cake, cover with the second cake and spread the remaining cream. Finally, sprinkle the praline on top.

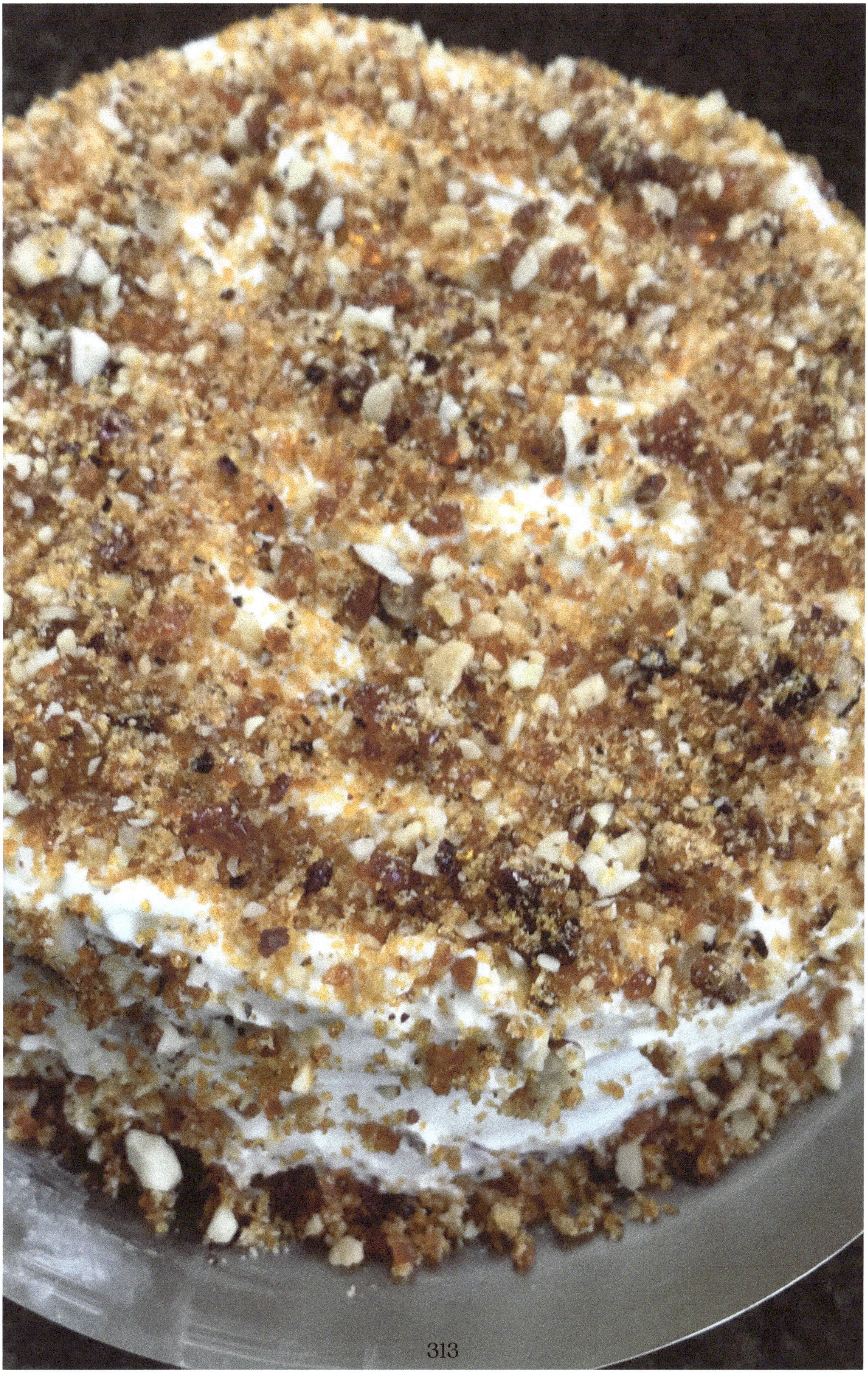

Tishpishti

(Greek honey cake soaked in syrup)

Honey cake is traditionally eaten at Rosh Hashanah, the Jewish New Year. The honey symbolises hope and it's eaten wishing that the ensuing year will be also sweet. There are many traditional versions and they roughly resembles each other. I have chosen this particular recipe because its different - it's soaked in a sugar syrup and has no eggs, so the consistency is different and more similar to the sweet pastries you find in the Middle East and Greece.

225g butter or margarine
1 cup coffee, freshly brewed
1 cup honey
1 cup sugar
½ cup orange blossom water or rose water or brandy
1 teaspoon cinnamon
1 teaspoon mixed spice
1 teaspoon salt
480g plain flour, sifted
2 teaspoons baking powder
1 teaspoon bicarbonate of soda
1 cup raisins
1 cup almonds coarsely chopped (any almonds or mixture of almonds)

For the syrup
   2 cups sugar
   ½ cup honey
   ½ cup water
   ¼ cup orange blossom or rose water or brandy
   juice of 1 lemon

Preheat the oven to 180C/Gas Mark 4.
Generously grease a 22 x 32cm (9 x 13 inch) baking pan.

Combine the flour, baking powder, bicarbonate of soda and salt.

In a medium saucepan, bring to the boil the butter, honey, sugar, coffee, orange blossom or rose water, salt and spices. Let the mixture cool for 10 minutes. When cool, stir in the flour mixture to form a smooth batter. Fold in the raisins and nuts. Pour into the prepared baking pan and smooth the surface.

Bake in a preheated oven for about 45 minutes. It may take longer, depending on the oven.

Meanwhile make the sugar syrup - put all the ingredients, apart from the lemon juice, in a saucepan, bring to the boil and boil for 5 minutes. Add the lemon juice and continue to stir until the mixture thickens.

Remove the cake from the oven when ready. With a sharp knife, cut through the hot cake into squares and diamonds while it's still in the pan.

Cool for 5 minutes, then spoon the syrup over the cake so that it's well covered and the syrup is absorbed between the pieces and around the edges. Return to the oven for a further 5 minutes.

Remove from the oven and let the cake stand for at least 24 hours to allow the flavours to mix.

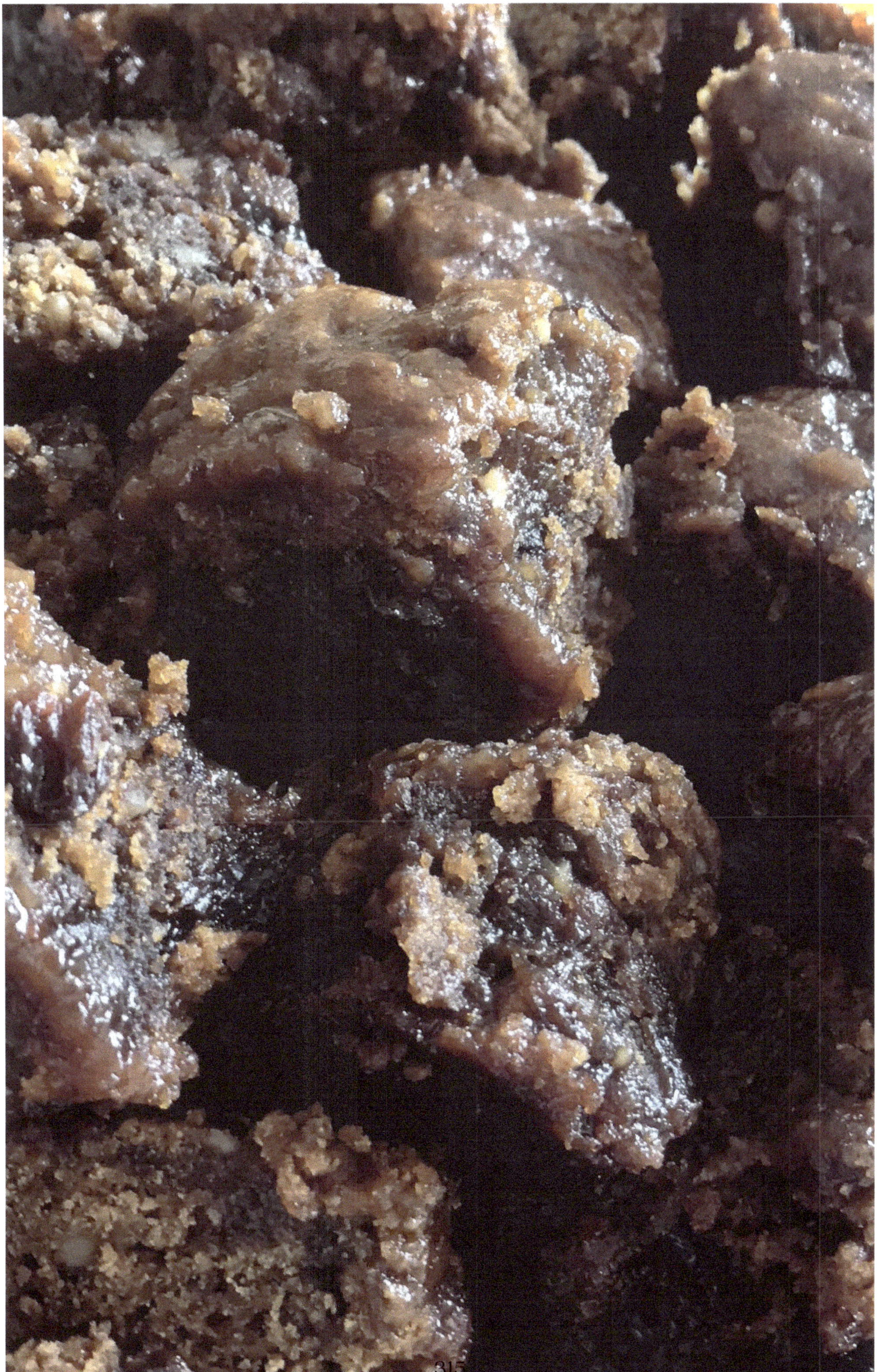

Almond, orange and semolina cake with lemon syrup

I found this recipe many years ago at the back of a semolina packet I had bought from a supermarket called Safeway, which has long since disappeared. I have lost count of the number of times I have made this cake – I like the combination of semolina, almonds, oranges and lemons topped with a light syrup, which is very common in many Mediterranean and Middle Eastern sweets. It's delicious when served with Greek yoghurt or crème fraîche.

Cake
    grated rind and juice of 2 oranges
    200g icing sugar
    250g unsalted butter
    115g self raising flour
    115g fine semolina
    50g ground almonds
    1 teaspoon baking powder
    3 large eggs
    115g sultanas
    60ml fresh orange juice

Lemon syrup
    150g granulated sugar
    100ml boiling water
    rind and juice of 2 lemons
    6 cardamom pods, shelled and crushed

Preheat the oven to 180C/Gas Mark 4.
Grease and line the base and sides of a 20cm (8 inch) cake tin.

In an electric mixer or with a handheld one, cream the butter, icing sugar and orange rind until light and fluffy. Add the eggs one at a time, mixing well between additions.

Sift the flour in a bowl, add the semolina, ground almonds and baking powder. Add the flour mixture to the egg mixture and beat until combined. Add the sultanas and orange juice and mix again.

Pour the mixture into the prepared cake tin. Smooth the top and create a depression in the middle- this will prevent the cake from developing a domed appearance.

Bake oven in the preheated oven for 45-50 minutes or until the sides have shrunk slightly and a skewer inserted in the centre comes out clean. Wait for about 20 minutes, then un-mould the cake and place it on a plate large enough to hold the syrup.

Prepare the syrup – place the sugar in a medium saucepan and add boiling water. Stir until dissolved. Add the lemon rind and the crushed cardamom pods and slowly bring to the boil. Simmer for about 5 minutes or until thick. Add the lemon juice, mix well, bring to the boil again and pour over the cake.

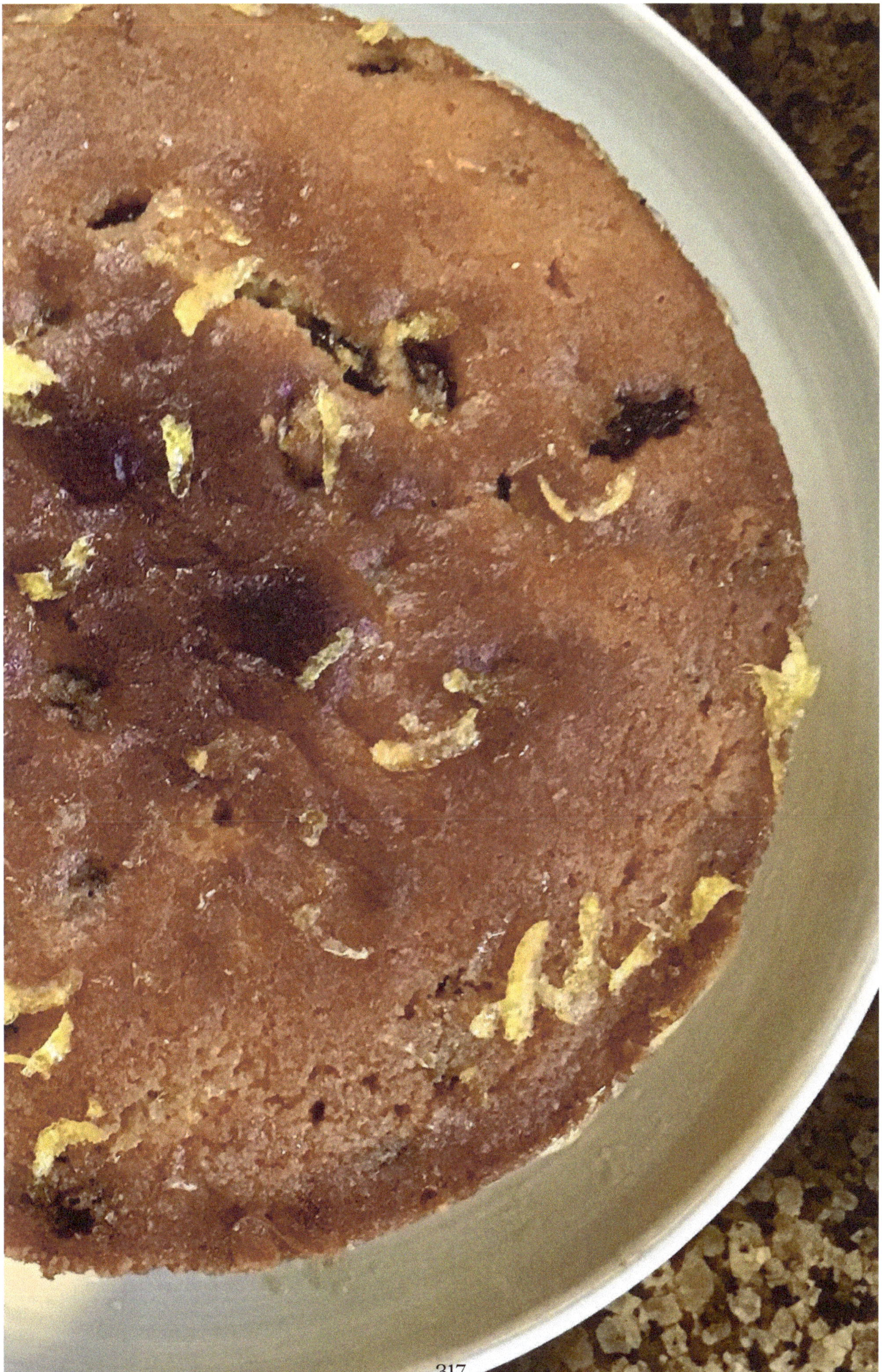

DESSERTS
Dulcerias
Halaweyaat

Quince in jelly

1kg quinces (2 large fruits)
juice of ½ lemon
100g sugar
600ml water

Wash the quinces well. Peel and cut them into 2cm (1 inch) slices, leaving the cores and pips, as they will produce the jelly.

Place the quinces in a large pan, add the lemon juice and sugar and cover with 600ml water.

Simmer for about 1 hour until the fruit is tender and the syrup starts to turn into a reddish jelly - it takes at least that long for the jelly to form. If the fruit becomes tender too quickly, lift out the slices on a plate and continue to cook the syrup until reduced.

Return the slices to the pan and continue cooking until the syrup becomes reddish and thick.

Lift out the quince slices and when cool, cut away the cores with a sharp knife.

Arrange the slices in a serving dish and pour the syrup on top. It will turn to jelly when it cools.

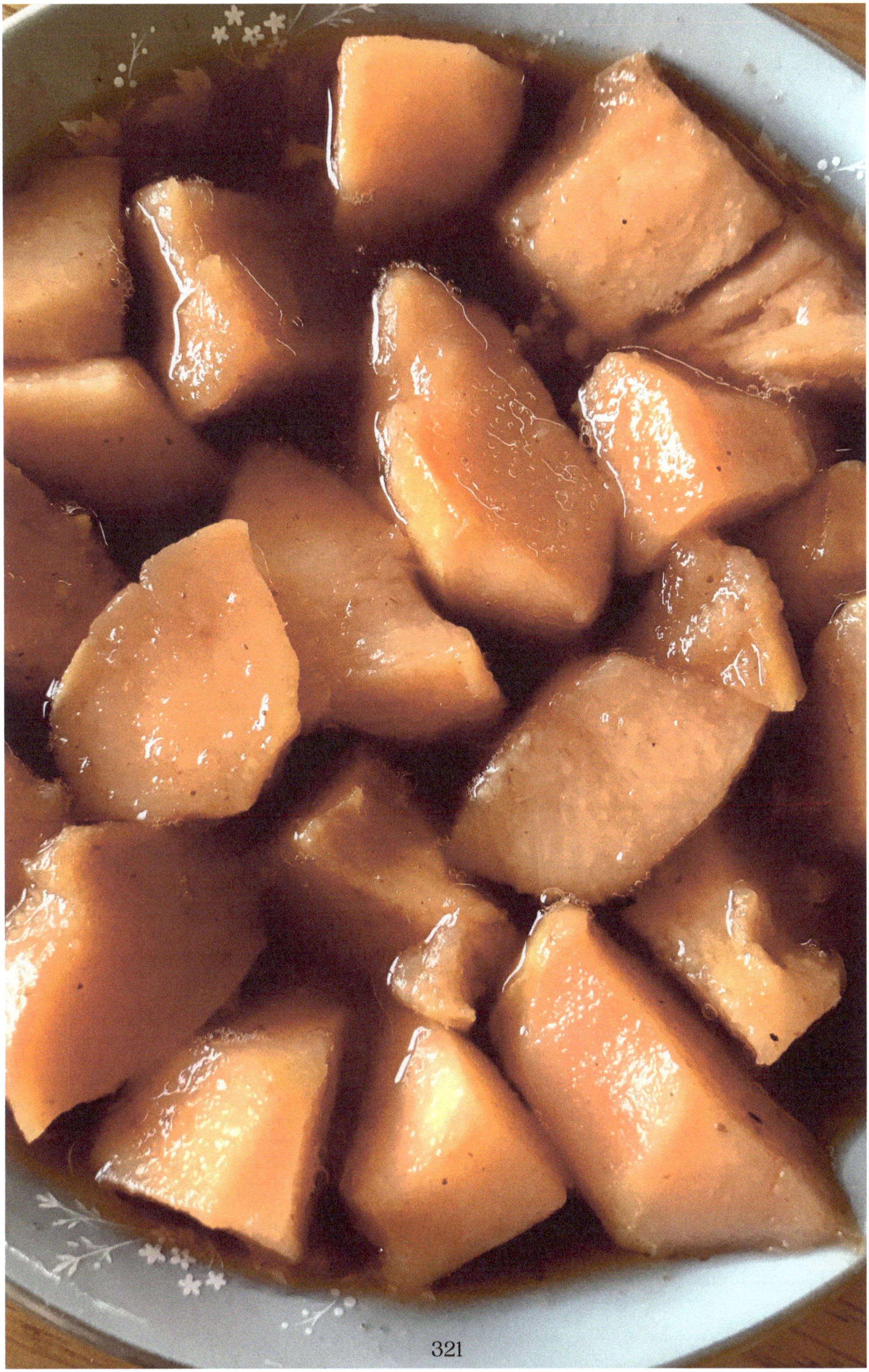

Rice pudding with raisins

This rice pudding is different because it uses arborio rice and eggs. It's rich and creamy and one of those comfort food you can have at any time. Add some whipped cream for that extra touch of luxury

120g arborio rice or short grain (pudding) rice
30g sugar
2 teaspoons vanilla extract
65g butter, melted
400ml full cream milk
3 large eggs, beaten
75g raisins
ground nutmeg and cinnamon for sprinkling

Preheat the oven to 180C/Gas Mark 4.

Mix the sugar with the vanilla extract and set aside.

Wash the rice well, drain and cook in some water for 10-15 minutes to soften it. Rinse under cold water and drain.

In a bowl, mix the melted butter and milk and add the beaten eggs. Add the partially cooked rice and raisins and mix all the ingredients together.

Lightly grease a 25 x 18cm (10 x 7 inch) baking dish and pour in the mixture. Sprinkle with ground cinnamon and nutmeg.

Fill a very large baking pan (larger than the one with the rice mixture) halfway with water, then carefully place the baking dish with the rice pudding into this pan – this is called a bain marie – make sure that none of the water gets into it.

Bake in the preheated oven for 1 hour until all the milk has been absorbed.

Remove from the oven and let the rice pudding cool.

Cassata Siciliana

One of my most vivid memories of Cairo is Groppi, the legendary tea rooms situated in the heart of downtown. Its owner, Giacomo Groppi, was the first to introduce Chantilly cream and ice cream to Egypt and the chocolate that was served was of the highest quality and famous all over the world. In its heyday, Groppi was a gathering place for writers, journalists, artists and stars. This was where people went to meet, gossip and be seen. My parents were introduced to each other by mutual friends in Groppi. We often went there for a drink late afternoon and Sundays and my favourite dessert was always the Cassata Siciliana. I have attempted to recreate something that resembles it, though of course it will never match the original.

1 large fresh sponge cake
225g soft cream cheese
275ml double cream
50g caster sugar
125g pistachio nuts, chopped
100g glacé fruit or mixed fruit
50g grated chocolate
2½ tablespoons orange liqueur (optional)
zest of 1 orange

Chocolate icing (optional)
225g dark chocolate
4 tablespoons strong coffee
175g unsalted butter, chilled and cut into cubes

Slice the sponge cake horizontally into 1-2cm (½ - ¾ inch) slices.

Beat the cheese, cream and liqueur, if using, until smooth. Stir in the pistachios, fruit, chocolate and zest and mix together.

Lay one slice of sponge on a plate and cover with a thick layer of the mixture. Add another slice of sponge and so on until all the sponge mixture is used up. Smooth the sides and make compact. Top with a final layer of the cream mixture if not covering with chocolate icing.

Refrigerate for about 2 hours before serving.

If covering with chocolate icing, melt the chocolate and coffee in a double saucepan until smooth. Remove from the heat and beat in the butter. Beat until the mixture is smooth and allow to cool until it has a spreadable consistency. Use a palette knife to spread the mixture evenly on top and all sides. Refrigerate overnight before serving.

Note – King Farouk of Egypt was particularly fond of Groppi chocolate. During World War II, he sent 100 kilograms of chocolate to King George, as a gift to his daughters, Princesses Elizabeth and Margaret.

Chocolate and date mousse

There are many recipes for chocolate mousse. This one uses puréed dates, which are whisked into an egg and chocolate mixture. The mixture will set as the chocolate cools. You can replace the dates with the same quantity of dried apricots, but dates have a more distinctive taste.

120g chopped dates
2 tablespoons brandy or water
125g dark chocolate
2 large eggs, separated
50g caster sugar
120ml whipping cream
50g grated chocolate

Put the dates in a small bowl, cover with the brandy or water and leave to soak for a minimum of 2 hours. Place the dates and brandy or water in a food processor and blitz to form a paste.

Boil some water in a large pan and lower the heat to simmering. Place the chocolate in a smaller pan and melt over the simmering water, making sure the pan does not touch the water.

Beat together the egg yolks and sugar. Stir in the melted chocolate and date paste. Whip the cream until it holds its shape and add to the chocolate mixture.

In a clean bowl, whisk the egg whites until firm peaks form. Fold them into the chocolate mixture.

Spoon the mousse into a large bowl or individual glasses and chill in the fridge for a minimum of 3 hours, or overnight. Dust with grated chocolate.

Chocolate mousse cake

This cake involves baking some of the mousse mixture and when cool, pouring the uncooked mouse on top. It's more of a dessert than a cake and it's ideal for serving at Passover, as it's light and doesn't contain flour.

250g dark chocolate
8 eggs, separated
65g caster sugar, plus an extra 3 tablespoons
200ml double cream
cocoa powder, for dusting

Preheat the oven to 150C/Gas Mark 2.
Grease a 22cm (9 inch) springform cake tin and line with baking parchment.

Melt the chocolate over a pan of simmering water.

Beat the egg yolks with 65g of the sugar in a bowl until thickened. When the melted chocolate has cooled slightly, pour into the egg yolk mixture, folding to combine.

In a separate bowl, whisk the egg whites until they reach stiff peaks, then add 3 tablespoons sugar, a spoonful at a time, whisking well after each addition, until you have firm and glossy peaks. Stir a large spoonful of the egg whites into the chocolate mixture, then gently fold in the rest.

Pour around three quarters of the mixture into the prepared tin (put the rest in the fridge) and bake for 40 minutes or until set, but not too hard in the middle. Allow to cool completely in the tin.

Whip the cream into soft peaks and fold it into the remaining mousse mixture. Chill until needed.

Gently spread the cream mixture over the cooled cake and dust with cocoa powder.

Place in the fridge for several hours or allow to set overnight.

Sutlach
(Fragrant rice pudding)

Sephardic Jews from Turkey and Greece call this rice pudding Sutlach. It's different, because ground rice or rice flour are used, instead of the customary short or long grain rice. This gives the pudding a smooth and creamy texture. It is traditionally served after the Saturday Shabbat morning service and for the festival of Shavuot. My mother regularly made it for us when the weather was chilly.

4 heaped tablespoons ground rice or rice flour
1000ml (1 litre) whole milk
3 tablespoons caster sugar, or to taste
1 tablespoon rose water

ground cinnamon for topping

Optional toppings
   chopped pistachios
   flaked almonds, toasted
   desiccated coconut

Blend the ground rice or rice flour with some of the milk until you have a smooth paste.

In a large saucepan, bring the milk and sugar to the boil over medium heat. Remove the pan from the heat as soon as the milk has boiled and stir in the rice flour mixture.

Return to the heat, stirring continuously for 2 minutes and then reduce to medium heat.

Continue stirring in a clockwise direction for about 15 minutes or until the mixture thickens and coats the back of a spoon. Be sure to stir constantly and scrape the bottom and sides of the pan, as this prevents the pudding from forming lumps and catching the bottom of the pan.

Remove from the heat and stir in the rose water.

Pour into individual serving dishes and ramekins and sprinkle with cinnamon. Top with any of the optional toppings.

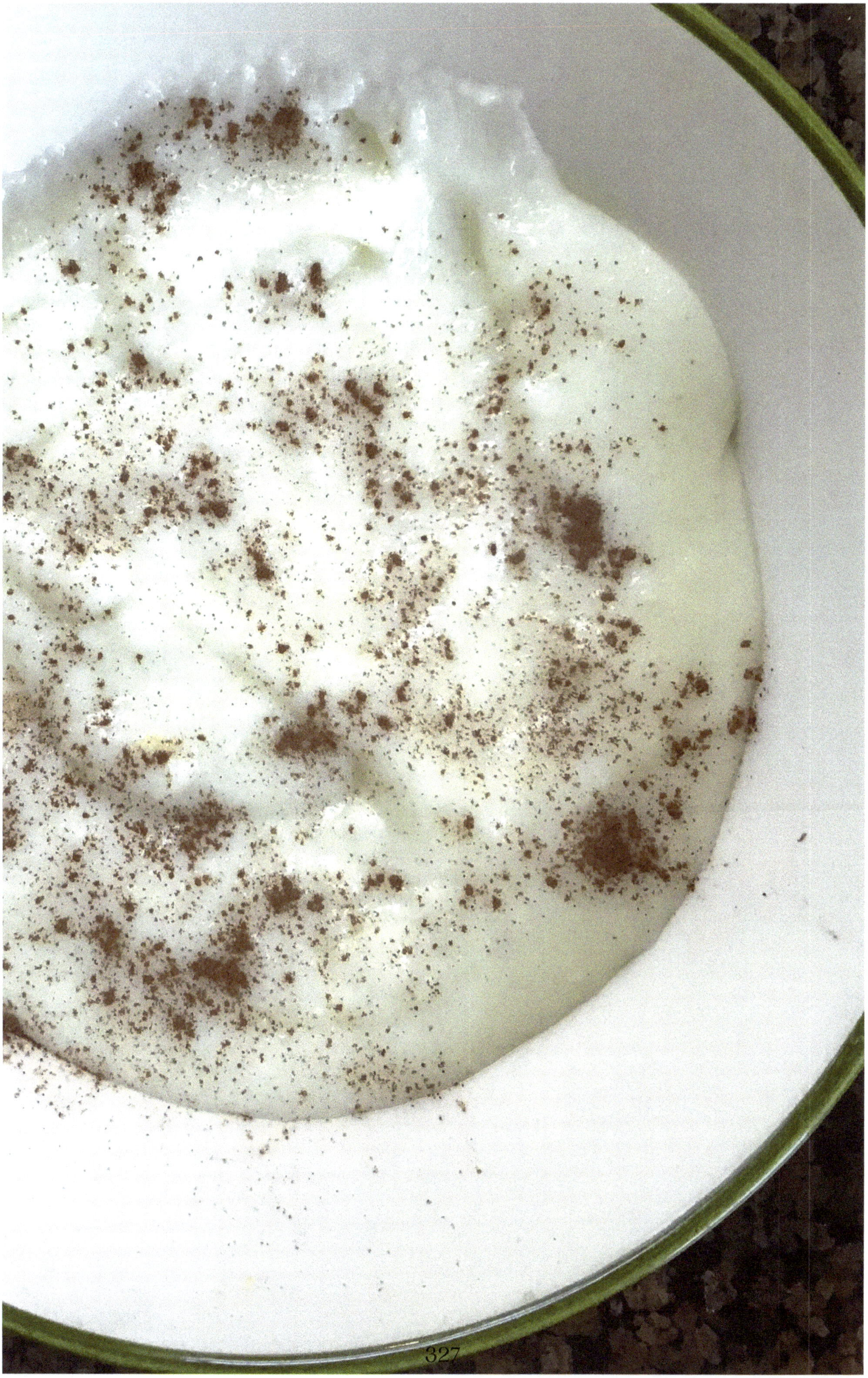

Ice cream with nuts and candied fruit

Nowadays, there is an excellent choice of shop bought ice creams, but it is nice to make your own sometimes. This way you get to choose which flavours and fillings to use. There are endless possibilities and you can mix and match, in fact anything goes. This recipe is for a no churn ice cream. It is incredibly easy and quick to make and you do not require an ice cream maker.

40g raisins
40g currants
½ cup water
2 large eggs
¼ teaspoon salt
100g sugar
60ml water
50g walnuts, roughly chopped
40g candied peel, chopped
40g glacé cherries, roughly chopped
125ml double or whipping cream
a few glacé cherries and nuts for decoration

Put the raisins and currants in a bowl and soak for 30 minutes. Alternatively, place in a saucepan and heat to simmering, remove from the heat and cool. Drain the soaked fruit.

In a small bowl, chop the glacé cherries and candied peel, add the walnuts and set aside.

Beat the eggs with the salt in an electric mixer until frothy. Put the sugar and water in a small saucepan, bring to the boil and boil for 3 minutes. Pour the sugar syrup in a thin streak over the frothy eggs, whisking all the time. Cool the mixture.

Whip the cream until thick, but not stiff.

Stir the nut and fruit mixture into the cooled egg mixture and lastly fold in the whipped cream.

Transfer to a container and freeze.

Note – it is better to whisk the eggs in an electric mixer, as you can slowly pour in the syrup over the eggs while the mixer is still going. If using a hand held mixer, try to get someone to pour the syrup for you whilst you are whisking.

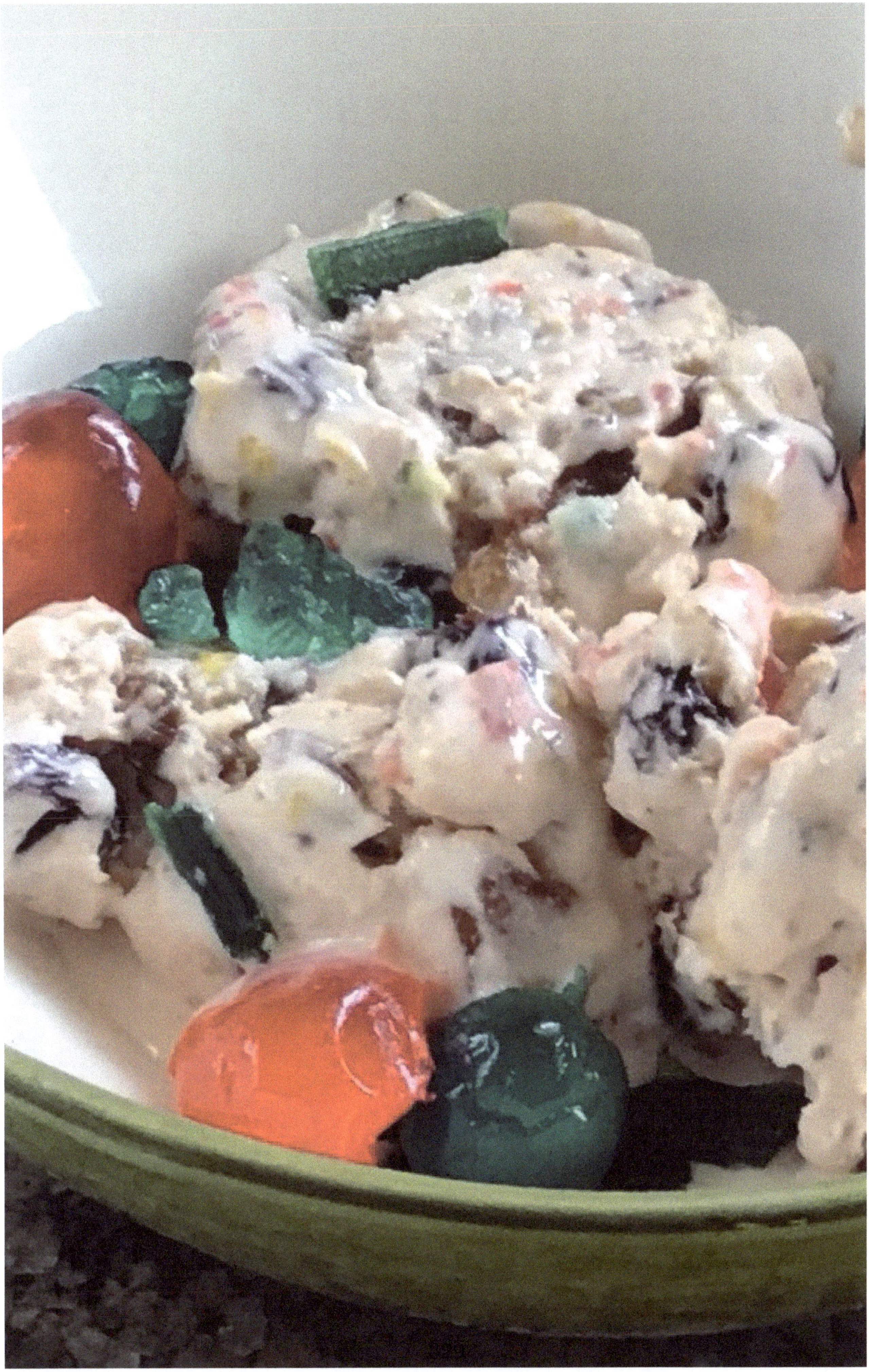

Date- nut pastries

This is a dessert which takes very little time to prepare. Serve with ice cream or simply as an afternoon treat with a cup of tea or coffee. It's also useful for Passover, as it doesn't contain any flour.

3 eggs
100g sugar
115g chopped walnuts
120g dates, chopped
½ teaspoon ground cinnamon
½ teaspoon mixed spice

Preheat the oven to 180c/ Gas Mark 4.
Grease and line a 20cm (8 inch) square baking pan.

Beat the eggs with the sugar until light. Mix with all the other ingredients.

Pour the mixture into the prepared pan and bake in the preheated oven for 30-40 minutes.

Autumn fruit compote

Use any fresh fruit available, but it's important to include plums, as they roast nicely in the oven. You can substitute the orange blossom or rose water with port or a sweet red wine.

750g plums
2 conference pears
2 apples, any variety
6 firm fresh figs
150g dark brown sugar
3 tablespoons honey
1 tablespoon orange blossom water
2 tablespoons rose water

Wash the plums, cut in half and remove the stones. Peel the washed pears and cut into thick slices. Peel the washed apples and cut into thick slices. Wash and carefully peel the figs. Leave them whole if they are small or cut larger figs in half.

In a large ovenproof dish arrange the plums, cut side down and cover with half the brown sugar. Place the slices of pears and apples on top of the plums and sprinkle with more brown sugar. Arrange the figs around the pears and apples. Sprinkle the remaining brown sugar.

Add the honey, orange blossom water and rose water.

Bake in a preheated oven 170C/Gas Mark 4 for about 1 hour or longer until the fruit is soft.

Serve with Greek yoghurt, crème fraîche or vanilla ice cream.

Greek honey tart

This Greek honey tart is also called melopita. It is very versatile and can be made many ways - like a pie with a bottom and top crust, like a tart or simply without a crust entirely. The curd cheese can be substituted with ricotta.

250g butter, chilled
250g plain flour
½ teaspoon salt
3-4 tablespoons water
500g curd cheese
4 large eggs
125-150ml honey
2 teaspoons cinnamon
2 tablespoons demerera sugar

Preheat the oven to 180C/ Gas mark 4.
Lightly grease a deep 25cm (10 inch) pie dish.

Mix the salt into the flour. To prepare the crust, work the chilled butter into the flour with your hands. You can also quickly do this in a food processor for 10 seconds. Gradually add 3-4 tablespoons water, just enough to make the dough hold together in a soft ball. Do not handle it any further and chill in the fridge for about 30 minutes.

Line the pie dish with the dough and pat it gently with your hands. Bake in the preheated oven for 10 minutes.

In the meantime, make the filling. Mix together the cheese, eggs and 125ml honey to start with. Taste before you add any more honey. Add 1 teaspoon cinnamon and blend well.

Cool the empty pastry shell – this is important, as it will disintegrate otherwise. Pour the cheese mixture gently all over the pastry and return to the preheated oven for about 35 minutes until it is firm and the top golden.

Dust with 2 tablespoons demerera sugar mixed with 1 teaspoon cinnamon and cool before serving.

Note – it is very important that chilled butter is used for the preparing the dough, as softened butter will result in a doughy pastry. I used a Polish curd cheese called Twarog, available from Polish and Tesco supermarkets.

Mango ice cream

This mango ice cream is something you can't buy in the shops, it has the real flavour of mangoes and does not feel in the least artificial. It's also creamy and can be easily scooped.

3 ripe yellow mangoes
1 x 395g can condensed milk
2 x 284ml tubs double cream

Wash the mangoes, remove the skin and cut into small cubes. Purée in a food processor or blender until completely smooth.

Transfer the mango purée to a large mixing bowl and stir in the condensed milk. Mix until throughly combined and smooth.

Whip the double cream until stiff, about 8-10 minutes.

Add the whipped cream to the mango mixture and fold until thoroughly combined.

Transfer the mixture to a freezer proof container, cover well and freeze until soft serve consistency or overnight.

Note – the ice cream will be frozen solid if kept in the freezer continuously. Allow to thaw at room temperature for 10-15 minutes before scooping.

Mango mousse

This is an eggless mousse which can be enjoyed all year round. You can use fresh ripe mangoes when they are in season and canned mango pulp when they are not. I find the latter a little too sweet, so I prefer to add a fresh mango if possible.

1½ tablespoons vegetarian gelatine powder
125ml water
2 tablespoons warm milk
1 large mango, preferably ripe or 2 medium ones
400ml mango pulp
300ml whipping cream
1 tablespoon caster sugar

Dissolve the gelatine in 125ml water by sprinkling the gelatine over the water and leaving it to rest for 10 minutes. Do not stir.

Peel the mango and cut into small chunks. Place in a food processor, add the mango pulp and blitz for a few seconds until smooth.

Gently dissolve the gelatine in 2 tablespoons warm milk and mix well. Pour the gelatine over the mango mixture and blitz for a few seconds.

Whip the cream with 1 tablespoon sugar until stiff.

Pour a little mango pulp at the bottom of a serving bowl or individual glasses. Pour a layer of cream and gently cover with the mango pulp Top with the remaining cream.

Chill for at least 3 hours until set. Serve garnished with a few mango slices.

Torta di riso
(Ricotta and rice cake)

As the name indicates, this is an Italian inspired dessert, using ricotta cheese and candied peel. I managed to find a jar of cherries in syrup, but leave out if not available and sprinkle with crumbled amaretti biscuits instead.

500ml milk
375ml single cream
2 tablespoons caster sugar
¼ teaspoon ground cinnamon
150g arborio or carnaroli rice, washed and drained
5 large eggs
80ml runny honey
3 tablespoons almonds, roasted and chopped
40g unsalted butter, softened
50g raisins
50g candied citrus peel, chopped
zest of 1 orange
250g ricotta cheese

¼ cup sour cherries in syrup, drained, syrup reserved
50g amaretti biscuits, crushed

Preheat the oven to 170C/ Gas Mark 3.
Grease a 22cm (9 inch) round cake pan and line with baking paper.

Place milk, cream, sugar and cinnamon in a medium saucepan. Bring to the boil over medium heat, stir in the rice and lower the heat. Cover and simmer for 35 minutes or until the rice is soft and creamy. Remove mixture from the heat and cool.

Beat the eggs and honey in a bowl and add the cooked rice. Stir in the nuts, butter, orange zest, raisins and citrus peel. Gently fold through the ricotta, leaving some chunks and stir well to combine.

Pout the mixture into the cake pan and bake in the preheated oven for 55- 60 minutes until set.

When cool, top with the drained sour cherries, syrup and crushed amaretti biscuits.

Note – I have used short grain pudding rice, which also works well.

Mango squares

This is the perfect dessert for anyone who likes mangoes. It's easy to prepare and using dried mango means you don't have to worry if fresh ones aren't available.

100g chopped dried mango
150g plain flour
60g icing sugar
60g butter
3 tablespoons water
200g packed brown sugar
50g plain flour
½ teaspoon baking powder
¼ teaspoon salt
2 eggs, beaten
½ cup chopped nuts
icing sugar for dusting

Soak the dried mango in warm water for 1 hour. Drain and set aside.

Preheat the oven to 180C/ Gas Mark 4.
Line a 22 x 22cm (9 x 9 inch) baking tin with parchment paper.

In a large bowl, mix the flour with the icing sugar. Cut in the butter and mix with your hands until the mixture resembles coarse breadcrumbs. Add enough water to bind the pastry. Press into the prepared baking tin. Bake the crust in the preheated oven for 15-20 minutes, until lightly browned.

In a medium bowl, blend the mango, brown sugar, remaining 50g flour, eggs, chopped nuts, baking powder and salt.

Pour the mixture over the baked crust and bake in the oven for around 20 minutes, until the filling is set.

Dust with icing sugar when cool. Cut into squares to serve.

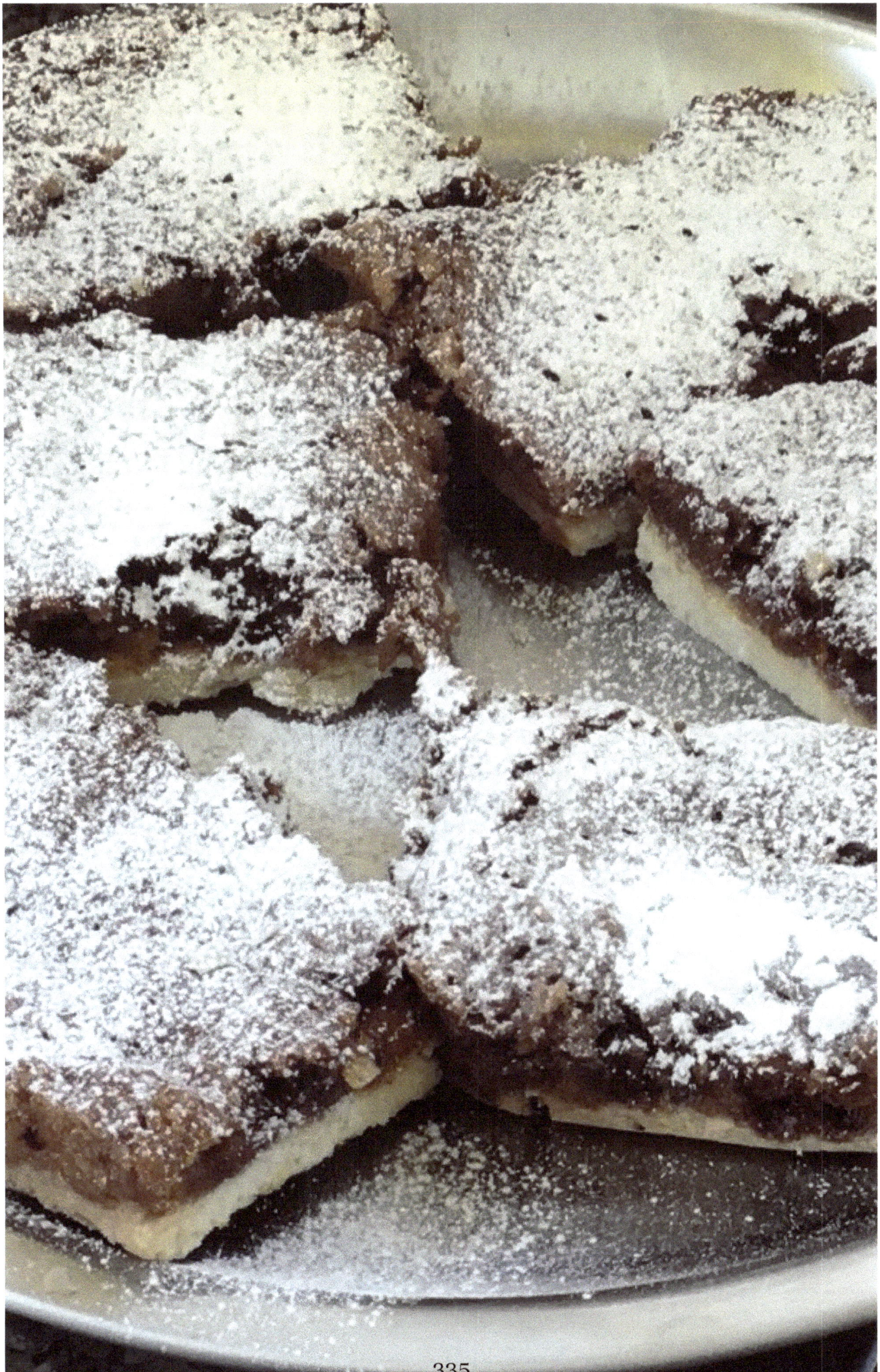

Dessert de pommes de terre douces

(Sweet potato dessert)

I have called the sweet potatoes by their French name, because it's how my mother referred to them and that's how I like to remember them. She used sweet potatoes to make a dessert, which is unusual. I don't know anyone else who cooks them this way, but it was a favourite of ours in winter. It's lovely served with vanilla ice cream, crème fraîche or Greek yoghurt.

2 large sweet potatoes
½ cup water
3 tablespoons maple syrup
3 tablespoons brown sugar
1 tablespoon honey

Peel and wash the sweet potatoes, cut them into medium size chunks and cook them covered in boiling water for 10 minutes until they are soft. Do not overcook or they will fall apart. Drain and arrange the slices in a shallow serving dish.

Put the water, maple syrup, brown sugar and honey in a saucepan. Cook uncovered over a medium heat until the sauce has reduced and thickened.

Pour the sauce over the sweet potatoes, making sure they are all covered.

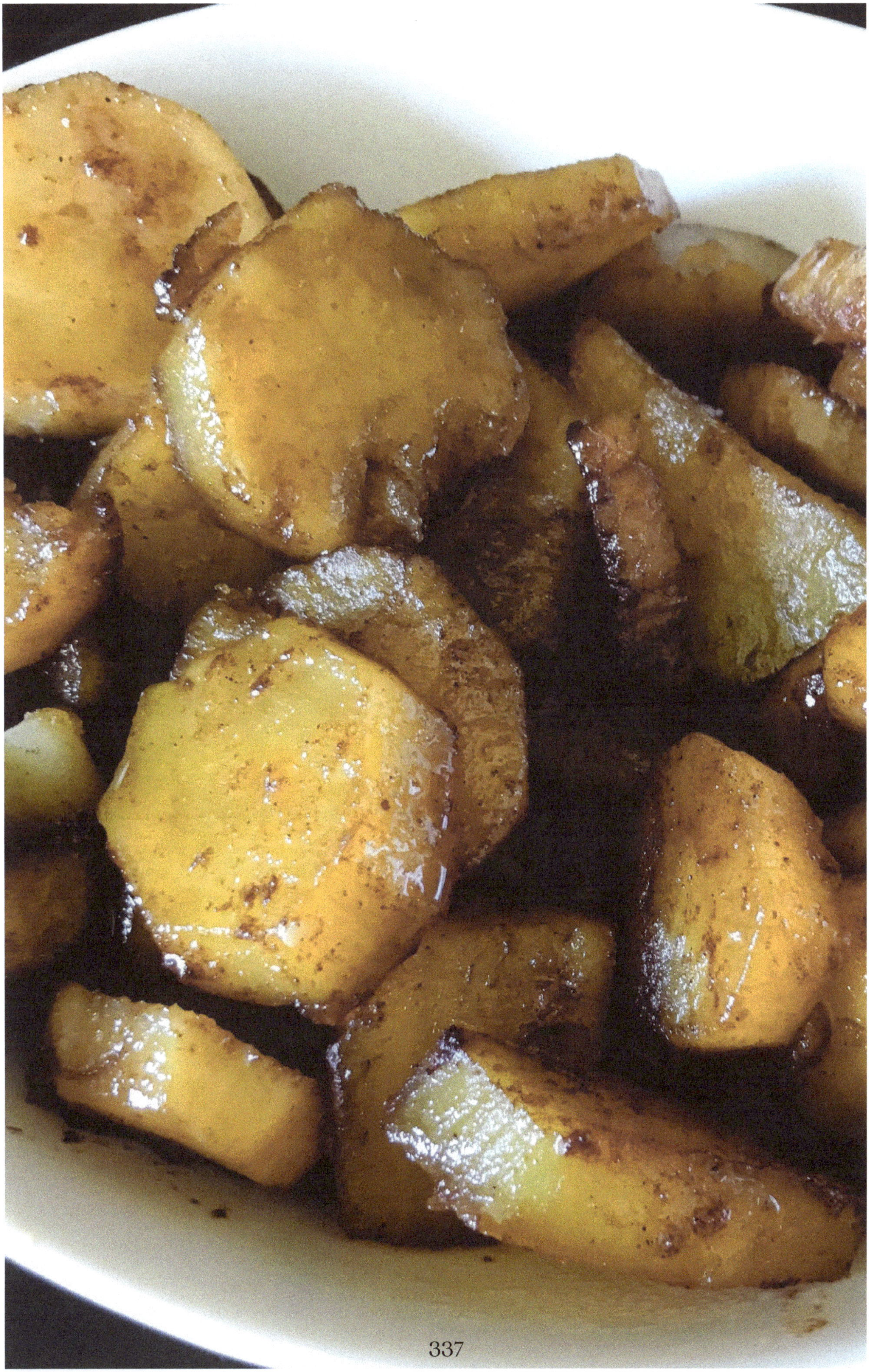

JAMS & MISCALLENEOUS
Mermelada
Murabba

Bimbriyo

(Quince paste)

Quince paste and the use of the quince fruit in savoury dishes is one of the characteristic features of Judeo-Spanish gastronomy.

2kg quinces
1kg sugar
juice of 1 lemon
water to boil the quinces

Wash the quinces well, peel and quarter them, but do not core them (it's much easier to cut and peel the quinces if you boil them first for 10 minutes to soften them).

Put the peeled and quartered quinces in a large heavy pan and cover with water. Add the lemon juice and cook for 2 hours. Lift out the quinces and reserve the liquid. When they have cooled, remove the seeds and cores and mash or process the fruit to a purée.

Boil down the liquid to about 175ml. Add the sugar and the purée and cook, stirring often with a wooden spoon, over a very low heat. Be careful not to let it burn. Keep stirring until the purée thickness and begins to splutter - continue until it turns to a rich garnet colour and comes away from the sides of the pan.

Let it cool a little before pouring into a wide shallow pan or tray lined with cling film or grease proof paper. Spread out to a thickness of about 1½cm (1 inch). Leave for a day or two to dry out in a warm, airy place.

Turn out the firmed paste and cut up with a sharp knife into 1½cm (1 inch) squares or lozenges. Roll the pieces in granulated sugar and pack them in an airtight container.

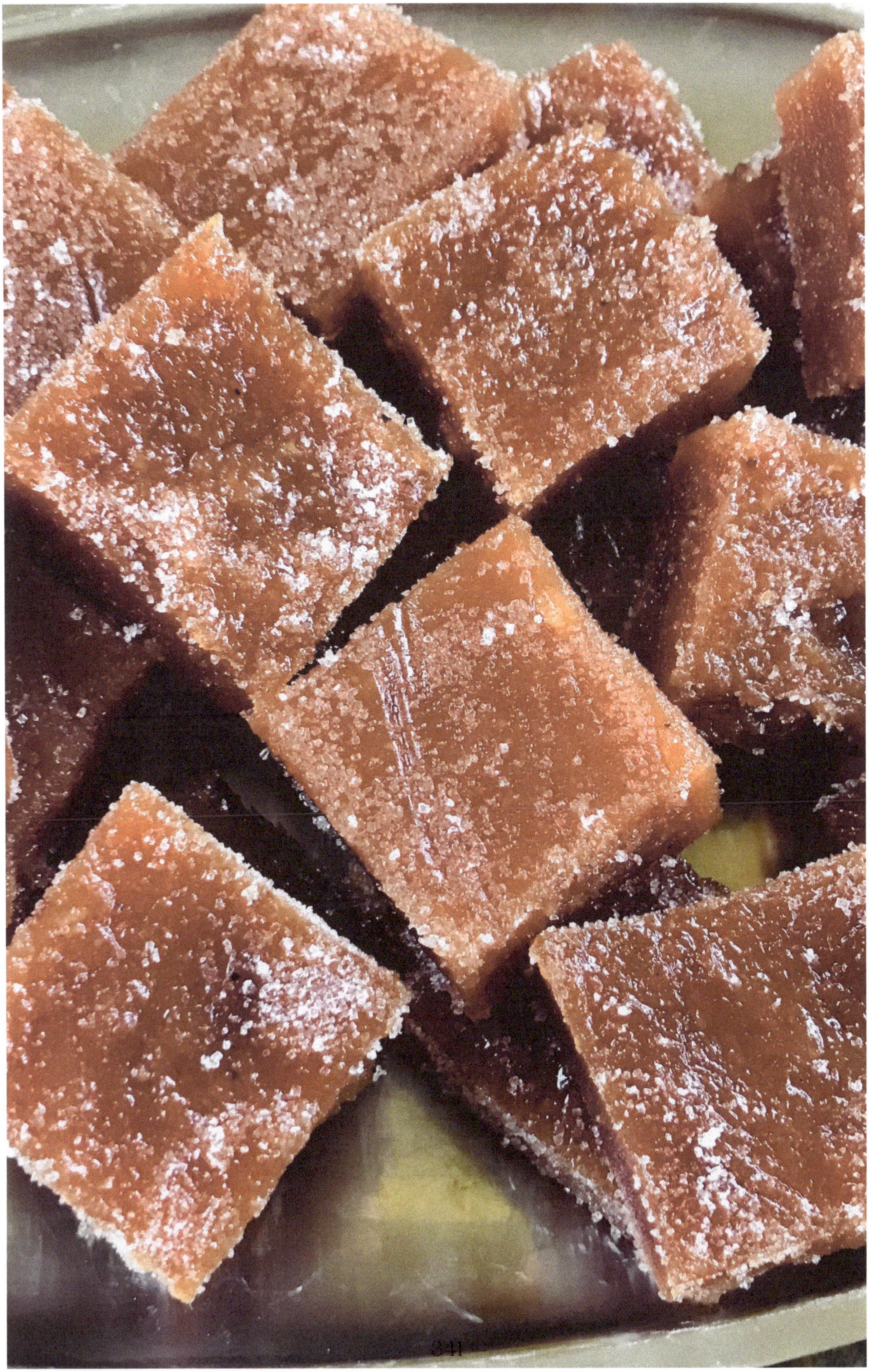

Amardeen

(Apricot sauce)

I like to keep a batch of this sauce in the fridge and often add a couple of tablespoons towards the end of cooking, as it gives a certain sour/sweetness to the dish. There are two ways of making this apricot sauce, either with amardeen or more simply with dried apricots. Amardeen is very popular in Middle Eastern countries, especially during Ramadan when it is used to make a refreshing drink. It consists of pressed sheets of dried apricot paste and can be found in most Middle Eastern and Turkish supermarkets.

Apricot sauce made with amardeen

400g packet amardeen
water

Separate the sheets of apricot paste as they are all stuck together. Cut them in small pieces, place them in a bowl and cover with boiling water. Leave overnight.

Put the apricot paste, which should be very soft, together with its water in a saucepan - you may have to add a little more water. Cook on a very low heat uncovered until you have a smooth runny paste. Store in the fridge and use as needed.

Apricot sauce made with dried apricots

500g dried apricots
200g sugar
juice of ½ lemon
about 2 cups water

Cover the dried apricots with water and leave them to soak overnight. Cook them in their water for 30 minutes until soft - the water should have reduced and you should be left with a light syrup. Transfer to a food processor and blitz until soft. Return to the saucepan, add 200g sugar (or to taste) and cook uncovered for a few minutes, stirring all the time. Keep in the fridge and use as needed.

Apricot jam

The Jews originating from Spain often used something called a kucharera - or tavola di dolci in Ladino. It was a silver vessel used for presenting sweets to welcome guests. The custom had its origin in the need to express joy over the visit and was one of the characteristics of hospitality amongst Jews of the Ottoman Empire. The tray was made of silver and had an ornamental container in its centre, a kucharera (the word kuchara means spoon) with a place for hanging spoons and forks. On the tray there were two or more small plates containing two kinds of marmalade and water glasses. The guest took some of the sweets with a fork or a spoon and placed it in the centre of the container when he/she had finished eating, then drank the water. The kind of fruits presented were usually fruit marmalade like naranjes, an orange marmalade or kayisi, an apricot one.

600g dried apricots
400ml boiling water
300g sugar
juice of ½ lemon and zest

Pour boiling water over the apricots and leave to soak overnight or for at least 6 hours.

Blitz the apricots with their water in a food processor.

Place the apricots in a large saucepan, along with the sugar, lemon zest and juice. Heat gently until the sugar has dissolved, then boil rapidly until the jam sets – this should take 20-25 minutes.

Spoon into sterilised jars.

Note - Apricot is one of my favourite jams and the good thing is that you can make it with dried apricots any time of year, as it tastes nearly as good as when you use fresh apricots. The jam will keep up to a year in a cool dark place. It can be served with a cheeseboard. Like Spanish membrillo quince paste, it goes very well with cheese.

Candied grapefruit peel

In Egypt, fruit preserves were usually presented on a decorative silver platter to welcome guests. The customary ritual was for the guest to sample a mouthful of the jam or preserve, which was offered in crystal bowls with a little spoon from a silver spoon holder, accompanied by small glasses of chilled water to cleanse the palate.

skin of 4 grapefruits, sliced into 2cm (1 inch) strips - about 500g
equal weight of sugar
500ml water
juice of ½ lemon

To extract the bitterness from the grapefruit peels, put them in a large saucepan with enough water to cover them and bring to the boil over medium heat. Reduce the heat, cover and simmer for 1 hour, or until the skins can be easily pierced with a fork. Drain and let them cool.

Using a slotted spoon, transfer the skins to a bowl of cold water. Keep changing the water frequently, about 5 times in the day. Before each change of water, wring out the outer skins throughly. Repeat this for 2 days.

After the last soak, allow the skins to dry for 3-4 hours or overnight. Roll the peels against a work surface, white pith side up, until they form spirals. Tie every six or seven spirals together with a thick thread to prevent them from unravelling. They will look like beads on a necklace.

In a large saucepan, bring the sugar and water to a boil over medium heat. Add the grapefruit necklaces, return to a boil and immediately reduce the heat. Simmer gently for about 1 hour, until the peels are tender.

Lift the grapefruit necklaces from the pan and let them cool at room temperature in the syrup. Remove the threads and transfer the grapefruit peels and syrup to sterilised jars.

Refrigerate for up to six months.

Coconut jam

My mother always used to make this jam for Passover. For some reason, it was never made at any other time of the year, but that's probably because it's nicest when eaten with matzah crackers.

250g unsweetened desiccated coconut
250g granulated sugar
75ml water
1 tablespoon lemon juice
1 tablespoon orange blossom or rose water
50g chopped pistachio nuts (optional)

Sprinkle the coconut with enough cold water to moisten it well and fluff it with your hands. Leave overnight to soften.

Make a syrup by simmering the sugar with 75ml water and lemon juice for a few minutes. Add the coconut and bring to the boil again slowly, stirring constantly. Continue stirring for 5-10 minutes until slightly thickened and remove from the heat.

Let the jam cool at little before pouring into sterilised jars. Serve in a bowl sprinkled with chopped pistachio nuts.

Fig Jam

There is nothing nicer than home made fig jam, when you can actually taste the fruit. Years ago, we used to go to Provence regularly for our summer holidays. I could never resist the beautiful fresh figs available in the markets and always ended up buying too many. The practical way to use the surplus was to make it into jam, which I then brought back home. There was enough to last all year round and, every time I had some, it reminded me of sunny days and filled me with nostalgia.

1kg fresh figs
500g sugar
1 cup water
juice of ½ lemon
1 sachet Tate & Lyle pectin

Wash the figs and cut them into chunks. There is no need to peel them.

In a large saucepan put the sugar and water and bring to the boil, stirring constantly.
When the liquid has reduced – about 10 minutes – throw in the figs and the juice of ½ lemon. As soon as the mixture boils, add a sachet of pectin - this is optional but I find it helps the jam set quicker.

Lower the heat and cook until the jam thickens, around 15 minutes. Keep an eye on it and stir constantly.

Turn off the heat, allow to cool and transfer to sterilised jars.

Chocolate truffles

Makes around 30

Homemade chocolate truffles are surprisingly easy and quick and make a lovely gift for a special occasion.

320g dark chocolate, finely chopped
300ml double cream
30g salted butter, cubed
100g cocoa powder
100g roasted hazelnuts, chopped

Put the chocolate in a medium bowl.

In a small pan, heat the cream and butter until the cream is steaming and take off the heat before it boils.

Mix in the melted butter and pour the mixture over the chocolate. Leave for a minute to allow the chocolate to melt, then stir to combine.

Set aside to cool, then cover and chill for 2 hours.

Put a teaspoon or melon baller in a mug of just-boiled water, then use it to scoop equal-sized balls of chilled chocolate ganache.

Briefly roll each ball between your palms and place on a board. Dust your hands with cocoa powder and roll each truffle again to even out the surface.

Spread out the remaining cocoa powder and chopped hazelnuts on 2 plates. Roll each truffle through one of the coatings until evenly covered.

Chill on a clean plate for one hour.

Note – the truffles will keep chilled in an airtight container for up to 1 week. Serve at room temperature.

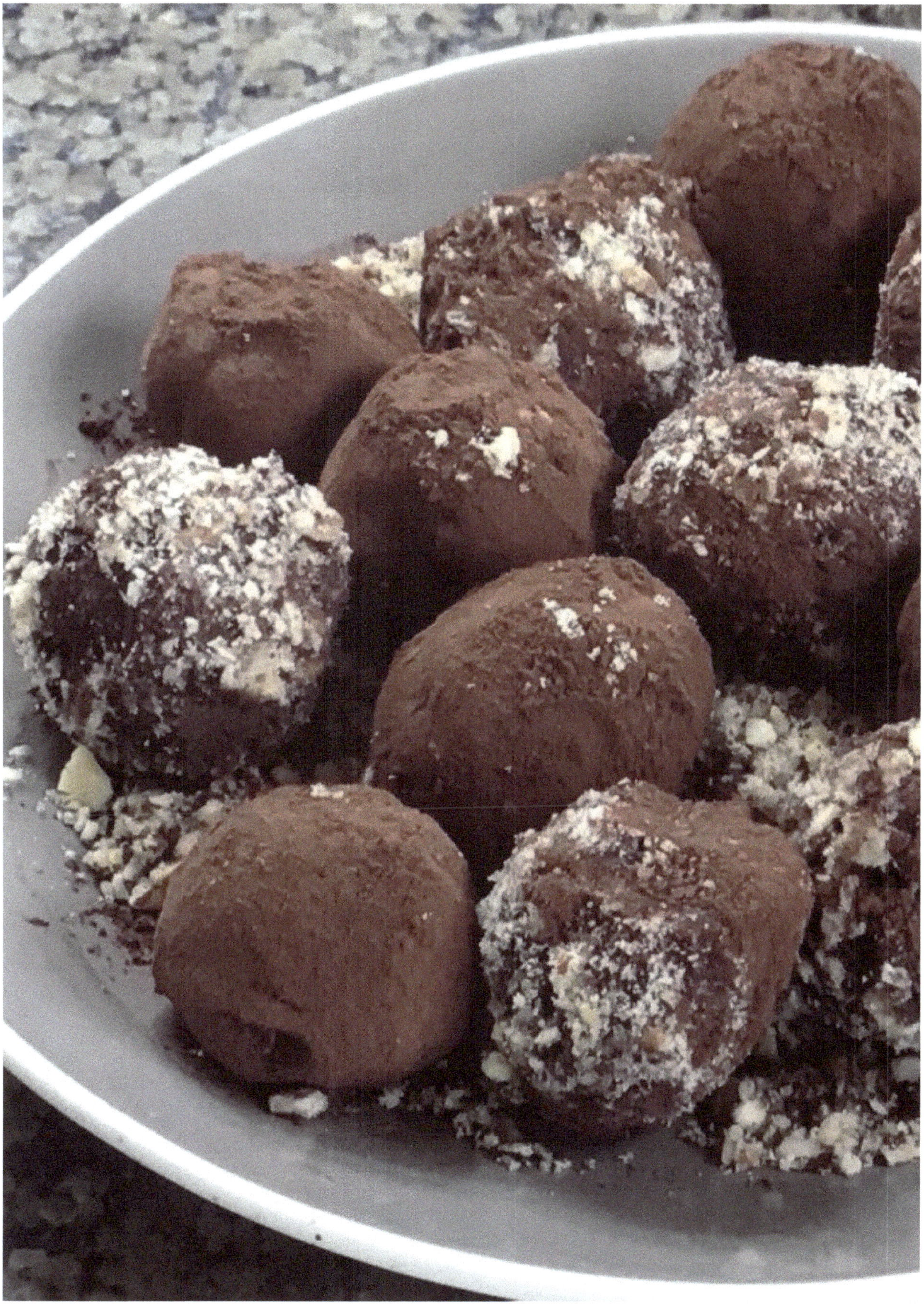

Quince Jam
(recipe 1)

Quince (or quince apples) cannot be eaten raw, but they are very versatile in cooking. As the season is very short my mother used to make a lot of jam. I remember opening the large fridge which was in the corner of the dining room in Egypt and staring at jars and jars of many varieties of preserves. That's actually what the fridge was for, since we cooked from fresh every day.

1kg quinces
600g sugar
juice of ½ lemon
1 sachet Tate & Lyle pectin (optional)

Begin by washing the quinces thoroughly. Peel, quarter and place them in a large saucepan. Do not remove the cores or pips. Cover with water and boil for about 1 hour or more until the fruit is very soft.

Lift out the quinces and keep the water they were boiled in. Remove the cores and pips, discard them and mash the quince with a fork.

Add 600g sugar to the saucepan with the water and boil for 10 minutes on high until the sugar has dissolved, stirring all the time. Add the juice of ½ lemon, the mashed quinces and the optional pectin sachet.

Cook for 10 minutes, stirring constantly. Remove from the heat as soon as the jam becomes a lovely dark pink.

Note - use a large saucepan as the jam will splutter a lot once it starts cooking.

The quantity I have given can easily be doubled.

Safargel Quince jam
(recipe 2)

Safargel is the Arabic word for quince jam. This is an alternative recipe for making it and It involves grating the fruit first, rather than boiling it. Both methods produce equally good results.

1kg quinces (about 3 large ones)
500g sugar
2 cups water
juice of 1 lemon

Prepare the quinces by washing and cutting them in half. Working around the core, grate the quince flesh, including the peel, with a cheese grater.

Pour 2 cups water in a thick bottomed pan and bring to the boil. Add the quinces, lemon juice and lemon zest, reduce the heat and simmer until the quinces are soft, about 10 minutes.

Add the sugar and bring to the boil again. Stir to dissolve the sugar and lower the heat to medium high. Cook uncovered, stirring constantly, until the jam turns pink and reaches the desired consistency.

Massapan
(Judeo-Spanish marzipan)

Makes around 22

Spain is the birthplace of marzipan and was first created in the fifteenth century. Jews adopted this as a candy after a meat meal. Almond paste became the basis of many sweetmeats and the jewel in the crown of Sephardi pastry-making and confectionery. It was served on such occasions as births, weddings and barmitzvahs. Spain remains the largest commercial producer of marzipan and Toledo is the centre of the trade. Jewish communities have different ways of making it and different flavourings, such as orange blossom water, rose water, lemon juice, cinnamon and cardamom.

The following recipe is the classic Judeo-Spanish way of making marzipan. Real Sephardic marzipan included a few bitter almonds but these are no longer available, so a few drops of almond essence approximates the flavour.

260g ground almonds
200g sugar
125ml water
juice of ¼ lemon
2-3 drops almond essence

Boil the sugar and water with the lemon juice in a pan for 5-10 minutes, until the syrup is thick enough to coat the back of a spoon. It must not colour or caramelise, or it will be too hard.

Add the almonds and almond essence and stir vigorously over a low heat for 3-4 minutes, until the paste no longer sticks to the pan. Let it cool.

Lightly oil your hands, take little lumps of paste and roll into 2½cm (1 inch) balls. Roll them in caster sugar.

Nareng

(Orange slices in syrup)

Seville oranges work well because of their thick skins and unique bitter taste. They were a big part of our cuisine in Egypt, as most traditional dishes requiring oranges used them, rather than the sweeter naval variety. My mother always kept a few jars of these delicious candied oranges in the fridge, but my aunt Marie's were the best. I remember having them as a treat on a regular basis when I lived with her in Milan.

1kg of Seville oranges peel, cut into 4cm (1½ inch) strips
1kg sugar
1 litre water
juice of ½ lemon

With a small pointed knife, cut straight lines down the sides of the orange, from the point of the stem end, converging at the other end. Carefully peel off the segments formed, without breaking them. Weigh the peel, as you will need an equal weight of sugar. Soak the peels in water for 2 days, changing the water frequently.

Drain and boil the peels in water for about 20 minutes, until soft. Drain again. Roll up the strips of peel, one by one, and thread them on to a thick thread with a needle, like beads on a necklace, tying about 7 or 8 strips together at a time. Tie the ends of the thread together.

Make a syrup by boiling the water, sugar and lemon juice. Drop the necklaces in the syrup and simmer for about 1 hour. Lift out and cool on a plate. Remove the threads and drop the coils of peel in sterilised jars. When slightly cooled, pour the syrup over them.

Store in the fridge for up to 1 year.

Note - the candied peels can sometimes be chewy, so grate some of the zest before cutting the oranges into segments - this will help soften them.

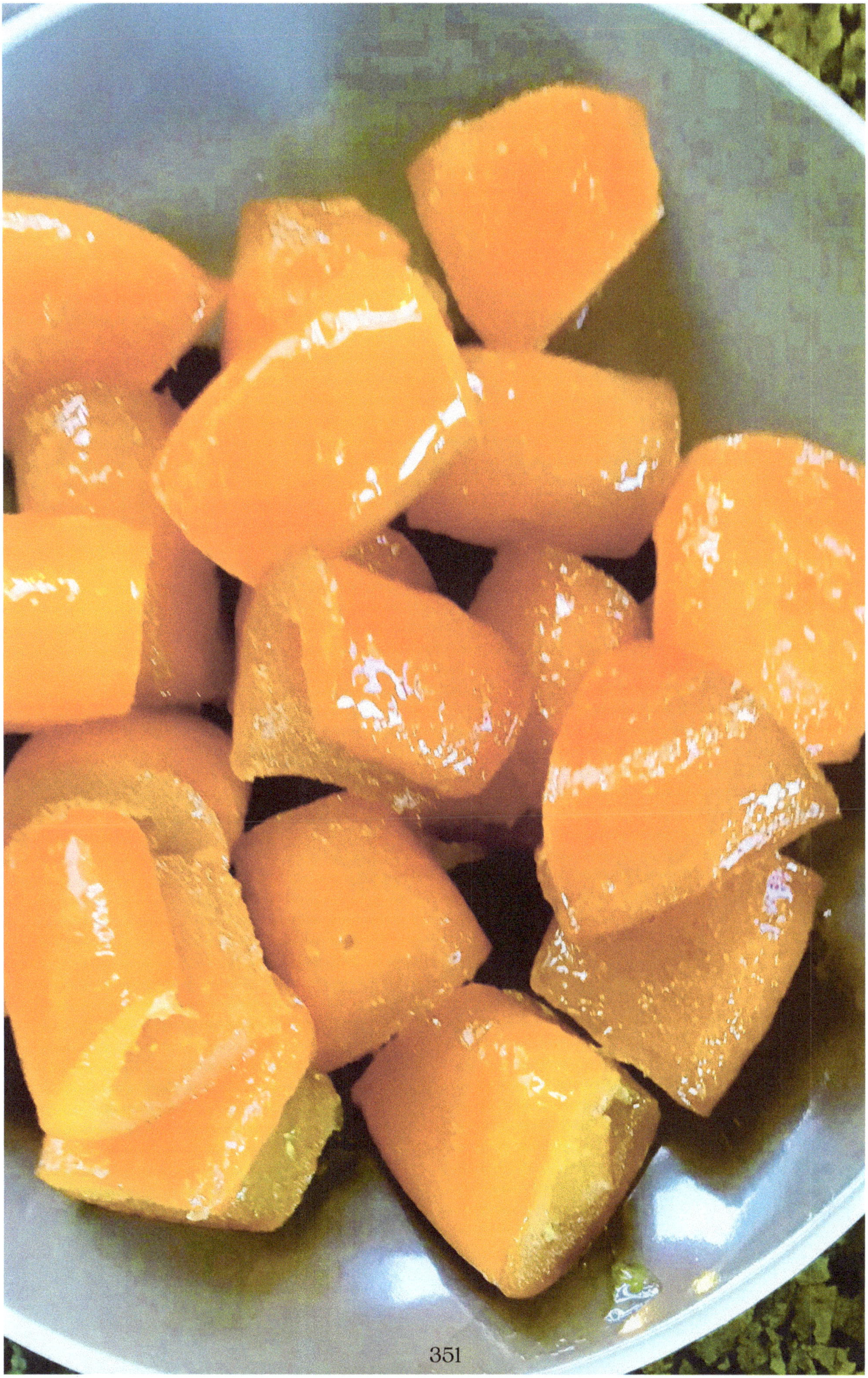

Pineapple jam

For some reason, pineapple jam reminds of when we first arrived in England in 1956. After spending an initial three months in a hostel near Stroud, in Gloucestershire, we were transferred to London and a flat in Kensington. My mother and I enjoyed taking the no 49 bus to Portobello Road market, which was always bustling and full of life. Along with other shopping, my mother always bought a jar of pineapple jam from one of the small shops. It was always the same jam and I don't know why she chose to buy this and no other variety, but we liked it anyway.

1 large pineapple, peeled and cut into chunks (about 450g)
150-200ml water, depending on the ripeness of the pineapple
300g jam sugar
juice of 1 lime
juice of 1 lemon

In a food processor, blitz the pineapple chunks with the water for a few seconds only.

Place the mixture in a pan and cook for about 20 minutes. Add the jam sugar, lime and lemon juices and cook for another 25-30 minutes.

Spoon into sterilised jars and keep in fridge.

Note – you can substitute the jam sugar with the same quantity of granulated sugar, mixed with 1 sachet of sugar pectin. It is important to use either alternative, as pineapple does not have any pectin and the jam will not set otherwise.

Glossary

Ashkenazi - Jews from Eastern France, Germany and Eastern Europe.

Barmitzvah - 'Son of the commandment'. A boy reaching the age of thirteen and the ceremony commemorating that event.

Batmitzvah - 'Daughter of the commandment'. A girl reaching the age of twelve and the ceremony commemorating that event.

Haleb - the Arabic name for Aleppo. It means 'milk' or 'the milked', referring o the ancient legend of Abraham's passage through the city, during which he fed the poor with the milk from his goats on the city's slopes.

Ladino - also known as Judeo-Spanish and Judezmo, Ladino is essentially 15th century Spanish, but it also has words mixed in from Portuguese, French, Italian, Arabic, Greek, Turkish and Hebrew. It was once the primary language spoken by Sephardic Jews throughout the Mediterranean and is now very nearly extinct.

Passover (Pesach) - a holiday commemorating the Exodus from Egypt. It also marks the beginning of the harvest season. Celebrated for eight days, bread is banished and matzoh, unleavened bread, is eaten. More than any other Jewish holiday, Passover has its own special cuisine.

Purim - a holiday celebrating the rescue of the Jews from extermination in the hands of Haman, the chief minister to the King of Persia, through the intercession of the Jewish Queen Esther.

Rosh Hashanah - the High Holy Day marks the beginning of the Jewish New Year. It is observed in September or October, a date determined by the lunar calendar. It is a day for family gatherings and dining. Certain ritual foods are served and the diners offer prayers for the New Year. Eating apples dipped in honey will guarantee a sweet year and pomegranate seeds will promise fertility.

Seder - Yiddish word for Order. It refers to the festival meal eaten on the first night of Passover, because what is eaten and the ceremonies performed follow a precise order.

Sephardic, Sephardim - Jews originating from Spain and Portugal and their descendants. The word Sephardi is derived from the Hebrew word for Spain. They are the descendants of Jews who lived in the Iberian Peninsula for centuries, before the expulsion from Spain in 1492. Those who refused conversion to Christianity were burned at the stake as heretics. Others converted in name only but continued to practice their Jewish religion secretly (they were known as conversos or marranos). Most fled to North Africa and the Middle East, especially to Turkey.

Shavuot - The Jewish festival which celebrates the giving of the Ten Commandments to Moses on Mount Sinai. Dairy dishes in place of meat are preferred during this time.

Yom Kippur - the Day of Atonement, a day set aside for fasting and repenting from the sins of the previous year. It is observed ten days after Rosh Hashanah and is the holiest of the Jewish holy days. On this day, there is complete abstinence from food and drink from the afternoon of one day until the evening of the second.

Bibliography

Abadi, Jennifer Felicia A Fistful of Lentils: Syrian Jewish Recipes from Grandma Frietzie's Kitchen, Boston: Harvard Common Press   2002

Alchech Miner, Viviane From my Grandmother's Kitchen, Triad Publishing Company   1984

Cohen, Stella Stella's Sephardic Table, The Gerald and Marc Hoberman Collection   2012

Cohen, Viviane Si la Table m'était contée, Editions du Cosmogone   2007

Dweck, Poopa Aromas of Aleppo, HarperCollins Publishers   2007

Eldaief, Dyna The Taste of Egypt, The American University in Cairo   2016

Kalla, Joudie Palestine on a Plate, Jacqui Small LLP   2016

Marks, Gil Olive Trees and Honey, Wiley Publishing Inc, Hoboken, NJ   2005

Phillips, Denise New Flavours of the Jewish Table, Ebury Press   2008

Roden, Claudia A New Book of Middle Eastern Food, Viking   1985

Roden, Claudia The Book of Jewish Food, Viking   1997

Shooter, Anne Sesame & Spice, Headline Publishing Group   2015

INDEX

aish el saraya (the palace bread) 194
albondigas de pishkado (fish balls in tomato sauce) 86
almodrote de berendjena (aubergine flan) 78
almodrote de kalavassa (courgette flan) 76
almond filo cigars (assabih bel loz) 266
almond custard (muhallabeya) 214
almond franginpane-filled filo triangles (sansaticos) 280
almond, orange and semolina cake with lemon syrup 316
amardeen (apricot sauce) 342
anise biscuits 275
apio (lemony celeriac and carrot) 25
apio con avas (veal stew with cannellini beans and celery) 108
apple cake, Passover 242
apricot jam 343
apricot pudding (muhallabeya bil amardeen) 215
apricot sauce (amardeen) 342
arroz pilaf con berendjenas y piniones (rice pilaf with aubergines and pine nuts) 184

Artichoke
    and broad bean salad 26
    and cheese casserole (carchof jiben) 75
    and vegetable soup 48
    bottoms stuffed (kharshouf mah'shi) 115
    soup (sopa de endjinaras) 60
    soup with rice 49
    with potatoes and meat (endjinaras con patatas y carne) 111
    assabih bel loz (almond cigars) 266
    aubergine
    and feta kofta 158
    and leek casserole 159
    and potatoes with a coconut sauce 175
    and tomato bake 160
    and walnut ragu 162
    aubergine parmigiana 80
    baked with cheese (berendjenas con keso) 68
    dip (mutabbal) 36
    feta, aubergine and sweet potato bake 70
    flan (almodrote de berendjena) 78
    khoresh 11
    pilaf with pine nuts 184
    roasted aubergine and goat's cheese tart 258
    salad (salatet el rahib) 38
    salad with dates and chickpeas 20
    salad with figs, feta cheese and bulgur 30
    sandwiches (betingan bil firan) 22
    stuffed with cheese (berendjenas rellenas de keso) 164
    stuffed with quince (betingan mah'shi bi safargel) 170
    autumn fruit compote 330
    avgolemono (lemon chicken soup) 50

baby spinach salad with tomatoes and mozzarella 32
baclawa (nut-filled pastry) 192
baked cauliflower with potatoes 176
baked fish with a coriander and tomato sauce (samak b'kamoun) 93
baked fish with fereek (samak fil forn b'fereek) 97
baked fish with tahini sauce 102
baked fish (samak fil forn) 98
baked sweet potatoes with fried shallots 166
bamia b'mishmosh (okra with prunes and apricots) 188
banana, medjool date and chocolate cake 305
barazeh shami (Damascus sesame biscuits) 268
basbousa bil laban zabadi (semolina cake with yoghurt) 223
basbousa cake with cream 196

Beef
    and aubergine stew, sweet and sour 109
    meat pizzas (lah'meh b'ajeen) 120
    stew Aleppo style 108
    stew with chickpeas, kale and tahini 110
    sweet and sour 130
    with artichokes and potatoes (endjinaras con patatas y carne) 111

beignets de Paques (matzo fritters) 228
berazeh shami (Damascus sesame biscuits) 268
berendjenas con keso (baked aubergines with cheese) 68
berendjenas rellenas de keso (Sephardic stuffed aubergines) 164
bessara (Egyptian fava bean and herb dip) 197
betingan bil firan (fried aubergine sandwiches) 22
betingan mah'shi bi safargel (stuffed aubergines with quince) 170
bimbriyo (quince paste) 340
biscochos (Sephardic biscuits) 284
borek with aubergine filling 246
borekas (small cheese pies) 262
borekas de espinaka (spinach pies) 249
borekitas (Sephardic cheese-and-potato pies) 264
borekitas de espinaka (spinach pies) 249
borekitas, sweet 285
boyikos de rayo (cheese scones) 259
boyos with cheese or aubergine filling 252
braised chicken with quince and almonds 134
bread pudding, Egyptian (Om Ali) 218

brisket, Sephardic style 127
brownies with halva and tahini 279
brown lentils with rice (megadarra) 210
bulemas with cheese and basil filling 250
bulgur and meat pie (kibbeh bil sanieh) 106
burgul bi kousa (burgul with courgettes) 169
butter biscuits, Egyptian (ghorayebah) 222
butternut squash, sweet potato, chickpeas and freekeh salad 23

cabbage, stuffed (malfoof) 178

Cakes
    almond, orange and semolina cake with lemon syrup 316
    apple cake, Passover 242
    banana, medjool date and chocolate cake 305
    basbousa cake with cream 196
    chestnut and coffee cake with marrons glacés 294
    chocolate, almond and pear cake (Passover) 229
    chocolate and macaroon cake, Passover 232
    citrus lavender syrup cake, Passover 234
    clementine cake, Passover 233
    coconut cake, Passover 240
    eggless chocolate cake 298
    fig and almond filo tart 299
    fig and almond tart 302
    fig and raspberry crumble cake 303
    fresh fig with a crumb topping 304
    glazed mango sponge 306
    hazelnut sponge, Passover 237
    membrillo, buttermilk and poppy seed traybake 296
    orange Passover cake 226
    Ottoman style sponge cake 311
    pan di Spagna (Spanish sponge cake) 308
    pomegranate cake 292
    raisin streusel cake, Passover 241
    Rosh Hashanah honey cake 309
    semolina cake with yoghurt (basbousa bil laban zabadi) 223
    seville orange and honey cake 300
    spiced date, prune and walnut loaf 310
    sponge cake with whipped cream and praline 312
    tishpishti (Greek honey cake soaked in syrup) 314
    Tunisian pistachio and orange cake 295

candied grapefruit peel 344
canella (cinnamon nut cookies) 269
carchof jiben (Syrian artichoke and cheese casserole) 75
carrot and sweet potato soup 48
cassata Siciliana 323
cauliflower and potatoes, baked 176
cauliflower florets stew (karnabit frita) 186
cauliflower salad with tahini and onions 33

celeriac and Jerusalem artichoke soup 52
cheese and basil bulemas 250
cheese scones (boyikos de rayo) 259
chestnut and coffee cake with marrons glacés 294
chicken and potatoes sofrito 136
chicken and rice soup 52
chicken and vegetable soup 63
chicken breasts on a bed of green vegetables 145
chicken in a coconut and ginger sauce 137
chicken, aubergine and sweet potato stew 142
chicken tagine with apples 153
chicken with dates 140
chicken with pomegranate and walnut sauce 152
chicken with quince 153
chicken with rice, chickpeas and vermicelli 137

Chicken
    braised with quince and almonds 134
    breasts on a bed of green vegetables 145
    in a coconut and ginger sauce 137
    lemon chicken with sweet potatoes 138
    Moroccan chicken Qdra 150
    orange chicken with fresh figs and raisins 151
    rice with chicken giblets and livers 144
    saffron chicken and potato casserole 148
    sofrito with potatoes 136
    stew with aubergines and sweet potatoes 142
    sweet and sour with apricots 146
    tagine, with apples 153
    with dates 140
    with pomegranate and walnut sauce 152
    with quince 153
    with rice, chickpeas and vermicelli 137

chocolate, almond and pear cake, Passover 229
chocolate and date mousse 324
chocolate mousse cake 325
chocolate truffles 346
cinnamon nut cookies (canella) 269
citrus lavender syrup cake, Passover 234
clementine cake, Passover 232
coconut cake, Passover 240
coconut jam 345
cod roe fritters (taramokeftedes) 94
cooked salad (salata matbucha) 28
corn soup 53

Courgette
    filo pie 69
    flan (almodrote de kalavassa) 76
    salad with leek and walnut 37
    stuffed with cheese (kalavassas reynada con keso) 71
    stuffed with lemon mint sauce 168
    with burgul (burghul bi kousa) 169

Damascus sesame biscuits (berazeh shami) 268
date and marzipan slices (ma'aroud) 272
date and raisin preserve (haroset) 236
date-nut pastries 330

Desserts
   almond custard (muhallabeyah) 214
   apricot pudding (muhallabeyah bi amardeen) 215
   autumn fruit compote 330
   cassata Siciliana 323
   chocolate and date mousse 324
   chocolate mousse cake 325
   date-nut pastries 330
   dessert de pommes de terre douces 336
   Egyptian bread pudding (Om Ali) 218
   Egyptian dried fruit salad (khoshaf) 205
   Egyptian pumpkin milk pudding (kar'assaly) 204
   Egyptian syrup-drenched doughnuts (zalabia) 220
   Greek honey tart 331
   ice cream with nuts and candied fruit 328
   konafa with cream 209
   konafa with mixed nuts (konafa bil mikassarat) 208
   mango ice cream 332
   mango mousse 332
   mango squares 334
   matzah pudding 240
   quince in jelly 320
   rice pudding with raisins 322
   sutlach (fragrant rice pudding) 326
   torta di riso (ricotta and rice cake) 333
   the palace bread (aish el saraya) 194

dried fruit salad, Egyptian (khoshaf) 205
dukkah (Egyptian nut, seed and spice blend) 198

Eggless chocolate cake 298
egg free chocolate cupcakes 278

Egyptian
aish el saraya (the palace bread) 194
   baclawa (nut-filled pastry) 192
   basbousa bil laban zabadi (semolina cake with yoghurt) 223
   basbousa cake with cream 196
   bessara (Egyptian fava beans and herb dip) 197
   dukkah (Egyptian nut, seed and spice blend) 198
   ful medames (cooked fava beans) 201
   ghorayebah (butter biscuits) 222
   kahk (savoury small bracelets) 202
   kahk bi sukar (shortbread cookies) 206
   kar'assaly (pumpkin milk pudding) 204
   khoshaf (dried fruit salad) 205
   kishk (rice with yoghurt and caramelised onions) 199
   konafa bil mikassarat (konafa nests with mixed nuts) 208
   konafa with cream (cream-filled konafa pastry) 209
   koshari (rice, lentils and macaroni) 212
   lamb fattah 200
   megadarra (rice with brown lentils) 210
   molokheya (also known as the green soup) 213
   muhallabeya (almond custard) 214
   muhallabeya bil amardeen (apricot pudding) 215
   Om Ali (Egyptian bread pudding) 218
   sharkaseya (walnut sauce for chicken) 219
   ta'ameya (Egyptian falafel) 216
   zalabia (Egyptian syrup drenched doughnuts) 220

endjinaras con patatas y carne (artichokes with potatoes and meat) 111
eshkaneh (Persian onion soup) 51

falafel (Egyptian ta'ameya) 216
fasoulia (green beans with tomatoes) 172
fava bean and herb dip (bessara) 197
fava beans cooked (ful medames) 201
fennel, apple and pomegranate salad 32
feta, aubergine and sweet potato bake 70
fig and almond filo tart 299
fig and almond tart 302
fig and raspberry crumble cake 303
fig jam 345
fig, walnut and goat's cheese salad 34
fil fil mah'shi bi fireek (stuffed peppers with freekeh) 173
filo triangles with cheese 253
filo pastry with nuts (baclawa) 192
filo spinach triangles 260

Fish
   baked with a coriander and tomato sauce (samak b' kamoun) 93
   baked with fereek (samak fil forn b'feeek) 97
   baked with tahini sauce 102
   baked (samak fil forn) 98
   cod roe fritters (taramokeftedes) 94
   fish balls in tomato sauce (albondigas de pishkado) 86
   salmon couscous 100
   salmon with a creamy dill sauce 92
   salmon with a honey and garlic sauce 92
   sea bass with tahini sauce 96
   sea bream on a bed of potatoes 101
   tagine 90
   tuna croquettes in tomato sauce 88
   with egg and lemon sauce (pishkado con agristada) 89
   with walnut sauce 88

fish balls in tomato sauce (albondigas de pishkado) 86

fish roe dip (taramasalata) 6
fish tagine 90
fish with egg and lemon sauce (pishkado con agristada) 89
fish with walnut sauce 88
fresh fig cake with a crumb topping 304
ful medames (cooked fava beans) 201

ghorayebah (Egyptian butter biscuits) 222
glazed mango sponge 306

Gratins and egg dishes
    artichoke and cheese casserole (Syrian carchof jiben) 75
    aubergine flan (almodrote de berendjana) 78
    baked aubergines with cheese (berendjenas con keso) 68
    courgette filo pie 69
    courgette flan (almodrote de kalavassa) 76
    courgettes stuffed with cheese (kalavassas reynadas con keso) 71
    feta, aubergine and sweet potato bake 70
    leek-and-cheese matzah pie (Sephardic mina de prasa) 80
    leek and courgette pie 74
    leek and dill pie (kurraath b'saniya) 81
    leek and matzah bake 75
    leek and potato patties (keftes de prasa y patatas) 72
    leek and potato gratin (prasifutchi) 77
    poached eggs in creamed spinach 82
    potato and leek bake (prasa quajado) 66
    spinach and potato frittata 79
    spinach and potato pie (sfongo) 79

Greek barley soup (sopa de cebada) 59
Greek honey cake soaked in syrup (tishpishti) 314
Greek honey tart 331
green beans with tomatoes (fasoulia) 172
green vegetable soup with lemon and rice 54

halva and sumac shortbread 274
halva and tahini brownies 279
hamin de kastanya (lamb with chestnuts) 112
haroset (Passover date and raisin preserve) 236
hashweh (one pot rice) 114
hazelnut Passover sponge 237
honey cake, Rosh Hashanah 309

ice cream with nuts and candied fruit 328

Jams and miscellaneous
    Amardeen (apricot sauce) 342
    apricot jam 343
    bimbriyo (quince paste) 340
    candied grapefruit peel 344
    chocolate truffles 346
    coconut jam 345
    fig jam 345
    massapan (marzipan, Judeo-Spanish) 349
    nareng (orange slices in syrup) 350
    pineapple jam 352
    quince jam recipe 1 348
    quince jam recipe 2 (safargel) 348

Jerusalem artichokes with carrots and potatoes 174

kahk (Egyptian savoury bracelets) 202
kahk bi sukar (shortbread cookies) 206
kalavassas reynadas con keso (courgettes stuffed with cheese) 71
kale, chickpeas and freekeh soup 55
karabij (nut filled ma'amoul with naatif cream) 269
kar'assaly (Egyptian pumpkin milk pudding) 204
karnabit frita (cauliflower florets stew) 186
keftes de espinaka con keso (spinach patties with walnuts) 165
keftes de prasa y patatas (leek and potato fritters) 72
kharshouf mahshi (stuffed artichoke bottoms) 115
khodar b'mishmesh (sweet and sour vegetable stew) 182
khoresh betingan (aubergine khoresh) 116
khoshaf (Egyptian dried fruit salad) 205
koshari (Egyptian rice, lentils and macaroni) 212
kibbeh bil sanieh (layered bulgur and meat pie) 106
kishk (rice with yoghurt and caramelised onions) 199
kofta bil karatz (meatballs in a sour cherry sauce) 117
kofta mishmisheya (meatballs in apricot sauce) 128
konafa with cream 209
konafa with mixed nuts (konafa bil mikassarat) 208
koshari (Egyptian rice, lentils and macaroni) 212
kurraath b' saniya (leek dill pie) 81

lah'meh b'ajeen (Syrian meat pizzas) 120

Lamb
    and quince stew 112
    Egyptian lamb fattah 200
    slow roast leg of lamb with spices 118
    with broad beans and almonds 118
    with chestnuts (hamin de kastanya) 112

Leek
    and carrots, Sephardi style 29
    and cheese matzah pie (Sephardic mina de prasa) 70
    and shallots with cinnamon and prunes 156
    courgette pie 74
    dill pie (kurraath b'saniya) 81
    matza bake 75
    potato patties (keftes de prasa y patatas) 72

potato gratin (prasifutchi) 77
potato soup 53

lemon chicken soup (avgolemono) 50
lemon chicken with sweet potatoes 138
lemony celeriac and carrots (apio) 25
lentil and chickpea soup 62
lentil and tahini dip 34
lentil, aubergine and pomegranate stew 185
lentil, red pepper and feta cheese salad 24

ma'amoul aux figures (ma'amoul filled with figs) 282
ma'amoul stuffed with nuts 270
ma'aroud (date and marzipan slices) 272
mafrum (meat stuffed potatoes) 129
mah'shi (stuffed vegetables) 124
mah'shi basal (stuffed caramelised onions) 122
mah'shi batatas (stuffed potatoes) 126
malfoof (stuffed cabbage) 178
mango and pepper salad on a bed of couscous 31
mango ice cream 332
mango mousse 332
mango squares 334
mankouche au halwa 288
massapan (Judeo-Spanish marzipan) 349
matzah pudding 240
matzo fritters (beignets de Paques) 228

Meat
    artichokes and potatoes and meat (endjinaras con patatas y carne) 111
    artichoke bottoms stuffed with meat (kharshouf mah'shi) 15
    aubergine khoresh (khoresh betingan) 116
    beef stew Aleppo style 108
    beef stew with chickpeas, kale and tahini 110
    brisket, Sephardic style 127
    bulgur and meat pie (kibbeh bil sanieh) 106
    Egyptian lamb fattah 200
    hashweh (one pot rice) 114
    lamb and quince stew 112
    lamb with broad beans and almonds 118
    lamb with chestnuts (hamin de kastanya) 112
    meatballs in apricot sauce (kofta mishmisheya) 128
    meatballs in a sour cherry sauce (kofta bil karatz) 117
    meat stuffed potatoes (mafrum) 129
    slow roast leg of lamb with spices 118
    stuffed caramelised onions (mah'shi basal) 122
    stuffed potatoes (mah'shi batatas) 126
    stuffed vegetables (mah'shi) 124
    sweet and sour beef and aubergine stew 109
    sweet and sour beef layered 130
    Syrian meat pizzas (lah'meh b'ajeen) 120
    veal stew with cannellini beans and celery (apio con avas) 108

meatballs in apricot sauce (kofta mishmisheya) 128
meatballs in a sour cherry sauce (kofta bil karatz) 117
meat stuffed potatoes (mafrum) 129
megadarra (rice with brown lentils) 210
membrillo, buttermilk and poppy seed traybake 296
menenas (ma'amoul with date filling) 286
Middle Eastern pies (sambusek) 257
mina de prasa (Sephardic leek-and-cheese matza pie) 80
molokheya (Egyptian soup) 213
monk's aubergine salad (salatet el rahib) 38
Moroccan chicken Qdra 150
muhallabeyah (almond custard) 214
muhallabeyah bil amardeen (apricot pudding) 215
muhammara (walnut and roast pepper paste) 9
mutabbal (aubergine dip) 36
my mother's Passover biscuits 230
my special chicken soup with vegetables 63

nareng (orange slices in syrup) 350
nut filled filo pastry (baclava) 192
nut filled maa'moul with naatif cream (karabij) 269
nut and raisin pastries 274
nut, seed and spice blend, Egyptian (dukkah) 198

okra with prunes and apricots (bamia mishmosh) 188
okra with tomatoes 179
Om Ali (Egyptian bread pudding) 218
orange cake, Passover 226
orange chicken with fresh figs and raisins 151
orange slices in syrup (nareng) 350

Pan di Spagna (Spanish sponge cake) 308

Passover
    apple cake 242
    chocolate and pear cake 229
    chocolate and macaroon cake 232
    citrus lavender syrup cake 34
    clementine cake 233
    coconut cake 240
    date and raisin preserve (haroset) 236
    hazelnut sponge 237
    matzah pudding 240
    matzo fritters (beignets de Paques) 228
    orange cake 226
    Passover biscuits, my mother's 230
    Passover biscuits (sablés de Paques) 238
    raisin streusel cake 241

pastelicos (small pastries filled with beef and pine nuts) 256
pastelles (Sephardic meat and rice pies) 254

Pastries savoury
- borek with aubergine filling 246
- borekas (small cheese pies) 262
- borekitas (Sephardic cheese-and-potato pies) 264
- borekitas de espinaka (spinach pies) 249
- boyikos de rayo (cheese scones) 259
- boyos with cheese or aubergine filling 252
- bulemas with cheese and basil filling 250
- Egyptian small savoury bracelets (kahk) 202
- filo triangles with cheese 253
- pastelles (Sephardic meat and rice pies) 254
- pastelicos (small pastries filled with beef and pine nuts) 256
- roasted aubergine and goat's cheese tart 258
- spinach filo triangles 260
- sambusek (Middle Eastern pies) 257
- Tapada (large Sephardic pie) 248

Pastries sweet
- anise biscuits 275
- assabih bil loz (almond filo cigars) 266
- berazeh shami (Damascus sesame biscuits) 268
- canella (cinnamon nut cookies) 269
- egg free chocolate cupcakes 278
- Egyptian butter biscuits (ghorayebah) 222
- Egyptian nut filled konafa (konafa bil mikassarat) 208
- halva and sumac shortbread 274
- halva and tahini brownies 279
- karabij (nut filled ma'amoul with naatif cream) 269
- kahk bi sukar (Egyptian shortbread biscuits) 206
- ma'amoul aux figues (maamoul with figs) 282
- ma'amoul stuffed with nuts 270
- ma'amoul aux figues (ma'amoul with figs) 282
- ma'aroud (date and marzipan slices) 272
- mankouche au halwa 288
- menenas (ma'amoul with date filling) 286
- nuts and raisins pastries 274
- nut-filled filo pastry (baclawa) 192
- sablés à la confiture (shortbread biscuits with a jam filling) 276
- sansaticos (almond frangipane-filled filo triangles) 280
- Sephardic biscochos 284
- sweet borekitas 285
- travados (Sephardic nut pastries) 283

pastries with nuts and raisins 274
peppers and tomatoes with eggs (shakshouka) 166
peppers stuffed with freekeh (fil fil mah'shi bi fireek) 173
Persian onion soup (eshkaneh) 51
pineapple jam 352
pishkado con agristada (fish with egg and lemon sauce) 89
poached eggs in a creamed spinach sauce 82
pomegranate cake 292
potatoes stuffed with meat (mafrum) 129
prasa quajado (potato and leek bake) 66
prasifutchi (leek and potato gratin) 77
pumpkin milk pudding, Egyptian (kar'assaly) 204

Quince
- jam recipe 1 348
- jam recipe 2 (safargel) 349
- in jelly 320
- paste (bimbriyo) 340

raisin streusel cake, Passover 241

Rice
- hashweh (one pot rice) 114
- pilaf with aubergines and pine nuts (arroz pilaf con berendjenas y piniones) 184
- pudding (sutlach) 326
- pudding with raisins 322
- ricotta and rice cake (torta di riso) 333
- with a vegetable and lemon sauce (roz hamud) 161
- with brown lentils (megadarra) 210
- with chicken, chickpeas and vermicelli 137
- with chicken livers and giblets (riz aux abattis) 144
- with lentils and macaron (Egyptian koshari) 212
- with raisins and pine nuts 179
- with yoghurt and caramelised onions (Egyptian kishk) 199

Rosh Hashanah honey cake 309
roz we hamud (rice with a vegetable and lemon sauce) 161

sablés à la confiture (shortbread biscuits with a jam filling) 276
sablés de Pâques (Passover biscuits) 238
safargel (quince jam) 348
saffron chicken and potato casserole 148

Salads and dips
- artichoke and broad bean 26
- aubergine dip (mutabbal) 36
- aubergine with dates and chickpeas 20
- aubergine with figs, feta cheese and bulgur wheat 30
- baby spinach with tomatoes and mozzarella 32
- butternut squash, sweet potato, chickpeas and freekeh 23
- cauliflower with tahini and onions 33
- courgette, leek and walnut 37
- fennel, apple and pomegranate 32
- fig, walnut and goat's cheese salad 34

fried aubergine sandwiches (betingan bil firan) 22
leeks and carrots Sephardi style 29
lemony celeriac and carrot (apio) 25
lentil and tahini dip 34
lentil, red pepper and feta cheese 24
mango and pepper, on a bed of couscous 31
salata matbucha (cooked salad) 28
salatet el rahib (Monk's aubergine salad) 38
salmon salad with a honey dressing 40
spinach and artichoke dip 41
spinach and orzo 42
taramasalata (fish roe dip) 36
walnut and roast pepper paste (muhammara) 29

salata matbucha (cooked salad) 28
salatet el rahib (Monk's aubergine salad) 38
salmon couscous 100
salmon salad with a honey dressing 40
salmon with a creamy dill sauce 92
salmon with a honey and garlic sauce 92
samak fil forn b'fireek (fish baked with fereek) 97
samak b'kamoun (fish baked in a tomato and coriander sauce) 93
samak fil forn (baked fish) 98
sambusek (Middle Eastern pies) 257
sansaticos (almond frangipane-filled filo triangles) 280
savoury small bracelets (Egyptian kahk) 202
sea bass with tahini sauce 96
sea bream on a bed of potatoes 101
semolina (basbousa) cake with cream 196
semolina cake with yoghurt (basbousa bil laban zabadi) 223
Sephardic almond filled crescents (travados) 283
Sephardic biscochos 284
Sephardic brisket 127
Sephardic egg and bulgur soup (sopa de huevos y bulgur) 61
Sephardic leeks and carrots 29
Sephardic leek-and-cheese matzah pie (mina de prasa) 80
Sephardic meat and rice pies 254
Sephardic nut pastries (travados) 283
Sephardic pie (tapada) 248
Sephardic potato and cheese pies (borekitas) 264
Sephardic style tomatoes stuffed with cheese 181
Seville orange and honey cake 300
sfongo (spinach and potato pie) 79
shakshouka (peppers and tomatoes with eggs) 166
sharkaseya (walnut sauce for chicken) 219
shorbah freekeh (freekeh and pinto bean soup) 56
shorbah sabanekh (Syrian spinach and yoghurt soup) 58
shortbread biscuits, Egyptian (ghorayeba) 222
shortbread biscuits with jam filling (sablés à la confiture) 276
shortbread cookies (kahk bi sukar) 206
small cheese pies (borekas) 262

small pastries filled with beef and pine nuts (pastelicos) 256
smoked aubergine salad with fig, feta cheese and bulgur 30
sofrito chicken with potatoes 136
sopa de cebada (Greek barley soup) 59
sopa de endjinaras (artichoke soup) 60
sopa de huevos y bulgur (Sephardic egg and bulgur soup) 61

Soups
artichoke and vegetable 48
artichoke soup (sopa de endijanaras) 60
artichoke with rice 49
carrot and sweet potato 48
celeriac and Jerusalem artichoke 52
chicken and rice 52
corn soup 53
egg and bulgur (sopa de huevos y bulgur) 61
freekeh and pinto bean (shorbah freekeh) 56
Greek barley 59
green vegetable with lemon and rice 54
kale, chickpeas and freekeh 55
leek and potato 53
lemon chicken soup (avgolemono) 50
lentil and chickpea 62
molokheya (Egyptian soup) 213
my special chicken and vegetable soup 63
Persian onion soup (eshkaneh) 51
Syrian spinach and yoghurt soup (shorbah sabanekh) 58
tomato and rice 60
Turkish mixed légume (tandir corbasi) 46

spiced date, prune and walnut loaf 310
spinach and artichoke dip 41
spinach and orzo salad 42
spinach and potato frittata 79
spinach and potato pie (sfongo) 79
spinach filo triangles 260
spinach patties with walnuts (keftes de espinaka con keso) 165
spinach pies (borekas de espinaka) 249
spinach salad with tomatoes and mozzarella 32
sponge cake, hazelnut, Passover 237
sponge cake Ottoman style 311
sponge cake, Spanish (Pan di Spagna) 308
sponge cake with whipped cream and praline 312
stuffed artichoke bottoms (kharshouf mah'shi) 115
stuffed cabbage (malfouf) 178
stuffed caramelised onions (mah'shi basal) 122
stuffed potatoes (mah'shi batatas) 126
stuffed vegetables (mah'shi) 124
sutlach (fragrant rice pudding) 326
sweet and sour beef, layered 130
sweet and sour vegetable stew (khodar b'mishmesh) 182

sweet and tart chicken with apricots 146
sweet borekitas 285
sweet potato dessert (dessert de pommels douces) 336
sweet potatoes with fried shallots, baked 166
Syrian artichoke and cheese casserole (carchof jiben) 75
Syrian meat pizzas (lah'meh b'ajeen) 120
Syrian pinto bean and freekeh soup (shorba fireek) 56
Syrian spinach and yoghurt soup (shorba sabanekh) 58
syrup-drenched doughnuts, Egyptian (zalabia) 220

tapada (large Sephardic pie) 248
taramasalata (fish roe dip) 36
taramokeftedes (cod roe fritters) 94
ta'ameya (Egyptian falafel) 216
the palace bread (aish el saraya) 194
tishpishti (Greek honey cake soaked in syrup) 314
tomato and rice soup 60
tomatoes stuffed with cheese, Sephardic style 181
torta di riso (ricotta and rice cake) 333
travados Sephardic nut pastries) 283
tuna croquettes in tomato sauce 88
Tunisian pistachio and orange cake 295
Turkish mixed légume soup (tandir corbasi) 46

veal stew with cannelloni beans and celery (apio con avas) 108

Vegetarian
    aubergine and feta kofta 158
    aubergine and leek casserole 59
    aubergine and tomato bake 160
    aubergine and walnut ragu 162
    aubergine parmigiana 180
    aubergine pilaf with pine nuts 184
    aubergines stuffed with cheese (berendjenas rellenas de keso) 164
    aubergines stuffed with quince (betingan mah'shi bi safargel) 170
    baked cauliflower with potatoes 176
    baked sweet potatoes with fried shallots 166
    cauliflower florets stew (karnabit frita) 186
    courgettes stuffed with a lemon mint sauce (mah'shi leban) 168
    courgettes with burgul (burghul bi kousa) 169
    green beans with tomatoes (fasoulia) 172
    Jerusalem artichokes with carrots and potatoes 174
    layered aubergines and potatoes with a coconut sauce 175
    leek and shallots wIth cinnamon and prunes 156

lentil, aubergine and pomegranate stew 185
okra with prunes and apricots (bamia b'mishmosh) 188
okra with tomatoes 179
peppers and tomatoes with eggs (shakshouka) 166
peppers stuffed with freekeh (fil fil mah'shi bi fireek) 173
rice pilaf with aubergines and pine nuts (arroz pilaf con berendjenas y piniones) 184
rice with a vegetable and lemon sauce (roz hamud) 161
rice with raisins and pine nuts 179
spinach patties with walnuts (keftes de espinaka con muez) 165
stuffed cabbage (malfoof) 178
sweet and sour vegetable stew (khodar b'meshmesh) 182
tomatoes stuffed with cheese Sephardic style 181

vegetable stew, sweet and sour (khodar b'meshmesh) 182
walnut and roast pepper paste (muhammara) 29
walnut sauce for chicken (sharkaseya) 219

zalabia (Egyptian syrup drenched doughnuts) 220

Photo courtesy of *91 Ways to Build a Global City*

Illustration and Graphic Design by Liane Aviram

A culinary legacy Recipes from a Sephardic Egyptian kitchen, 2021

I grew up in Cairo in a Sephardic Jewish community, but I was too young to appreciate the wealth of cultures and traditions around me. I took them for granted, as I did everything else back then. I became interested in cooking much later in life, but mostly concentrated on baking. Covid 19 and the various lockdowns gave me time, a precious commodity which I had not acknowledged before. Something which started as a vague idea soon became a full blown project and the result is a collection of recipes which I hope reflect the heritage of both sides of my family - the Syrian and Judeo Spanish styles of cooking, as well as some quintessential Egyptian dishes. Cooking them has brought back many memories and a lot of nostalgia.

Lightning Source UK Ltd.
Milton Keynes UK
UKHW020427230322
400389UK00006B/106